"The American Statesmen Series was a pathbreaking venture in its time; and the best proof of its continuing vitality for our time lies in the testimony of the introductory essays written by eminent scholars for the volumes of the Chelsea House edition—essays that not only explain the abiding value of the texts but in many cases represent significant scholarly contributions on their own.

"Chelsea House is contributing vitally to the scholarly resources of the country—and, at the same time, helping us all to understand and repossess our national heritage."

—*Professor Arthur M. Schlesinger, jr.*

Other titles in this Chelsea House series:

CHARLES FRANCIS ADAMS, *Charles Francis Adams, Jr.*
JOHN ADAMS, *John Quincy Adams and Charles Francis Adams*
JOHN QUINCY ADAMS, *John T. Morse, Jr.*
SAMUEL ADAMS, *James K. Hosmer*
JOHN C. CALHOUN, *Hermann E. von Holst*
LEWIS CASS, *Andrew C. McLaughlin*
SALMON P. CHASE, *Albert Bushnell Hart*
HENRY CLAY, *Carl Schurz*
ALBERT GALLATIN, *Henry Adams*
ALEXANDER HAMILTON, *Henry Cabot Lodge*
PATRICK HENRY, *Moses Coit Tyler*
ANDREW JACKSON, *William Graham Sumner*
JOHN JAY, *George Pellew*
THOMAS JEFFERSON, *John T. Morse, Jr.*
JAMES MADISON, *Sydney Howard Gay*
JOHN MARSHALL, *Albert J. Beveridge*
JAMES MONROE, *Daniel Coit Gilman*
GOUVERNEUR MORRIS, *Theodore Roosevelt*
JOHN RANDOLPH, *Henry Adams*
CHARLES SUMNER, *Moorfield Storey*
MARTIN VAN BUREN, *Edward M. Shepard*
GEORGE WASHINGTON, *John Marshall*
DANIEL WEBSTER, *Henry Cabot Lodge*

Forthcoming titles in this Chelsea House series:

JOHN P. ALTGELD, *Harry Barnard*
THOMAS HART BENTON, *Theodore Roosevelt*
JAMES G. BLAINE, *Edward Stanwood*
DANIEL BOONE, *Reuben G. Thwaites*
WILLIAM JENNINGS BRYAN, *M. R. Werner*
AARON BURR, *James Parton*
PETER COOPER, *R. W. Raymond*
STEPHEN A. DOUGLAS, *Allen Johnson*
DAVID FARRAGUT, *Alfred Thayer Mahan*
ULYSSES S. GRANT, *Louis A. Coolidge*
NATHANIEL GREENE, *Francis Vinton Greene*
MARCUS ALONZO HANNA, *Herbert D. Croly*
SAM HOUSTON, *Marquis James*
HENRY KNOX, *Noah Brooks*
LUTHER MARTIN, *Paul S. Clarkson and R. Samuel Jett*
ROBERT MORRIS, *Ellis Paxson Oberholtzer*
FRANKLIN PIERCE, *Nathaniel Hawthorne*
WILLIAM H. SEWARD, *Thornton K. Lothrop*
JOHN SHERMAN, *Theodore E. Burton*
WILLIAM T. SHERMAN, *B. H. Liddell Hart*
THADDEUS STEVENS, *Samuel W. McCall*
ROGER B. TANEY, *Carl Swisher*
TECUMSEH, *Glenn Tucker*
THURLOW WEED, *Glyndon G. VanDeusen*

JUDAH P. BENJAMIN
PIERCE BUTLER

INTRODUCTION BY
BENNETT H. WALL

American Statesmen Series

GENERAL EDITOR

ARTHUR M. SCHLESINGER, JR.

ALBERT SCHWEITZER PROFESSOR OF THE HUMANITIES

THE CITY UNIVERSITY OF NEW YORK

CHELSEA HOUSE

NEW YORK, LONDON

1980

Cover design by Zimmerman Foyster Design

Library of Congress Cataloging in Publication Data

Butler, Pierce, 1873
   Judah P. Benjamin.

   (American statesmen)
   Reprint of the 1907 ed. published by G. W. Jacobs,
Philadelphia, in series: American crisis biographies.
   Bibliography: p.
   Includes index.
   1. Benjamin, Judah Philip, 1811-1884.   2. United
States--Politics and government--1849-1861.
3. Confederate States of America--History.   4. Legis-
lators--United States--Biography.   5. United States.
Congress. Senate--Biography.   6. Lawyers--United
States--Biography.   7. Lawyers--Great Britain--
Biography.   I. Title.   II. Series.   III. Series:
American crisis biographies.
E467.1.B4B9 1980   973.7'13'0924 [B]   80-20134
ISBN 0-87754-198-1

Chelsea House Publishers
Harold Steinberg, Chairman & Publisher
Andrew E. Norman, President
Susan Lusk, Vice President
A Division of
Chelsea House Educational Communications, Inc.
70 West 40 Street, New York 10018

CONTENTS

*Publisher's Note: All arabic folios from the 1906 edition
have been retained in the Chelsea House edition.*

General Introduction

BLAZING THE WAY
Arthur M. Schlesinger, jr.

THE ORIGINAL AMERICAN STATESMEN SERIES consisted of thirty-four titles published between 1882 and 1916. Handsomely printed and widely read, the Series made a notable contribution to the popular appreciation of American history. Its creator was John Torrey Morse, Jr., born in Boston in 1840, graduated from Harvard in 1860 and for nearly twenty restless years thereafter a Boston lawyer. In his thirties he had begun to dabble in writing and editing; and about 1880, reading a volume in John Morley's English Men of Letters Series, he was seized by the idea of a comparable set of compact, lucid and authoritative lives of American statesmen.

It was an unfashionable thought. The celebrated New York publisher Henry Holt turned the project down, telling Morse, "Who ever wants to read American history?" Houghton, Mifflin in Boston proved more receptive, and Morse plunged ahead. His intention was that the American Statesmen Series, when complete, "should present such a picture of the development of the country that the reader who had faithfully read all the volumes would have a full and fair view of the history of the United States told through the medium of the efforts of the men who had shaped our national career. The actors were to develop the drama."

In choosing his authors, Morse relied heavily on the counsel of his cousin Henry Cabot Lodge. Between them, they enlisted an impressive array of talent. Henry Adams, William Graham Sumner, Moses Coit Tyler, Hermann von Holst, Moorfield Storey and Albert Bushnell Hart were all in their early forties when their volumes were published; Lodge, E. M. Shepard and Andrew C. McLaughlin in their thirties; Theodore Roosevelt in his twenties. Lodge took on Washington, Hamilton and Webster, and Morse himself wrote five volumes. He offered the authors a choice of $500 flat or a royalty of 12.5¢ on each volume sold. Most, luckily for themselves, chose the royalties.

Like many editors, Morse found the experience exasperating. "How I waded among the fragments of broken engagements, shattered pledges! I never really knew when I could count upon getting anything from anybody." Carl Schurz infuriated him by sending in a two-volume life of Henry Clay on a take-it-or-leave-it basis. Morse, who had confined Jefferson, John Adams, Webster and Calhoun to single volumes, was tempted to leave it. But Schurz threatened to publish his work simultaneously if Morse commissioned another life of Clay for the

Series; so Morse reluctantly surrendered.

When a former Confederate colonel, Allan B. Magruder, offered to do John Marshall, Morse, hoping for "a good Virginia atmosphere," gave him a chance. The volume turned out to have been borrowed in embarrassing measure from Henry Flanders's *Lives and Times of the Chief Justices.* For this reason, Magruder's *Marshall* is not included in the Chelsea House reissue of the Series; Albert J. Beveridge's famous biography appears in its stead. Other classic biographies will replace occasional Series volumes: John Marshall's *Life of George Washington* in place of Morse's biography; essays on John Adams by John Quincy Adams and Charles Francis Adams, also substituting for a Morse volume; and Henry Adams's *Life of Albert Gallatin* instead of the Series volume by John Austin Stevens.

"I think that only one real blunder was made," Morse recalled in 1931, "and that was in allotting [John] Randolph to Henry Adams." Half a century earlier, however, Morse had professed himself pleased with Adams's *Randolph.* Adams, responding with characteristic self-deprecation, thought the "acidity" of his account "much too decided" but blamed the "excess of acid" on the acidulous subject. The book was indeed hostile but nonetheless stylish. Adams also wrote a life of Aaron Burr, presumably for the Series. But Morse thought Burr no statesman, and on his advice, to Adams's extreme irritation, Henry Houghton of Houghton, Mifflin rejected the manuscript. "Not bad that for a damned bookseller!" said Adams. "He should live for a while at Washington and know our *real* statesmen." Adams eventually destroyed the work, and a fascinating book was lost to history.

The definition of who was or was not a "statesman" caused recurrent problems. Lodge told Morse one day that their young friend Theodore Roosevelt wanted to do Gouverneur Morris. "But, Cabot," Morse said, "you surely don't expect Morris to be in the Series! He doesn't belong there." Lodge replied, "Theodore . . . *needs the money,*" and Morse relented. No one objected to Thomas Hart Benton, Roosevelt's other contribution to the Series. Roosevelt turned out the biography in an astonishing four months while punching cows and chasing horse thieves in the Badlands. Begging Lodge to send more material from Boston, he wrote that he had been "mainly evolving [Benton] from my inner consciousness; but when he leaves the Senate in 1850 I have nothing whatever to go by. . . . I hesitate to give him a wholly fictitious date of death and to invent all the work of his later years." In fact, T.R. had done more research than he pretended; and for all its defects, his *Benton* has valuable qualities of vitality and sympathy.

Morse, who would chat to Lodge about "the aristocratic upper crust in which you & I are imbedded," had a fastidious sense of language. Many years later, in the age of Warren G. Harding, he recommended to Lodge that the new President find someone "who can clothe for him his 'ideas' in the language customarily used by educated men." At dinner in a Boston club, a guest commented on the dilemma of the French ambassador who could not speak English. "Neither can Mr. Harding," Morse said. But if patrician prejudice improved Morse's literary taste, it also impaired his political understanding. He was not altogether kidding when he wrote Lodge as the Series was getting under way, "Let the Jeffersonians & the Jacksonians beware! I will poison the popular mind!!"

Still, for all its fidelity to establishment values, the American Statesmen Series had distinct virtues. The authors were mostly from outside the academy, and they wrote with the confidence of men of affairs. Their books are generally crisp, intelligent, spirited and readable. The Series has long been in demand in secondhand bookstores. Most of its volumes are eminently worth republication today, on their merits as well as for the vigorous expression they give to an influential view of the American past.

Born during the Presidency of Martin Van Buren, John Torrey Morse, Jr., died shortly after the second inauguration of Franklin D. Roosevelt in 1937. A few years before his death he could claim with considerable justice that his Series had done "a little something in blazing the way" for the revival of American historical writing in the years to come.

New York
May, 1980

INTRODUCTION
TO THE
CHELSEA HOUSE EDITION

Bennett H. Wall

When Stephen Vincent Benét came to Judah P. Benjamin in his poem *John Brown's Body,* his portrait of that inscrutable Confederate leader captured both the full flavor and essence of the man. Biographers before and after Benét have fleshed out Benjamin, but no one perceived the great Southerner better. Benét first described Benjamin at a Confederate Cabinet meeting:

Judah P. Benjamin, the dapper Jew,
Seal-sleek, black-eyed, lawyer and epicure,
Able, well-hated, face alive with life,
Looked round the council-chamber with the slight
Perpetual smile he held before himself
Continually like a silk-ribbed fan.
Behind the fan, his quick, shrewd, fluid mind
Weighed Gentiles in an old balance. . . .

I am the Jew. What am I doing here? . . .
And we are colleagues. And we speak to each other. . . .

Later Benét described General Robert E. Lee's battered army on its way to Appomattox and wrote about Benjamin:

Benjamin is with them for some few days,
Still sleek, still lively, still impeccably dressed,
Taking adversity as he took success
With the silk-ribbed fan of his slight, unchangeable smile.
Behind that fan, his mind weighs war and defeat
In an old balance.

   One day he is there and smiling.
The next he is gone as if he had taken fernseed
And walked invisible so through the Union lines.
You will not find that smile in a Northern prison
Though you seek from now till Doomsday. It is too wise. ...[1]

That tells the story of the man well.

Judah P. Benjamin, as one scholar phrased it, "had almost as many careers—and was almost as lucky—as the nine-lived cat."[2] He began life in the Virgin Islands (St. Croix, then a British possession) in 1811, and he died in Paris in 1884. He received his education in the Carolinas and at Yale, from which place he departed under a never-resolved cloud of suspicion. Almost penniless when he went to New Orleans, he studied law and soon became renowned as the leading commercial lawyer in the city. He gained both a local and national reputation as a fine speaker. Benjamin also pursued a career as a planter. At Belle Chasse he conducted experiments in sugar-making and with sugar cane, which he dutifully wrote about in *DeBow's Review*. In 1852 a raging Mississippi flood and his acceptance of responsibility for a note he had endorsed forced him to sell his plantation. He returned to New Orleans and built a fine home.

After a political career in Louisiana, he won election to the United States Senate as a Whig. When that party expired he became a Democrat and a close ally of Louisiana's John Slidell. Always a realist, Benjamin foresaw the breakup of the Union and sought to warn his peers of the coming struggle. When Louisiana seceded, Benjamin resigned from the U.S. Senate, becoming in succession Attorney General, Acting Secretary of War, Secretary of War, and Secretary of State in the new Confederate government. After Lee surrendered in April 1865, Benjamin fled in company with other Confederate leaders. Breaking away from the rest, he made his way to England. There he successfully claimed English citizenship and, though fifty-five years of age, soon emerged as a leading English commercial lawyer. He adorned the British legal profession for almost twenty years, receiving many honors when he retired in 1882.

Benjamin was a legal scholar and during his career edited two digests of law, one in the United States and the other in England. While studying Louisiana law, he kept full notes, and these were often borrowed by other lawyers. In 1834, with the aid of his friend Thomas Slidell, he published his *Digest of the Reported Decisions of the Superior Court of the Late Territory of Orleans and the Supreme Court of the State of Louisiana.* After he found asylum in England in 1865, he began a second manuscript while preparing for the bar examination. In 1868, when the volume *A Treatise on the Law of Sale of Personal Property, with Reference to the American Decisions, to the French Code and Civil Law* appeared, it was enthusiastically received and quickly became a legal classic known as "Benjamin on Sales."

Benjamin spoke French and Spanish with equal fluency, and frequently other lawyers consulted him about cases involving those languages. On occasion he tried cases in French and Spanish jurisdictions. Small wonder that the Confederate President, Jefferson Davis, praised him as "a master of the law."

All biographers of Benjamin have confronted the same problem, the absence of personal papers. As Pierce Butler noted in the first full biography, "It was Mr. Benjamin's rule to destroy at once all his correspondence." Butler reported that Francis Lawley, who once planned to write Benjamin's life, had interviewed his subject shortly before his death and asked about personal papers. Benjamin replied, "I have no materials available for that purpose. I have never kept a diary, or retained a copy of a letter written by me. No letters addressed to me by others will be found among my papers when I die. With the exception of Mrs. Jefferson Davis, no one has many letters of mine." In the last hours of the Confederacy, Benjamin and his staff burned most of his papers. In France shortly before his death he did the same thing. These actions add to the mystery. No person except, perhaps, Jefferson Davis ever knew him well. Part of his reticence could have been occasioned by an unhappy marriage that dragged out fifty years. On the surface he appeared charming, ever pleasant, and to friends, completely congenial. But always a very private person, he injected little of himself into his social activities, reserving personal emotions for his family. To them he appeared the ideal son, brother, and father.

Butler, Benjamin's first biographer, was born on January 18, 1873, and grew up in the post-Civil War South. He belonged to the Natchez Butlers and from them heard tales of the Old South. He received his education at home, at Tulane, at the Sorbonne, where he received an M.A., and at Johns Hopkins University, where he received a Ph.D. in English. He manifested his interest in history throughout his life through membership in the American Historical Association and through his various writings. In 1902 Butler joined the Newcomb College (New Orleans) faculty, where he taught English, history, and French. In 1906 he became full professor of English, and in 1907 head of that department. Finally, in 1920, he was appointed second dean of Newcomb. When that college merged with Tulane University and moved to the present uptown campus, he continued as dean until 1938. Because of his family background and his

personal accomplishments, he enjoyed pleasant relations with upper-class New Orleanians. Through
them he made contact with Benjamin's relatives
and friends.

In 1905 he contracted with the publisher George
W. Jacobs and Company, of Philadelphia, to write
a life of Judah P. Benjamin for the American Crisis
Biography Series. The volume, published in 1907,
still remains a fine example of the biographer's art.
While writing about Benjamin, Butler utilized the
then recently published *War of the Rebellion: A
Compilation of the Official Records of the Union
and Confederate Armies*,[3] visited Belle Chasse,
and borrowed letters and papers from Benjamin's
friends and family. He interviewed many persons
who had known his subject—oral history. Familiar
with the sugar industry, Butler wrote expertly
about Benjamin's career as a planter. Because he
did not travel to England, Butler found few sources
detailing Benjamin's career as an English lawyer.
Hence this portion of the life did not receive full
coverage. Butler was a felicitous writer, and his
organization of the biography became the model
for later biographers of Benjamin.

In 1933 Rollin G. Osterweis, a Yale history professor, published *Judah P. Benjamin, Statesman of
the Lost Cause*.[4] Because of the pronounced simi-
larity of much textual material in this volume to
that in Butler (and other sources), G. P. Putnam's
Sons sought to withdraw it from the market. For

whatever reasons, few copies and fewer reviews of the Osterweis volume are known to exist.

In 1931 Robert D. Meade began a study of Benjamin that required twelve years for completion. His *Judah P. Benjamin, Confederate Statesman*[5] came out in 1943. Meade's research encompassed virtually all major manuscript collections in both England and America plus many letters and documents in private hands. His use of English sources enabled him to provide more information on Benjamin's dramatic English legal career than did Butler. He also put to rest the hallowed myth that the statesman had been Queen Victoria's personal lawyer. In fact, Benjamin never did receive appointment as Queen's Counsel; rather did he receive the "patent of precedence," a rank above all future Queen's Counsel. However, to the detriment of his volume, Meade included many editorial asides and inconsequential judgments. He went into some detail about Davis's transfer of Benjamin from his cabinet post as Secretary of War to that of Secretary of State. Unlike Butler, Meade pointed out the War Secretary's errors of judgment and explained his feuds with several state governors and such military commanders as Joseph E. Johnston and P. G. T. Beauregard. He carefully analyzed the one confrontation between Benjamin and General Thomas J. "Stonewall" Jackson. In these cases Meade indicated that all parties erred and were equally guilty of poor judgment. With reference to his work as War Secretary, Meade concluded, "Except in his personal relations with certain generals . . . Benjamin's administration had been an almost unqualified success."[6]

Meade covered fully Benjamin's work as Secretary of State. He emphasized that his diplomacy had to depend on Confederate military success and that all his brilliance and cleverness could not overcome the defeats inflicted on the Confederate armies. Meade did not judge his subject in this role; rather he detailed his actions, leaving to the reader the final judgment. Still, in Meade's opinion, Benjamin in all three of his cabinet roles served as a buffer for Jefferson Davis. Much of the criticism of Benjamin resulted from actions taken under direct instructions from Davis (including the Stonewall Jackson affair). Benjamin took praise without becoming conceited and endured unjust complaints and attacks without flinching. Characteristically, he rarely struck back.

Two other accounts of Benjamin as a Confederate leader deserve mention—Burton J. Hendrick, *Statesmen of the Lost Cause: Jefferson Davis and his Cabinet*,[7] and Rembert W. Patrick, *Jefferson Davis and his Cabinet*.[8] Hendrick's admiration of Benjamin was evident throughout his volume. He contended that when Davis, whom he detested, came to appoint a Secretary of State, Benjamin overshadowed all others mentioned for the post. Patrick's volume is by all odds the best evaluation yet written of the civil leaders of the Confederacy. It reflects thorough research and careful exposition. Patrick viewed Benjamin as "the Confederacy's jack-of-all-trades. And far from being good at none, he was capable at all. Preeminently an able lawyer, he was also a good administrative officer and a perfect advisor to the man who presided over the Confederacy." Yet Patrick, in judgment, concluded that "on his own accomplishments, Judah P. Benjamin was a failure as Secretary of State."9

Only two volumes, those of Butler and Meade, cover the full career of Benjamin, and both authors had difficulty grappling with their subject. While numerous articles have been written about Benjamin, few add to the information in the biographies; like the Hendrick account mentioned above, they deal largely with Confederate diplomacy. Neither revisionists nor other historians have attempted in recent years to pull together the mixed threads in the life of this brilliant and enigmatic American who carved out distinctive careers under three flags. Therefore persons interested in Benjamin must still turn to Butler and Meade for the flavor of the man, the statesman, and the enigma.

New Orleans, Louisiana
June, 1980

NOTES

1. Stephen Vincent Benét, *John Brown's Body* (New York, 1941), 65, 353.

2. Frank L. Owsley, review of Robert D. Meade's *Judah P. Benjamin: Confederate Statesman, American Historical Review*, XLIX (April, 1944), 506.

3. Washington, 1880-1901.

4. New York and London, 1933.

5. New York, 1943.

6. *Ibid.*, 207.

7. New York, 1939.

8. Baton Rouge, 1944.

9. *Ibid.*, 202-9.

AUTHOR'S PREFACE
TO THE
1906 EDITION

AMERICAN history, certainly, scarcely contains the record of a personality more intrinsically interesting than that of Judah P. Benjamin, the Jewish lawyer and statesman who, after conspicuous success at the bar in this country, after continuous service in the leadership of the Confederacy, again achieved the most honorable triumphs at the bar of England. Were his own life otherwise quite barren of interest—which it is not—the mere story of his share in the great Civil War, if properly told, should prove a fascinating record. Therefore it is that the present writer is bold enough to hope that the mere interest of the subject and the substance of this narrative may help to atone for his own errors and shortcomings.

But a further plea for the indulgence of my readers is necessary. The extreme difficulty of collecting adequate and reliable materials for this biography can be thoroughly appreciated only by those who may attempt, as I hope some will, to do better than I have. Yet the general reader may judge of the obstacles to be overcome in this respect when he learns that it was Mr. Benjamin's rule to destroy at once all of his correspondence—everything that might aid or enlighten a biographer. Mr. Francis Lawley, who had begun the task of collecting materials for a biography of Mr. Benjamin, thus writes down what the latter told him on April 27, 1883 : " Even if I had health, and desired ever so much to help you in your work, I have no ma-

terials available for the purpose.   I have never kept a
diary, or retained a copy of a letter written by me.
No letters addressed to me by others will be found
among my papers when I die.   With perhaps the exception of Mrs. Jefferson Davis, no one has many letters
of mine ; for I have read so many American biographies which reflected only the passions and preju-
dices of their writers, that I do not want to leave behind me letters and documents to be used in such a
work about myself."   Indeed, Mr. Benjamin was very
reserved concerning his private affairs, as well as
matters of professional or official business within his
ken.   Just as he had devoted his last day in Richmond to the burning of the secret service papers of the
Confederacy, so he was busy during the last weeks of
his life in destroying such private papers and letters as
remained ; and "when he died," writes Mr. Witt, one
of his executors, "he did not leave behind him half a
dozen pieces of paper." [1]   Moreover, his nephew, Mr.
E. B. Kruttschnitt, of New Orleans, wrote to Mr. Lawley : "I do not know what material you have at hand
to aid you in writing Mr. Benjamin's biography, but I
would say that I have always found it extremely difficult to learn anything about his life prior to the Civil
War with any degree of accuracy.   The older members of the family know nothing but the most general
facts, and have never been able to give me details
which would be extremely interesting in reference to
the political campaigns in which Mr. Benjamin was
engaged, his two candidacies, and election to the United
States Senate, etc.   When I first joined the bar in this
city, in 1874, many of Mr. Benjamin's contemporaries

[1] *Lawley MS. ;* see also Callahan, pp. 12, 20, 23.

were still alive, and some of them could speak most interestingly about his earlier career, but all of these persons are now dead [1897], and I do not know of any one who from personal recollection could give any matter of real importance to a biographer. . . . The task of preparing such a work is one which I at one time seriously considered, but I was appalled by the amount of research and labor which would be necessary, in order to obtain the information required to prepare such a work. My aunt, Mrs. J. P. Benjamin, who was then alive, was quite desirous that I should undertake the task when I last saw her on a visit to Europe in 1886. Neither she, nor Mr. Benjamin's daughter, had any papers, however, which could be of the slightest assistance to me, and I could not then see where I could get the material for more than a short sketch."

Confronted by a situation thus discouraging, I nevertheless persevered in my endeavor to find sufficient material to give form to this work. A careful investigation of the valuable files of newspapers preserved, or rather allowed to exist, in the City Hall in New Orleans, revealed many details of interest about Mr. Benjamin's earlier career in that place. I made an examination of these newspapers from 1830 to 1865, being especially careful for those of the years after 1842; and for this labor I was amply rewarded by the mass of news and of editorial comments upon which some of the earlier chapters of the present book are based.

Through the generous help of the publishers and of Mr. Kruttschnitt, I was enabled to secure the materials, still quite inchoate, collected by Mr. Lawley, which gave much most valuable information for the treatment of Mr. Benjamin's career in England.

Again through the kindness of Mr. Kruttschnitt and of other members of his family, I was given such details of family history as they could furnish. And at length they discovered and put at my disposal a most interesting collection of letters, about two score, dating from 1864 to 1883, from Mr. Benjamin to various members of his family, the only considerable number of letters I have been able to find. I have drawn largely upon these, though always, I trust, with due regard for the manifest wish of Mr. Benjamin to leave unharmed the sanctity of family relations.

Mr. Max J. Kohler, of New York, also furnished me with a copy of his excellent monograph upon Mr. Benjamin, and put me upon the track of several other possible sources of information. The most fruitful of these proved to be a small collection of letters from Mr. Benjamin to Messrs. James A. and Thomas F. Bayard. Mrs. W. S. Hilles, of Wilmington, Del., daughter of Hon. Thomas F. Bayard, deserves especial thanks for her care in copying and sending to me these letters, as well as certain notes upon Mr. Benjamin made by her father, which, though few in number, contained items of great interest and importance.

Finally, the record of Mr. Benjamin's public acts as an official of the Confederate Government, now in possession of the United States Government, at Washington, is sufficiently full to enable one to follow this part of his career with accuracy. Some of this material has been published [1] or is in course of publication by

---

[1] The Hon. J. D. Richardson's *Compilation of Messages and Papers* was not available until my task was practically completed.

authority of the Federal Government; much, however, still remains in manuscript in the archives of the Treasury Department, to whose custodians I wish to make acknowledgment for their courtesy and assistance in the examination of the documents.

Since the author is, by ancient and precious custom, permitted to introduce himself to the reader in his own way in the preface, I may venture upon a word or two of explanation in regard to the method of treatment and the point of view that I have sought to maintain in the following pages. First, as to the proportion or amount of space devoted to the various periods of Mr. Benjamin's life, I may say that I have tried to give due preponderance to what seemed most vital and interesting. For example, the political career both before and during the Civil War has received fuller treatment than the purely legal career. The significant characteristics of the great advocate, and the important cases that should claim popular attention, have been presented; but the author has sought to avoid technicalities of the law, that might be of doubtful interest to a limited number of students; for Mr. Benjamin was something more than a lawyer, and we should but lose sight of the larger activities of the man in attempting to make a professional study. It has likewise seemed proper to treat in greater detail the whole story of Mr. Benjamin's life in America; for, undoubtedly, it was in this land that he "found himself." His fame was made before he went to England, and his successes there were but the culmination, and, indeed, the continuation, of those here. Though he transferred his formal allegiance to Great Britain, whose child he chanced to be, he could no more for-

get America than he could make the English forget
what they called his "American accent."

Secondly, it seems proper to say that the aim
of the book has been to treat quite frankly the life of
one who, active in the politics of a very stormy period
of our history, did not escape the criticisms and calumnies of politics.   Every charge against Mr. Benjamin
of any moment whatever, so far as known, has been
set down in these pages; where justification or excul-
pation seemed proper, it has been attempted; but
where his conduct seemed indefensible, no defense has
been made,—merely the statement of such facts as
could be established.   The character of the man, I
believe, should outweigh petty accusations; hence I
have not wilfully neglected to notice them all where I
found them.   Finally, in discussing the delicate political questions of the period from 1850 to 1865, I have
sought to present the view, as I conceived it, of the
South, but always with such comment as the fairer and
clearer vision of our own time appeared to call for.   It
seemed futile to attempt to understand the Confederacy
if one treated it in hostile or unsympathetic mood; it
seemed equally absurd and unworthy of history to
follow blindly the political teachings of apologists for
a lost cause.   The most difficult matter, perhaps, has
been to present adequately the diplomatic history of
the Confederacy, so as to show, if possible, that because she failed of securing that foreign recognition which was the stake for which she played in
diplomacy, it does not follow as a necessary consequence that the fault was in the diplomacy.   The historic prestige of success, of course, is with the Union
cause; but it should not be forgotten that, though

victory may follow the biggest battalions, the smaller may have been ably commanded.

It remains for me to express my thanks for assistance of various kinds from the many to whom I have found it necessary to apply in the course of this work. The names of all I cannot give here; but at least I should not fail to mention Mrs. E. A. Bradford, of New Orleans, widow of Mr. Benjamin's law partner and intimate friend; Mr. Joseph Lebowich, of Harvard College, author of a useful Bibliography on Mr. Benjamin, who has been most kind in putting at my service materials and references collected by him; Mrs. Mary Pohlman, custodian of the archives in the New Orleans City Hall, who assisted me greatly in my search through the newspapers; Mr. William Beer, of the Howard Library, who has allowed the utmost freedom in consulting the valuable collections there upon the history of Louisiana; and Mrs. Jefferson Davis, who has written full and interesting letters, furnishing details about one with whom she was so intimately associated during Richmond's ordeal by fire. For care in the reading and revision of the proofs, I must thank Professor John R. Ficklen, of Tulane University.

CHRONOLOGY

1808—Philip Benjamin and Rebecca de Mendes, married shortly before in London, emigrate to St. Thomas.

1811—Judah Philip Benjamin born in St. Thomas, August 6th.

1816–1818—The Benjamins remove to the United States, settling first at Charleston.

1825—Benjamin enters Yale College, but leaves in 1827, without taking a degree.

1828—Comes to New Orleans, earning his living by teaching, and studies law as a notary's clerk.

1832—Called to the bar, December 16th, and three months later is married to Natalie St. Martin.

1834—Benjamin and Thomas Slidell publish their *Digest* of Supreme Court Decisions.

1842—Having made secure his position at the bar, Benjamin enters politics; elected to the lower house of the General Assembly on the Whig ticket.

1844–1845—Delegate to the Louisiana Constitutional Convention.

1846–1847—Summons his mother and family from South Carolina, and establishes them on "Bellechasse" plantation. Relinquishes much of his law practice to devote himself to sugar planting. Death of his mother, 1847.

1852—Elected to the State Senate; to the Senate of the United States; most influential delegate to the Louisiana Constitutional Convention. During this period is prominent in the affairs of the Jackson Railroad and the Tehuantepec Company.

1856–1858—Speech on the Kansas question in the Senate; taking sides in the growing bitterness of the slavery question. The Whig party goes to pieces, and Benjamin finally becomes a Democrat.

1859—Reëlected to the Senate.

1860—Split in the Charleston Convention (April) of the Democratic party. Benjamin takes sides against Douglas, and
approves of the secession of Southern delegates. Absent in
California as counsel in the New Almaden mines case when
Congress assembles. December 3d, takes his seat soon after
the meeting, and declares for secession. December 31st,
delivers a great speech in defense of the Southern position.

1861—South Carolina having seceded on December 20, 1860,
Louisiana follows, January 26, 1861. February 4th,
Benjamin and Slidell bid farewell to the Senate. Benjamin
returns to New Orleans, and on February 25th, is named
Attorney-General in the Confederate Cabinet. February
18th, inauguration of the provisional government of the
Confederate States. March 4th, inauguration of President
Lincoln. April 12th, firing on Fort Sumter. July 21st,
Bull Run. September 17th, Benjamin named acting
Secretary of War, and confirmed in the office by the
Confederate Senate in November. November–December,
Mason and Slidell sail as Confederate Commissioners to
England and to France respectively; are captured by the
United States SS. *San Jacinto*, and released upon the de-
mand of England.

1862—January–February—Confederate disasters at Roanoke Island,
Fort Henry, and Fort Donelson. Censure of Benjamin as
Secretary of War. February 22d, formation of the per-
manent government of the Confederacy. President Davis
names Benjamin Secretary of State. August–September,
second battle of Bull Run, Lee crosses into Maryland, but is
checked at Sharpsburg or Antietam; frustration of Confederate hopes of intervention on the part of England or
France. September 22d, Lincoln issues Proclamation of
Emancipation.

1863—May 1st–3d, Chancellorsville, death of Stonewall Jackson.
Lee invades Pennsylvania: July 1st–3d, Gettysburg.
July 4th, fall of Vicksburg. The Confederate cause henceforth really desperate, though the struggle is kept up with
vigor.

1864—March 3d, Grant appointed Lieutenant-General, assumes
command of Union armies; in June he begins the attack
upon Richmond from the South. September–December,
Sherman advances to Atlanta. Duncan F. Kenner sent to
Europe with full powers by the Confederacy.

1865—February 3d, fruitless conference between Confederates and Lincoln at Fortress Monroe. April 2d, evacuation of Richmond, retreat of the Confederate Government. April 9th, Lee surrenders at Appomattox. April 14th, assassination of Lincoln. May 10th–11th, capture of President Davis. Benjamin makes his way to the Florida coast and escapes, landing in England in September.

1866—June, Benjamin called to the bar in England.

1868—Publication of *Benjamin on Sales* establishes his reputation.

1872—Made Queen's Counsel; his wrecked fortune is repaired.

1880—Severely injured by a fall from a tram-car in Paris.

1883—Retires from practice, and in June bids farewell to the bench and bar at the Temple banquet.

1884—May 6th, dies in Paris.

To the late
Ernest Benjamin Kruttschnitt,
through whose generous and ever
kindly help it was made possible,
this book is gratefully dedicated.

JUDAH P. BENJAMIN

CHAPTER I

BIRTH AND TRAINING

OF the ancestry of Judah P. Benjamin little can be given with sufficient accuracy to warrant me in reproducing it. "I suppose there never was a family," writes one of his nephews, "whose members seemed to know so little of their own history." Beyond the fact that, on the mother's side at least, his family were Portuguese Jews, little is known with certainty. Yet some items of interest may be ascertained, and of these I must first speak.

According to the recollection of one of the older generation of the family still surviving (Mr. Benjamin's niece), the home of Rebecca de Mendes, the mother of Judah P. Benjamin, was near Finnsbury Circus, London. How many members of the family there were, and what was their occupation, are points that are not known. But it is clear that they were people of some education and refinement, though probably poor. There were several daughters in the family, and at least one son. Tradition reports that two of the daughters were remarkable for their beauty. Two of them married West Indian planters and moved to the islands before the marriage of the youngest to Philip Benjamin. The date of this union is uncertain; but

there seems reason to fix it not long before 1808. In
the materials collected by Mr. Lawley for his proposed
Life of Benjamin it is simply stated that "little is
known of his parents beyond a vague rumor that
when resident in London they occupied a shop in one
of the streets leading into Cheapside, near Bow Church,
where they made a little money by selling dried fruit."
Mr. Lawley knew Mr. Benjamin personally, and may
have had his authority for this rumor; but it cannot
be verified; and the present writer is inclined to the
belief that, though Philip Benjamin may have lived
near Bow Church, it was before his marriage.

When taking out his naturalization papers at Charleston, S. C., in 1826, Philip Benjamin stated that he
was then forty-four years of age. He would therefore
have been twenty-six in 1808. It seems hardly probable that he was married much younger than that; and
it is positive that he and his wife went to the island of
St. Croix, or St. Thomas (there is some doubt as to
which), in 1808, where their eldest child, Rebecca,
was born in the following year. He was of a restless
disposition, a rolling stone, and apparently never successful, and so not long satisfied anywhere. The removal to the West Indian island may have been made
immediately after his marriage. And his selection of
the West Indies as a place in which to seek new fortunes
was not unlikely due to the fact that his bride had
relatives there who had prospered. At all events,
there are no certain evidences that the Benjamins lived
any part of their married life in England; and their
story really begins in St. Thomas.[1]

[1] Benjamin himself declares for St. Thomas; see below, Chapter
XIII.

This island at the time was a British possession, having been juggled about among the great powers then engaged in the titanic wars of Napoleon. Though small, and long since fallen from its high estate, it had been and for a time continued to be somewhat important as an *entrepôt* for the thriving West Indian trade, and as a base for naval operations. What business the Benjamins were engaged in we do not know; but they did not prosper. And being in very straitened circumstances while there, they probably left no such impression as would justify our putting trust in the report that, some years ago, the house in which they lived, and where their distinguished son came into the world, could still be identified.

Judah Philip, the second child, was born in St. Thomas, on August 6, 1811, and his early boyhood was spent there. Nearly all the published accounts of Mr. Benjamin state it was merely chance that he should have been born under the Union Jack, since his parents, sailing from England for New Orleans, stopped at St. Thomas only because the British fleet was already blockading the mouth of the Mississippi, previous to the outbreak of the War of 1812. The facts thus far given are certainly sufficient to disprove this statement: there was no blockading fleet in 1808; and if it had been Philip Benjamin's intention to go directly to the United States, he could easily have done so. When the removal was made is not altogether certain: dates as early as 1816 and as late as 1825 have been suggested, and by those who knew Mr. Benjamin in his youth; but the later date is altogether out of the question, since he always spoke as though he had been brought to the United States when too young to re-

member anything clearly about his first home. With
a man of Philip Benjamin's rather aimless habits, it is
not unlikely that the mere transfer of the islands from
England to Denmark, would have been sufficient to urge
him to move from a place where fortune had not smiled
on him ; and this would also point to the earlier date.

There was a brisk trade in those days between the
West Indies and the Carolinas, where some of Mrs.
Benjamin's relatives were already settled, one being a
merchant in Fayetteville, N. C. Philip Benjamin and
his family went to the Carolinas, and first settled at
Charleston.

Here they seem to have lived for some time, their
fortunes, as always, at a very low ebb ; for the father
was "that *rara avis*, an unsuccessful Jew." The family
were strict Jews, and Mrs. Benjamin, at least, had a full
share of that pride which is a distinguishing characteristic of the well-bred of her race. Her granddaughter
remembers even now the stern and severe rule of the
old lady, resolved to hold her head high in spite of
poverty. On one occasion the prosperous sisters in the
West Indies, probably suspecting the true state of affairs, sent generous chests of linen and other luxuries.
Mrs. Benjamin never opened them, but returned them
with thanks, and the assurance that her needs were
provided for. But the less offensive kindness and
assistance of friends and relatives nearer at hand was
not rejected ; and to this the children owed their education. The family had increased since the move to
Charleston. Besides Rebecca and Judah, there were
two brothers, Solomon and Joseph, then Julia, Harriet,
and Penina, the last born in 1824, when Judah was
finishing his school-days.

As a boy, his brightness and aptness had attracted attention in Charleston. His preparation for college was had in Fayetteville, N. C., where he and his sisters Rebecca and Harriet lived with relatives. The Fayetteville Academy was one of the few institutions of its kind in the South,—one of the oldest, and probably the best, with a full and good corps of instructors, and nearly two hundred pupils. Perhaps we had best try to look at Judah through the eyes of a schoolmate. Mr. R. C. Belden, of Spout Spring, N. C., wrote as follows [1] in 1897 :

"In the year 1825 [1822 ?] Judah, with his brother, Solomon, and sister, Hannah [Harriet], came to Fayetteville, N. C., and lived with their aunt, Mrs. Wright, and uncle, Jacob Levy, the former of whom conducted a fancy dry-goods store, the latter a commission merchant and largely engaged in the West Indian trade. Judah soon entered the Fayetteville Academy, and was a pupil of the Reverend Colin McIver. In many respects he was a singular boy. Reserved in manner, he never had an intimate associate while at school ; and during recess, when the boys were at play, he was making preparation for the coming lesson. As a scholar he was uniformly at the head of his class, and was the brightest intellect in the school. His residence in Fayetteville was short,—about eighteen months.

"Judah and myself were classmates during his school-days in Fayetteville. Solomon, Judah's brother,

---

[1] *Lawley MS.*, from which, and from Mr. Kruttschnitt's family I get most of the details for this chapter. Allowance must be made for certain errors of memory on the part of this octogenarian classmate, errors which I have corrected as far as possible by insertions in brackets.

and the writer were great friends. I previously stated that Judah was the brightest boy in the school; I will now add, I never knew him to make an imperfect recitation, and the ease with which he mastered his studies was a marvel to every one in the school, teachers and all.

"I think I stated in my former note that I was eighty-six, and that there was but little difference between mine and Judah's age.

"The 'Fayetteville Academy' was established in 1796, and incorporated by act of the Legislature. The town made a tax levy to purchase the site and erect the building, and to the amount thus raised the leading citizens of the place made generous contributions. The school soon acquired distinction, and was largely patronized by scholars from many of the Southern states. Men of national renown, including Willie P. Mangum, for many years Senator in Congress, and William R. King, also a Senator, and Vice-President of the United States, were prepared for college at this school. The academy was destroyed in the fire of 1831, and never rebuilt. The number of scholars, in both departments, at the time that Judah was a student, must have been between two and three hundred."

Scanty as are the facts here given of Benjamin's schooling (we know nothing more), the letter itself is a testimony, I think, to the simple thoroughness of the training in this lost institution. After completing his preparation at Fayetteville, young Benjamin returned to Charleston. Thence he went to New Haven, Conn., and entered Yale in 1825. It has been repeatedly asserted that the family was unable to pay the expenses of his college education, and that he was again fortunate in finding generous friends. The Charleston tradition is that the necessary money was supplied by Moses Lopez, a wealthy Jewish merchant, and president of the Hebrew Orphans' Aid Society. But Professor Samuel Porter, of Gallaudet College, Washington, who was a member of his class at Yale, stated that "his expenses were defrayed by a charitable lady of Massachusetts." It is a matter of not much moment, indeed; but the inference from his own letter below is that neither of these statements is correct.

From the records at Yale, it appears that Benjamin attended the college for nearly three sessions, his name appearing in the catalogues of 1825, 1826, and 1827. There is no proof of his attaining really marked distinction; still it is a pleasure to note that there is some tradition placing him among the best scholars, and that this tradition is supported by the testimony of Professor Simeon North, afterward President of Hamilton College, who was Benjamin's "guardian" at Yale, and who took charge of certain of his effects when he left, including a Hebrew Psalter and a Berkleian prize-book inscribed by President Day "for excellence in scholarship."[1] Any laurels he may have won, however, were blasted by a cruel calumny that was of the spawn of bitter partisanship at the time of the Civil War. I shall mention it and dismiss it here, though events must be anticipated; for it is pleasant to feel that one has done with such a matter.

Just prior to the Civil War, when political animosities tarnished so many fair names and embittered so many lives, a newspaper article purporting to come from a classmate went the rounds of the Northern press

[1] Kohler, *Publications Amer. Jewish Hist. Soc.*, No. 12, p. 68.

with the assertion that the needy Jewish student at
Yale had been both a desperate gambler and a thief.
One night after he had gone to bed, said the writer,
and when Benjamin believed him asleep, he had
caught his roommate going through his pockets: to
avoid exposure and summary expulsion, the young
man had left Yale. Immediately upon hearing of
this attempt to poison his life-story at the very source,
Mr. Benjamin employed counsel who, being in the
North, could best serve him in running the libel to
earth and prosecuting those responsible for it. Of the
advice he received from Charles O'Conor and S. M.
Barlow, his counsel; of the peculiar embarrassment
of his position; and of the rallying of friends to his
side, one learns from two letters to his devoted
friends, James A. and Thomas F. Bayard.[1] The first
is dated at Montgomery, from the Department of
Justice of the Confederacy, March 19, 1861, and is in
answer to a letter from Mr. James A. Bayard of February 26th :

"I preferred a suit to an indictment for several
reasons, principally because it gave the man a better
chance to exhaust all possible means of proving the
truth, and thereby render it out of his power to say
that if he could have taken testimony under commission, he would have succeeded in establishing a justification of his infamous calumny. But O'Conor, instead of bringing suit, writes a letter to Barlow, . . .
the tone and temper of which are so manly and generous, and at the same time so apparently discreet and
wise, that he has almost unsettled me. I shall advise
with my friends about it in New Orleans. . . .

[1] Copies of these and other interesting letters were kindly furnished me by Mrs. W. H. Hilles, daughter of T. F. Bayard, Wilmington, Del.

"I am decided in one conviction; that it is not advisable to have any publication in any manner or form on the subject, whether from myself or friends. I feel fully your kind offer to make a communication to the editor of the Confederacy [*sic*] but of what use, with such infamous scoundrels as those who have evidently delighted in circulating this attack, would it be to establish the absolute *impossibility* by a comparison of dates? I left college in the fall of 1827, in consequence of my father's reverses rendering him unable to maintain me there any longer. I was studying law in New Orleans in February, 1828, and maintaining myself whilst so doing, by giving private instruction in two families in New Orleans. The statement in the libel is that the facts occurred in the *fall* of 1828, with one Dyer Ball, whose name I never heard before in my life. Suppose all this shown in a publication by the most conclusive proof. The next week the same men come out and say they were mistaken in the *year*; that it was not in 1828, but in 1827—and the whole affair again goes the round of all the newspapers at the North, with the most malignant comments that can be invented. If I get friends that were college mates to state that no such thing ever occurred, the answer will be that only a few were engaged in the scheme for exposure of the culprit, and that they promised secrecy as is asserted in the libelous article itself. I am satisfied that *nothing* is advisable, unless it be a suit that will sift the whole story, so as to make it *impossible* to evade the result of verdict by cutting off all equivocations. Yet O'Conor, who agrees that this is the only mode, advises so strongly against it, that I must mistrust my own judgment.

"I send you an article cut from the *New Orleans Delta* of 1st March,[1] which appeared since I left there. I have but a single copy, as the paper was forwarded to me marked, by whom I know not, which with the exception of some trifling errors, gives you a fair his-

[1] Should be 2d March.

tory of my life, leaving out of course the emphasis of eulogium contained in it. One error is of time—I have lived in New Orleans thirty-three years instead of twenty-seven—I did not pay my way through school and college by labor, but was thrown on my own resources early in the fall of 1827, when I was just sixteen years old, having been born on 6th August, 1811. . . . [The article] seems to show O'Conor's view to be right, but I will not determine finally till I consult my friends further."

Added reflection led him to the view that Mr. O'Conor and the *Delta* were right, and that it were better to rest his defense on the honor and uprightness of his life rather than on any mere specific attack upon this calumniator. The suit at libel, moreover, would have been a practical impossibility, for the next letter, to Mr. T. F. Bayard, is dated April 5th, less than a fortnight before the firing on Sumter. In it he says: "I have your kind favor of the 30th ultimo, and am exceedingly touched by the warm and genial sympathy which it expresses. When I look back a few weeks I am myself somewhat ashamed that I could have allowed myself to be moved so deeply by such a cause, and yet there was something so inexpressibly loathsome and revolting at the bare idea of having one's name published in the newspapers in connection with so degrading a charge, that it is scarcely to be wondered at, that feeling should usurp the place of judgment. However, I have determined to yield to the advice of my friends, and to let a lifelong career of integrity and honor make silent and contemptuous answer to such an attack. If anything could compensate for the mortification necessarily incident to such an abominable outrage, it is the constant receipt from

valued friends of just such letters as that which I have
been gratified in receiving from you. I, however,
needed nothing from you nor from any one bearing
your name to feel assured in advance of the light in
which such a publication could be received."

The article in the *Delta* to which reference is made,
showed that Mr. O'Conor's advice had indeed been
judicious, and with this quotation we may close the
account of the student days at Yale: "'We have
seen a letter from the Hon. J. P. Benjamin to a gentleman in this city, announcing his intention to depart
from the established rule of his life so far as to prosecute for libel some one or more of the more prominent
of those who have given publicity to the infamous
calumny in reference to his conduct at Yale College
years ago.' The above, from the Louisville *Courier*,
relates to one of the vilest and most infamous attempts
ever made to blacken the reputation of a public man
whose great talents, astonishing energy, patriotic and
dignified bearing in the public councils have elicited
the applause and admiration of the whole country.
The story was hatched by Abolition malice, and the
place and time of the incidents in it were selected with
cunning regard to the difficulty of refutation. . . .
[The calumny] has served to revive, in the memories
of all who are familiar with his remarkable career, the
recollection of the innumerable instances of his generosity, his devotion to his relatives and friends, the
prodigality, we may say, of his beneficence, and the
remarkable absence of all sordidness in his whole nature and conduct."

CHAPTER II

LAW AND SUGAR

FROM New Haven Benjamin returned to his family; but he was of a spirit too self-reliant and proudly independent to trust to them for support, even if his father had been in a position to help him. Philip Benjamin had a small shop in King Street, Charleston, but had made no success of his business. The eldest daughter, Rebecca, to whom Judah was particularly attached, had been married, while he was at Yale, to Mr. Abraham Levy, in 1826. And it was not long after this that the rest of the family removed to Beaufort, S. C., where they lived for ten or fifteen years, and where, during the latter part of this period, they were supported by Judah, the father having proved utterly unable to maintain them. The boy could not have remained long in Charleston, for he came to New Orleans early in 1828, arriving, it is said, with less than five dollars in his pocket.

In his need, any employment was welcome, and in spite of his marked intellectual proclivities, he seems first to have found a position in a commercial house. An old friend, Mr. J. R. Hamilton, said[1] he had often heard Benjamin declare that the familiarity he then acquired with commercial forms and procedure, and bookkeeping, stood him in good stead in after years. Nothing, however, but a memory of this mercantile

[1] *Lawley MS.*

episode remains. One cannot even say with what firm or in what business he was employed ; and it could not have been for long, since we soon find him at what must have been a more congenial occupation, as clerk to a notary. From the first Benjamin had made use of every spare moment to prepare himself better for the battle with the world. After business hours he studied law ; and he was acute enough to recognize at once, not only that New Orleans offered him unusual facilities for acquiring French and Spanish, but that a thorough familiarity with French, particularly, would profit him immensely in any career, mercantile or professional. Accordingly, he sought private pupils who wanted coaching in any of the branches he felt prepared to teach—and his education, even so unhappily truncated as it had been, was certainly far above the average. From some pupils he received fees ; with others an exchange was affected, he teaching English and learning French.

The notary with whom Benjamin served, and under whose friendly care he studied law more regularly than he could possibly have done by himself, was Mr. Greenbury R. Stringer. The friendless and all but penniless young Jew seems to have been very fortunate in finding his way into this gentleman's service ; for Mr. Stringer had a large amount of notarial business, and therefore many clients who might subsequently remember the young man studying law in his office ; and he was moreover highly respected as a man, and a good friend to his clerk and pupil. One day a gentleman from the country, a sugar-planter of means and high social position, wrote to Mr. Stringer to ask whether he could recommend any likely young man for a tutor. Mr. Stringer replied that he thought he could name a suitable person; would the gentleman call at his office on his next visit to the city? The gentleman came, was introduced to Benjamin, and had an interview with him. "I'm sorry," he told Mr. Stringer afterward, "but your young man won't do." "What's the matter? Can't he teach the subjects you want?" "Oh, yes, and more besides; the fact is, he's perfectly wonderful. But he's so fascinating that I'm sure my girl would fall in love with him and run away before the month was out." [1]

The story itself is very likely apocryphal; but it shows the impression the young man made on those around him. Moreover, while teaching English to Mlle. Natalie St. Martin, Benjamin not only learned French of the best sort and in the most thorough fashion, but fell in love himself. The young lady was strikingly beautiful, and witty; she had, besides, great musical talent and "the voice of a prima donna." Benjamin was called to the bar on December 16, 1832, and within a few months later he was married.

The marriage contract, fixing the property relations between the future spouses, was passed before Louis Peraud, Notary Public, February 12, 1833, signed by Judah Philip Benjamin and Natalie St. Martin, daughter of Auguste St. Martin and Françoise Peire. The witnesses were Greenbury R. Stringer and Charles Maurian on the part of the husband, and Samuel Herman and Alonzo Morphy, at one time a justice of the Louisiana Supreme Court, on the part of the bride. The exact date of the marriage ceremony is not

[1] Anecdote from the late Dr. Davidson, of New Orleans, in a clipping from the *N. O. Democrat*, 1880, which I cannot date.

known; but it is customary to pass the notarial act on
the day of the wedding, or not long before. Mrs.
Benjamin, just previous to her death, wrote that she
had been married on February 16, 1832; the year is
manifestly a mistake of failing memory; but she would
have been less likely to make a mistake as to the day
of the month, which accords well enough with the date
of the notarial act.[1]

The bride was a Creole, *i. e.*, of French parentage,
but born in a colony, her parents being refugees from
the black horror of St. Domingo. Though socially attractive, she was not a fit companion intellectually for
her husband, caring far more for brilliant society than
for domesticity. And she was a devout Catholic. Mr.
Benjamin had been brought up a Jew, and was too
proud of his hereditary religion, however slight the
hold of its forms and practices upon him in after life,
ever to accept the Roman Catholic or any other creed.
Marriages between persons of different faiths are rarely
wise; and when neither party is sufficiently indifferent
to compromise, they can hardly help proving ill-
assorted and unhappy. If there ever was a man who
loved the home, and knew how, even when preoccu-
pied with affairs in the great world, to give himself up
to the little loving services that count so much in the
daily lives of the family, that man was Judah P. Benjamin. He did not care for wealth for himself; he
wished to make ample provision for the comfort of all
those dependent on him; he wanted a home. But Mrs.
Benjamin did not share his simple tastes; and though
he hid his unhappiness most scrupulously from the
world, from his most intimate friends, and even from

[1] Letter from Mr. Kruttschnitt, *Lawley MS.*

his own family as far as he could, his married life could
not have been other than a disappointment to him.

Since Mrs. Benjamin really entered so slightly into
his career, we may as well anticipate events just enough
to complete the little that need be said of her life in
America. Mr. Benjamin was soon in a position to
supply her liberally with means, and she entertained
her friends, he sharing in it all as far as his occupations would permit. Their home was at first in the
city, on Bourbon Street; but after he secured an interest in "Bellechasse" plantation, Mrs. Benjamin
tried life there, and found it "*triste.*" There was but
one child who lived beyond infancy, Anne Julie Marie
Natalie Benjamin, and when the little girl was between
four and five years old her mother moved permanently
to France to educate her, and Mr. Benjamin saw them
only on his summer trips, almost annual, to Paris.

When Judah P. Benjamin was married, in 1833,
he had his own living to make; he was already contributing something to the support of his mother and
sisters, and was soon to have to provide for their entire
maintenance. In a young and vigorously growing
American city like the New Orleans of that day, fortunes were more readily and rapidly accumulated than
now; still, Mr. Benjamin's rise was marvelous, or
what the newspapers sometimes call "meteoric." His
service in the notary's office had been good training; it had taught him much of legal forms and legal
procedure which others had to acquire in the course of
their profession; it had made him a ready penman,
and developed that exquisitely neat and accurate chi-
rography which distinguished him always; it had
probably brought him into personal contact with a

large number of clients who would now come to the
young lawyer. But unquestionably the most potent
factors in his success were his native ability, his pleasing personality, his tremendous energy, and his capacity for hard work.

It has been stated repeatedly that Benjamin began
his practice in partnership with Thomas Slidell, or
with C. M. Conrad, or with both of them in the firm of
Slidell, Benjamin, and Conrad. He was early associated with the former in the preparation of a "Digest
of the Reported Decisions of the Superior Courts in the
Territory of Orleans and State of Louisiana" (1834),
which brought him considerable reputation ; and he
was also intimate with Mr. Conrad ; but I have been
unable to find any authority for the statement that he
was then in partnership with either of them. It would
have been more like him to be self-reliant and start in
his profession by himself. Furthermore, such is the report given me by a member of the family ; and the
early directories of New Orleans confirm this by assign-
ing Benjamin, Slidell, and Conrad to separate offices.

Clients come but slowly at first to every young lawyer ; therefore during the first year of his practice
Benjamin had leisure to prepare the "Digest" mentioned above. It had been originally intended only
for his own use, brief annotations accompanying the
résumé of facts and analysis of the court's ruling in
notable cases. But, encouraged and assisted by Mr.
Slidell, he added to the scope of the notes, and included more cases, until fellow lawyers right and left
found it very convenient to borrow the manuscript,
whose real value thus became apparent. Then the
two friends revised it, and published it in book form.

While of course not ranking as a creative work or a standard treatise discussing fundamental principles— for it really required little more than care and accuracy in compilation, with the ability to write an intelligent synopsis—the "Digest" was recognized as a very useful work to the Louisiana lawyer, and had sufficient sale to warrant another printing within a few years. This revised edition, in fact, continued to hold the field for many years.

Very soon after he began his practice, however, Benjamin had cases before the Supreme Court of Louisiana;[1] and but a glance at the court reports subsequent to 1834 is necessary to show the constantly increasing frequency with which his name appears. Many of these early cases, doubtless such desperate ones as generally come to young practitioners eager to undertake anything, are lost, and in not one does the sum involved or the issue decided appear to have been important. Yet the volume of legal business indicated by these recorded cases is noteworthy. Before his apprenticeship at the bar is ended, Benjamin's name becomes at least as frequent in the reports, if not in connection with the larger causes, as those of able attorneys who had several years' start of him. Among these men, some of more than local renown, some much older and some younger than Benjamin, were the Slidells, John, afterward Senator, and Thomas, afterward Chief Justice of Louisiana ; Pierre Soulé, foreign born (like Benjamin), a famous orator, and one day to be Minister to Spain, when he will sign that famous Ostend Manifesto that startles the Union in 1854 ;

---

[1] Louisiana Reports, VI, 100., Baron *vs.* Duncan, Executor, *et. al.;* and 182, Spurrier *vs.* Sheldon *et. al.*

Christian Roselius, also a foreigner, risen from the hardest poverty to be a lawyer whose opinion is highly prized, a man whose sturdy honesty all respect ; F. B. and C. M. Conrad, both prominent in the politics of the South ; Mazureau, the greatest of the Creole lawyers ; John R. Grymes, some time, like John Slidell, to be a serious political rival of Benjamin ; and a host of others—Levi Peirce, L. C. Duncan, E. Seghers— whose names are now less familiar because they preferred law to politics. It was a very able bar, and a very large one for a town of less than fifty thousand inhabitants. But the volume of commercial business then flowing through New Orleans was out of all proportion to the population. Benjamin had chosen wisely in coming here to begin his life-work, for the town had already grown and for thirty years was to continue growing with that marvelous rapidity which has become so common, under improved conditions of communication, that it ceases to be a marvel. Given a favorable situation, such as that of New Orleans at the mouth of a great river, and steam applied to transportation would work wonders. Already to New Orleans the Mississippi boats brought a vast business, soon to be added to when steamships replaced the sailing vessels and railways supplemented the steamboats. It was a thriving commercial city, where fortunes were quickly made. And where commerce thrives the lawyer does also.

This partly explains, no doubt, Benjamin's rapid success. There were many men at the bar of far less brilliance than he who nevertheless made handsome fortunes ; for any attorney of fair talent could not fail to find plenty to do. It was in the field of commercial

law that Benjamin labored. He certainly had more
than average ability; and he worked, said a contemporary, "as few men have, before or since." Pains-
taking and accurate to the smallest detail in getting up
his cases, he had then as always an immense capacity
for work, and he labored with such intensity and con-
centration that he completed his task with what
seemed incredible celerity. Scarcely one of those who
have told of his achievements at the bar has failed to
note his powers of logical analysis; with the most
complex matters of fact or of law before him, his mind
at once singled out the essential, the vital point at
issue; and seeing this clearly himself he could present
his view disencumbered of confusing details. But this
quickness of apprehension, and power of logical presentation, which might have been a temptation to care-
lessness and superficiality was, as we have said, guarded
by the most thorough mastery of detail. The perfect balance of Benjamin's temperament, his complete
self-command and easy good-humor under the most
trying conditions, and the deceptive air of being
always unpreoccupied and free to devote his time to
things other than business, gave many the impression
that his learning was easily acquired. On the contrary, his legal knowledge was the fruit of hard labor;
whatever of genius there may have been, there was
also plenty of steady work.

To the lay reader any extended treatment of the
suits in which Benjamin appeared would prove tedious.
Most of these suits, moreover, deal with commercial
law, and hence do not in any way bring up issues of
general public interest. But in 1842 Benjamin, at that
time with Slidell and Conrad, had a case, or rather a

series of cases, that attracted wide attention, involving as they did international complications that might have led to a serious clash with England. The brig *Creole*, engaged in the coasting slave-trade, shipped a lot of negroes at Richmond, Norfolk, and other points in Virginia, for New Orleans. While on the high seas, nineteen of the slaves mutinied, killed the agent of one of their owners, seriously wounded the captain, and obtained complete control of the vessel. They then forced the crew to change the course and make for Nassau. On arrival there the mate jumped into the quarantine boat, was taken ashore, and appealed to the American consul for protection for the ship. The British officials guarded the *Creole*, and kept the slaves from landing or holding communication with other boats. In due time the Attorney-General for the island, accompanied by magistrates, boarded the vessel and took depositions on the mutiny, establishing the guilt of the nineteen leaders, whom they proposed to hold for the murder of the agent and assault upon the captain and crew. Thus far both parties are in agreement; of the subsequent happenings there are two versions,—that of the American crew and passengers, and that of the British officials. The former alleged that the Attorney-General and the magistrates, after establishing the guilt of the actual mutineers, announced to the rest of the negroes that they were free to go ashore, and that, being once on British soil, they would no longer be slaves. This was directly contradicted by the British, who testified that this announcement was made by a passenger, and that the responsible officers of the vessel, standing by, made no protest, and no effort to hinder their landing.

The Commercial Court of New Orleans first considered the suits brought by the owners of the liberated slaves to recover from the insurance companies. There were a number of separate suits, *e. g.*, McCargo *vs.* The New Orleans Insurance Company, and Lockett *vs.* Merchants' Insurance Company,[1] in which F. B. Conrad, T. Slidell, and J. P. Benjamin represented the insurance companies. The case of McCargo *vs.* The New Orleans Insurance Company will serve for what brief comment we can make. The suit was lost in the lower court, judgment for $18,400 being given against the underwriters. The brief on appeal to the State Supreme Court was prepared by Benjamin, and was an exhaustive consideration of the wider aspects of the case; the judgment of the lower court was reversed. Benjamin's argument is most elaborate and lucid, clearly establishing that the liberation of the slaves was not due to "foreign interference" (covered by the policy), but to "the force and effect of the law of nature and of nations on the relations of the parties, against which no insurance was or could be legally made." This is the eighth and final point in the argument to prove that the insurance company was not liable, the others being based on more technical grounds and supported by copious legal references. And this point is the more interesting to us because its proof involves an examination of the status of slavery in the law of nations. Mr. Benjamin, himself a slave-owner, and afterward in the Senate one of the most able defenders of the institution, here quotes the very passage of the Roman law about which he was later to have a debate with Seward: "Slavery is

[1] 10 Robinson's Louisiana Reports, 202 and 339.

against the law of nature; and although sanctioned by the law of nations, it is so sanctioned as a local or municipal institution, of binding force within the limits of the nation that chooses to establish it, and on the vessels of such nation on the high seas, but as having no force or binding effect beyond the jurisdiction of such nation." [1]

The "Creole case" involved issues that made it not only a *cause célèbre* but a matter for diplomatic negotiations. With these we are not concerned; but this suit was probably the first which spread Benjamin's name over the Union. His brief was printed in pamphlet form and widely circulated; and it seems rather prophetic, when we look at it from our vantage ground of sixty years, that his name should thus first have become widely known in connection with slavery.

But Benjamin's reputation as an attorney depended not on "Creole cases." Already, in 1842, he very likely had a practice as lucrative as that of any lawyer in New Orleans. Fees regarded as enormous in those days were given to retain him, or to secure his opinion. Unfortunately, the details of all this business can only be guessed at; but we have an index to his reputation in an interesting little volume that was issued in New Orleans in 1846: *Sketches of Life and Character in Louisiana.* The sketches, originally appearing in the New Orleans newspapers [2] were anonymous, but are known to have been by Judge Whitaker, afterward a quite distinguished member of the bar whose famous members he described. What he says of Mr. Benjamin is for the most part so apt and so useful, as

[1] 10 Robinson's Louisiana Reports, p. 279.
[2] *The Bee* and *The Jeffersonian.*

giving a contemporary view, that I shall quote liberally :

"Benjamin is emphatically the *Commercial* Lawyer of
our city, and one of the most successful advocates at
our bar.   .   .   .   He is remarkable for the vivacity of
his features, his sparkling and intelligent eyes, the
perfect neatness and elegance of his costume, and the
finished courtesy of his manners.   He is rather below
the middle height, though well proportioned.   From
his appearance, he would scarcely be taken for a
student, though perhaps as industrious a man as there
is in the city, and to be found at his office early and
late, never neglecting business for social enjoyments,
or the calls of pleasure.   Mr. Benjamin is a man fitted
to adorn any circle, however distinguished for elegance
or refinement, and yet at the same time, we find him
the severe and untiring devotee to his profession.

"As a speaker, he is calm, collected, forcible, though
sometimes a little too rapid in his elocution.   His voice
has a silvery, mellifluous sweetness, and seldom jars
upon the ear by degenerating into shrill or harsh tones.
His style is distinguished for its conciseness and close
adherence to the matter in hand.   He never goes in
search of flowers or metaphors, and yet, when occasion
offers, uses them with skill and appositeness.   His
manner and gesture are graceful and finished ; and his
language the purest and most appropriate English.
To his many scholarly acquirements he adds the French
language, which he speaks with fluency and elegance.
In his converse with the world he is sociable and
agreeable, and, I believe, generally admired and liked
by those who know him intimately.

"Mr. Benjamin is by birth, and as his name imports,
an Israelite.   Yet how far he still adheres to the religion of his fathers, I cannot tell, though I should
doubt whether the matter troubled him much.   In his
politics, he is a Whig, and one of the lights of the
party in this city.   He is, too, if I mistake not, some-

thing of a writer, and has contributed his quota to the literature of the South. . . . It is very evident that Mr. Benjamin seeks rather the distinction of being a thorough and accomplished lawyer, than that of a literary man or politician. In business he is ever ready, never for a moment at a loss. This readiness, this activity of mind, are the fruits of labor and of study ; he has not been a close student for nothing.

"Mr. Benjamin cannot be more, certainly, than thirty-six, and yet deserves a niche among the veterans of our bar. I dwell long upon this picture, as I think it may be studied with advantage by young practitioners who seek distinction."

Accompanying the sketch of Benjamin is one of Randell Hunt ; and the writer's contrast of the two is in some points instructive :

"Composure, coolness, and perfect self-possession characterize the manner of Benjamin, while Hunt, in his fondness for display, is more excited, more passionate, more energetic. With Benjamin every word has a meaning, every expression is germane to the matter. . . . The peculiar department of law to which the younger counselor has directed his attention has probably conduced to the severity of his style, and the plain, businesslike features by which it is characterized. . . . Mr. Benjamin in his peculiar walk, is the best lawyer of the two, and the more attached to his profession for the love of it. Mr. Hunt aims, we should think, greatly more at political distinction, though we should not be in the least surprised if the younger counselor got the start of him."

There are several significant points in this little bit of gossipy character-drawing that tempt one to pause for comment. In the first place, the closing remark was an apt prophecy; for Hunt was soon to be quite distanced in public life by his competitor. Besides this, one cannot help noting the reference to Benjamin's religion. In the absence of direct evidence it is impossible to speak with decision, but it may be doubted if he had in any way kept up his connection with the Jewish church since his arrival in New Orleans. He had undoubtedly been reared to a very strict observance of his faith; and the fact that he was known as a Jew at Yale, and that he possessed there a copy of the Hebrew Psalter, would indicate that up to that time he had remained a professing Jew. But soon after his coming to New Orleans, an intensely Catholic community, we find him intimately associated with Catholics, rather than with those of his own race. His marriage to a devout Catholic, too, would in itself indicate apathy, at least, toward his faith. And we have direct evidence to show how very lax were the few Jews in New Orleans at the time. Even if he had been temperamentally religious,—and he certainly was not—or inclined to elect his associates from among the Jews, the atmosphere of the city would have been most unfavorable. A writer in the *Allgemeine Zeitung des Judenthums* [1] reports that, though there were about seven hundred Jewish families in New Orleans, only four kept a Kosher table, and only two observed Saturday as Sabbath. The synagogue accommodated only about fifty persons, and "the former Rabbi, a Dutchman, had married a Catholic wife, who was restrained with difficulty from sending a crucifix to his grave with her husband on his death." [2]

[1] 1842, Vol. VI, p. 294.
[2] Quotation and references from Kohler, p. 68.

In such an atmosphere, the faith of his fathers was not apt to retain its hold upon the successful lawyer and aspiring politician, of whom a newspaper could say, in the height of that first "native American" hysteria with which he was inclined to sympathize, "Of Mr. Benjamin's religious views we know nothing." [1] He did not forswear Judaism or conceal his Jewish origin; he remained always (so testifies an old friend who held many arguments on the subject with him in later years) a firm believer in immortality and in a personal Divinity; he was not ashamed, rather justly proud, of his lineage, and in temperament always retained much of the best of the traits of his people; but he had ceased to hold any active communion with Judaism.

These habits of indifference must have become firmly fixed within the first ten or fifteen years of his residence in New Orleans; for long before that time had passed he was in circumstances sufficiently prosperous actively to renew his association with his family in South Carolina. Almost yearly, in the dull summer season, he used to visit his mother and sisters, taking with him supplies of such things as would add to their comfort or conduce to their pleasure. Always there was a trunk full of the latest books; and during his stay it was his delight to read the thrilling novels to them, to tease them by breaking off short whenever one of Mr. G. P. R. James's lone horsemen or distressed maidens was found in a predicament more than usually unhappy. Into all their pleasures he entered with the hearty zest of a boy on his holidays, and it was a holiday for him. He was by this time practically

[1] New Orleans *Courier*, Nov. 23, 1844.

their sole support, and was maturing plans to bring
them nearer him, where he could more constantly
see to their well-being.

The large profits of his practice before the bar were
not squandered, though generously expended. In the
early forties, he acquired an interest in a large sugar
plantation, "Bellechasse," in the Parish of Plaquemines, below New Orleans, and on a visit to his
mother in 1846, he was able to announce to her that
they should soon have a home of their own in Louisiana.
But about this time he was to suffer a reverse that for
awhile plunged him into despondency, and ultimately
led to his temporary retirement from the bar.

The severity of the strain to which he had subjected
his health, and particularly his eyesight, had not been
realized in the buoyancy of success. Now his eyes
suddenly gave out, so that for some months he was
utterly incapacitated for the pursuit of his profession,
and as thoroughly depressed as energetic and ambitious temperaments are by what seems an entirely useless and incomprehensible check upon progress. One
of his contemporaries used to recall this as a period
when even Mr. Benjamin was despondent and moody.[1]
It is small wonder that he was so, for the blow came
at a time when he was just beginning to feel himself
secure in the anticipation of unselfish pleasures for
which he had labored devotedly. But the period of depression did not endure long. He resolved to relinquish his practice, and give himself more assiduously to the fascinating occupation of cultivating
sugar-cane.

At the time when Mr. Benjamin became interested

[1] The late Mr. Henry J. Leovy.

in sugar-making, that great Louisiana industry was
yet in its infancy. Many of the plantations in what
is now the great sugar and rice district of the state
were still devoted to the growing of cotton, though the
soil was by no means well adapted to that plant.
Much of the land now under cultivation was yet un-
cleared of the dense growth of timber, the forest
primeval of majestic live-oak and impenetrable cane-
brakes; much was believed to be incapable of cultivation because of bad drainage, being swamp-land subject to overflow from the great river and from every
freshet in the numerous bayous and chains of lakes
that honeycomb southern Louisiana. Furthermore,
where sugar was cultivated, the methods were extremely crude. The absolute essentiality of good
drainage was understood, but the drainage systems
were very imperfect, laid out in rough-and-ready
fashion that too often accomplished the minimum of
good at the maximum of cost. Few planters realized
the necessity of fertilizing a soil apparently so rich,
but soon exhausted by the cane; few even understood
the advantage of rotation of crops, but used one field
till it was exhausted and then cleared a fresh tract of
timber. The possibility of improving the plant by
careful selection of the seed, and by importation of
new varieties, was but little appreciated. And when
the crop was grown, the cane was ground in little,
primitive mills that could extract but a small proportion of its saccharine juice, which, scarcely freed
from even its grosser impurities, was then boiled in
large "open kettles" to the point of granulating;
then laboriously ladled out into shallow wooden boxes
called "coolers," where the wet sugar, brown with

impurities, would settle to the bottom, leaving a large proportion of delicious but uncrystallizable "cooler molasses" on top. There was no science in the process, and consequently much waste. For in the excessive production of molasses alone the planter lost a great proportion of the most valuable product of his cane, sugar being worth many times what molasses was.

Those of us who can remember the delights of the old "open kettle" process, with its delicious by-products of *sirop de batterie, cuite,* and cooler molasses, may have a lingering regret that improved methods have brought more sugar out of the cane juice, and infinitely more money into the pockets of the planters, at the expense of all these good things. Mr. Benjamin became interested in the subject just when some half-dozen progressive planters were beginning to attempt improvements in the manufacture of sugar. He was by no means a pioneer, though he was among the earliest successful experimenters. Unquestionably, however, his intelligence, added to his superior advantages through foreign travel, knowledge of foreign languages, and naturally scientific habit of mind, gave him a preëminence in a business in which men who had been at it all their lives regarded him somewhat enviously and contemptuously as an unpractical theorist and tyro. These points merit some emphasis at our hands because there was a good deal of jealousy and ill-feeling at the time, and because various biographical notices of Mr. Benjamin have set up unwarranted claims for him. His just due is quite enough, without making extravagant assertions, as if he were the father of sugar chemistry and the pioneer in the new process of boiling sugar in vacuum.

The explanation of the fact that Mr. Benjamin has been given credit for things which he never dreamed of claiming as his own, lies in this: He was a clear and fluent writer, and was the first, in Louisiana, to print really accurate, lucid, and scientific descriptions of the improved methods used by others as well as by himself. Plunging into the theoretic side of the question with his usual enthusiasm,—throughout his life it was noted that, even for a lawsuit, he would subject himself to any amount of labor in order to learn all about any practical or theoretical points involved, from sailing a ship to building a railway—he quickly mastered the essentials of the discoveries then being made by the French chemists, saw their practical application, and proceeded to advocate the new methods in a series of papers published in the once famous *De Bow's Review*.

These articles, though necessarily filled with technical details, are wonderfully readable, and could still be perused with profit, despite the continuous improvement in the making of sugar. For the great majority of their readers (and the periodical had a wide circulation), they first elevated the whole process, from the cane-field to the finished white sugar, into a science where nothing was to be left to luck or done without forethought of its effect; where every item of expense and of profit was calculated; where chemical principles that ignorance had despised as of no practical use were shown to have the most direct practical bearing in dollars and cents. Even now there are many, especially of those engaged in agricultural pursuits, who, to their cost, despise pure science. To these people it would seem a barren fact, that a liquid in vacuum will boil at a temperature much lower than that necessary in the open air. But with such a demonstration as Benjamin was able to give, that the application of this principle and others of like apparent remoteness from common sense and the teachings of their fathers meant an immense increase in the money returns from sugar, prejudice was constrained to yield at last. For his efforts at popularizing useful scientific knowledge Mr. Benjamin would deserve to be remembered in the agricultural history of the country, even had he done nothing else.

In the first article, "Louisiana Sugar,"[1] he gives general comment and useful practical suggestions on drainage, planting the cane, fertilization, cultivation, and improvement of the seed-cane. But the major part of the paper is devoted to a popular presentation of the improved process of manufacture, with tables of figures to show the practical results on his own plantation and on others where experiments had been made. He gives a chemical analysis of the sugar-cane, inaccurate in the view of more recent research but sufficient for the purpose, and explains the structure of the plant, as well as the old wasteful methods of extracting and boiling the juice. He then describes the improved methods. There were two rival processes at that time, each with its advocates. Both applied the principle of boiling the cane-juice in vacuum, whereby a much greater proportion of sugar was produced in place of the molasses. They differed chiefly in certain technical points of arrangement, which cannot be explained without the use of technical terms. In the

[1] *De Bow's Review*, Vol. II, pp. 322–345, November, 1846.

apparatus of M. Rillieux, which Benjamin had installed at "Bellechasse," the juice was boiled in a series of "vacuum pans," always kept from contact with the air till it reached the point of granulation in the fourth and last pan, and the evaporated steam from one pan was used to assist in boiling the syrup in the next. In that of Dérosne and Cail a part of the process took place in the open air, the syrup being allowed to flow over a series of pipes heated by steam, a portion of the apparatus known as a "double effect," modifications of which have been used since. The champion of the Dérosne and Cail apparatus was M. Valcour Aime. In both systems scientific principles were applied to the problems of extracting a maximum of juice from the cane, filtering and defecating the juice to remove impurities, and economizing fuel by making use of steam in place of a direct flame to boil it. Mr. Benjamin's argument in favor of the superiority of the apparatus employed on his own plantation is sound in theory, and supported by a good array of facts. It may be well to mention here that subsequent improvements in the art have also rather justified his view, though both of the rival systems have contributed to the apparatus now used in modern sugar refineries. It is perhaps needless to remark that, while mechanical improvements have been made, as in the successful construction of mills with far heavier rollers to crush the cane, the greatest advances since have been merely developments on the scientific side, such as more accurate chemical analysis of sugar and cane, the application of the principles of polarization, and the use of the centrifugal for drying the sugar instead of the primitive method of allowing

the molasses to drip from the wet sugar placed in barrels over a cistern.

In a second paper,[1] an address on "Agriculture" intended to be delivered before the meeting of the Agricultural and Mechanics' Institute of Louisiana, Mr. Benjamin discusses several phases of possible improvement in agricultural methods. He tells of some new things seen on his last visit to France, among others—a dream still to be realized—a steam plow which he saw tried in that country. But he recurs to sugar chemistry, recording the recent advances made in France. He describes, also, an apparatus since successfully introduced, a "slicer" for cutting and slicing the hard bark of the cane before it goes to the mill, with the experiments in soaking the crushed cane with lime-water and recrushing it, all of which would, it was believed, increase the percentage of juice extracted, a theory since fully proven. And with pardonable pride he quotes from the recent report of Professor R. S. McCulloch, a chemist sent out by the Federal government to study sugar-culture in Louisiana and Cuba, describing the efforts of Messrs. Benjamin and Packwood to make chemically pure sugar direct from the cane-juice, without the slow process of the "cooler" and subsequent refining. It would be tedious to give an account of the experimental methods, using a tank with a perforated bottom called a "tiger," by which Benjamin and Packwood were enabled to give McCulloch a specimen of sugar found to be chemically pure : "Its crystalline grain and snowy whiteness are also equal to those of the best double refined sugar of our northern

[1] January, 1848, Vol. V, pp. 44–57.

refineries. To these two enterprising men must, therefore, be awarded the merit of having first made directly from a vegetable juice, sugar of absolute chemical purity." Mr. Benjamin gives the credit for the success of this experiment to his partner, Mr. Packwood, under whose careful supervision all of the practical work was done.

As early as 1846 the State Agricultural Society had awarded the first prize for loaf sugar to Benjamin and Packwood. But, as Mr. Benjamin himself confesses in the article just reviewed, the attempt to make pure sugar in the "tigers" was only an experimental success, interesting but not really practical on a large scale. The claim made on the basis of McCulloch's report, however, led to some ill-feeling at the time, whereby Mr. Benjamin did not escape caustic censure, in spite of his express statement that all credit for the experiments at "Bellechasse" was due to Mr. Packwood. I refer the curious in such matters to Valcour Aime's article in *De Bow's Review*.[1] We are not writing the history of sugar in Louisiana, and our interest in the controversy ends here.

The last of the *De Bow* articles[2] introduces us to an instrument whose use led to the greatest improvement in the art of sugar-refining. It is a description of "Soleil's Saccharometer," the earliest usable instrument applying the polarization of light to determine the percentage of sugar in a given amount of juice. Only the practical sugar-maker could appreciate what a revolution the "polarizer" has effected, and so I shall not attempt to show its application. Mr.

[1] Vol. V, pp. 249, 289.
[2] Vol. V., pp. 357–364, April, 1848.

Benjamin gives a detailed description of the instrument, explains the optical and chemical principles involved, and the method of its use in the sugar-house, with the consequent gain to the intelligent planter.

It is not very surprising that a trained student and scholar of broad culture and keen intellect should have taken such an interest and achieved such results in the more theoretical departments of farming. But Mr. Benjamin was not the typical gentleman farmer, proud of his cabbages at one dollar a head. Until misfortunes beyond human foresight to avert came upon "Bellechasse," it was a successful plantation, though perhaps no small share of the credit for this should go to Theodore Packwood, who was a practical man, and who took charge of the actual work. That Mr. Benjamin's theories were not altogether visionary, one is at least led to surmise, since the machinery installed by him at "Bellechasse" was still serviceable and in use as late as 1895; not till then was it deemed necessary to remodel the sugar-house which he had constructed half a century before. But there is certainly ground for the belief that, without the practical knowledge and the restraining conservatism of his partner, he would have been tempted into fruitless and costly experiments; for he was by nature not only fond of new things,—experimental toys—but also prone to be too sanguine, fascinated by vaguely magnificent schemes where his fervid imagination could revel, in consideration of the immense results, without being hampered by the cold facts that must be faced ere those results could be made realities. One of the household at "Bellechasse" recalls that Mrs. Packwood used to say, despairingly: "There goes

Theodore with Mr. Benjamin! I never see them riding about the field together without trembling for the consequences. Mr. Benjamin can talk him into buying any new-fangled pot or pan he's pleased with for the moment, and then Theodore has the worry of trying to make the thing work." And the same witness remembers several expensive and useless toys of the kind Mrs. Packwood complains of, among other things a domestic ice machine, which produced, or was supposed to produce, ice in long candles when you turned the crank. In spite of this fondness for experiment, however, and whether the ice machine worked or not, "Bellechasse" was a financial success.

Early in 1847 Mr. Benjamin wrote to his mother that she, his widowed sister, Mrs. Levy, and the latter's young daughter, should come to take possession of the plantation home he had prepared for them; his wife had found it too lonely. To the youngest member of the trio it was all a delightful surprise, a romance whose charms she longed to taste. [1] They made the long trip from Beaufort by sea, and arrived safely in New Orleans one bright spring morning. The next day they took the steamboat down to "Bellechasse," of which Mr. Benjamin would tell them nothing till they saw it. And the quaint old Creole house then occupying the place—rooms all in a long row, galleries front and back, walls tinted in delicate colors and frescoed with the queerest scenes of beribboned gondolas and fantastic shepherds,—the lovely garden, the mighty live-oaks, certainly did charm them. More precious to them and to him, however, was the thought that now at last there was a home. They

[1] Conversation with Mrs. Popham.

deemed the old house quite good enough, but he had already planned the larger mansion which still stands and which soon replaced the smaller and less comfortable one.

Mr. Benjamin's mother, however, did not long survive, dying in the autumn of 1847. Then Mrs. Levy was installed as mistress of the new house, which her devoted brother was determined to make as pleasant a home as loving thought could, and to which came other members of the family. She was a little older than himself, and had always been looked up to as a sort of superior being. Indeed, those who knew her bear witness to her wonderful intellect, her wit, her charm of manner,—in all things like her brother, and always the sharer of his perplexities, his triumphs, his troubles, as much as if she were part of himself.

Though the plantation was remote from the city, they were not cut off from the world. Before their coming, Mr. Benjamin, recovering the use of his eyes, had partially taken up his practice in New Orleans again, and, in fact, was just at this time coming into wider prominence. In 1847 he had been appointed counsel to the California Land Commissioners, on behalf of the Federal government. In this position his familiarity with French and Spanish, and with the Spanish system of law, similar to that of Louisiana, gave him an extraordinary advantage. His services so added to his prestige that he was sought and received big fees, for many important cases involving California lands; and in October, 1848, he was admitted to practice before the Supreme Court of the United States. Whatever the charms of "Belle-chasse," it was manifest that destiny would not let him rest a sugar-planter. He did not live on the plantation, therefore, but in New Orleans, going down to it every week-end, and only occasionally indulging himself in a longer stay there.

Both he and his sister delighted in entertaining, and understood the art. Almost every Saturday Mrs. Levy learned to look for a boat-load of guests, old and young, to enliven the house for a few days ; and sometimes even this excellent housekeeper was put to it to provide for the comfort of more company than she had counted on ; and though "J. P.," as he was affectionately called, generally brought with him a generous lot of provisions, fruit, and delicacies from New Orleans, it sometimes necessitated very careful manipulation of the available "loaves and fishes" to feed the hungry. Among those who came so frequently as to be almost a member of the household was M. Auguste St. Martin, Mr. Benjamin's father-in-law, a most delightful old gentleman, who could tell the young folk thrilling tales of the horrors of the great West Indian slave insurrection. Then there were the two Huntington brothers, with whom Mr. Benjamin kept bachelors' quarters on Polymnia Street in the city. And frequently, for quite long visits, came the dried-up little chemist, Rillieux, always the centre of an admiring and interested group of planters from the neighborhood as he explained this or that point in the chemistry of sugar or the working of his apparatus ; for by this time had begun that immense expansion of the sugar industry, thanks to the persistent experiments of such pioneers as the Fouchers and Valcour Aime and now Benjamin, and thanks also to the substantial tariff Congress had been induced to put upon the product.

"Bellechasse" became not only a sort of social focus for the planters of the neighborhood, but the scene of a symposium, as it were, on sugar. Who would have believed that scarce fifty years had passed since the time when it had been firmly believed that Louisiana cane would not make sugar!

But though the host naturally delighted in the companionship of such men, he was always ready to enter into the pleasures of the younger people. His niece, then just entering womanhood, found him her most sympathetic confidant in any girlish troubles, and many a situation, seeming tragic to her young heart, was made easy after a stroll about the garden with the great lawyer, who was to her like one of her own age, only more wise and gentle than any other. For young girls he had a great affection. When they gathered about the table of an evening, it was his favorite custom to test their wits in the sport of capping verses—a pastime long obsolete one suspects only because of the inferior culture in literature, for in those days people read and learned by heart the classics with which we now decorate locked bookcases. Mr. Benjamin had a wonderful stock of verse in his memory, and would pour forth scrap after scrap, with a challenge to them to place the quotation. Or when midnight approached in stormy season, and the nervous tension of his auditors prepared them for such experiences, he told some horror tale, working carefully up to the awful catastrophe and suddenly crying out, "Boo!" Whereat at least one in the group (his younger sister, afterward Mrs. Kruttschnitt), invariably shrieked, to his great delight.

Unforeseen disasters, however, were soon to end the

pleasant days at "Bellechasse." The great river rose and overflowed its banks. Though his own front levees held, there were crevasses on neighboring places that let in the backwater. Up and up it crept, into the yard, to the very steps of the house, the yard being filled with cattle seeking the high ground, and even deer driven from the swamps in this emergency for safety near man. The growing crop was destroyed, for cane perishes quickly under water; even the seed-cane was gone. And then a friend, for whom Mr. Benjamin had endorsed a note of $60,000, failed to meet his obligations, and the endorser was called upon to pay. He had to give up the expensive home at "Bellechasse," and resume with all his old energy his practice in New Orleans. The family, removing for a short time to another plantation above the city, then went to live in a house he bought for them, at the corner of Nashville and Naiades (now St. Charles) Avenues, where they were to remain till expelled by the Federal troops. The locality was then too remote from the city for him to live with them, though there was a railway connecting the suburb of Carrollton with what seemed the distant city, now grown miles beyond this point. He continued to reside with the Huntingtons, on Polymnia Street, but dined almost every day with his family, sometimes notifying Mrs. Levy that he expected to bring guests, or longed for one of his favorite delicacies. "Have broiled chickens for dinner," he would say, "also plenty of butter on 'em; you know how I like it done."

So ends the plantation episode of this varied career, in disappointment and financial disaster, through no fault of his own. But there was no check apparent to the world in the triumphant career. Few even of his intimate friends knew the extent of the loss; and with undiminished zeal and hopefulness he set about re-building the shattered fortune.

Before we turn to take up other threads of the life, it may be well to note some of the lessons of this plantation experience. As owner of "Bellechasse," he had also become a slaveholder, and had thus had practical knowledge of the slave system. From this he could judge how false were the lurid pictures of Louisiana plantations drawn by the Northern radicals. Some few of his slaves were still living a year or two since, and would tell visitors all sorts of tales of the master of long ago;—none but kindly memories, and romantic legends of the days of glory on the old place, such as the setting up of the plantation bell, still there, into whose molten metal Mr. Benjamin is said to have cast two hundred silver dollars to give it sweet tone. Slavery in practice, then, was familiar to him, and seemed no wrong, certainly far from the thing it was pictured to be. Moreover, in the actual business of planting, it was inevitable that the wider aspects of agriculture in the South should be revealed to his trained mind. His subsequent views of the economics of the slavery question would take their coloring from his own experience, an experience which enlisted his head as well as his heart on the side of the planter to whom emancipation conveyed the threat, almost the certainty, of financial ruin and the gravest social perils. And in the lull of continuous hammering away at the law, in the greater leisure, brief though it was, of plantation life, his mind was left free for speculations other than legal or forensic. It is perhaps no mere barren coincidence that just at this time he engaged in politics, as if suddenly aware of the importance of things that had not interested him before.

CHAPTER III

POLITICS AND CONSTITUTION MAKING

INTELLIGENT English observers, such as Mr. Bryce, have noted that a very large proportion of American public men are lawyers, at least in training if not in practice. This was more true in the old South, perhaps, than it is to-day; scores of the notable men of that by-gone society are betrayed by the title of Judge, while even the Generals and Colonels (as abundant then as now) will frequently be found to be merely lawyer-politicians masquerading in those most unexceptionable and useful martial titles. Most politicians, in fact, were lawyers, and it might be said that most lawyers were also politicians. It is therefore not surprising to discover Mr. Benjamin very early seduced from law into politics.

Before the first decade of his life in New Orleans had passed, we find him taking a share in local politics, serving on city or parish executive committees, and occasionally making a speech that the newspapers consider of sufficient moment to mention, but not at first himself a candidate. In order to understand many of the points that will arise in our discussion of Mr. Benjamin in public life, it will be necessary briefly to explain some of the peculiar features of politics in Louisiana in the forties.

In the first place, quite irrespective of party, the population of Louisiana, and of New Orleans in particular, was divided by differences of language and nationality that, on rare occasions, might cause almost as much mutual distrust as if the one party or the other had been actually hostile foreigners. There were two languages, recognized not merely under the law, by the printing of the constitution in French and English, and by similar dual publication of all public documents, but by custom as well, in the daily practice of those who still formed a considerable proportion of the total white population of the state. The French, more numerous, though not in the majority in the southern portion of Louisiana, and the English, settling in constantly increasing numbers in the Felicianas, in the rich alluvial parishes from Red River to the Arkansas line, and in the hilly northwestern parishes, might oppose each other on some points quite without regard to supposed party affiliations. The French Creole might be a Democrat, or he might be a Whig, but in the eyes of his English neighbor he was always a Frenchman, constitutionally opposed to development and progress.

It should be said, in justice, that such narrow prejudice very rarely led to serious conflict, and that ordinarily the only distinctions of moment in politics were those between the Whigs and the Democrats. Of the still vigorous party inspired by Webster and Clay, Mr. Benjamin was from the first a warm supporter, and no small share of the flashes of success that came to it in the last decade of its existence in Louisiana is attributable to his energy and political sagacity. This was a time of desperate struggle for the Whigs, threatened at first by defeat at the hands of the new and popular Democracy with its Jacksonian cult; then menaced by insidious Native American attacks, and at last suddenly and forever extinguished in the storm clouds of the conflict whose coming there was no longer a Webster or a Clay to hinder. And in the fierce party fights that I shall have to record, not the most spotless gentleman could hope to escape with reputation unassailed. Mr. Benjamin, being often in the forefront of his party as campaign manager or as candidate, came in for an extra share of scurrilous abuse from opposition newspapers at a time when American journalism was incredibly coarse and brutal.

Louisiana had been rather steady as a Whig state, having a conservative electorate under the rather restrictive suffrage qualifications of the state constitution of 1812. But about 1840 the waves of Democracy were rising steadily, and nothing but efforts of an extraordinary vigor could long secure Whig victories in Louisiana. In the local elections in New Orleans in April, 1842, the Whigs were defeated, and hence redoubled their exertions to win at least some offices in the state campaign, which then took place in July. For the first time, Mr. Benjamin threw himself into the contest with that energy which had already won signal triumphs in his profession. He was a candidate for the lower house of the General Assembly, and his office on Exchange Place was frequently the meeting-place, and, on election day, the headquarters of the Whig executive committee.[1]

Elections in New Orleans in those days were always characterized by fraud, attempted or achieved, and not infrequently by violence and bloodshed. Though the suffrage was restricted by property and other qualifications, the professional voter was far more in

See New Orleans *Bee*, April 4, 20; June 4, 25; July 1, 4, 5.

evidence and far more dangerous than now; and as
there was no system of registration,—only the most
cumbrous and uncertain method of deciding, at the
very polls, whether or not the voter presenting himself
was properly qualified,—"repeating" became so easy
as to cease to be a crime in the eyes of many, and a determined and reckless minority could, by precipitating
contests at the polls, or by actual violence, either re-
tard the election or actually drive away hostile votes.
The more candid members of both parties admitted
and deplored these irregularities; but naturally the
defeated faction, of whatever party, was loud in charges
of fraud on the part of the victors.

In this particular election the Whigs were, in the
main, successful, and the Democratic papers, such as
the *Jeffersonian* and the *Courier*, made allegations of
extraordinary fraud in New Orleans, naming Benjamin
as the person chiefly responsible. Under the property qualification clause of the constitution, it had been
held that ownership of a carriage or cab, proved by
payment of a license tax, was sufficient to qualify a
voter. The Democratic papers attributed the suggestion of this idea to the acute lawyer who had taken so
conspicuous a part in Whig councils. They stated,
moreover, that licenses had been issued on cabs which
had no existence except in the necessity for Whig
votes, and that hundreds of votes had been cast by
this ingenious trick, since the inspectors at the polls
had no time or opportunity to examine into the real
existence of the cabs, but must accept the license receipt as evidence of *bona fide* ownership.

There were frauds, no doubt, in the election; but
there is nothing but partisan accusation based on ex-

aggerated suspiciousness to show either that the number of fraudulent votes was very considerable, or that Mr. Benjamin had anything whatever to do with the "cab votes." [1] Following a rule almost inviolate with him, he made no public denial of the newspaper calumnies, though it must have been exasperating to have this same charge raked up and vociferously urged at every election in which his name came before the people—in 1844, in 1848, in 1852, in 1858.

With or without "cab votes," Mr. Benjamin was elected to the legislature, [2] and served in the last sessions held under the old constitution of the state. As a legislator he showed himself businesslike and resourceful, but no measure of importance was considered during his term ; for the nation was just catching its breath between the great financial panics that marked the Jacksonian era, and Louisiana was preparing to call a convention to give a constitution that would, by some yet undiscovered method, prevent wild-cat banks and hydrocephalous trusts without throttling finance and commerce, and that would tie up the General Assembly in knots of limitations which might prevent it from robbing the people and yet leave it freedom of action in case it should by any chance prove honest and capable. With this increasing distrust of the democracy for its own chosen representatives, Benjamin was then heartily in sympathy. He approved of the convention which was to work such marvels for Louisiana, and was put forward as a candidate for membership in it in the spring of 1844.

[1] Cf. the New Orleans *Bee*, July 9 ; *Jeffersonian*, July 6, 1842; *Courier*, July 3, 5, 6, and Aug. 3–9, 1844, etc.
[2] New Orleans *Bee*, July 5, 1842.

In this election one hears the first suggestions,—really quite without serious foundation—that Benjamin was an adherent of the American or Know Nothing party. Since the most vital of the ill-considered principles of that mushroom party were open hostility to citizens of foreign birth and scarce concealed hostility to Catholics, and since Benjamin was himself foreign born, his wife a Catholic, and he himself absolutely tolerant of the religious as of the political opinions of others, it would seem that the mere suggestion of his being a Know Nothing would have been sufficiently absurd to refute itself. But, strange to say, there were facts to lend color to the charge.

By 1844 Mr. Benjamin had become interested not only in other matters than law, such as the cultivation of sugar and the life of a planter, but his view of political questions had broadened till he was capable of foreseeing from what quarter danger threatened not Louisiana only but the whole South, with its entire social and agricultural system dependent on slavery. He was already, as we shall see from a significant speech in the convention, making plans for the defense of Louisiana. In what he says there, and in the imperfectly reported fragments of political speeches during the preceding campaign, it is made very clear that he considered unrestricted naturalization[1] of immigrants into the state, whether "foreign born" or migrating from the Northern states, a source of danger to the community. In so far his opinions seemed to coincide with those of the American party.

[1] Here and in a following chapter I use the term "naturalization," meaning acquisition of the suffrage in the state, because it is so used by the contemporary papers; naturalization, strictly speaking, is controlled by the Federal government.

But Benjamin was too intelligent and too broad-minded to become an adherent of such a party. At first he was favorably impressed by the strict naturalization requirements proposed by them, and expressed his approval in such fashion as to compromise himself to some extent. But he soon discovered that this organization, with a no more definite policy than the exclusion of foreigners from citizenship and office, and proposing to introduce into democratic American politics the methods of the Carbonari, the Mafia, or other Italian secret society, was no fit guardian of democratic privileges.

Throughout the campaign which, for reasons to be explained presently, was a long one, Benjamin and his colleague, C. M. Conrad, were frequently assailed as Know Nothings by the Democratic papers. Part of this, it is true, was merely for political effect; without regard to its veracity, a Democratic paper of 1844 would make any assertion that it thought likely to help its faction, even if the lie were detected—after election. The Louisiana *Courier*, in particular, makes repeated attacks on this score; and they are, so to speak, double-barreled, the paper being published half in French and half in English. It boldly asserts, in its two tongues, that Benjamin and Conrad are [1] "opposed to the Catholic religion because they belong to and act with a party that avows its opposition to that mode of faith. Mr. Conrad, we believe, was brought up in the Protestant church. We know nothing of Mr. Benjamin's religion." Nay, it appears from the *Courier* that these two gentlemen were notorious for sullying "the purity of the ballot box," and, most horrible of all, both are guilty

[1] See *Courier*, Nov. 19, 20, 23, 1844.

of *lèse majesté*, having dared to maintain that they thought Judge Hall was perfectly right in imposing a fine on General Andrew Jackson for some of his high-handed proceedings in New Orleans! All of which rather moves us to smile, and to doubt, especially when we discover that this diligent champion of the purity of the ballot has next to nothing to say of the notorious Plaquemines election, in which Democratic voters by hundreds were carried from New Orleans to the voting place in that parish.

Though supported by one of the Know Nothing papers, Benjamin continued to act with the Whigs. In December, 1844, he and many other leading citizens of New Orleans signed a public call for the formation of a "Louisiana American party." [1] This was not really a Know Nothing organization; its purposes were reform, especially reform of the ballot, and reform of the naturalization laws. But its existence, as an independent party, was precarious, and Benjamin's connection with it was certainly little more than the signing of the call in the hope of bettering local political conditions. His loyalty as a Whig was never again impeached until the party ceased to have any real existence.

This campaign, in which Benjamin manifested interest in matters other than local, may be said to be the formal beginning of a political career henceforth without interruption. It may be of value, therefore, to note his opinions at this important period. Fortunately, an accidental indisposition gives us a better chance to get an idea of these views. He was

[1] See the *Tropic*, Dec. 24; the call is signed by Glendy Burke, W. C. C. Claiborne, W. A. Violett, etc., etc. Cf. *Tropic*, Nov. 20.

announced to address a Whig meeting in New Orleans on June 20th. If he had spoken, the Whig papers would have garbled and praised the "most eloquent and argumentative effort it has been our pleasure to hear in New Orleans"; but he was unable to speak, and consequently sent a written statement of his views to the papers a few days later. [1]

We find that he believes, in contrast to the extreme Democrats, that the powers of the constitutional convention for which he is a candidate are not limited, but unrestricted, the members being not mere legislative representatives: "If there be a feature of our republican institutions to which we may point with honor and pride, it is peculiarly this,—that with us changes of government are peaceful revolutions, and not the fruit of civil war or dreadful strife; and that it is at all times within the power of a well ascertained majority of the people to effect such changes without danger and without commotion. As some honest doubts are, however, entertained on this subject, I should deem it advisable . . . that the labors of the convention should not take effect till ratified by the people." He is in favor of reducing the suffrage qualifications, being more democratic in this than on any other point; but he advocates something that was regarded as tyrannous and unrepublican in those days: "a registry system to prevent the fraudulent usurpation of the electoral franchise by those [not] really entitled to it." He shares the prevailing fear of wild-cat banks, and would restrict the powers of the legislature in regard to the formation of certain kinds of corporations. And the following views on state banks are

[1] See *Tropic*, June 25, 1844.

decidedly more conservative than those prevailing a generation before the Federal government had established its system of national banks. "It is too late at the present day to question the right of the states to charter banks, although I must confess that the strong bearing of my mind has always been against the constitutionality of the exercise of such power by the states. I have found it very difficult to reconcile the idea of the coexistence of such a power with those confided by the Constitution of the United States to the general government of coining money, regulating its value, and regulating commerce, and with the prohibitions by which the states are prevented from coining money, emitting bills of credit, or making anything but gold and silver coin a tender in payment of debt. . . . I shall vote, if elected, to prohibit the legislature from confiding to any body of individuals the power of doing banking business as corporators unless such corporators be individually liable for the debts of the corporation to the whole extent of their fortunes."

His program for the judiciary is also extremely conservative. He advocates a judiciary appointed by the governor and for good behavior, perhaps to be retired after reaching the age of sixty ; but he notes that such a provision would have deprived New York of the best services of Chancellor Kent, and the Federal government of the best services of Marshall, a difficulty which might be avoided by sanctioning reappointment for short terms of judges who would otherwise be retired in the plenitude of their powers.

In all this it will be noted that there is little tendency to Democratic views, and no trace whatever of Know

Nothingism, or, as it was more irreverently called, "Sammyism."

The election resulted in the choice of Conrad and Benjamin to represent New Orleans in the convention. As usual, there were complaints of fraud on both sides ; but in this case Whigs and Democrats vied with each other in condemning the disfranchisement, by election inspectors, of a considerable body of voters who held naturalization papers said to have been irregularly issued by a judge who was impeached and convicted about this time. But not till long after the election do we hear of any accusation against Mr. Benjamin, or any hint that his right to a seat in the convention was likely to be disputed.

The convention met on the appointed day, Monday, August 5, 1844, at the little town of Jackson. This was a mere village, with no sufficient accommodations for the delegates, with no watchful daily press (except one poor little sheet that eked out a sort of parasitic existence upon the official printing), and peculiarly inaccessible even now, sixty years later, being situated about fifteen miles from the river which was at that time the great artery of communication. The selection of such a place, suggestively named Jackson, represented a victory of the Democrats in the legislature which had called the convention. With all of his might, Benjamin, aided by the members from New Orleans, had fought against attempting to manufacture a constitution in a corner, and at a season when the state was liable not infrequently to devastating epidemics of yellow fever ; but the Democrats, and indeed most of the members from the rural constituencies, had, and still have, the most unreasoning and uncontrollable jealousy and fear of New Orleans. When the convention met, however, and began to organize, it was manifest that, although the Democrats elected their candidate for presiding officer, the Whig element was stronger.

At the first informal roll-call, Benjamin and Emile La Sére, a Democrat, responded for New Orleans, and both were allowed seats. Mr. Conrad, Benjamin's duly elected Whig colleague, did not appear in the convention for several days, but his name was registered by a friend before his arrival. It was evident that the seats held by Benjamin and Conrad were to be contested by the Democrats; but so little heed was paid to the possibility of a dispute that, before the Committee on Elections brought in its report on the credentials of members, Benjamin was appointed to the Committees on Contingent Expenses, on the Third Article of the Constitution (Executive Department), and on the Bill of Rights (Ninth Article), Mr. Conrad also serving on the last named. That same day, however (August 10th), the president, Joseph Walker, submitted to the convention "letters from Emile La Sére and J. B. Planché, claiming to be entitled to seats in the convention, as having been duly elected from the Parish of Orleans." The letters were referred to the Committee on Elections.

Before this committee there was a vigorous fight, echoes of which reach us through the debates of the convention. Neither side won a decisive triumph, but the strategic victory was on the side of Benjamin and Conrad, who continued to occupy their seats and act as members of the body. The committee, not being able to settle the question, reported the contest back to the convention. It appeared that the Whig candidates had been chosen by a fair majority on the face of the returns, but the contestants declared there had been serious irregularities in the election, and submitted proof of their allegations. The most important piece of evidence was from the parish Judge, Charles Maurian (a political opponent of Benjamin and Conrad), whose duty it was to make the election returns, and who had done so, adding marginal notes on the very documents themselves to show that, in his opinion, the returns from certain wards should be thrown out because only one inspector had signed them. With these wards eliminated, the Democratic candidates would have been elected by a small margin. Benjamin, in answer to this, very properly contended that he and Conrad had a right to have evidence too, since the committee had undertaken to go behind the returns; and he now applied to it for process to be directed to the city of New Orleans to take testimony to sustain his allegations and to rebut those of the contestants.

In the convention this contest was to occupy the whole of the session at Jackson. Mr. Conrad spoke for hours, and repeatedly, on the subject, while General Solomon Downs and other Democratic leaders replied at still greater length. Benjamin spoke, also, though not so much; and there is nothing in the speeches of his opponents to disturb our conviction that he was in the right and duly elected. The difficulty seemed to be no nearer settlement than at the beginning, when, on August 21st, the convention having already agreed to adjourn to meet again in New Orleans on the second Tuesday in January, 1845, Benjamin and Conrad stated

that they would, just before adjournment, resign their
seats and stand for reëlection, if their opponents
would abide by this decision. La Sère and Plauché
agreed, the new election was held on November 25th,
and the Whigs were again elected, by a much larger
majority.[1]

Very little was attempted or accomplished in the
three weeks that the convention sat in Jackson. The
members were all too busy in the trial of strength between the Whigs and the Democrats on the seating of
Benjamin and Conrad, and on the adjournment of the
convention to New Orleans. The "little member
from Orleans," with his untiring energy, his affable
manners, and his tactful readiness to meet the views
of others half-way in order to gain his object, was
credited with having a good deal to do with the
decision on the latter point. The Democratic minority
presented a protest against the adjournment to New
Orleans, signed by twenty-nine members, which is so
typical of the "party thunder" of two generations
ago that I must quote a part of it; the contrast between this, which smacks of Solomon W. Downs, and
Benjamin's style should be noted. When the convention met in Jackson, say the Democrats, "all was
bright and cheering as in the morning of time; party
spirit recoiled to its bed; the passions of men were
soothed, from the happy reflection that a glorious era
had come in Louisiana; the demon of discord aroused
not from his lair, but peace prevailed universally and
without interruption. . . . But the evil day came,

[1] For this contest, see *Debates of Convention*, 1844–1845, *passim;*
and newspapers, especially *Tropic*, Sept. 30, Nov. 14, and *Courier*
Nov. 19–26, 1844.

and with it a postponement of the labors enjoined upon the convention. . . . The fiat has gone forth, regardless of reason and the demands of the people. No epidemic darts from the noonday beams or hangs upon the curtain of night to alarm the stranger or discompose the citizen; no foreign enemy is upon our borders to lay waste our fields and eat our substance; and no internal commotion, political or religious, disturbs the peaceful quietude of the country in which we are called to deliberate; but notwithstanding this favorable state of things for the accomplishment of the grandest object ever assigned to man, the millennial day of Louisiana is still left distant in the womb of time." No one would have taken more pleasure than the fun-loving Benjamin in remarking *sotto voce* to General Downs "that it was still there."

On the reassembling of the convention[1] in New Orleans, it became immediately apparent that, though a temporary combination of votes had caused its removal from Jackson, the jealousy of the country members toward the city was very active, and would occasion the most violent conflicts. Benjamin had not been elected as the head of the city delegation; such a position might rather have been claimed by the eloquent and fiery Frenchman, Pierre Soulé, or the honest, sturdy German, Christian Roselius, both of whom, though certainly already surpassed at the bar by this extraordinary young man, were older and more experienced politicians. But in the actual adjustment of the matters in dispute between the city and the

---

[1] Newspaper reports of proceedings are very meagre, hence I rely in the following pages chiefly on the *Debates*, giving specific reference only for matters of importance.

country, Benjamin took the lead, and brought about a settlement which, though not satisfactory to him or to his colleagues, was better than their uncompromising methods would ever have attained.

In connection with this matter, Benjamin spoke several times. So extreme was the jealousy of New Orleans that, although the city had nearly one half of the total population of the state, it was attempted to restrict her representation to twenty members, even to eighteen, in a house of one hundred ;—nay, to provide that, whatever the city's population, not more than one-sixth of the one hundred members should be from New Orleans. Finding himself unable, in the committee which had charge of the apportionment of representation, to get anything like justice for the city, Benjamin had consented to a compromise. He was full of the spirit of concession. Even such an opponent as Downs, the leader of the extreme Democratic faction, said :[1] "Mr. Benjamin, with that spirit of truth and candor for which he is justly distinguished, has come into our midst in the spirit of conciliation and harmony ; . . . and if any good should result from his offer, . . . to him alone should belong the honor and the credit of the final settlement of this difficult question." This particular compromise was not successful ; but, as I have said, the arrangement was on the basis of mutual concessions suggested, and supported in spite of some ill-natured comments, by Benjamin, whose attitude toward opponents throughout his political life is well indicated in one of the short speeches he made in the endeavor to win over his obstinate colleagues from New Orleans :

[1] *Debates*, March 3, p. 382 ; for Benjamin's speech, March 6, p. 387.

"How can any one expect that he can induce those who differ with him to change their opinions, when he begins by telling them that he is impracticably wedded to his own, and that whatever may be their arguments he will not change that opinion? This question, I am sorry to see, has been discussed in such a spirit of intolerance as to have caused much warmth of feeling, and to have provoked personalities that ought to have been avoided. . . . One of my brother delegates [Mr. Roselius] has told us that he will never consent to a compromise of principle, and so persuaded is he that he is right in that doctrine, that I have no hopes of inducing him to yield his support to my proposition. I think he is wrong, and I regret his determination. With similar resolutions, it may be said to be impossible to form a constitution. We have the knowledge that there were great divergences of opinion in the Federal convention,—and it is a notorious fact that the Constitution never would have been formed had there not been mutual concessions on the part of its illustrious framers. If a similar spirit had not pervaded the Virginia convention, to which reference has so frequently been had, and in which some of the same distinguished men participated, the constitution of that state would never have been formed. . . . It appears that the delegation from the city must make concessions . . . or withdraw from the convention. There is no other alternative. I am as anxious as my colleagues can be to insist upon the just proportion of power belonging to the city, but as I am met by the determined and impracticable resistance of the majority of this body, I am willing to make some concessions, provided the country is disposed to meet us in something like a similar spirit, and will not expect the city to make all the sacrifices."

Throughout the session of the convention, which was extraordinarily prolonged by the interminable debates, the endless and useless motions to reconsider, on such questions as the basis of representation for the state, the apportionment of representatives, the boundaries of senatorial districts, and the qualifications to be exacted of members of the legislature, Mr. Benjamin was almost constantly in attendance. With morning and evening sittings, we can only wonder how a man busy with an extensive law practice, and devoting at least part of his time to his plantation interests, could find it possible to be present day in and day out at the convention, from January 14th to May 16th. He did go, somehow, and not infrequently his presence enabled him to frustrate schemes hostile to the city, as when some unscrupulous member, noting that the house was thin, would move to reconsider the never-ending apportionment of members in the legislature, which the city delegation had fondly hoped was finally settled by the last three-hour wrangle. No member from the city, indeed, was so regular in attendance, or so active in many matters before the convention; and the fact that Benjamin bore the lion's share of the actual work, —the drawing up of articles for consideration, the correction of absolutely glaring errors in those submitted by others, the mere auditing of accounts and keeping track of the printing on behalf of the Committee on Contingent Expenses,—is manifest in the debates, and was recognized by the newspapers then and when the next convention assembled.

We should be utterly mistaken, however, if we imagined that he was either an interminable or an incessant speaker. He spoke frequently, for he had something practical or sensible to say or some definite object in saying it, on most of the important matters to be considered; but he does not approach the Democratic leader, Downs. He never made a long speech, again in agreeable contrast to his oratorical opponent. And it will be seen from the fragments of his addresses which I shall find occasion to give, that his style is simple, direct, lucid, so plain as to come near baldness were it not for the skill with which he handles it; this, too, is in marked contrast to the Gothic splendors of American forensics at that time. Perhaps legal training, especially in the unemotional commercial law to which he had chiefly devoted himself, had something to do with this peculiarity of style, a peculiarity which has its exact analogue in Mr. Benjamin's commonsense businesslike methods in this convention and in other similar bodies. It was most unprofessional, from the point of view of the politician, this acting on the assumption that the making of a constitution was a business, and should be attended to like any other business, with the object of getting it done as speedily and in as workmanlike a manner as possible.

As indicated in the statement of his opinions before election, Benjamin was extremely conservative in most of his views. His vote was given unhesitatingly for an appointed judiciary; he advocated an appointed secretary of state; and he wished to make amendment of the constitution even more difficult than it was finally made by the convention. He spoke and voted, vainly, in favor of an article requiring a registration

law, which he and Mr. Conrad advocated on grounds
that are now the axioms of political science—foremost
of all, the inevitable temptation to corruption,—but
the Democrats declared registration un-American,
derogatory to the dignity and independence of freemen,
dangerous, oppressive, tyrannous, and more corrupt
than absolutely unregulated voting.[1]

But there are two important questions on which Mr.
Benjamin spoke and voted in a way which, then and
afterward, rendered him liable to attack. The first
of these was "naturalization" (by which, as noted
above, was meant the acquisition of the suffrage), and
the special qualifications to be imposed upon candidates for the General Assembly and for the governorship. The second was the basis that should be adopted
in computing representation in the legislature.

When, on January 21st, the question was discussed,
whether or not it would be advisable to require
a term of residence in the state as a pre-requisite to
membership in the legislature, Benjamin was among
the considerable minority who voted in favor of insisting that no man should be a representative who had
not been four, even five years, a resident and citizen.[2]
And when the matter came up again two or three
days later, he made a remarkable speech in favor of a
similar limitation, saying : "Any stranger that would
have entered this room during any stage of our discussion would have supposed that we were debating a
constitution for Europeans, or the people of the other
states, and not for Louisiana. For the whole burthen
of what has been said has been rather what privileges

[1] *Debates.* pp. 187, 289, 406; cf. *Picayune,* Feb. 8.
[2] *Debates,* p. 88; *Picayune,* Jan. 24.

should be granted to strangers coming among us, than what rights and what guaranties we should secure to ourselves. . . . The question before us, divested of all the extraneous matters with which it has been clogged, is a simple one.[1] It is a question of security. This state is peculiarly situated, and her position exacts some measures of prudent forethought, in order to shield her from assaults upon a vulnerable point. Her peculiar institutions are liable to attack, and it is to preclude the danger which menaces her that some measure, similar to the one under discussion, is deemed of vital importance. . . . What is really the matter in dispute? It is this, that no one shall be eligible to the General Assembly who has not resided four years in the state, if he be a citizen of the United States by birth or by adoption. What objection can there possibly exist to this provision? It is assumed that it is an unequal, unjust, and anti-republican restriction. . . . Where is the impropriety of protecting, by requiring residence the institutions we have met to remodel and to perfect? . . . All are willing that two years' residence, should be required. That is con-

---

[1] The debates are miserably reported, and there was complaint of this at the time. The reporter, incredible as it may seem, was not a stenographer, and we can quite believe, as one member remarked in excusing him, that " it was very difficult to report the remarks of gentlemen that spoke with the fluency and rapidity of the delegate from New Orleans "—meaning Benjamin. Speeches are rarely reported in direct discourse, and on the present occasion the ingenious reporter has mingled direct and indirect discourse indiscriminately. I have taken the liberty, here and elsewhere below, of reproducing simply the direct discourse. Where there is such inaccuracy, it would not be just, of course, to accept any speech as a sample of the speaker's oratory; but the reports are sufficiently trustworthy on mere matters of fact to warrant us in taking them as fairly representing the speaker's opinions.

ceded to be correct. But four years is 'aristocratic,' an attempt to create a 'privileged class,' a 'nobility.' . . . There is one subject that I approach with great reluctance. It is a subject of vital importance to the Southern states, and should produce at least unanimity in our councils, to avert a common danger. It is not the part of wisdom, however we may differ, to wrangle where the safety of all may be compromitted. I would scorn to appeal to party considerations. A question may arise in a few months that will obliterate all party distinctions, when there will be neither Whigs nor Democrats; when the whole South will coalesce and form a single party, and that party will be for the protection of our hearths, of our families, of our homes. That man must be indeed blind not to perceive from whence the danger comes. The signs are pregnant with evil. The speck upon the horizon that at first was no bigger than a man's hand, overshadows us, and there is not a breeze that blows that does not sound the tocsin of alarm. The light is shut out, and we should prepare ourselves to meet the emergency, whenever it may come. Our organic law would be deficient if it did not provide a bulwark, if it did not guard us from the machinations of an insidious foe. The course of events within the last few months proves that we must rely upon ourselves and our Southern confederates to maintain our rights and cause them to be respected, and not upon the stipulations in the Federal compact. We must insist for ample security for those rights."

Mr. Benjamin was considered an alarmist when he spoke thus in 1845. He was still so regarded when he repeated the substance of his warning in 1855. Whether the means with which he proposed to meet the danger were adequate or not, events have proven his fears too well-founded. It is clear from this speech and others on similar subjects that, as noted above, two years of experience in public life had enabled him to rise above mere Whig partisanship to something like a broad view of the conditions affecting not only Louisiana but the whole South. In this particular instance his policy was for the safeguarding of Louisiana alone. He would have inserted in her constitution every provision, however remote its application might appear, to preclude the possibility of her own *bona fide* citizens losing control of the government of the state. The justification of slavery is quite aside from the purposes of this comment. Slavery has long since ceased to be an academic question or a question of any sort. In the Northern states at this time it was an academic question. In Louisiana, and to Mr. Benjamin and the great majority of the people, it was not an academic question, but merely a question of their right to their own property, a right which was menaced by Abolition activities. The idea that the slave was property, just like any other property, was as old, certainly, as the Constitution, though at first it had been but a vague, inchoate notion. Little by little finding articulate expression till it became a part of the Southern political creed, it was vigorously re-asserted in broader terms in the Dred Scott Decision. To the exposition, the extension and the advancement of this idea, *viz.*, that the slave was property, and that therefore protection in the enjoyment of this property must be assured to the owner by the Federal government, Benjamin was from this time forth to devote much of his talent as a debater.

The same purpose on Mr. Benjamin's part, crops
out, though not openly avowed, in another remarkable
speech on his proposition that the governor should be
a native of the United States—he would have preferred to say, a native of the state. This speech[1] was
made in reply to several long ones by those whose
views were more popular, especially Pierre Soulé,
himself a native of France, who was so radical in his
opinions that he had been compelled to leave his home,
and who had since won a high and honorable rank as
lawyer, politician, and orator, in his adopted state.
In his opening words Mr. Benjamin avows his entire
responsibility for the proposition under discussion, and
that, "it was at my suggestion that the word 'native'
[the gist of the controversy] was inserted in the section now before us for our consideration. If therefore,
sir, there be censure to be cast upon any one for that
apparently objectionable word, upon my shoulders it
must in justice fall." He then replies to, or rather
utterly demolishes the constitutional arguments offered
by Soulé,—an easy task in this case, for Soulé had
nothing to stand on when he maintained that it would
be unconstitutional for the state to require, like the
United States, that its chief executive should be a
native,—showing that an article similar to the one
under discussion had been adopted in the constitutions
of Virginia, of Arkansas, of Alabama, and of Missouri, and had been sanctioned by the action of Congress in the case of the last three.

"In a word, then, sir, I assert that our power to insert the clause disputed is not a doubtful question;

[1] *Debates*, Feb. 14, pp. 221-224.

that we have the power to do so constitutionally, and
the only question we now have to decide is, Is it expedient for us to do so? My own impression is that
we should unhesitatingly insert it, if we study our own
interests. When I first proposed to the committee to
insert it in the section, it was a natural instinct that
prompted me to believe that it was necessary. Since
then I have given the subject calm and serious deliberation, and I have daily, nay, hourly, become
more and more convinced of the necessity and propriety of the measure.

"Sir, I have listened with delight to the eloquent
eulogy pronounced by the delegate from New Orleans
[Soulé] on the brave men who lent us their aid in 1815
—on Savary, St. Gemes, and their associates. I have
witnessed in imagination the memorable scenes so
graphically and eloquently described by the honorable
gentleman from Rapides [Mr. Brent], and I have felt
my heart glow with feelings of gratitude toward the
brave and generous men who, amidst the smoke and
carnage of battle breasted the British bayonets, and,
side by side with American citizens, periled their
lives in our country's cause. Honor and gratitude to
them all! And I will yield to no man in expressing
on all occasions, and in all suitable manner, the
acknowledgments that are due to their eminent services. But, sir, let us not allow our feelings to obtain the mastery over our judgment. Those brave
men were the sons of France, and the enemy was the
hereditary foe of France. Sir, does the gentleman,
can any man, believe that, if our invaders had been
French, these gallant men would have gone to battle
against their countrymen? Sir, they would have recoiled with horror at the forethought [*sic*] with the
same instinctive abhorrence as if called on to smite
the cheek of the mother that bore them. How then,
sir, can we place as the commander-in-chief of our
armies an individual who in the event of war with the
country of his birth would be exposed to this conflict

of duties and of feelings? The honorable gentleman tells us that in an event like this, a gallant spirit, stifling all that love of country, of our natal soil, that the Creator has implanted in the breast of every man, would take for his motto, ' *Fais ce que dois, advienne que pourra.*' Sir, this may sound very finely in theory, but every feeling of our nature would recoil from its practice. I call on the gentleman to point out to me the man, nay, sir, I ask if he himself, and surely there is none whose eminence as a citizen would render him more worthy of so exalted a station,—I ask if he himself, as commander of our armies, were called to lead our forces into the field against the country of his birth, would he not feel his inmost soul revolt at the bare idea? Whether the bare sight of the flag of his native country would not bring back upon his memory every thought and feeling of his childhood and his youth, and whether he could steel his heart to the task of carrying death and carnage into the midst of those in whose ranks might, perchance, be found the playmates of his childhood, the companions of his youth, nay, perhaps a brother or a parent? Never, sir, never could he do it. It is our duty then, sir, in making this organic law, to provide in such a manner as to render it impossible, in any contingency, for our chief magistrate to be placed in such a position. The necessity is too apparent to admit of doubt. . . .

"Once again, sir, let not the feelings which dictated the proposal of this measure be misunderstood. Let it not be said that it is an attack directed against the naturalized citizen. He is received with open arms into the country. Every avenue to fortune which cupidity could desire, every path to office which the most unbounded ambition can aspire [to], are all opened to him. Is it too much to ask that there should be one small spot reserved for the native of the soil? that the chief magistracy of the state, as that of the United States, shall be regarded as a temple within whose precincts none but the American people themselves shall ever be permitted an entrance? Our duty to our country makes it necessary that we should so determine, and I trust that such will be the vote of this convention."

For one who was himself an adopted citizen, as he said, but "sixteen years a resident in the state," and whose career might certainly lead him to the governorship if he had any desire for it, this was a remarkable position to assume. He was not satisfied with, though he reluctantly accepted, the article as finally put into the constitution, prescribing fifteen years' residence for the office. And the motive underlying this and other extreme undemocratic opinions was a wish, which cannot but seem exaggerated, to "provide a bulwark in our organic law against the machinations of an insidious foe."

It was not often that Mr. Benjamin showed himself lacking in tact and consideration for the feelings of others. Sometimes, it is true, such an opponent as the rather pompous Downs furnished so tempting a mark for ready sarcasm as to be absolutely irresistible, and Mr. Benjamin would succumb to temptation, and afterward have to exert all of his affability to smooth the ruffled dignity of his victim. But the closing part of this speech is not judicious : the arguments adduced could not carry conviction ; they might and did give serious offense to the hypersensitive Creoles. The next day the valuable time of the convention was taken up by fiery vindications of the unimpeachable patriotism of the Creoles of Louisiana, all of which may be found in the *Debates*, printed at state expense. Among those who spoke, the most remarkable and the most effective was one long celebrated in local annals,

—Bernard Marigny, whose immediate ancestors for
several generations had been Chevaliers of the Order
of Saint Louis ; who had squandered more money,
certainly, than any man in Louisiana ; who had been,
in 1803, the leader and pattern of the *jeunesse dorée;*
who had served in the first state convention of 1812 ;
who had visited and been received by that temporary
monarch, Louis Philippe, in return for hospitality
once accorded by the Marignys to a certain young
Louis Egalité with no place to lay his head ; and who,
finally, in spite of all this personal and ancestral connection with aristocracy, was almost a radical democrat. His reply, though less polished than Benjamin's
speech, and marred by outbursts of somewhat inco-
herent passion, is really sufficient to demolish Benjamin's main point, *viz.*, that a man would not lead an
army against his countrymen.

We have yet to consider Mr. Benjamin's position on
the basis of representation, which may sound as if it
ought to be a matter of no importance and capable of
easy adjustment, but which really brings us at once
face to face with the slavery question.

The distribution of slave inhabitants in Louisiana
was really the cause of the whole difficulty. Then as
now, the hilly parishes in the northern portion of the
state enjoyed a preponderance of white over negro
population. In the sugar district (which may be
roughly defined as lying south of Baton Rouge, exclusive of New Orleans), and in the alluvial parishes
in the cotton district, such as Tensas and Concordia, the slaves were plainly in the majority. Moreover, a very large proportion of the taxable wealth of
Louisiana lay in or was produced by these negro par-

ishes.   New Orleans alone, in the southern part of the
state, could really claim a heavy preponderance of
whites over blacks and at the same time a heavy proportion of taxable wealth.   When people representing
interests as varied as those of the parishes of De Soto,
Lafourche, and Orleans attempt to find a basis for
representation that will give fair political weight to
the sturdy white farmers who own no slaves, and who
are few in numbers and poor, with the same for the
wealthy planters who are also few in numbers but whose
slaves make so much wealth for the state, and again
the same for the merchants and white laborers of the
one great city in the state, difficulty is not far to seek.

A similar obstacle, it will be remembered, had been
met and overcome by the framers of the Federal Constitution :   Shall the slaves of Virginia count as much
as the freemen of Massachusetts ?   Virginia said, yes ;
Massachusetts said, no.   Hence the compromise :
" Representatives and direct taxes shall be apportioned
among the several states . . .   according to their
respective numbers, which shall be determined by adding to the whole number of free persons, including
those bound to service for a term of years, . . .
three-fifths of all other persons."   Thus the " Federal
basis" came to be applied in those states that had to
deal with the problem of slave representation in their
legislatures.   There were two other bases that might
be used for the computation : the "total population
basis," and the "qualified electors basis," the latter
susceptible of various slight modifications.

The committee in charge of the article involving this
question brought in a report (February 4th) providing
for the "Federal basis."   Mr. Benjamin, then and when

the article again came up for discussion a month later, denounced the proposition in terms more than usually uncompromising and vigorous.[1] "I ask you if the Federal basis of representation, as adopted in the report, is not a clear departure from the very principle and essence of democratic government? For, what does it propose? It proposes taking a part of the power of representation from the electors, to whom alone it belongs, and conferring it on the slaves. And those who raise their voices against so flagrant a proposition are, it is insinuated, favoring the views of the Abolitionists! Why, . . . it is the party who make the accusation who are upholding the doctrine of the Abolitionists; they are for giving the slaves political consequence,—the very thing for which the Abolitionists have been for years contending. I am for regarding them as they are regarded by the law— mere property. Is it not so? . . .

"Slaves are, by our laws, nothing but property. But, says the delegate from Lafourche [Mr. Beatty], we should allow them to form a part of the basis of representation because they are productive labor, and labor should be represented. If this argument hold good, then it might, with equal propriety, be urged that we should allow representation to horses, oxen, etc., which are attached to the glebe, and which are equally productive labor. This is the first time that I have ever heard the notion that labor should form a part of the basis of representation, . . . and especially that particular kind of labor. . . .

"By the principle which they [his opponents] lay down, would not a man owning five minor slaves have

[1] *Debates*, pp. 156, 360, 368–371; cf. *Picayune*, Feb. 5.

a representation equal to four votes, whilst a man having five minor children would have a representation of but one vote? If property is to be represented at all, why not all property? Why not houses and lands? . . . Or if at all, why not make it a qualification for voting?"

Even more distinctly, in the later speech, he states that, "when in the committee, I opposed the insertion of [the Federal] basis, not because I did not think New Orleans would get as much by adopting that as by taking any other basis that might be selected. On the contrary, I think New Orleans would gain by it in that respect; but I opposed it because I thought it radically wrong. . . . I opposed it because I thought it would operate unjustly. I regard representation as a correlative term; I believe that there can be no representation unless from the choice of those represented; and I am opposed to any other basis than that of free white population."

Once later on he proposed apportionment on the total population basis, which would have been just two-fifths more unfair and undemocratic than the Federal basis; but this was merely a compromise offered in desperation and soon abandoned. He contended persistently, and with ultimate success, against the Federal basis or any other basis that involved representation of slaves. And his statement of the case against the principle involved is so perfectly simple and clear, so free from the casuistry with which he was accused of upholding more doubtful cases in law and in politics, that one cannot forget it.

On the many minor points of Mr. Benjamin's activities in the convention of 1845 we need not pause to comment. In all essentials he lived up to the promises he had made before election; and where he deviated from them, it will be found that he did so in behalf of some compromise which would at least accomplish part of the desired end. After a careful examination of the press, and particularly of the opposition press, always ready to find fault, I find no criticism of his conduct that merits the least mention. And that his own party endorsed his action is sufficiently established by their continued confidence.

For six or seven years after 1845 there is little in Mr. Benjamin's public career that needs comment. This was the time of his plantation success and disaster, of which we have already spoken, and of the renewed activity as a lawyer that was to follow planting losses, of which we shall also have something to say later on. He was still ready with his advice when the party required it, and did not by any means cease to take part in state campaigns; but of the scores of political speeches it were worse than useless to remark in detail unless they express opinions of more than local or temporary interest. Like nearly all Southerners, he was in favor of that war with Mexico which our better judgment constrains us to condemn as indefensible. He was a Presidential elector on the Whig ticket in the campaign which justified the victory over Mexico by the election of Taylor. And he was too good a Whig and too good a Louisianian not to stand by the candidate of his party and his state, though his undisguised admiration for Clay and Webster could not fail to make him feel that the party had chosen the man who could be, rather than the man who should have been, elected.

CHAPTER IV

WHEN the Compromise of 1850, admitting California as a free state, but extending the possible area of
slavery over the remainder of the territory taken from
Mexico, came before the people, Mr. Benjamin's
opinions on several points underwent a change which
seemed sudden, but which I venture to believe had
been long prepared for.

The first expression of this change of views arose
from his dissatisfaction with the constitution of 1845.
He threw himself into the movement to call a new
convention to remodel that constitution, which had
not yet been six years in operation. There were several
reasons for this displeasure. One that was almost
personal had to do with an enterprise in which he had
recently become much interested—the Tehuantepec
Railroad Company, whose formal incorporation had
been much interfered with by the rigid and needlessly
restrictive provisions of the old constitution. Of this
it will be more convenient to speak when we consider
other similar commercial enterprises in which Benjamin took a part. Quite aside from this personal
motive for dissatisfaction, neither Benjamin nor any
other New Orleans Whig could be content with the
apportionment of representatives, while the Democrats generally were dissatisfied with the whole basis
of representation, as not sufficiently popular. Reason-

able men from both parties had recovered from the panic that had led to the insertion of provisions seriously restrictive of banking or other corporations, now sorely needed to aid in developing the resources of the state. In the popular mind distrust of the legislature had somewhat given place to distrust of the executive; people were no longer so much afraid that their own representatives in the legislature would rob them as they were that the governor, with his extensive powers of appointment, would exercise almost despotic control over the administration. Some of our historians have remarked that, at the time of the framing of the Constitution, America had a dreadful bugaboo constantly in mind,—George III—and consequently hedged the President about as if there were imminent danger of his developing into a Sulla, a Cromwell, or a Governor Tryon (to use an illustration that might have occurred to them). There is still a little of this feeling among us, and the result is that sometimes we allow our judges to be selected for long terms by the governor, and then again we have a recurrence of the ultra-democratic fever and leave the choice of these officers to the inscrutable wisdom of the ballot box. These were the sentiments that inspired the calling of a constitutional convention in Louisiana in 1852.

But before we tell of Mr. Benjamin's part in this convention it will be necessary to mention several other matters political.

Following his usual custom, Benjamin went abroad in the summer of 1851. He had not returned in time for the meeting of the local Whig convention in October, but, along with Mr. Robb, his associate in many large enterprises, he was nominated for the state Senate. The issues in the state were so well defined that the local party platforms are quite understandable even now. That one upon which Benjamin was nominated, and which his friends assured the voters, during his absence, he would accept, declared in favor of a constitutional convention to remodel the existing constitution so as to provide for an elective judiciary, a well regulated system of free banks, the delegating to the legislature of powers to enact liberal laws for railways, manufactories, etc., and other items of less note. Unfortunately, the memory of man doth run to the contrary, when the length of the course is but six years. Benjamin was no sooner nominated than the Democratic papers, and even some that were by no means Democratic, called attention to the fact that, in 1845, he had voted against every measure of a liberal character; but "Mr. Benjamin being absent in Europe, his friends, who put him in nomination, are safe in making whatever professions they choose in his name."[1] His friends did, indeed, promise in his name, and their promises were made good. They also, to some extent, attempted to explain Mr. Benjamin's votes in 1845, and to account for the change of views that must be presupposed if he could honestly stand on their platform; in this they were by no means very successful, so far as convincing one's reason is concerned. They seemed to have no difficulty, however, in persuading the voters that Mr. Benjamin was all right, even if it did look a little queer to have him supporting in the legislature of 1852 many measures

[1] *True Delta*, Oct. 28; see also *Orleanian*, Oct. 17, Nov. 7; *Delta* Oct. 9, 10, 14.

he had opposed in the convention of 1845, and he was elected without serious trouble.

Scarcely had he been elected, when it became clear that he was the strongest candidate for the United States Senate. Two of the more influential papers of his own party at first told him good-naturedly that such plums were for his betters, or at least his seniors in party service, though he had been a very good young man. Duncan F. Kenner is preferred by one paper, and Randell Hunt by another. And one journal, highly approving of his nomination for the state Senate, has a comment so significant of the impression which Mr. Benjamin's boyish appearance (in his fortieth year) still made on people, that I cannot forbear quoting : [1]

"He is sagacious, possesses great tact, and would make a very brilliant and effective senator. His appearance in that body would startle the gossips at Washington. His boyish figure and girlish face,— his gentle, innocent, ingenuous expression and manner, —his sweet and beautifully modulated voice, would render him decidedly the most unsenatorial figure in that body of gray heads and full grown men. But, when he should arise in the Senate, and in the most modest and graceful manner proceed to pour forth a strain of the most fluent and beautifully expressed ideas, of the most subtle and ingenious arguments, of the most compact and admirably arranged statements,—casting a flood of light over the dryest and most abstruse subjects, and carrying all minds and hearts with him by his resistless logic and insinuating elocution,—then would the old senators stretch their

[1] New Orleans *Delta*, Oct. 10, 1851.

eyes and mouths with wonder, whispering to one another, 'That's a devilish smart little fellow,'—then
would all the ladies declare, 'What a love of a man !'
—what a perfect Admirable Crichton,—so beautiful,
yet so wise,—so gentle, yet so terrible in sarcasm,—so
soft-toned, yet so vigorous in logic !   The *quid nuncs* and
politicians would join in the general wonderment, and
give their decided opinion that he was a psycholog-
ical, physiological, and intellectual phenomenon.
But, with all his genius, his universal talents and
eloquence, Mr. Benjamin will hardly be elected to
the Senate, because he is too valuable and necessary a
man in this state.   He is the acknowledged leader of
several great enterprises, in which our state and city
have a greater interest than in being ably represented
in the United States Senate."

When the time for the election came on, however,
the vote for Benjamin in the caucus of his own party
was overwhelming.   He was nominated on the second
ballot, receiving thirty-seven votes to Kenner's nineteen, Hunt's eleven, and two scattered.   And in the
actual election a Whig victory was certain, that party
having a clear majority of the General Assembly.
Benjamin was a popular candidate, and won some
Democratic votes, being elected by a majority of
twelve over his old antagonist of 1845, Solomon W.
Downs.   To supporters of Hunt or Kenner, like the
Delta, Benjamin's easy victory over them in the
caucus came as a surprise.   But this paper [1] probably
hit the true explanation :   "The country members
rather preferred a gentleman . . . who . . .
was a sugar planter, and had, therefore, a common

[1] Jan. 29, 1852 ; see also Jan. 27.

interest and sympathy with them. Another great advantage enjoyed by Mr. Benjamin was in the fact of being a prominent member of the legislature. . . . Mr. B. made good use of this advantage. He not only rendered himself very agreeable to the members of the legislature, but he manifested a zeal, industry and capacity in the preparation of business for the legislature,—digesting and framing bills, and drawing up reports, etc.,—which produced a most favorable impression as to his great practical talent and usefulness."

We might step aside here for a moment to mention some of the praises bestowed upon Benjamin in the little sketch of his life that follows the comment just quoted. His amazing versatility, his rapid rise in his profession,—" though not yet forty, he has reached the topmost round of the ladder of distinction as an advocate and counselor in this state "—and his amiable, fascinating personality caused most frequent remark. What a ring of a by-gone age it has, when the worthy editor undertakes to account for " astonishing versatility, such as we have never seen in any man we ever knew," in this fashion : " His head, phrenologically speaking, is fully developed in all the faculties. He has a fine imagination, an exquisite taste, great power of discrimination, a keen, subtle logic, excellent memory, admirable talent of analysis." But the most astonishing thing in the senator-elect,— and here we must agree with the *Delta*,—is that, while attending to a very heavy law practice, " he has had time to look after one of the largest sugar plantations in the state, to pay a yearly visit to Paris, to see to the interest of the great Tehuantepec enterprise, to fulfil all of the duties of an active partisan, of a public-spirited citizen, of a liberal gentleman, with a taste for the elegancies, the social pleasures and refinements of life."

Mr. Benjamin's term in the Senate of the United States was not to begin until March 4, 1853. In the meanwhile there was more activity in political life than at any time before. He did not, of course, resign from the State Senate, of which he had just been elected a member, and took a prominent and very eager part in the actual work of the legislature during January and February, 1852, making a long and successful fight in behalf of the Citizens' Bank of New Orleans, which brought down upon him the unsparing censure of its many enemies.

Of the Citizens' Bank it is only necessary for us to say here that it was a financial institution which had suffered in the panic of 1839, had suspended specie payments, and, failing to resume within the time prescribed by the legislature, had since been struggling to protect itself from enforced liquidation under unfavorable conditions. Mr. Benjamin was one of those who believed that the interests of all concerned in the bank could best be served by permitting it once more to resume control of its own affairs.[1]

The Whigs, having obtained control of the legislature, strained every nerve to win the by-elections in the state, and above all to control the constitutional convention which was to assemble in July. Even the city election, in March, was conducted on national party lines, the Whigs making a vigorous fight in the face of a dangerous opposition and a split in

[1] *True Delta*, Feb. 15, March 3, 11 ; *Delta*, Feb. 18.

their own ranks. In a speech at a great Whig meeting on the eve of the election (March 21st), Benjamin urged his hearers to vote in favor of the proposed constitutional convention and for delegates to it, and to remember that in voting at this election they would be helping to decide whether the next four years of national administration should be Whig or Democratic. For this excessive partisanship he was justly condemned ; the only excuse which can be offered is that, as in 1845, he was intent on issues of far greater importance than those that lay on the surface. The people were in favor of the convention, and the Whigs elected at least a part of their ticket in the city.[1]

Delegates were to be chosen on June 14th, and again the Whigs, with Benjamin and Roselius among their candidates, made a strict party fight. Not only was this course deprecated, but the *Delta*[2] very pertinently commented on the Whig ticket : "It includes two gentlemen who were prominent members of the convention of 1845, and who, in that body, were conspicuous for their maintenance of those very restrictions which have excited the hostility to the constitution that has led to the present movement to change it. Mr. Benjamin, if not the author, was the ablest supporter of the bank prohibition clause ; he was also in favor of restricting the suffrage ; and, though foreign born himself, voted for the provision requiring naturalized citizens to reside here two years after acquiring citizenship before they could vote. Mr. Roselius voted for the same clause."

[1] *Delta,* March 22.
[2] May 21 ; cf. May 8 and 18, and June 13 and 15.

But Benjamin and Roselius succeeded in convincing the people that they had modified their views on other important issues, if not on suffrage restriction, and the Whig delegation was elected by a very substantial majority. Meanwhile, before the convention met, the Presidential canvass had begun, and Benjamin bore his share of the campaign work. A speech which, for its courtesy and eloquence, won warm praise even from his most persistent and uncompromising critic, the *True Delta* (not to be confounded with the *Delta*) was delivered at a great ratification meeting on July 1st. Though a regular campaign speech, full of "party thunder" in places, it is remarkably felicitous in expression and tactful in matter. There is a touching tribute to the dead Clay, the lost leader. Fillmore, he said, would have been the first choice of Louisiana, and Webster, whom he eulogizes in a few apt phrases, the second. But he praises Scott without fulsomeness, and in the campaign that followed he did his best in the losing fight for him. As the campaign progressed, in September, he stumped the state for the General. As one paper put it,[1] "the gentle, persuasive, bird-like notes of that oratorical siren, J. P. Benjamin [enchained] the wild cattle that roam the prairies of Opelousas."

The constitutional convention met at Baton Rouge on July 5th. Though the changes it made were in many cases radical, it was not so important a body, and excited less popular interest than the previous convention. In 1845 it had taken nearly five months to patch up a constitution which was not so very different from the one it replaced; which was full of com-

[1] *Delta*, Sept. 19; also 9.

promises that satisfied no one ; and which lasted but
seven years.   In 1852 it took less than a month—from
July 5th to July 31st—to enact a constitution in
which one can easily count twelve or fifteen changes
of capital importance.   When such an amount of
work was accomplished in the time named, it is almost superfluous to remark that there was little debate ; the ideal of this body was to do with certainty
and celerity those things upon which the majority
were agreed.   Except for special reasons, speeches
were rigidly limited to half an hour.   Article after
article of the old constitution, involving no contro-
verted points, was adopted without change.   With
relentless and monotonous frequency the majority
voted to table indefinitely amendments that might
excite dispute ; and Benjamin voted with, and was
the directing spirit of, that majority.[1]

It would be tedious as well as profitless to enumerate
the points of difference between the constitutions, but
we must indicate such as are significant of a change of
opinion on the part of Mr. Benjamin.   In 1845, he
who had advocated appointment, and appointment for
life, in the case of the judges of the supreme court
and other officers, now advocated, and carried through,
articles providing for elective judges of the supreme
court (term ten years) and of district courts ; for
an elective superintendent of public instruction ; for
elective boards and commissions, etc.   Similarly, he
voted for annual sessions of the legislature ; for increased liberality in the acquisition of citizenship ;
for the abolition of all restrictions, except that of be-

[1] The chief source for the facts in this and following paragraphs
is the *Journal* of the Convention, which gives no debates.

ing a " free white male citizen over twenty-one years of age," imposed upon members of the legislature. The voter could now acquire the suffrage after one year's residence, and if he were but twenty-one he was as eligible to the senate as to the house. In 1845 the governorship seemed so precious a thing in the eyes of the convention, that they provided that the occupant of the office must be at least thirty-five years of age, and have resided in the state at least fifteen years. Mr. Benjamin, it will be remembered, then wanted to make the provision still more conservative. Now he voted for a provision setting the age at twenty-eight, the residence at four years.

All these are striking enough by themselves to bring upon Mr. Benjamin the facile and irrefutable charge of inconsistency. There is something more singular still, which we shall leave till we mention two or three of the new clauses in the constitution.

With small difficulty, where before he had encountered hopeless opposition, he got passed a clause providing for the free registration of voters in New Orleans—population was so sparse elsewhere in the state as to render such a law of little use. He had learned that there could be as great folly in throttling corporations as in permitting South Sea Bubbles or wild-cat banks. He therefore favored liberal modifications of the existing provisions on banks and corporations, and himself was chiefly instrumental in having inserted a special clause legalizing the Citizens' Bank and the acts already passed in support of it. After the long depression in the train of the great panics that had stopped all commercial enterprise, the Southern states in particular were beginning to feel a

revival of business prosperity, and a consequent revival of projects, often all too ambitious, for the building of railways and other internal improvements. In
this current enthusiasm Benjamin shared, and so
united promptly and effectively with those who helped
to enact a whole new section (Articles 130–134) in the
constitution, providing for the fostering of internal
improvements, with an elective board to administer
the same.

It is scarcely necessary to remind any one of Mr.
Benjamin's opinion on the proposition to adopt the
Federal basis of representation. With simple logic and
statement of the facts so undisguised and straight-
forward as to be overwhelmingly convincing, he had,
in 1845,[1] denounced the principle of slave representation in any form as unjust and iniquitous. The question of the basis of representation was, naturally, an
interesting one in the new convention, one of the few,
in fact, which brought on warm debate. And Mr.
Benjamin voted and spoke in favor of basing representation on the total population, slaves and all.[1]
Indeed, whether justly or not, the opposition papers
accuse him of being the person responsible for the
final adoption of that basis, of exerting his eloquence
to persuade and his sarcasm to drive reluctant members to vote for this most distasteful measure. And
" after adjournment, Mr. Benjamin mollifies the subjects of his sarcasm by his pleasant smile, his silvery
laughter, or—greatest concession—allows them to ex-
cel him in a game of ten-pins!"

There was, of course, opposition in the convention,
though far less than one would have supposed. From

[1] *Journal*, p. 65; *Delta*, July 27, 29, and Aug. 3.

the nature of the question involved, however, this opposition was bitter, and the denunciation in the press
fierce. Ten of the city delegation voted against the
total population basis, including Randell Hunt and
E. A. Bradford, soon to become Benjamin's partner.
The city press generally, Whig or Democratic, disliked the provision ; some gulped, made faces, and
swallowed it; some were courageous enough to de-
nounce it. The *True Delta*, in particular, always daring to the point of intolerable insolence and not over-
nice in its "distinction of epitaphs," returned to the
assault again and again. The practical effect of the
provision can be very clearly appreciated when one
examines the census. To keep in touch with the
opinion of the time, we may as well use the figures
given by the *True Delta*[1] with its comment.

The seven parishes of West Baton Rouge, St.
Charles, West Feliciana, Pointe Coupée, Concordia,
Tensas, and Madison (alluvial lands, chiefly produc-
ing cotton) had a white population of 11,264, a
negro population of 47,373, making a total of 58,637.
The thirteen parishes of Livingstone, St. Helena,
Washington, Sabine, Jackson, Bienville, Franklin,
Caldwell, Union, Catahoula, Calcasieu, St. Bernard
and Vermillion (chiefly upland pine country) had a
white population of 35,681, a negro population of
23,819, making a total of 59,500. "By this most
atrocious arrangement, 11,264 residents of seven
parishes are clothed with as much political power as
35,681 residents of thirteen parishes among the most
prosperous of the state." This should make it clear
how unequal and unjust in its operation would be the

[1] Aug. 8; also Sept. 9 and 11.

provision now sanctioned by the state constitution. As I have noted elsewhere, such parishes as Concordia and Tensas had an enormous preponderance of slaves, who formed a minority in such parishes as Union or Sabine. The slave owner was given a tremendous political advantage. "The one hundred negro slaves of J. P. Benjamin, of Plaquemines, are made just as good as one hundred citizens."

In the abstract, one cannot defend the constitution of 1852. The best that can be said for it, I think, is that its makers recognized its shortcomings and provided for a much more rapid process of amendment than had prevailed. It has, however, one merit which may be overlooked; though its ends be not wise, it at least has the courage to seek them by direct means, and to declare itself for a principle. And when we remember that this was a period of growing hysteria on the slavery question; that Louisiana, once liberal in her encouragement of the enfranchisement of slaves, but now frenzied by incessant Abolition agitation at the North, was passing draconic laws in her black code; that even in the convention itself members not to be classed as radical in their views proposed articles absolutely prohibiting any master from freeing a slave unless said slave were deported from the state, and absolutely prohibiting free negroes from entering the state, under penalty of forfeiture of their freedom,[1]—when we remember all this, it should not be difficult for any person endowed with common knowledge of and sympathy with man as he is, to understand the impulses that led to the adoption of that constitution, and perhaps to justify them on the

[1] *Journal*, p. 26.

principle of the inherent tendency to defend our own property by any and all means.

The truth is, that there was some foundation for the charge made against the Whig leaders, and particularly against Benjamin, in regard to this constitution. They boasted, it was said, that the instrument would guarantee Whig control in Louisiana at least for the next generation. The Whigs had come to be regarded as conservatives, as the party in favor of safeguarding existing rights, privileges, and conditions, North as well as South. A very large proportion of the wealthy and prominent families of the state were Whigs, who regarded the Democrats as certainly dangerous in politics, and quite as certainly not fit to associate with them on an equal footing in society. These people were, in the main, still the largest owners of slaves. And a provision which gave them representation for their slaves ought, in the nature of things, to have secured their influence over the affairs of the state.

But the causes that brought about the disintegration of the Whig party as a national force were quite beyond the control of Louisiana politicians, and those causes were already at work. The death was to be a lingering one; indeed, the exact instant of final dissolution can scarce be detected:

> " As virtuous men pass mildly away,
>   And whisper to their souls to go ;
>   Whilst some of their sad friends do say,
>   ' Now his breath goes,' and some say, ' No.' "

The party may be said to have been really *in articulo mortis* when Scott met defeat in the autumn of this same year. And the provisions of the Louisiana constitution of 1852 could not consolidate the Whig party in that state when the national organization was destroyed.

There is no denying Benjamin's radical change of front; but though his motives may have been mistaken, it would certainly be nothing but narrow prejudice to condemn him without at least attempting to discover those motives. The *True Delta*, more apt in criticism than profound or just, baldly declares [1] that Mr. Benjamin's sole motive was a small and almost selfish one. In 1845, it states, he was a lawyer owning no slaves; in 1852 he was a sugar planter, and a large slave-owner. The facts are not exact, and the suggestion is little short of puerile malignity. Unfortunately, with his habitual indifference to journalistic censures, Mr. Benjamin, so far as I can discover, vouchsafed no explanation. Under such circumstances, I feel justified in suggesting one which seems to me reasonable.

Unquestionably, he still held the views expressed in 1845, *viz.*, that a conflict was fast approaching between slavery and Abolition, and that in preparation for this conflict a well-knit Southern party must be formed. He repeats this idea, we shall see, in 1855. His legal training taught him to seek, if possible, a peaceful solution of the problem rather than allow matters to come to a crisis. Even his defeated opponents frequently bore evidence, on other occasions, to the fact that he was not an unscrupulous antagonist, not a partisan who would attain his own ends by trampling upon others; but that he was preëminently tactful and conciliatory. His marked partisanship in this con-

[1] Sept. 11.

vention and in the political campaign was commented on because it was unusual. Was it not due
to his determination to make one final and desperate
effort in behalf of his chosen principles? If he could
gain a victory for the Whigs, and if they, as a national
party, should make up their minds to stand by the
South, certainly a critical point would have been
gained. He could not foresee that the great party
would fail so utterly to respond to the needs of the
hour, to change with the changing times. He himself
was too clear-headed, too rational to cling with desperation to principles that were no longer, to use a
recent phrase, "live issues." Accordingly, he had
yielded with the majority of his party in Louisiana to
the popular demand for democratic or liberal measures, though his own choice would certainly have been
different. He could not carry the Northern wing of
the party into the policies which he thought might
have given it a chance for continued prosperity, a new
lease of life.

CHAPTER V

COMMERCIAL INTERESTS

THE year 1852 was not to pass without still further political excitement for Mr. Benjamin. After the election to the United States Senate, the session of the legislature, the election for the convention, service in that convention, the Presidential campaign, and the election in November to ratify the constitution, there came, to cap the climax, a determined and alarming assault upon the validity of his election as senator. As early as November 6th, one of the city papers remarked:[1] "The friends of a certain distinguished gentleman, who is known to aspire to a seat in the Federal Senate, are said to speak of the probability of Mr. J. P. Benjamin's being unseated."

It is highly probable that this attempt to unseat Benjamin was at least partly the natural outcome of the hard feeling which was engendered by the campaign of the spring and summer, and especially by his somewhat ruthless partisanship. As it is an interesting example of the extremes to which party feeling and trickery can go, the case is worth reviewing. Even though they must have known that the attempt could not succeed, the enemies of Mr. Benjamin manifested an unholy joy at the prospect of his being "hoist with his own petard"—the petard in this case being the constitution of 1852, said to be of his manufacture.

[1] *True Delta.*

The grounds on which Benjamin's election was asserted to be illegal and void involved a very subtle quibble in constitutional law. Acting under the mandate of the constitution of 1845, the General Assembly of 1846 had passed a law relative to the election of United States senators, and this law was still in force. It provided that, on the first Monday following the meeting of the legislature (January), in the session thereof commencing in the year in which the term of office of the senator or senators would expire, the two houses should meet and proceed to the election.

Since the Louisiana legislature convened biennially, in the even years, '46, '48, '50, '52, and as the terms of senators always expire in the odd years, no session of the legislature "commencing in the year in which the term of any senator or senators" would expire could ever occur, unless such session should chance to be an extra or special one. Having carefully provided for what, in all human probability, would never happen, the law very wisely proceeded to put in the one clause that was worth all the rest, prescribing that, in case a session of the legislature should not occur in the same year, the election should take place in "the year next preceding." Under this provision Benjamin had been duly chosen in January, 1852.

But the same legislature which elected him, and which had a Whig majority, sent forth the call for the constitutional convention. That convention, still dominated by the Whigs, enacted a new constitution, one of whose provisions was for *annual* sessions of the legislature, meeting, as before, in January. The constitution had been ratified by the people; it was to go into effect immediately, allowing only time for new elections. Throughout the summer, however, and in the November elections, the Whigs had been losing ground, until finally, at the election for members of the new legislature which was to assemble in January, 1853, the Democrats found themselves secure in the lower house of that body. The term of Solomon W. Downs, whom Benjamin had been expected to succeed, expired on March 4, 1853. Here was a law commanding that the election for senator should be held in the same year in which the senatorial term expired. Here was a session of the legislature—and a Democratic House—in the same year in which one of the two Democratic senators was to be replaced— by a Whig? or by a Democrat?

The temptation was far too strong for the average politician. Before the legislature met, the partisan press discussed the pros and cons; when it did assemble, the Democratic caucus hesitated somewhat, but finally took up the matter, and decided by a vote of thirty-nine to fifteen that they would bring up the senatorial election, and support it as a party measure. According to the program, on the 24th of January, a Democratic member from New Orleans introduced a joint resolution, that the House, with the assent of the Senate, proceed to an election for senator to succeed Downs, thus treating Benjamin's election as absolutely null and void. There was a postponement of action, however; then the motion was lost; then a motion to reconsider was rushed through in a thin house by one vote. Meanwhile, the Senate, still Whig, sent the resolution to the Judiciary Committee, and ordered five thousand copies of their adverse report printed.

The disgraceful episode was closed, so far as the legislature was concerned, by an adverse vote on February 10th. But it had been a hot fight, in and out
of both houses. The report of the Senate Judiciary
Committee had been freely circulated as a Whig
document, and Whig members of the legislature had
done their best to influence public opinion in favor of
the validity of Benjamin's election. One of the ablest
of these defenses is that by T. G. Hunt, brother of
Randell, in the *Picayune* of February 6th. And the
Democrats had held mass meetings in New Orleans
and in Baton Rouge, with the object, so said the Whig
press, of intimidating the General Assembly ; while the
Democratic or opposition press teemed with arguments,
so-called constitutional, against Benjamin's right to
his seat, and insinuations of the wildest nature regarding him personally. Thus the *True Delta* suggests
that there are some doubts whether Benjamin, although
he exhibited such an " intolerant and restrictive spirit
in relation to adopted citizens," has himself complied
with all the formalities necessary to naturalization.
And one writer, usurping the name of "John Hampden," filled columns in several issues of that journal urging all the specious quasi-constitutional arguments against Benjamin, and revealing his own
want of faith in his argument by dark hints that the
senator's election was the result of deep and sinister
Whig designs, born of amazing prescience that the
party would lose in the elections of 1852, and that
his only chance would be in the legislature of that
year.

For the first time, we find John Slidell, who was a
brother of Thomas Slidell, and had always been a

Democrat, acting as Benjamin's friend. The fight
was lost in the legislature, but a forlorn hope of Democrats carried it still further. Some of them no doubt
were acting conscientiously, being really confused by
the speciousness of the argument advanced. But the
real animus of the attempt to unseat Mr. Benjamin
was narrow partisanship. In the United States Senate
Pierre Soulé, on March 7th, presented a petition
signed by twenty members of the legislature, protesting against Benjamin's taking his seat, on the ground
of his having been illegally chosen, and of his being
a native of the Island of St. Thomas. Benjamin had
already been sworn in, without opposition, on March
4th. The petition was formally presented by Soulé,
but to his honor be it said, he distinctly stated that
he would do no more than this, and it was laid on
the table.[1]

It was not long after this that the Democratic legislature of Louisiana had the privilege of electing a
senator. Soulé was despatched as American envoy to
Spain, and Benjamin's friend, John Slidell, was chosen
to fill the vacant place in the Senate. Though almost accidental, this replacing of Soulé by Slidell
must be credited with not a little influence on Benjamin's subsequent political career. He had known
Slidell for years, of course, but had never been so
intimately associated with him. And though he was
a man of too much intelligence and character to be
dominated by another, he was unquestionably influenced by his associates, as one would expect from a

[1] *True Delta*, Jan. 11, 13–16, 19–23, 25–29, Feb. 1, 3, 8–11, 13
and 16 ; *Picayune*, Jan. 25, Feb. 4, 6, 8, 9, 11, 13, March 17 and 18.

disposition rather impressionable, given to enthusiasms, above all, fond of being on good terms with his
fellows. From this time on we find the names of Benjamin and Slidell almost constantly associated in the
opposition press.

Mr. Slidell was a man of unquestioned ability as a
politician, and his personality, though neither fascinating by its urbanity, like that of Benjamin himself,
nor commanding respect by its fire and earnestness
and gentleness combined, like that of Jefferson Davis,
as his admirers saw him, was yet a strong one. As a
lawyer and as a speaker, he was much inferior; as a
political tactician, he was probably superior to Mr.
Benjamin. His methods aroused much suspicion almost always among the Whigs of his state; and his
name was frequently connected with transactions that
induced the most bitter feeling, and brought upon him
the most violent denunciations. It is unfortunate
that in much of this Benjamin's name is put beside
that of Slidell; but it is a fact that, at the same
time, no charges of corrupt practice are made against
Mr. Benjamin, and that those which are uttered
have no surer foundation than the partisanship of a
very vituperative press.

The circumstances of Mr. Benjamin's entrance into
the Senate, in a contested seat at a time when there was
still some doubt as to the political complexion of that
body, at first attracted pretty general attention to
him. His reputation as a lawyer and as a debater,
too, had preceded him, while it was generally known
that President Pierce had offered him a seat on the
Supreme Court, which he declined, not only because
he preferred the more active life in politics but prob-

ably also because he needed for his family more money than a Supreme Court Justice received. During his first two years in the Senate there is little of importance sufficient to warrant extended comment. He was working hard at the time, and no careful survey of the *Congressional Globe* for those years is needed to convince one of his assiduity. But the presenting of petitions and local bills is a matter in which the public of two generations later can hardly feel a keen interest. Then, too, Benjamin was as yet acting constantly and loyally with the dwindling Whig party during a Democratic administration, so that little opportunity offered itself for a conspicuous share in the making of laws. He delivered several speeches, but none of first-rate ability, though they must have been sufficient to establish his reputation as a ready debater, and to prepare for greater efforts.

When he went to Washington, he did not lose touch with local affairs. Mrs. Benjamin, who was always rather French than American in her tastes and interests, moved to France permanently, so that there was no opportunity for him to establish a home at the capital. He was compelled to relinquish his hold as a sugar planter, since attendance in the Senate, his practice, and numerous other occupations, added to the actual misfortunes of the overflow, were enough to render it impossible for him to attempt to continue in a business so notoriously precarious. But though thus obliged to abandon one project dear to his heart, there were many others, of great utility for the state, to which his devotion was hardly relaxed by political exigencies. The most notable of these were the Tehuantepec Railroad and the Jackson Railroad.

The dream of trans-isthmian communication, now so near the most perfect realization, was never so vivid, so truly oriental in its exuberance, as during the middle of the century which has just closed. Then the imaginations of all people, even the Mexicans, were fired by ideas and predictions and statements about railways which soon were proved to be utterly fanciful and unwarranted. The facility of organizing companies was taken as an indication of the ease with which roads could be constructed. With more than the impracticability and enthusiasm of Alnaschar, the world dreamed of railways which it would have taken a century to build; and the bewilderment and ruin were proportionately greater when the crash came. Difficult as were the problems of construction, obtaining materials and equipment, and remunerative operation, in the United States, they were as nothing compared to those to be solved in southern Mexico. And yet men of intelligence spoke of a railway across the almost unknown, unsurveyed wilds of Vera Cruz and Oajaca as if they expected to make a journey on it next week. It was very near the end of the century before the first locomotive crawled over a line similar to that of which Mr. Benjamin and his friends spoke with such great confidence in 1850. For this man, with all of his practical sense and his experience, was often unaccountably sanguine, too ready to believe what he wished very much to believe, and apt to take on trust statements which he afterward discovered, by personal investigation, to be quite unreliable.

It was in the fall of 1849 and the spring of 1850 that the scheme of the Tehuantepec Railroad began to take definite shape as a matter in which the citizens of New

Orleans were interested.[1] But there had been eight
years of deferred hope before that. In 1842 (March
1st) Santa Anna, then nominally president and really
dictator of Mexico, issued a decree giving to Don
Jose Garay, a citizen of Mexico, the exclusive right to
effect inter-oceanic communication across the Isthmus
of Tehuantepec. The grant[2] was very generous in its
terms, permitting him to open a canal, or to build
first a carriage road and then a railway. The grantee
or his assigns were to have protection in all their
rights as well as aid in the work, and the privilege
of fixing tolls for fifty years on the canal or railway.
All vacant land, to the extent of ten leagues on both
sides of the proposed route, went to Garay. In
return, he was to agree that the canal or railway was
to be neutral ; that the work on the line should begin
within two years after the completion of the preliminary survey ; and that any colonists introduced to people the land granted to him should become citizens of
Mexico.

Garay seems to have been what we, in the days of
Hooleyism, should call a "promoter," having neither
the means, nor perhaps the intention of undertaking
the work of railway building himself. But the chronic
disturbance in Mexican politics encouraged him to
make a show of beginning, in the hope, probably, of
obtaining further concessions. He did succeed in ac-
complishing this object, and from time to time secured
extensions of the period of his grant. In December,

[1] Newspapers of 1850–1852 are filled with items ; the most important, as giving a full history of the matter, are the *Delta* and
Picayune of Aug. 9, 1851.
[2] *True Delta*, July 31, 1851.

1843, during one of the kaleidoscopic reappearances
of Santa Anna, the date for commencing work on
the Isthmus was extended from July 1, 1844, to
July 1, 1845, some sort of a survey having meanwhile
been accomplished, though so carelessly that no port
had been definitely selected on either side of the
Isthmus for the terminus of a railway that certainly
could not live without ports.

The approaching difficulties with the United States
furnished Garay with still another excuse for seeking
an extension of the period within which he must begin
actual work. In June, 1845, just before the time set
would have expired, he sought another extension,
with still further privileges. The lower house of Congress considered his appeal approvingly, and passed a
law, which was then sent up to the Senate. There it
had been favorably reported from a committee, and
was on the eve of being acted on, when, to quote Mr.
Benjamin's report,[1] "there occurred one of those
events unfortunately too frequent in the history of our
neighboring republic. The administration of Praedes
was attacked and subverted by Mariano de Salas, at the
head of an armed force." In other words, Praedes
had lost his hold on the "army," Salas having bought
enough of the "soldiers" to make himself dictator,
which he proceeded to do. He was something of
a benevolent despot, introducing various reforms, permitting liberty of the press, etc. He was certainly
benevolent toward the Tehuantepec scheme. Says
Mr. Benjamin again : "Whilst Salas was thus exercising, *de facto*, the supreme power of the government ;
whilst his dictatorship was thus unquestioned, his at-

[1] *Delta*, Aug. 9, 1851.

tention was called to the law which was on the eve of being passed when the Congress was dissolved; and after examination of the subject, he promulgated his decree of the 5th of November, 1846, which is a copy of the law that had passed the Mexican House of Representatives and the committee of the Mexican Senate.

"By the terms of this decree, the delay of commencing the works on the Isthmus was prolonged to the 5th of November, 1848. The work was actually commenced prior to that date, as is established by the official reports of the Mexican authorities on the Isthmus."

The validity of the grant, endorsed by so many of the half-dozen administrations which had in turn enjoyed a precarious existence since 1842, certainly should have been beyond question, however prejudicial it may have been to the best interests of the country; however outrageous in its disregard of public policy; however doubtful may have been the means used to secure such a public franchise. Its force was still further recognized, directly and indirectly, by subsequent administrations. When the United States had taken the edge off its keen martial appetite at the expense of Mexico, the Polk administration sought to secure what advantages it could from the vanquished foe. Unfortunately, neither the direction nor the immediate application of our diplomacy was in very able hands, and so, with General Scott bickering with Mr. Trist, and Mr. Trist misunderstanding Mr. Polk and finally patching up a treaty without any very clear right to do so, we did not get quite all we wanted. In regard to this Tehuantepec matter, Mr. Trist had been instructed to offer fifteen millions of dollars for a right of way across the Isthmus. The Mexican commissioners replied that "Mexico could not treat on this subject, because she had several years before made a grant to one of her own citizens, who had transferred his rights, by the authorization of the Mexican Government, to English subjects, of whose rights Mexico could not dispose." Therefore the treaty of Guadalupe-Hidalgo (1847) was concluded without any Tehuantepec rights for us, and with a most positive recognition by Mexico of the grant to Garay, and of his transfer of the same to Messrs. Manning and Mackintosh, a firm of English bankers in the City of Mexico.

This was the situation of affairs when the United States began to have a more direct interest in Tehuantepec. A Mr. P. A. Hargous, who was really a Pennsylvanian by birth and residence, but who had carried on much business with Mexico, purchased the Tehuantepec rights, known as the Garay grant, from Manning and Mackintosh. The inside history of transactions with the Latin American republics is always more interesting than the outside; but we can here catch only a glimpse of the inside, and cannot be quite sure of what we really do see. However, the gossip of New Orleans had it, that Mr. Hargous paid only $25,000 for the Garay grant. While this sum is surely a great underestimate, it is also certain that a shrewd business man would not pay any very large sum for privileges that first Garay and then the English bankers had been six or seven years trying to dispose of.

Hargous, like Garay, had no intention of undertaking actual construction himself. He had business connections and acquaintances in New Orleans. He came to that city in 1850, and soon had ten or twelve of the more enterprising and wealthy citizens interested in Tehuantepec. Mr. Benjamin was the most conspicuous of these, the one who was almost invariably the spokesman and the representative in the perplexities which were to envelop the Tehuantepec Company. It is customary to speak of it as the Tehuantepec Company, though without real warrant. When those who first became interested sought to obtain the coöperation of the public, and Benjamin issued a sort of manifesto with glowing accounts of their hopes, their first desire was to become incorporated, so that they might be empowered to issue and sell stock, bonds, etc. To their chagrin, they discovered that the constitution of 1845 was so rigid in its restrictions that no suitable charter could be had without the special action of the legislature. It was nearly two years before its next regular session, and Mr. Benjamin, with his customary enthusiasm and energy, thoroughly enlisted in favor of what seemed to him a splendid project, headed a delegation to Baton Rouge to petition Governor Walker to call an extra session. Not seeing wherein the expense to the public would be justified, that magistrate declined to assist Mr. Benjamin and his friends in this fashion. The would-be incorporators, nothing daunted, formed a temporary organization, with Benjamin as Chairman, and Bernard Fallon as Secretary.

This company, unlike the previous purchasers of the right of way across Tehuantepec, seems really to have been in earnest in its desire to avail itself of the privileges acquired. Mr. Benjamin was certainly very much in earnest; he rightly believed that the posses-

sion of a railway, with good harbors at each end, across
the one hundred and sixty or seventy miles of the Isthmus of Tehuantepec would revolutionize the fast-grow-
ing traffic with California; would give command of the
trade of the East; and that New Orleans would gain
immensely should this communication be opened.   He
was always ready to take advantage of an opportunity
to explain to his fellow citizens the peculiar benefits that New Orleans could hope for from the successful completion of this undertaking.   In a speech
before the Southwestern Railroad Convention, held in
that city in January, 1852, Benjamin had been describing the prime needs of the South in the matter
of railways, the most important of which was the route
north and south to be begun by the Jackson railway.
He continued, "This straight line of railroad [the Jackson, or what is now known as the Illinois Central] will
stop at New Orleans, but it will not cease there as a
line of travel. That line carries us straight across
the Gulf of Mexico to the narrow neck of land which
divides the Pacific from the Atlantic, whereon Nature
has bestowed every blessing of soil and climate, where
she has even lowered the hills as if purposely to point
out the way for a railroad; and when we cross this
Isthmus, this Isthmus of Tehuantepec—what have we
before us? The Eastern World! Its commerce has
been the bone of many a bloody contest. Its commerce makes empires of the countries to which it flows,
and when they are deprived of it they are as empty
bags, useless, valueless. That commerce belongs to
New Orleans!" [1]

Immediately after its organization, the company

[1] *Picayune*, Jan. 7, 1852.

started to take steps to secure its rights. The Mexican authorities of the hour were applied to for passports for a party of engineers to re-survey the route. These were readily granted, and a body of men, under Major Barnard, an army officer well known throughout the lower Mississippi valley, proceeded to the gulf side of the Isthmus, and went to work on it immediately. Meanwhile, application was made to the Washington administration to secure the protection of the United States, and to ascertain "beyond a doubt the honest intention of Mexico to forward this great enterprise," before beginning actual labor.

Webster, at that time Secretary of State, under Fillmore, was favorably impressed by the plans as presented to him first by Hargous and then by Benjamin. Accordingly, our Minister to Mexico, Mr. Letcher, was instructed to make overtures for a treaty giving joint protection to the work. The American proposals were favorably received by the Mexican President and his Cabinet, and a treaty was put in form by them, subject to ratification by the Senates of the respective countries. This provisional treaty also contained a clause, slightly modifying the terms of the Garay grant, to the effect that tolls were to be regulated by joint control of the two governments,—not by the grantees alone, and to this modification, of course, the consent of the grantees was to be obtained before the ratification.

When this draft treaty reached Washington, the representatives of the Tehuantepec Company were invited to examine it, and found that, though the general tenor of the document was entirely satisfactory, there were certain ambiguities, to remove which they pro-

posed some amendments. The treaty then went back
to Mexico, where it was again favorably received—by
a brand new President and Cabinet—and returned to
Washington with the changes desired by the Tehuantepec Company.   So far, all had gone as well
as could be wished. Both governments seemed of one
mind in the determination to assist in the great project. And even the most suspicious of the local papers
sheathed their rapiers and smiled on Benjamin, while
they indulged in fantastic predictions of the gain to
New Orleans when the canal or railway should be
completed. The friendly journals even sent special cor-
respondents with the Barnard surveying party, from
whom we find long letters from time to time.

It was in one of these letters that the public first
learned what the directors of the company had probably
known for some time ; namely, that things were not
safe in Mexico. The report was that the Mexican
Senate, after one of those violent tornadoes which so
frequently and unaccountably changed its political
complexion, had declared the Garay grant null and
void. The facts were, that another new President,
Arista, and his advisers, were hostile to the Tehuantepec Company, and had passed a law through Congress
declaring the decree of Salas, November 5, 1846, *ultra
vires* and hence null and void ; indirectly, this would
abrogate the grant absolutely, since the delay authorized by Salas was all that stood between it and forfeiture on the ground of non-compliance with its terms.[1]

Almost simultaneously with this disquieting news
from Mexico comes the announcement that Letcher's
treaty has gone to Washington ; that Webster has in-

[1] Cf. *Delta*, April 12, 1851.

vited the company (February 18, 1851) to inspect it; that the same has been declared satisfactory, and will be at once ratified by the Senate of the United States. But the *Delta's* "correspondent" with the Barnard expedition writes from Tehuantepec[1] that there is no doubt the Arista faction will forfeit the grant; that there is great excitement on the Isthmus; and that, as he expresses it with more force than propriety, "in good time, h—— will be to pay." It was not long, indeed, before news came of the expulsion of Barnard and his party, and of the closing of those ports which a friendly administration had opened to admit the supplies and materials of the company.

The tone of the New Orleans press becomes either less hopeful, or altogether hostile. Losing sight of the fact that Mr. Benjamin and his fellows had already expended a considerable sum, out of their own pockets, in promoting the survey; that the interests of New Orleans, or of any citizen of New Orleans, certainly could not be injured, and might be greatly advanced by the success of the scheme, the papers declared the whole thing a fraud. Simply because he declined to take the public into his confidence on matters of business concerning the company, it is hinted that,[2] "Mr. J. P. Benjamin has the good or ill luck to be prominently identified with mysterious projects; . . . we do not doubt that, as the agent of Mr. Hargous, . . . he earnestly aims to benefit his adopted city by the promotion of the Tehuantepec route; but we complain of the movements set on foot by him, inasmuch as they are unusual, strange,

[1] Date March 10th, in *Delta*, April 12th.
[2] *True Delta*, May 18, 1851.

and most suspicious." More and more hysterical
becomes the *True Delta*, till it quite earns the nick-
name bestowed by the *Courier:* "*L'Isthmophobe
. . . le nom seul de l'isthme de Tehuantepec lui
donne des accès de fureur et de rage.*"

It was vain for Benjamin to maintain a cheerfulness
and apparent unconcern which observers noted as
characteristic in a later and far graver crisis. It was
vain for him to refer in speeches to the probable return of reason and common honesty in Mexico; to
publish cards in the papers with encouraging reports
from Major Barnard ; to advertise for and buy
steamers; to employ five hundred laborers, in behalf
of the company. Public confidence could not be expected to revive in the face of the news from Mexico.
Benjamin went to Washington in July, having lingered in New Orleans just long enough to hear the
worst—President Arista's proclamation ordering the
expulsion of Barnard. Webster had just left the
capital, so Benjamin followed to Marshfield to urge
his claims. The interview was full of good promise,
and Benjamin came back to New Orleans and published a long and very interesting "Address to the
People of the United States," setting forth the history
of the Garay grant up to date, and making an unan-
swerable plea for its validity. It is from this article
that I have taken some of the facts in this account.

There was a lull in affairs concerning Tehuantepec
during the remainder of 1851, and the New Orleans
company by no means gave up hope. Their surveyors
had located a good route, had discovered a practicable
harbor on the Pacific, and had published this information in an interesting report (March, 1852). Benja-

min, presiding at a meeting of the directors on April 10, 1852, reported these facts, and in addition stated that a responsible firm of contractors had proposed to build the entire line of railway, one hundred and sixty-six miles, at the rate of $40,000 per mile. He had now succeeded in getting the State Department to take action in the matter. Webster had written to Letcher: "Perhaps, if on a suitable occasion, you were to hint . . . that the money due to Mexico for the extension of the limits of our territory, pursuant to the treaty of Guadalupe Hidalgo, had not yet been paid in full, and that contingencies might happen which would warrant the Government in withholding it, an impression might be produced favorable to the result of your negotiations."

But this mild threat proved quite ineffective. Though Mexico had protested violently and with Latin heroics that she would never permit the Tehuantepec Railway to be built by foreigners, Arista and his Congress authorized a new grant to a foreigner, Colonel A. G. Sloo, of New Orleans. Mr. Benjamin had pretty clearly intimated in his "Address" that sinister influence had been exerted against his company by some foreign nation, and that the peculiar jealousy and distrust of Americans by Mexico was responsible for much of the difficulty. If Mexico had been resentful of American encroachments, surely no one could have blamed her honestly. But that such was not really the case was proved by her action in making the new grant, however much her politicians may have stirred up the people against one set of Americans before they sold out to another. The essential difference between the Sloo grant and the

Garay grant is that the new one proposed a payment to Mexico for the privileges at once.

Benjamin kept up the fight some time longer ; but it must have been evident to all now that if he had bought anything in the Garay grant he had bought not the right to build a railway, but, as one facetious critic remarked, the right to a lawsuit. Really, the only question henceforth was whether this lawsuit was to lie in the courts of Mexico, or in those of the United States. He carried it into the Senate, and sought to have it made an international matter. But the resolutions then introduced by Senator Mason were even more fruitless than such measures usually are. Benjamin wrote another pamphlet, showing the justice of the claims of his company and urging the government to act. He pictured the political condition of Mexico, with thirty persons claiming to have exercised supreme executive authority, within the last thirty-six years, and during that same period five forms of government intermediate between anarchy and absolutism. But Webster passed away, and a new and less friendly administration followed that of Fillmore. A humorous incident in connection with this stage of the matter is the threat by Benton's *Missouri Democrat*. One of the provisions of the Garay grant had been that colonists introduced should become Mexican citizens. This did not, of course, apply to the grantee or to the company. But the *Missouri Democrat* hinted that it might be well to inquire into the matter with the object of determining whether Mr. J. P. Benjamin, "who signs himself in his correspondence with Mr. Webster as 'Chairman of the Managing Committee' " of the Tehuantepec Company be really a citizen of the United States or of Mexico. Mr. Benjamin did not lose his seat in the Senate on the ground of his having become a Mexican, but neither did he get the United States to back the claims of the isthmian enterprise.

The last fight in the Senate was over the Gadsden treaty. This originally contained two articles protecting claimants against Mexico, and specifically naming the Garay grant. Mexico insisted on a clear statement that she did not recognize its validity, and the government of the United States was to assume the task of examining, before special commissioners, the claims under this grant, which might be paid out of a fund of five million dollars reserved from the whole sum of fifteen millions provided for in the treaty. The Senate, however, threw out these provisions when the treaty was finally ratified. [1]

This concludes, for the present at least, Mr. Benjamin's connection with the unfortunate Tehuantepec Company. What were the actual losses of those interested—and New Orleans people furnished practically all of the actual money expended—it is impossible to determine. Hargous made a claim for something more than five million dollars; but that was of course a

[1] In addition to the contemporary press, to which references have been given, interesting matter bearing upon the earlier and later fortunes of Tehuantepec may be found in: Williams, *Isthmus of Tehuantepec* (1852) ; *Memorial on the Isthmus of Tehuantepec*, by the Mexican Minister of Relations (1852); Trastour, *Summary Explanation respecting the Tehuantepec Canal* (1856) ; *Conventions and Treaties of the United States* (1889); Stevens, *Tehuantepec Railway* (1869); Eads, *Tehuantepec Ship-Railway* (1883) ; Corthell, *Atlantic and Pacific Ship-Railway* (1886). For the revival of the project under Benjamin's auspices, see Chapter VII.

fantastic figure including estimated damages in the loss of his valuable privilege. It is more likely that the one hundred thousand dollars mentioned by Mr. Benjamin in his address (published after the completion of the survey) would quite cover the loss; and a newspaper gossip reports that the total was really not over eighteen thousand dollars.

This undertaking brought him more harsh and ungenerous criticism than almost anything in which he was engaged. But he was not spared in connection with the Jackson Railroad, of which he was one of the foremost promoters. In the midst of the exciting political campaigns of the spring of 1852, the movement for a railway to connect New Orleans with the north via Jackson, Miss., took definite shape in New Orleans, though more than a year before this time there had been discussion of the matter. [1] Benjamin and Robb had spoken in favor of such a road at the Southwestern Railroad meeting in January. Benjamin spoke again at a meeting on April 15th. He gave an exposition of the advantages of the railway, a report of what had already been done by a provisional committee, and much technical information about the proposed route, the cost of construction, etc. He advocated a tax on property to aid this and the Opelousas Road, to be voted on by the people. [2]

Shortly after this meeting, the first election for directors of the company was held. There were to be

---

[1] *Delta*, April 22, 1851, Benjamin chairman of committee on incorporation, rendered difficult by restrictive laws; cf. *Delta*, April 30.

[2] *Picayune*, January 7, 8, and April 16; *Delta*, January 7 and 15, 1852.

twelve from Louisiana, and six from Mississippi; and among those chosen for Louisiana were Benjamin, Robb, J. P. Harrison, John Slidell, H. S. Buckner, and Emile La Sère—names which are still familiar to many in New Orleans. Benjamin was not only an active member of the directorate, but he was chief legal adviser of the company as long as his senatorial duties admitted of his being in Louisiana. In spite of a threatening opposition, the railroad advocates carried the day, getting a fair majority on the vote for the tax. And things progressed very satisfactorily in the preliminary work on the road, even to the actual construction, although there was more difficulty in Mississippi, owing to the bad financial reputation of the state and the consequent reluctance of capitalists to invest in anything that bore her name.

In Louisiana, too, there was some trouble, and much ill-feeling, in connection with the bonds of the company. Bonds bearing eight per cent. interest, and secured by the city tax on real estate, had been issued; but though Mr. Benjamin and other lawyers had given written opinions which were favorable to the validity of the charter, of the bonds, and of the tax, the Supreme Court of the state had not yet pronounced upon these questions. Mr. Robb was said to have bought $600,000 of these bonds at a discount of ten per cent., and a certain section of the press attacked the transaction as little short of dishonest, though there was nothing to show that they would have commanded any higher price at the time in the open market. However that may be, the city council thought it a fair opportunity to meddle in the affairs of this big corporation. Accordingly, they sent a committee to

Benjamin to demand of the directors all the particulars of the bond sale, on the ground that they, the council, were guardians of the public interest in the matter. Benjamin, at the time acting as chairman of the New Orleans, Jackson, and Great Northern Railroad Company, replied in a little legal communication polite but very firm, the plain English of which was that it was none of the council's business; that the directors were required by the charter to issue periodical statements to the stockholders, and to make special reports whenever a specified number of the stockholders should desire it; but that the councilmen, as councilmen, were not stockholders, and had no right to the information they sought. Of course, this position was perfectly proper; the move of the city council was inspired by political motives.[1]

But as Benjamin had chanced to be the representative of the company, all the wrath of the disappointed councilmen and their friends descended upon his head. Now that time has hushed all these voices, it is with amusement that we record the vicious remark of the *True Delta*, that Mr. Benjamin was always ready for "a nefarious blow aimed at popular rights or public justice"; and "that the same Mr. Benjamin would be found equally willing and ready to give his opinion, provided it were his interest to do so, to the effect that his Satanic Majesty is entitled by law to exercise archiepiscopal functions in this diocese, we have no more doubt than we have of his connivance in the sacrifice of the $600,000 of railroad bonds."

Not all of Mr. Benjamin's fellow citizens, however, shared the *True Delta's* splenetic dislike. He was

[1] *True Delta*, May 4, July 8, 12 and 14, 1853.

constantly in demand socially, and for those semi-social public gatherings where ladies were gently inducted into political mysteries by some honey-tongued orator, as well as popular meetings to express the hopes, fears, indignation, of the people. Thus he had been the speaker of the evening at the great annual dinner of the New England Society, December 22, 1852, the first at which ladies had ever been present. Mr. E. A. Bradford, soon to become his partner, responded to the toast of "Webster," and Benjamin to that of "Louisiana." It is unfortunate that we have only the newspaper's word,[1] and our own fancy, that both speeches were beautiful, "enchanting the fair auditors." Again he had stepped aside from absorbing local politics, in October, 1852,[2] to speak at a great indignation meeting over the treatment of the steamship *Crescent City* by the Spanish authorities in Cuba. The details of the incident are petty—concerning an individual named William Smith, whom the Spaniards, for the most excellent reasons, did not desire in Cuba,—but New Orleans was a filibustering city, and there was great excitement. Of Benjamin's speech we need only say that it was very remarkable for its tone of moderation. In response to his query, What should the people do to avenge the insult to America in the treatment of the *Crescent City*, hundreds of voices in the great throng that filled Lafayette Square shouted, "Fight! fight!" Mr. Benjamin said that we should first be sure we were right, then go ahead; it appeared that the Spanish government was ignorant of the insult which had been offered by Captain Gen-

[1] *Picayune*, Dec. 23, 1852.
[2] *True Delta*, Oct. 13.

eral Cañeda; if so, "let us make a dignified but peremptory demand for reparation, and wait till that is refused before we proceed to make war upon Spain."

But the crowning testimony to the esteem and good will of those who were associated with him is the great banquet given in his honor by members of the Boston Club (November, 1853), on the eve of his departure for Washington.[1]

With all the splendor of display and exquisiteness of cuisine in which New Orleans delighted and for which she was famous, the banquet of one hundred covers was laid at the St. Charles Hotel. Mr. Bradford presided, and when the time for toasts came, he opened with a little address, dwelling upon the pleasant and amiable traits of character that endeared their guest to them, his fellows of the club, and ending with one of those gracious "sentiments" so touchingly redolent of the days when gentlemen took time to be gentle and to cultivate "elegance"; he said that "the success of Mr. Benjamin in his public career could not equal the wishes nor exceed the expectations of his fellow citizens." Benjamin's reply, of which again we have but a poor report, reviewed his career in New Orleans, with all the happy and tender associations refreshed in his memory by the occasion of this banquet:—how he had come, a poor and friendless boy, twenty-six years ago, and had met with uninterrupted kindness, encouragement, and confidence. "In all that time he had never made a friend who had been alienated, or asked a favor, public or private, that had not been granted." It was no mere political banquet to celebrate a victory—of those there were

[1] *Picayune*, Nov. 23.

plenty. It was a spontaneous expression of a body of gentlemen of all shades of political opinion; and we need not wonder that Mr. Benjamin was moved by this unusual compliment to one who had been in political campaigns so bitter as those recently conducted in Louisiana.

With this pleasant God-speed, he returned to Washington for the short session of the Congress. As was noted above, the routine work to which he chiefly devoted himself is barren of interest for us. But, in the Senate and out, his abilities as a debater were attracting attention. One instance will suffice, an argument before the Supreme Court in the great McDonogh case, Benjamin appearing for the heirs of McDonogh against the cities of New Orleans and Baltimore, which had been made the chief beneficiaries. As a legal argument, it displays more subtlety than soundness, and it does not now carry conviction to our judgment any more than it did to that of Justice Campbell; but the reporter of the *Washington Union* waxes enthusiastic over its eloquence and power when delivered by Benjamin.[1]

He writes : " Whoever was not in the Supreme Court room this morning missed hearing one of the finest forensic speakers in the United States. In the case of the great McDonogh estate, Mr. Senator Benjamin made one of the most truly elegant and eloquent speeches that it was ever my good fortune to hear. His address is refined, his language pure, chaste, and elegant; his learning and reading evidently great; his power of analysis and synthesis *very* great; his argument as logical as the nature of the case will admit;

[1] Quoted in the *Picayune*, Feb. 2, 1854.

his rhetoric so enchanting as for the time to blind his hearers to the faults in his logic if any. . . . Mr. Benjamin contends that substantially the devise in the will is not to [the cities of New Orleans and Baltimore] as beneficiaries, but only as trustees for others; and you can judge of his powers as a debater when I say that I think he carried conviction to most all, if not all, of his hearers, at least during the time that he was speaking. So fascinating was his oratory that his hearers, at least one of them, lost sight of the fact that the city of New Orleans, to which the devise was made, was not that spot of earth or physical entity known as such city, but the community occupying that spot. . . . The man who has the power to render, for even a moment, such a question obscure, must be a finished debater."

CHAPTER VI

CHANGE IN POLITICAL VIEWS

FOR some years the health of W. C. Micou, with whom Mr. Benjamin had associated himself since 1849, was so poor as to increase his labors greatly. Benjamin had been accustomed to devote himself to the commercial cases—though occasionally engaging in criminal cases—leaving the jury work generally to Mr. Micou. But when his health began to give way, and the senior partner found more and more of his time engrossed by occupations outside of his profession, it became necessary to find another associate. For a short time John Finney, just starting out in practice, was connected with the firm of Benjamin and Micou. Then, in the early part of 1854, notice[1] is given that J. P. Benjamin, W. C. Micou, John Finney, and E. A. Bradford "have formed a partnership for the practice of their profession," an arrangement which lasted but a very few weeks, for Mr. Micou died in April, leaving the firm as it was to remain for six years,—Benjamin, Bradford, and Finney. Mr. Micou was a man of high character and good attainments as a lawyer, but not comparable to the new member.

Mr. Bradford, although of a very different type from Benjamin, was a man of most unusual force and intellect. As great a student as Benjamin, he was not distracted from his legal investigations by the allurements of politics. More quiet and colder, he was

[1] *Crescent*, March 24, 1854.

consequently not so good an orator; but these very limitations preserved him from the danger of being over-sanguine, made him less liable to be carried away by sudden enthusiasms, or misled by the fascinating ingenuity of an over-subtle plea. These were the defects inherent in a nature like Mr. Benjamin's, and occasionally noted even by his earnest admirers during his lifetime. Mr. Bradford was not so ingenious, so fertile in suggesting plausible pleas, or so subtle in elaborating an argument; but he had the same power of clear analysis, and those who have heard both say that his presentation of the facts to a jury was better than that of his brilliant partner. They worked together in harmony, agreeing to differ not infrequently on politics, but most devoted to each other personally,—united by bonds of friendship as long as Mr. Bradford lived, and long after the dissolution of the firm by the great conflict. After the death of Mr. Bradford, the intimacy with his family endured to the end.

In connection with the land claims before the California Commissioners, Benjamin had found his knowledge of Spanish and Spanish laws invaluable. He had since had frequent opportunity to perfect himself in the language in connection with the Tehuantepec Company. Already, indeed, local journals had suggested his fitness for a diplomatic mission to Mexico. But it was not as an ambassador that he was to find a singular use for his linguistic and legal accomplishments. In the autumn of 1854, the newspapers announce, mysteriously, that Mr. Benjamin has gone to the Pacific coast of South America. In January, 1855, they report his return "on his way to Washington, from Ecuador, from which government he bears a commercial treaty

with ours, in the execution of which he has been engaged for some months."[1]   As usual, this was only
half true.

The visit to Ecuador was on private business, though
it for a time seemed to be of sufficient magnitude to
interest others besides those directly concerned.   General Villamil, who had been a resident of New Orleans,
and had also been a minister from Ecuador at Washington, had purchased some sort of claim to one or more
of the Galapagos Islands, which lie about five hundred
miles off the coast of that republic directly under
the imaginary line from which it takes its name.
General Villamil had not been able to make Charles
Island, the one that he claimed, in any way remunerative ; nor was his title altogether clear.   He
had tried to organize a company, and then employed
Mr. Benjamin as counsel and got him interested in
the island on his own account.   Reports were circulated of very rich deposits of guano there and
the lawyer was induced to believe in the representations made to him so far as to undertake a personal investigation of this source of wealth untold.   He
went to Quito, and there argued Villamil's claim in
the courts—a feat which would have been considered
more than remarkable in any one with a less romantic
history, and which is certainly good evidence of his
familiarity with the language of the country.   But it
is only on hearsay that we can affirm that he himself
went to see Charles Island.   As they approached the
island, it is said, the black mounds and heaps covering
its surface were hailed as deposits of guano ; on investigation they proved to be a barren waste of gray

[1] *Picayune,* Jan. 2, 1855.

and brown boulders. It was as the New York *Times* said : Villamil had painted glowing pictures of the fertility of the island, and of the herds of cattle there, but he had said nothing of the volcanoes ; "he told a lot about the 'critturs,' but never a word of the craters." [1]

Before the public was informed of all this, however, there had been wild suggestions—that Benjamin had in his pocket a commercial treaty with Ecuador, protecting the guano trading rights ; that he had exceeded all bounds in thus usurping diplomatic functions in addition to his senatorial duties, that the United States was to purchase the Galapagos Islands for three millions ; and that somehow Benjamin had captured a fee of $200,000 for conducting the "negotiations." He did not buy the guano island, nor had he any thought of jumping out of the Senate after some petty diplomatic bait.

The condition of things at Washington was growing more and more serious for all Southern Whigs. Benjamin continued to act with the remnants of his party in 1854 and the early part of 1855 ; he had evidently not made up his mind what course to pursue. Yet so far is he from yielding to the political excitement of the moment that he delivers a lecture on " Law as Practiced at Rome in the days of Cicero," at Petersburg, Va. [2] For all this, one could not help seeing that the great slavery question, every time it made its appearance in Congress, was dividing the Northern from the Southern Whigs, and that no bridge of com-

[1] *Delta*, Jan. 7, 1855; cf. also Jan. 3 ; *Picayune*, Jan. 4 and 5; and *True Delta*, Jan. 6 and 7, and November 15.
[2] *True Delta*, April 17 ; *Picayune*, April 18, 1855.

promise could span the chasm. And, in their desperate
perplexity, Whig leaders in both sections of the
country were deserting to Democracy or to one or other
of the new parties.

In the North and West Abolitionists and Republicans were on the increase. The two had not yet
coalesced—never did entirely coalesce—for the man
and the hour had not come. The Republicans had not
yet made up their minds openly to favor even the
gradual emancipation of slaves, much less the rash and
impolitic measures proposed by radical Abolitionists.
But the party was at least a " Free Soil" party ; *i. e.*,
it desired to restrict slavery, and above all to keep it
from spreading into the territories now just being
opened in the West and Northwest. And the South
(not without reason, as history discovered) could not
distinguish Tweedledum from Tweedledee, hated and
feared the "Black Republican" Seward, deserter
from the sinking Whig ship, just as much as the Abo-
litionist Garrison. Besides these abhorred twins, so
very near alike, there was the Native American or
Know Nothing party, which had a large following in
certain states both North and South. Similar tenets
had been in vogue for a while during the early forties,
particularly in Louisiana ; but the revived Know
Nothings were far more active and ambitious than the
Native Americans whose doctrines Benjamin had
seemed to like in 1845.

In view of the approaching general election, and
perhaps remembering Benjamin's leanings toward
nativism ten years earlier, a handful of faithful old
Whigs in New Orleans addressed an open letter to
him, asking for an expression of his opinions on the

Know Nothing party. To this he replied[1] at considerable length, so that we shall have to content ourselves with noticing only a few significant portions.

He confesses that, "in the debate which occurred in the Senate of the United States, . . . on the Nebraska Bill, the mortifying conviction was forced on my mind that the Whig *national* party was no more." Northern Whigs had again and again refused to stand by the rights guaranteed to the South in the Constitution and now assailed by the Abolitionists. The next House would be controlled by the Free Soilers, who had boasted of their determination to couple a repeal of the Nebraska Law and of the Fugitive Slave Law with the general appropriation bill, and thus carry their point or bring the whole administration to a full stop. And though this attempt would be foiled in the Senate, the parties hostile to the South, call them what you will, were waxing stronger, bolder, more inveterate and unscrupulous in their encouragement of evasions of the Fugitive Slave Law and of Abolition activities North and South.

"Suppose," he continues, "a body of insane fanatics in this section of the Confederacy should avow their belief in the sinfulness of subjecting the animal creation to the domination and service of man, and should, under the dictates of this 'higher law,' act on their conviction of the duty of stealing from the Northern farmers the flocks and herds which form so large a portion of their wealth. Suppose that to effect this they should organize bands of robbers and incendiaries who should make the night lurid with the flames of their barns and granaries, and even threaten with the

[1] *Delta*, August 3 and 5, 1855.

torch the roofs that protect their families. Suppose
that in this course of conduct they were not only ex-
cused, but encouraged and applauded by the South,
and that Southern legislatures took pride in passing
laws for their protection and assistance,—how long,
think you, would the North remain as patient and as
forbearing as the South has shown herself to be?"

Now that our country, in common with the whole
civilized world, is at one in the belief that slavery is
morally and economically wrong, it can do no harm
for us to try to put ourselves in a frame of mind at
least patient of, if not acquiescent in, such views as
Mr. Benjamin here voices. To him, as well as to
hosts of good men, there was no moral wrong in
slavery ; but arguments on the ethics of the question
are futile, barren of everything but the possibility of
exciting bitterness. Another line of argument, however, should appeal to the reason and to the sense of
justice of all of us ; and this is the one stated by Mr.
Benjamin in the paragraph just quoted. Repugnant
to our feeling it may be, but it was nevertheless unde-
niably the right of the slave-holder to have as good
protection in the use of his property as was afforded to
the owners of any other species of property. It was
guaranteed to him by laws innumerable ; and he saw
in the attacks on slavery but the most unaccountable,
unwarrantable violation of what his whole Anglo-
Saxon temperament and training had taught him
to regard as the very foundation of social and political liberty—property rights of the individual. It
was no paradox to him to talk of the abolition of
slavery as infringing liberty ; whether or not slavery
was contrary to Seward's "higher law," his slave was

a very valuable piece of property, had cost him, probably, a good round sum ; and he could no more see
that it was right for Northern people to plan to rob
him of his slave than it would be for him to connive at
horse stealing.   Individual philanthropists here and
there may have been willing to emancipate their
slaves ; though even among the philanthropists there
is one well-known case which might be mentioned.   A
gentleman made such disposal of his vast wealth that
it still works untold good, and liberated his slaves ;
but, it will be found, upon investigation, that he devised an elaborate scheme by which the negroes bought
their own freedom ; that one of the conditions attached
to their freedom was that they should immediately
emigrate to Liberia ; and that—he bought more slaves.
When even this Southern millionaire of most benevolent disposition did not feel that he could afford to lose
his slave property, would it not be extraordinary if the
man of moderate means, whose sole productive capital
was his slave property, should contemplate with calm-
ness and patience the political success of those who
were planning to deprive him of what was his own ?
The South was not ready for emancipation ; it would
not have consented to it peacefully for many years.
Even with compensation for the actual slaves, it would
not have consented until economic changes had made
slavery as impossible as at the North ; for there were
many who, remembering Hayti and Jamaica, sincerely
and deeply dreaded the possible consequences of turning loose these hordes of half-tamed savages.

It was to a public firmly convinced of such facts—
slaves were property, the North was seeking to rob
them of this property, a policy not only cruelly dis-

honest but fraught with fearful perils for them—that
Mr. Benjamin addressed these words. He and count-
less other speakers were to repeat the substance of
them again and again, prophesying woe and wrath to
come, till the dread sound of war justified the prophets
and silenced their voices forever.

We have turned aside here to summarize conditions
with which most of us are probably painfully familiar,
but which we must keep in mind while following a
politician through the years just prior to the Civil
War. Mr. Benjamin himself summarizes them in the
address which is cited, but rather for his audience
than for one of our time. He proceeds to his consideration of the Know Nothings. Four-fifths of the
Whigs of Louisiana, instead of uniting " in one great
Southern party upon some platform similar to that of
Georgia, on which we can all stand together and meet
with firmness the coming shock," have been seduced
into joining that organization. This is not a national party ; it is objectionable because of its narrow,
mediæval hostility to Catholics, and on account of its
puerile oaths of secrecy and the like. But above all, it
is not a national party because it has no platform, no
principles ; it is " held together not by the ties of a
common belief in certain principles and measures of
public policy, but simply by their preference of themselves as the right kind of men for office holders " ;
and finally, it is hostile to the South.

With greater prescience than he displayed in his
later action, he then concludes : " Although the Democratic party is not yet so thoroughly disorganized as
the Whig party, it requires no political sagacity to
perceive that it cannot maintain itself as a national

party. . . . Impressed with these views of public affairs, I shall hold aloof from the present state canvass. I will not even join the attempt to revive the organization of the Whig party. Its ashes alone remain, and the Phœnix is equally a fable in political as in natural history. I shall await the fast approaching time when not only Louisiana but the entire South, animated by a single spirit, shall struggle for its dearest rights, and in defense of that Constitution which is their most precious heritage."

The battle contemplated by Mr. Benjamin, it is scarcely necessary to remark, was political, under the Constitution which he thought the best safeguard for North and South alike. He was not of the "fire-eaters" who exhausted themselves in threats of war; of that it would be time to speak when he saw that war was inevitable. Benjamin's great Southern party, of which for a while there was some talk (Alexander H. Stephens was to be its organizer), was of course hopeless of formation as of power if it had been formed. Such a party could not have had a majority in either house of Congress. It could at best have held the balance of power; and for all questions in which the South was vitally interested her representatives, whether calling themselves Democrats or Know Nothings, could already be depended on to vote together.

His letter was received with approval more general than usual; but some opponents pooh-poohed his apprehensions. Randell Hunt, one of the Whigs who had apostatized to "Sammyism," delighted a meeting of his followers by a sketch of Benjamin going forth to war, his short arm bared to the elbow, brandishing a huge and gory sabre.[1] Others advised him not to despair of the future, but to cast his lot with the Democrats, and all would be well. Not many weeks, indeed, were needed to convince Benjamin that his Southern party was a dream, and that the one chance of preserving the South from a hostile Congressional majority lay in immediate and hearty coöperation with the Democrats. Exactly when he arrived at the determination to become a Democrat one cannot say ; it was certainly as early as December, 1855 ; but he did not make any public announcement of the change, which was known to his friends, and manifested to the public by a slight increase of cordiality on the part of the administration.[2] Not till May, 1856, did he find a suitable opportunity to make a public confession of political faith. The telegraph first, and then the fuller mail reports—which even at that time took more than a week to reach New Orleans from Washington—announced Benjamin's first really powerful speech in the Senate, May 2d, on the Kansas bill.[3]

This is not the proper place to quote an address of much length ; but it is one of the two or three of so much importance in Mr. Benjamin's senatorial career that we must attempt to present some characteristic ideas inspiring it. Of its style in general the reader may judge from the extracts we can give ; throughout it is what the old-fashioned critics called "chaste," meaning that it is simple, very severe and restrained,

[1] *Delta*, Aug. 16; *True Delta*, Aug. 5.
[2] *Picayune*, Dec. 6, 13 and 23 ; *True Delta*, Dec. 7.
[3] *Globe*, 1855-1856, Part I, p. 1092 *et seq.* ; cf. *True Delta*, May 11, 1856 ; *Courier*, May 11, 15 and 16 ; *Crescent*, May 12.

not at all "flowery." Its arguments are not new—
who could hope even then to find new things to say
on such a question?—but they are marshaled with
unusual skill, and illustrated with a simplicity which
gives them greater force. Its view of the facts of our
constitutional history, though contrary to that presented in the great speech of Webster which Benjamin must have had in mind while framing his argument, is incontrovertible as history, however it may be
doubted as sound or practicable in public policy. In
temper it is sometimes severe and sarcastic, for Mr.
Benjamin had a caustic tongue and felt deeply upon
the questions involved; but it is mildness itself in
comparison with the bitter, savage, often coarse in-
vectives that senators from both sections hurled at
each other. There could be no better remedy for
exaggerated veneration of men and measures of a past
age than a perusal of some of those disgraceful pages
of the *Congressional Globe* when partisans so violent
as Foote or Wade had the floor. In this speech as in
all others, Mr. Benjamin does not forget that he is a
gentleman, and that he is speaking in an august body;
accordingly, he engages in a battle wherein the
weapons are purely intellectual, armed with the keen-
est and most fatal of rapiers instead of a thick blud-
geon, with which to smash his opponent.

After reviewing the history of the compromises,
all of which, he alleges, had failed to work satisfactorily, because of the bad faith of the North, Benjamin said: "The policy of seeking for some other
compromises than those which are contained in the
Constitution was a mistaken policy on the part of the
South. . . . She has no longer any compromises

to offer or to accept. She looks to those contained in the Constitution itself. By them she will live; to them she will adhere; and if those provisions which are contained in it shall be violated to her wrong, then she will calmly and resolutely withdraw from a compact all the obligations of which she is expected scrupulously to fulfil, from all the benefits of which she is ignominiously excluded."

This distinct and calm enunciation of the doctrine of the right of secession was the result of careful deliberation. In common with the very great majority of the leading political students of the South, Mr. Benjamin was confident of this right; as confident, one might venture to say, as were most of the framers of the Constitution, or "we, the people of the states of Virginia, Massachusetts," etc., when they voted to adopt that Constitution. That national life and national government on such a principle would be utterly impracticable, either did not occur to them or, if so, did not distress them in the least. Whether they called themselves Whigs or Democrats or Know Nothings, the people of the South were, and are, extremely democratic, and believe that local government is better than a centralized government; they had, and have, a very wholesome dread of that which we now call imperialism and paternalism. And Louisiana, which had certainly never had any sovereign rights to surrender to the Federal government, was just as sincere in asserting state sovereignty as was Texas, which had for ten whole years enjoyed autonomy. Mr. Benjamin restates the principle in this same speech.

"What, then, is the principle that underlies that

whole compact for our common government . . . ?
It is, sir, the equality of the free and independent
states which that instrument links together in a common bond of union—entire, absolute, complete, unqualified equality—equality as sovereigns, equality in their
rights, equality in their duties. This was the spirit
that presided over the formation of the Constitution ;
this is the living spirit that breathes through every
line of it ; this is the object professed by it of forming
'a more perfect union.'

> 'Great were the thoughts, and strong the minds,
>   Of those who framed in high debate
> The immortal league of love that binds
>   Our fair, broad empire state to state.'

Take away this league of love ; convert it into a
bond of distrust, of suspicion, or of hate ; and the entire fabric, which is held together by that cement, will
crumble to the earth, and rest scattered in dishonored
fragments upon the ground."

If this equality be a reality, he argues, not a mere
dead promise of a Constitution which the North con-
temns, should it not apply in the administration of
territory " acquired by treaty, purchased by the common treasure, or conquered by the common valor of
the country " ? And yet this territory, fit only for
agriculture, is to be closed to Southern settlers, *by the
Federal power*, since " almost [the] entire agricultural
population [of the South] consists of negro slaves, and
this is precisely the population which it is proposed to
exclude. So that we are insulted and mocked by the
offer to give us our portion of the common property,
coupled with a condition which makes it impossible

for us to use it, and which reserves it for the exclusive use of the North."

Upon the vital point involved in the discussions on the Kansas-Nebraska bill, *viz.*, Can Congress exclude slavery from a Territory? Benjamin, of course, is still in accord with Douglas. No ingenious Freeport doctrine has yet alienated the Southern following of the "Little Giant," and he and Benjamin can agree that "Congress has no power to exclude slavery from the common territory; it cannot delegate it; and the people in the Territory cannot exercise it except at the time when they form their constitution." They can unite in passing a bill in which, "we said . . . that we transferred to the people of that Territory the entire power to control, by their own legislation, their own domestic institutions, subject only to the provisions of the Constitution; that we would not interfere with them; that they might do as they pleased on the subject; that the Constitution alone should govern." This is the comfortable doctrine of "squatter sovereignty," as the South understood it, before Lincoln's simple question found and penetrated its weak point, so that Southerners could no longer shelter themselves beneath it.

We shall not pause over the more personal portions of the speech, having but a temporary interest. Yet it is but just to the South to give the other view, now that nearly all histories are (blatantly in some and with humility in others) accounting for the coming on of the Civil War by the desperate efforts of the "slave power" to maintain its ascendancy. After examining the motives that might inspire those who now seek to exclude the South from her share of the common territory, he determines that love of the negro is but a mask. They do not act consistently with their professions of desire to ameliorate the condition of the slave. The real motive is the desire for political strength : "The object is to attain such power as shall put these parties in possession of sufficient representation, in both branches of Congress, to change the Federal Constitution, and to deprive the South of that representation which is already inadequate to protect her rights. When that shall have been done—when she is reduced to a feeble minority, utterly incompetent to move hand or foot, and bound subserviently to the will of the North, then will the last act of the drama be played ; and then will the Abolition sentiments which they hide now, but which they entertain in their heart of hearts, be developed to the country, and ruin and desolation spread over fifteen of the states of this Union."

On the other side, what is the interest that invigorates the determined opposition of the South ? "Property, safety, honor, existence itself, depend on the decision of the questions which are now pending in the Congress—property, for $2,000,000,000 cannot purchase at a low average price the slaves which now belong to the people of the South, whilst no human calculation can reach the estimate of the destruction of other property which would necessarily be involved in any measure which should deprive us of our slaves ; safety, because our population, now kept in proper subjection, peaceful and laborious, would be converted into an idle, reckless, criminal population, eager for rapine and murder, led on to their foul purposes by inflamed passions,—passions inflamed by fanatical emissaries from another portion of a common country who formed a common government to cherish brotherly feelings; honor, because we should be degraded from our position of free, sovereign, self-dependent states, into a servile subserviency to Northern will; existence, aye, existence itself, because the history of Hayti is written in characters so black, so dark, so prominent, that we cannot be ignorant of the fate that awaits us if measures similar to those which have produced that result there are also to be inaugurated in our Southern states."

With all of his distrust of the ultimate designs of the Republicans, Mr. Benjamin pleads for an adjustment of existing difficulties under the Constitution rather than outside of it. He was too sensible not to perceive that there was a real and imminent danger in the situation, despite the insulting intimation that "the South couldn't be kicked out of the Union"; for he knew how earnest were his people; and he showed very convincingly, that if once established as independent of the United States, the Southern states would inevitably get from the northern neighbor much more effective provisions for the return of fugitive slaves. The United States would need extradition treaties and commercial advantages, for which the new power could drive a bargain to suit herself. But he also knew two other things that too rarely came into the calculations of the fire-eaters. The first was that the South was not "equal in population or military strength with the North." The second was that there could be no peaceable dissolution of the Union, whatever one might believe about the theoretical right of withdrawing from the "Federal compact." The people of the South, he said, "appeal to the guarantees of the Constitution, and when those guarantees shall fail, and not till then, will the injured, outraged South throw her sword into the scale of her rights, and appeal to the God of battles to do her justice. I say her sword, because I am not one of those who believe in the possibility of a peaceful disruption of the Union. It cannot come until every possible means of conciliation has been exhausted; it cannot come until every angry passion shall have been roused; it cannot come until brotherly feeling shall have been converted into deadly hate; and then, sir, with feelings embittered by the consciousness of injustice, or passions high wrought and inflamed, dreadful will be the internecine war that must ensue."

At the conclusion of his speech, Mr. Benjamin reviewed the political conditions, somewhat as he had done in the letter of 1855, but more in detail—how there were nineteen Whig senators when he took his seat in 1853; how this minority had been rent into "fragments that no mortal skill could ever re-unite, for the cement of a common principle is wanting"; how that spurious and illusive party called Know Nothing had risen, and had already displayed sentiments inimical to the South; how, finally, in this perplexity he had sought the only rational solution in joining the Democratic party. It was the natural and inevitable conclusion to be reached by a practical man. And it was less narrow and less dangerous than the formation of any new sectional party. This was the only chance of staving off for four years that conflict which Benjamin already deemed almost inevitable, but from which he shrank as long as shrinking could not be construed into disloyalty to the people whose interests he represented.

Though Mr. Benjamin's conversion to Democracy—if it could be called a conversion when he still openly worshiped the place where the Whig gods had stood, and as openly said he was a Democrat only because there were no more Whigs—had been anticipated, it nevertheless called forth much comment. "There was much rejoicing," says the *True Delta*, "over the repentant sinner in the United States Senate; and General Cass did not disdain to welcome the Louisiana senator into the ranks of a party he had for so many years lustily opposed." The more friendly papers remarked the earnestness, animation, and powerful effect with which he spoke; and only a few representing the forlorn hope of obstinate Whigs, indulged in criticism whose acerbity was a test of their sense of the loss sustained by the great party.

True to his promise, Benjamin went into the campaign of 1856 with great vigor. He spoke first[1] in New Orleans at a tremendous meeting held in Odd Fellows' Hall, September 23d; and then on several other occasions in the city. Moreover, he subjected himself to the great fatigue and discomfort of a tour through the state and appeared in a score or more of the towns. The speech at Odd Fellows' Hall was the finest effort, for it had to be a justification of his change of party before a critical audience and in a city then too often terrorized by the violence of the Know Nothings. His arguments we need not consider; they cover the same ground as before; but, strange as it may seem, this address was a revelation

[1] *Delta*, *True Delta*, and *Courier*, Sept. 24.

to some of his fellow citizens who had never heard
Benjamin on a political topic that called for the exercise of his full powers. The hall was crowded to the
doors, and many stood in adjoining rooms, hoping
to hear where they could not see. And even the
atrabiliar *True Delta* is amazed and lulled into sullen
submission by his admitted eloquence, while the *Delta*
cannot restrain its admiration of the orator, though
somewhat critical of the policy he advocated : "We
were proud of him as a Southern man, proud of his fine
capacity, energy, and pluck. . . . Mr. Benjamin
is usually a quiet and conversational speaker, gifted
with those peculiar graces which render the eloquence
of the bar almost an eloquence *per se ;* and we always
considered that he possessed the analytic capacity and
firm qualities of an Erskine rather than the vivid and
impetuous inspiration of a Sheridan. But we were
undeceived last night. The calm logician can become
the effective rhetorician when he pleases, and the
Hyperides of the Louisiana bar to our amazement and
delight suddenly grew into the proportions of a Demos-
thenes, and swept the hearts of his audience as a
minstrel might smite the chords of a harp. . . .
Mr. Benjamin . . . possesses enough of the *mens
divinior* to irradiate and beautify his ponderous knowledge ; and the man who is unequaled in the Supreme
Court at Washington need entertain very little fear of
rivalry on the stump in Louisiana."

In the roar of the tumult that came four years later,
we are apt to forget how bitter was the campaign of
1856, how very near our ship of state steered to the
breakers. Failure to elect Buchanan then would have
been the signal for disruption of the Union almost as

certainly as was the failure to elect Douglas in 1860.
Though plenteously besprinkled with the choicest
epithets of loathing by Whigs who had chosen the
Democratic party, Fillmore, who had allowed himself
to be seduced by the Know Nothings, was probably
the unconscious instrument of salvation. His can-
didacy was more harmful to Frémont than to Buchanan. The result is a matter of history; but it
was only by a narrow margin that the Democrat was
chosen, while the campaign brought out sharp divisions
between men who had formerly acted in the same
party and who were all too soon to face each other in a
sterner contest. With all of this it has struck the
writer as very remarkable that, throughout the canvass, Mr. Benjamin for once escapes hostile criticism
except of the most dignified kind. The Know Nothings tried to break up the Odd Fellows' Hall meeting,
and hustled the audience as it dispersed; but none of
the scurrility which had not infrequently marked
references to Mr. Benjamin appears now. Elected as
a Whig, he had in the midst of his term become a
Democrat and retained his seat: he was certainly
peculiarly vulnerable. But his motives seem to have
been so obvious and so universally approved that there
were few to find fault.

After the battle was won, however, and the South
breathed once more, bitterness again tinged many of
the references to him in the local press. His success
irked the envious; but above all, he could not be forgiven for being in the good graces of Mr. Slidell,
and practically assured of succeeding himself in the
Senate.

At Washington Benjamin was a frequent speaker,

and particularly ready to stand to his guns whenever the South needed defense. After the great Kansas speech of 1856, his reputation was as firmly established there as at home. And since that state, with her rival constitutions, occupied the attention of the whole Union throughout these troublous years, it is not surprising to find Benjamin making it the theme of another notable speech on March 11, 1858.[1] It is ostensibly a plea for the admission of Kansas under the Lecompton Constitution, a document which we now know to have been distinctly misrepresentative of popular sentiment in Kansas, proved to be a fraud soon afterward, and hopelessly lost. The law of nature, as so many have remarked, forbade slavery in Kansas ; and only blind partisanship could defend the attempt to force this constitution upon the people. It is surprising to find a man usually fair-minded and not given to narrow sectionalism defending the course pursued by the pro-slavery party in Kansas and by the administration. And the only excuse we can make, a poor one, is resolute loyalty to what was considered the need of the South, through thick and thin.

But though we cannot approve the advocacy of the Lecompton Constitution, this speech is another admirable statement of Southern views on slavery, and contains many eloquent passages. Benjamin took occasion to review the status of slavery under the English common law ; indeed, three-fourths of the speech is on that topic, not on Kansas at all, whose Lecompton Constitution gets but scant notice near the close. It will be sufficient here to quote his prelim-

[1] *Globe*, 1857-1858, Part II., p. 1065 *et. seq.*

inary statement of the points he proposes to establish, in order to show the character of the argument :

"Mr. President, the thirteen colonies, which, on the 4th of July, 1776, asserted their independence, were British colonies, governed by British laws. Our ancestors in their emigration to this country brought with them the common law of England as their birthright. . . . If I can show . . . that the nation thus exercising sovereign power over these thirteen colonies did establish slavery in them, did maintain and protect the institution, did originate and carry on the slave-trade, did support and foster that trade; that it forbade the colonies permission either to emancipate or export their slaves; that it prohibited them from inaugurating any legislation in diminution or discouragement of the institution,—nay, sir, more, if at the date of our Revolution I can show that African slavery existed in England as it did on this continent, if I can show that slaves were sold upon the slave mart, in the Exchange and other public places of resort in the city of London as they were on this continent, then I shall not hazard too much in the assertion that slavery was the common law of the thirteen states of the Confederacy at the time they burst the bonds that united them to the mother country."

He has little difficulty in presenting a strong argument to establish all but the fact of real existence of slavery in England after Mansfield's famous decision of 1771 (Sommersett case), and the selling of slaves in that country. The latter was undoubtedly common enough in one way—the sale of colonial property, including slaves, the slaves held in the colonies, but

the actual sale taking place in England. He then
proceeds to demolish the rather flimsy arguments of
Fessenden, Collamer, and Seward, that the Constitution does not recognize slaves as property, to be held
and protected as securely as any other species of
property. In reply to Collamer's argument, that
because a peculiar provision was made for slave property, the framers of the Constitution did not regard it
as other property, but as a thing that needed some
provision other property did not need, he makes
use of an illustration that has been quoted as one of
the few passages of pure ornament in his usually
very businesslike speeches: "There are numerous
illustrations upon this point [*viz.*, that where no
remedy is granted by the law of a state, a man cannot have title to his property, though his equitable
right may be unquestioned]—illustrations furnished by
the copyright laws, illustrations furnished by the
patent laws. Let us take a case, one that appeals to
us all. There lives now a man in England who from
time to time sings to the enchanted ear of the civilized world strains of such melody that the charmed
senses seem to abandon the grosser regions of earth,
and to rise to purer and serener regions above. God
has created that man a poet. His inspiration is
his; his songs are his by right divine; they are his
property, so recognized by human law; yet here in
these United States men steal Tennyson's works and
sell his property for their profit; and this because,
in spite of the violated conscience of the nation, we
refuse to grant him protection for his property."

Though Louisiana could not but be proud of the eloquence of her senator, attracting national attention,

there were many factions at home already scheming to prevent his reëlection on the approaching expiration of his term. The *True Delta*[1] hails with delight a report that Slidell is "setting the traps" to elect Representative J. M. Sandidge as his successor, "either on the expiration of Colonel Benjamin's term of office, or on the appointment of this gentleman to a special mission to Mexico, of which there is some talk." The military title with which Benjamin is here dignified is meant as a mark of the editor's supreme contempt, and is as fantastic as the mission to Mexico. As the time for the election draws nearer, the same paper reports that Slidell is scheming for the Presidential nomination, and to that end seeks for "Belmont the mission to Madrid, and for his colleague, Senator Benjamin, that to Mexico or France, the latter being, it is said, anxious to obtain the greater distinction in order to be near his family, who reside in the French capital. Both gentlemen are of the Hebrew faith, as is, I believe, Senator Slidell himself." But no hope remained of shunting Benjamin off on a diplomatic track. Several independent candidates for the senatorship were mentioned, and the *True Delta* exclaimed, that if such a candidate could not be chosen, "then, in God's name, let Slidell himself be chosen, for he may just as well have two votes in his own person as to be able, on every occasion, to command the servile accompaniment of his facile coadjutor."

The opposition to Benjamin seemed very formidable, and his political record was jealously scrutinized to discover vulnerable spots. The public was not al-

[1] April 30, 1857; also Feb. 2, 1858.

lowed to lose sight of the fact that he was a Jew and a foreigner. But this was manifestly insufficient to prejudice the party against so useful a leader. The main reliance of the opposition was placed upon his connection with the Houmas land claims; yet that too, though assiduously worked, proved no more damaging to Benjamin than to the principal rival for the senatorship, J. M. Sandidge, who had done quite as much in connection with the Houmas land bill in the House as Benjamin had in the Senate. The Congressional investigation of the case was not completed till 1860, but as its bearing on this part of Benjamin's career is most important, we shall anticipate so far as to present a résumé of it here.

It is almost impossible to discover the whole truth about the Houmas lands, so much were the facts distorted by political passions. Thus it was asserted even by newspapers which are counted conservative to-day, such as the New York *Times*,[1] that Slidell's holdings in these lands amounted to over a half million dollars, and that Benjamin had received ten thousand for getting the bill through Congress. Certain of the facts in the case, however, can be established with sufficient ease to cast discredit on these charges. The lands in question lay on the east bank of the Mississippi River, in the parishes of Iberville and Ascension,—a plantation there still bears that name—and had been purchased originally from the Houmas Indians in 1774 by Conway and Latil, with the sanction of the Spanish authorities. The original grant, which was added to, ran back from the river front the usual depth of forty arpents. Land was cheap in

[1] March 24, 1859, quoted by *True Delta*, March 29.

Louisiana in those days ; in fact, Spain was only too glad to entice colonists into its swamps by grants of the most magnificent extent and vaguest limits. Hence when Conway, in 1776, told the Spanish governor that there was no timber on his tract, or for two-score arpents back of it, and that he needed timber for plantation purposes, the Spanish surveyor went upon the land, marked out the side lines of the original forty arpents, and two arpents further to give the direction. That was the all but universal method of surveying. The neighboring proprietors were witnesses, and signed the surveyor's report of this proceeding. The governor granted the land, and Spanish and French authorities found no fault with the transaction, which was indeed not unusual ; nor did it seem to occur to them that there might ever come a day when people would wish to know how far back the new grant ran. Conway had asked for " all of the lands back " of his first claim, and such presumably was the intention of the Spanish governor. But did this, as was quite commonly understood in such grants, mean that those side lines, which the surveyor had run out only for two additional arpents " to give the direction," should continue to run until they met the next natural boundary, in this case a water course ? If this were so, then these lines would be twenty miles or more in length.

The back lands, however, were of no special value for half a century after the date of the grant. The claim of the original parties had, of course, passed into various hands. And as no particular attention was paid to the lands, squatters settled unmolested on certain portions of them. Meanwhile the United

States had tacitly acknowledged the validity of the title soon after the acquisition of Louisiana, but Congress had declined to pass a specific act on the subject. Then an agent of the Land Office, acting hastily, sold some of the lands to squatters and settlers (1835), and there were more complications, since some of these purchasers gave up their interests when the title was questioned, while others held on. At length efforts were made to have Congress quiet the titles of those who represented the original grantees, of whom Senator Slidell was one—his holdings under the claim amounting to about eight thousand acres, assessed at $15,000. A bill for that purpose was introduced in the second session of the Thirty-fourth Congress, but not acted on for lack of time. The same bill, favorably reported by the Committee on Private Land Claims, of which Benjamin was chairman, passed the first session of the next Congress, as one section in a bill to settle certain private land claims in Missouri and elsewhere.

This measure did not give absolute title to the Houmas claimants as against the other settlers on the land, but provided that suit should be instituted within two years by all who questioned the rights of the grantees, and that in case of failure to show a better title, the area in litigation should be held as rightfully the property of the latter or their present representatives. As soon as the fact of the passage of this bill became known in Louisiana there was great excitement among the many persons whose lands lay in what was known to be included in the Houmas district. Mass meetings were held, and the rising flame was fanned by the many enemies of Slidell. Protests were sent to Washington, and Benjamin himself, in the closing weeks of Congress, introduced a joint resolution to suspend the action of the law till the end of the succeeding session, since the time was too short for proper investigation immediately. On January 4, 1860, Robert Toombs presented another petition against the law, and after some discussion, the whole matter of the Houmas lands and the law of June 2, 1858, was, on Benjamin's suggestion, referred to a special committee for thorough investigation. On May 29, 1860, the report of this committee, of which Toombs was chairman, was taken up and debated, then and later, at great length.

The findings was adverse to the Houmas grantees, and Toombs and Benjamin, in particular, waxed warm in Congress over the matter. Benjamin's speech was remarkably subtle, but for once he seems to have been seeking to defend a doubtful position, and one in whose defense he might lose much, and could gain nothing. For Toombs's report had recommended but one change of any consequence in the law as it stood, and the concession of that point by Benjamin would have saved him from unjust suspicions without prejudice to public policy or to any *bona fide* rights of individuals. This change was to the effect that the Houmas grantees as well as all other parties whose titles were in doubt, should begin suit against the government for recovery of the land, within two years, and that on failure to establish the title it should revert to the government. But, a little vain of his familiarity with Spanish and French law, thoroughly convinced from his own investigations that the Houmas grants were valid (in 1840 he had been employed in an important case involving the examination of this title),[1] and angered by the foolish accusations against him and by Toombs's tactless and somewhat bullying manner, Benjamin fought to the bitter end. In spite of all his ingenuity and eloquence, the report was accepted, and the amendment proposed by the blunt and rather reckless Georgian was passed.

Those who were in Washington with Benjamin at the time knew that his connection with the Houmas affair had been in no way dishonorable, although most unfortunate and perhaps unwise. Men of the stamp of the Bayards, of Davis, of L. Q. C. Lamar, and of Mason, knew Benjamin, and their regard for him was not disturbed by the charges of corruption made by the press, delighted to have so easy a theme. But this same press spread the reports among those who did not know and could not discover the truth, who took insinuations for proved facts, and who held up their hands in horror. The echoes of the Houmas scandal followed Benjamin almost all the way through his subsequent career in America; and Mr. Slidell was never referred to by the New Orleans *True Delta* otherwise than as " Houmas John." [2]

When the Louisiana legislature met in January, 1859, more or less garbled accounts of these facts had run the rounds of the press. It is probable that private sources of information, nevertheless, enabled the members to form a fairly just judgment. When the Democratic caucus met, it had a stormy time deciding on a candi-

[1] Moore *vs.* Hampton, 3 La. Annual Rep., p. 192.
[2] For the full record of the affair, see the *Congressional Globe,* 1859-1860, Part I, pp. 323, 324 ; Part III, p. 2423, *et seq.;* p. 2588, *et seq.;* p. 2674. Cf. *Delta,* Apr. 13, 1859; *True Delta,* Apr. 3, 4, and 11, and June 9, 1860.

date. In a full meeting, thirty-six votes were needed
to establish the choice. After sitting all day, casting forty fruitless ballots, the caucus adjourned at
six o'clock to meet again at seven. On their reassembling, the struggle was resumed; and on the forty-
second ballot the vote stood: Benjamin, 25; Sandidge,
23; Gray, 19; Parham, 1. The members then adjourned till next morning at ten o'clock, when, after
more hopeless voting till three, they agreed to take one
more ballot, and in the event of failure to secure a candidate on whom they could unite, to cease balloting in
caucus. This vote gave thirty-five for Sandidge, just
one short of the requisite number. With supreme
daring, the Benjamin men had cast most of their votes
for Sandidge, presumably to convince the latter's
friends that there was no hope for them in any event.
Then the Benjamin faction proposed to continue the
voting, in spite of the agreement just reached, to which
the other factions refused to consent, and left the caucus. Assembling again at six o'clock with their fragment of a party, fifty members being present, Benjamin's supporters elected their man on the first ballot,
the vote standing twenty-six for Benjamin, twenty-three
for Sandidge, and one scattering. Benjamin was declared the nominee of the party; but the outlook was
not very cheering, since fifty-seven votes were requisite
for election in the legislature, and he had so far
shown nothing like that strength. To the consterna-
tion of the opposition, when the first vote was taken in
the Assembly, it gave Benjamin fifty-seven, Gray fifty,
and Randell Hunt, the Know Nothing candidate, five.
Said the *True Delta:* "George Wooley was the only
Know Nothing from the city of New Orleans who voted

for Benjamin, and when the vote was given, it aston·
ished and embittered against him all his colleagues
from the city. This vote was the last Know Nothing
vote given, and elected Benjamin. The friends of
Sandidge all went home with long faces, most of them
swearing that north Louisiana should have the senator
to be elected two years hence." And "two years
hence" there were no more senators of the United States
to be elected from Louisiana. The *Picayune* describes
this as " the most excited contest " for senator ever held
in the state; while the *Delta*, now favorable to Benjamin, remarks : " Without designing to be invidious,
we cannot refrain from congratulating the people of
this state at the result. . . . As a profound lawyer, Mr. Benjamin has stood for years at the head of a
bar that has no superior in the Union ; as an orator,
his reputation is as wide as the country itself, while
as a man his life has been singularly pure. His popularity is best proved by the fact that among all the various offices to which he has aspired—commencing in the
House of Representatives of this state, passing through
the Senate and constitutional convention, until he attained his present high station—we believe he has
never once known defeat." Still, this last election
was won by the narrowest margin.[1]

[1] The press teems with items of this contest; the best accounts
are in the *True Delta*, Jan. 15, 23, 25, and 26, 1859, and the *Delta*
and the *Picayune*, Jan. 26.

CHAPTER VII

THE perilous contest for reëlection in Louisiana had not been allowed to distract Benjamin's attention from his duties in the Senate, where his skill as a debater and his attractive personality were steadily increasing his power. Fond of social amusements, much given to playing cards, though not a rabid gambler, he was a general favorite, and had many friends among the very best set in Washington; but his principle, in friendships, seemed to be "entangling alliances with none." As the storm of the presidential election approached, party and sectional lines were drawn closer, and men found themselves attracted to or repelled from persons about whom they had felt very differently heretofore. Some few Southerners continued to the last— nay, even afterward,—on friendly terms with Northern colleagues whose politics they must fight relentlessly. Though there was often courtesy still there could be little intimacy; for to both parties, if for very different reasons, the Ohio seemed a Phlegethon. But Benjamin was remarkable all through life for having no close friends. He was personally so affable and uniformly courteous that he rarely offended even violent partisans on the other side, and had most friendly relations with nearly everybody; but scarcely one of the senators, North or South, could claim to be really intimate with him. Perhaps he was nearer this relation with the Bayards than with any other family. There is hardly a more remarkable instance in our history than that of successive generations of Bayards holding the best of Delaware's national offices, and always with the highest credit, for almost a century. At this particular time James A. Bayard was senator from Delaware, a staunch and honorable champion of what he held to be the constitutional rights of the states, rights now endangered by the spread of Republicanism. He was an enthusiastic admirer of Benjamin's eloquence ; and association in the Senate soon brought about the most pleasant relations with the family.

The next Bayard, Thomas F., later our Minister to England, gives some interesting reminiscences :[1] "I first saw Mr. Benjamin about 1856, at Washington, where he was a senator of the United States from the state of Louisiana, and most successfully conducting a leading practice in the Supreme Court of the United States. I was on a visit to my father, and at his house I met Mr. Benjamin, who, together with other leading members of the Senate, including Pearce and Pratt of Maryland, Hunter and Mason of Virginia, Bingham of North Carolina, Butler of South Carolina, Mallory of Florida, etc., was a frequent guest. Benjamin's personal appearance was not at all impressive,—short, fat, and 'pudgy' in figure, with few or none of the features which physiology or phrenology teach us to expect in individuals possessed of strong moral and intellectual characters ;—and then a half smile about his mouth, that sometimes seemed to degenerate into a simper, did not increase confidence. His manner, however, was most attractive,—gentle, sympathetic, and absolutely unaffected, and this restored confidence ;

[1] MS. notes copied by Mrs. Hilles ; also the letters cited below.

for he was endowed with a voice of singular musical timbre, high pitched, but articulate, resonant, and sweet. He excelled in conversation, with an easy flow of diction, embellished by a singular mastery of languages at the base of which lay the Latin and its fibres of the French and Spanish. All this gave grace and breadth to his conversation, enriched by anecdote and playful humor and gentle philosophy. He certainly shone in social life as a refined, genial, and charming companion. To my mother and her young daughters at her tea table he was an ever-welcome guest, and as a consummate player of whist, he was equally companionable to my father."

With the writer of this comment, Benjamin soon struck up a friendship, and the fruits thereof most appreciated by us are certain letters that passed between them from time to time, and which are almost the only letters available except those in the hands of his own family. One of the earliest contains some remarks about Seward, for whom Benjamin had a most cordial hatred that polite manners hardly veiled. Mr. Bayard had written to express the approval of his father and himself on the latest of Benjamin's expositions of Southern principles and his denunciation of the unscrupulous agitation of the Republicans, and Benjamin replied, May 3, 1858:

"MY DEAR SIR:—Maybe you think I have taken my full time to answer your kind favor of 24th March, and certainly appearances are against me; but I assure you the delay has arisen only from my desire to do something more than write a few hurried lines, and until now I have been utterly unable to do so. I closed my last cases for the term in the Supreme Court on Friday, and now hope to bring up the arrears of my correspondence, which has suffered terribly. I am of course very much gratified that you were pleased with my speech, and especially that you found in it anything new to you. I believe that the great error of the South has been in supineness, in neglect to meet and expose fallacies which to her appeared too shallow to serve any purpose of her enemies. But the older we get, the better satisfied we become that no statement of fact or principle, however monstrous, is without *some* influence. A generous mind will repel with scorn any imputation of dishonor against a person of tried integrity, yet if to-morrow a newspaper should publish a charge of bribery against the Chief Justice, some one would be found to believe it, at all events to suspect that it might be true.[1] Now Seward acts on this principle, and I charged him with it in a speech made four years ago on the Kansas question. You speak of shame on his part—why, I had scarcely finished my speech when he said to me, ' Come, Benjamin, give me a segar, and I won't be mad with you.' . . .

" Please present my best regards and remembrances to your mother and sisters, and tell Miss Mabel that I insist she shall send for her portrait if she values my peace of mind. Her father's pride in it is intolerable, and he turns a deaf ear to every suggestion that I will have a better one made if he will give me the one he now has for a model."

With all of his colleagues Benjamin was on terms at least of mutual forbearance. Even his enemies did not become angry with him personally, and he was so skilful a diplomatist that he frequently got what he wanted even from them. Indeed, he was in some ways well fitted for that mission to Spain for which his name was mentioned; but a diplomatic post had not

[1] See Chapter I for Benjamin's own experience.

sufficient attraction for him. Though the Spanish Minister would always have occupation enough in settling petty but irritating filibustering difficulties, the Senate offered greater and more congenial opportunities for his energies and talent.

Yet good nature alone could not always suffice to preserve at once friendly relations with rude antagonists and his own self-respect. It was in the Senate that there occurred a little incident of which much was made by the press,[1] though in itself trivial enough.

Jefferson Davis, at that time senator from Mississippi, was in very bad health, and the distress of his disease made him irritable and impatient of opposition. During a debate on the army appropriation bill, June, 1858, Senator Benjamin made a remark which Davis corrected in a very ill-natured and supercilious manner. The doughty Louisianian quietly repeated his statement in another form and Davis sneered again, adding that he considered what the former had said as an "attempt to misrepresent a very plain remark." There were more words which did no credit to Mr. Davis, and which gossip reported in less agreeable style than we find them in the official report of the *Congressional Globe*. He completely lost his temper, while Benjamin, resenting what had been said, maintained his position, in a dignified way, and declined to pursue the subject further in the Senate. Of what followed the *Globe* in its account of Davis's apologetic explanation, before that body, gives only a hint.

[1] *E. g.*, *Delta*, June 16, 1858; *Picayune*, and *True Delta*, June 16th; and for the account in the *Globe*, probably toned down, see 1857–1858, Part III, p. 2780, *et seq.*, and p. 2823.

As is quite well known, there was only one way of arranging such matters between gentlemen in those days, and accordingly rumor reported all sorts of things about the duel involving the two leaders. The most accurate account is that furnished in some private notes which were taken by Benjamin's warm friend, Thomas F. Bayard: "Benjamin peremptorily challenged Jefferson Davis for rude language in debate and brought the note to my father in the session to be copied and delivered. My father handed the note to Davis in the cloak-room of the Senate. He read it and at once tore it up, and said, 'I will make this all right at once. I have been wholly wrong.' [He] walked back to his desk in the Senate, and on the first opportunity rose and made the most distinct withdrawal of what he had said, and regretted any offense most amply. No one in the Senate but my father knew what had called forth from Davis this apology; for Benjamin had sat down in silence when Davis had made the rude interruption. But writing instantly at his desk, Benjamin called him to account by the note, which contained a direct challenge, without asking for a withdrawal or explanation. When the temper of the time is considered, the character of the two men is strongly illustrated."

Benjamin's unfailing suavity, his gentleness, his very looks deceived many people into thinking him deficient in courage; but he would resent an insult as readily as any blusterer. Fortunately for all parties, Mr. Davis had no need to fear any misconstruction of his motives, and made the sort of amends that only the truly courageous can make. Benjamin accepted the explanation in a few simple words, stating that

he could confidently appeal to his brother senators to
bear him out when he said that he had always striven
to be courteous and patient of differences of opinion;
that he had been hurt by the asperity in the tone
and manner of one whom he respected and admired;
but that he would be very glad to forget all between them "except the pleasant passage of this
morning." Thus simply closed an incident whose
like was, with less happy ending, too sadly frequent
in Congressional annals. Its importance was mag-
nified at the time, and the subsequent relations of
the two men made people attach an undue significance to it. Mr. Davis's respect for the Louisianian was no doubt increased by it, but acqaintance
did not of a sudden ripen into intimacy, as some
newspapers afterward said. Indeed, the two, while
friendly, continued to be often antagonistic in politics, though forces far more potent were inevitably
bringing them together.

Before we undertake to review the critical events
of the year preceding the Civil War, it may be well to
conclude here with some account of matters not per-
taining directly to politics with which Benjamin was
concerned. And in this connection, one of the most
important tasks will be to take note of his views
on our relations with Cuba.

His first public association with the Cuban question had been professional rather than political, and
it is hard to say how far he was acting as the lawyer. The irrepressible Lopez had organized an expedition in New Orleans, in 1850, ostensibly to sail
for Chagres, but really intended, of course, for Cuba.
There was the usual fiasco, not without its trage-

dies, and then a number of indictments were returned against the Americans who had taken more or less part in the purposed infraction of the neutrality laws, including General Quitman, the governor of Mississippi. It is not surprising that the government thought it necessary to employ additional counsel for the prosecution of these cases, in view of the fact that the District Attorney at New Orleans, whose attention had been called to Lopez's preparations in 1850, had replied to Secretary of State Clayton, May 14, 1850 : "You may rely on it, that in connection with the supposed expedition against Cuba,"—which had already sailed—"no law of the United States has been violated in this district. . . . The leaders of this enterprise have had good legal advisers !" [1]

The first case, against General Henderson, came on for trial in January, 1851, and Benjamin was associated with the District Attorney for the prosecution. There was a mistrial, the jury failing to agree. The case was tried again, with the same result, and again, and again,—until the government, realizing the impossibility of securing a conviction, gave up the prosecution and dismissed all of the suits. Public sentiment was too strongly in favor of the filibusters ; when the cases were closed, a salute of thirty-one guns (one for each state, and one for Cuba) was fired in Lafayette Square.[2]

The facts in the case seem very plain to unprejudiced eyes, and Benjamin's speech to the jury in the first trial, while not on a great subject, covered them all

[1] *Delta*, Jan. 3, 10, 11, 14, 18, and 23, 1851.
[2] *Delta*, Feb. 11, and 26 ; March 8.

and pointed out unerringly the violations of the neutrality laws. We need not consider the legal points in this address, but in view of his later attitude on Cuban annexation, we may quote a few passages that were very unpopular in such a community : "What a blaze of indignation fired the whole nation, a few years ago, when some British officers, provoked to madness by the aggressions of our own people, crossed over to our soil and burned a steamer within our territory. The blood mantled to every American cheek, and every arm was raised to repel and avenge the insult offered to our sovereignty. And yet, in the face of such facts, showing our own sensibility to attacks of this character, we are to listen day after day to verbal criticisms and metaphysical niceties of language, to show that . . . there has been no violation of law." He exposed the deceitful tricks and unworthy means used to get up this expedition, and the absolute failure of the "oppressed" Cubans to aid their "liberators" : "Not a single movement has been made in Cuba ; not a ripple disturbs the smooth current of the life of that people ; not a single proof is given of their dissatisfaction with their lot ;—these discontents exist only in the imaginations of our Cuban bondholders. The rich are busily engaged in rolling their sugar cane, gathering in their rich crops ; the poor are eating *tortilles*, smoking cigars, swinging in hammocks, and sucking oranges ; —they do not appear to be at all troubled by their oppression or disturbed with their lot. Their independence is to be achieved for them by our enterprising young men who rejoice in the outlandish name of 'Filibuster.' "

But neither evidence nor rhetoric could prevail

against what the *Delta* called "the spirit of the age."
Indeed, the acute and uncharitable reader may find
sufficient reason for the disagreement of the juries in
the following bill of fare which, says this paper,[1] the
first jury sent to the marshal, "and which was promptly
filled by that courteous officer: 'Soup: oyster and
turtle—plenty. Roasts: ducks and beef—with independent vegetables and separate gravies. Vegetables:
Irish potatoes, mashed; sweet potatoes, roasted; onions,
boiled. Tenderloin steak with mushrooms; venison
steak with cranberry jelly. Custards, tarts, oranges,
raisins, mince pies, and bananas. Liquors: brandy,
Madeira, hock, and whiskey. Dinner for twenty-four.
Liquors for forty-eight.'"

Benjamin was indeed running counter to the "spirit
of the age" in this matter; and such a menu alone
might well outweigh his best arguments. Then, too,
rumors were set on foot that the Spanish government
had employed him to prosecute, or persecute, the
would-be liberators of Cuba. To this insinuation he
replied in one of his rare letters to the papers:[2] "I
observe it stated in a letter from Mississippi, published
in your paper of this date (May 22d), that Governor
Quitman had asserted, in a public speech, that I had
received from the *Court of Spain* a fee of $25,000 (!)
for assisting in the Cuban prosecutions. The story is
so ridiculous that I should not have deemed it worth
noticing, if coming from a less responsible source; nor
can I now think it possible that a gentleman of Governor Quitman's high position can really have said
such a foolish thing. Your correspondent must have

[1] Jan. 24, 1851.
[2] *Delta*, May 23.

misunderstood him. Yet, as there is no limit to the credulity of some people, I beg to say that I have never been employed, directly or indirectly, by any other person than Mr. Hunton [District Attorney], acting under an order from Washington, which was shown to me when he employed me ; that I was never promised,—have never received—nor do I ever expect to receive, one cent of compensation for my services from any other source than from the government of the United States ; and in order that everybody taking an interest in my private affairs may be fully informed on the subject, I will add that I have not yet received one cent of compensation, even from our own government, and will feel much indebted to any kind gentleman that will take the trouble to procure for me the allowance of a reasonable fee from the authorities at Washington."

No doubt Benjamin was sincere in condemning the filibusters and their methods. Both common sense and common honesty must have convinced him that expeditions like those of Lopez could not succeed, and could not be anything but disgraceful to America if they did by any chance succeed. In several public utterances he showed that this was his view ; and he was rather conspicuous for his willingness to concede that there might be something to be said for Spain, when others were shouting for summary extinction of Spanish despotism in Cuba, and incidentally for the annexation of that valuable island. But the letter just cited seems to me to be the production of the politician, rather than of the man. Scores of libels, more absurd and more damaging than Quitman's nonsense, called forth no public reply from Benjamin ; why should he

choose to notice this one? It was not that he cared
for Quitman or his opinion, but that he might in some
measure mitigate the unpopularity that the lawyer had
brought on the politician by prosecuting the heroes
of the hour. It was bad enough, in all conscience, to
have been so employed professionally by his own government; it would have been almost certain political
ruin to have it thought that he was really pro-Spanish
in his sympathies. The letter, consequently, very
subtly leaves the impression, without actually saying
so, that Benjamin the lawyer of course did his best for
his clients in the case, but that Benjamin the politician might not, after all, really hold opinions such as
had been expressed to the jury, and had certainly no
relations with the enemies of Israel and the possessors
of Cuba.

In all seriousness, however, it would have been
politically impossible for Benjamin to have been anything except an annexationist, an expansionist; but
filibustering most frequently made at least a pretense
of aiming at the establishment of an independent government in Cuba, and a free Cuba would most certainly be no addition to the strength of the South. It
might, indeed, as he and others feared,[1] mean little
less than another San Domingo right across from
Florida. His action in the Senate, therefore, shows
him to have desired Cuba, though not with that
passion which would hurry him into union by Gretna
Green methods. There was to come a day when he
must have wished most devoutly that he could convince Spain that he had resolutely championed her

[1] See Rhodes, Vol. II, p. 25, and Benjamin's speech of Feb. 11,
1859, in the Senate.

cause, not only against filibusters, which he had done, but against the greed of his own people, which he had not done.

For some time we have heard nothing of the Tehuantepec scheme, which we left in a very tangled and unsatisfactory state, and which must now claim attention for a brief period of high promise and apparent prosperity. The Sloo contract[1] with the Mexican government had proved as unfortunate as its predecessors. Hargous, after the confirmation of the new grant, had not by any means given up his fight, though now he sought to secure his ends by indirect means. When Sloo, unable to construct his road or even to make the necessary payments to the Mexican government, borrowed the funds from F. P. Falconnet, an English banker residing in Mexico, Hargous obtained control of the grant by buying up this debt. Since the debt to Falconnet, carrying a lien on the property, antedated the Tehuantepec Company formed in New Orleans with Emile La Sère as president, it was rather hard to see that this corporation was anything but "the shadow of an insubstantial corpse," as one journalist remarked. In the early summer of 1857, La Sère went to Washington, conferred with Hargous and his attorney, Benjamin, and agreed to an arrangement that would once more protect the various interests involved. Benjamin could probably have entirely disregarded the claims of

[1] For the statements on this part of the Tehuantepec episode, see *Senate Executive Documents* 221, 1st Session 36th Congress; *Treaties and Conventions of the United States*, (1889), p. 697 and p. 1356; *Picayune*, July 29 and Sept. 14, 1856; Aug. 2, Sept. 29, Oct. 13, 1857; *Delta*, Aug. 6, Sept. 29 and 30, Oct. 1 and 12, 1857; *True Delta*, Sept. 29, Nov. 1 and 13, 1857.

La Sère's company; it would have been neither honest nor good policy, however, to have done so, for many of his fellow citizens had invested their money in this venture, and he knew that the ultimate success of the scheme under any management would depend upon its good name and upon the support of these very people.

Once more we find the advertisement of a Louisiana Tehuantepec Company, its charter dated July 30, 1857. This charter, similar otherwise to that of previous companies, carries an obligation to take up financial responsibilities that fairly stagger one. Omitting details, suffice it to say that it assumes, first, the positive debt of $600,000, plus interest, to Falconnet; second, that stockholders and trustees of both old companies are to be paid in stock of the new company, dollar for dollar; and third, that all just liabilities of the La Sère company are likewise to be paid. But even more discouraging than this beginning with liabilities amounting to between three and four millions, scarcely a pretense at effective work had been made on the railroad, and even the carriage-road was largely a fiction of the Mexican imagination, while another chapter of uncertain and perhaps expensive negotiations with Mexico must be gone through with to ratify the forfeited Sloo grant once more.

In the charter of the new company, Benjamin and La Sère were specially designated as the commissioners to arrange for this ratification. On August 2d, these two, representing the now consolidated interests, sailed for Mexico on the steamship *Texas.* Another passenger was Pierre Soulé,[1] representing a rebellious faction of the extinct Sloo company. Before

[1] Cf. Diary of a Public Man, *North American Review*, 1879, p. 264.

starting on his journey Benjamin had secured the good will of President Buchanan. This was chiefly due to the personal friendship existing between Mr. Slidell and the Chief Executive. The former had become interested in Tehuantepec, and through him Benjamin had an opportunity to present the plans, prospects, and hopes of an undertaking, which, if successful, would be of national consequence. What the particulars of the interview were we shall never know; but the President so far favored Mr. Benjamin's project as to send special instructions to Mr. Forsyth, Minister to Mexico, informing him that Benjamin and La Sère came on a mission approved by the administration; that they possessed the confidence of Mr. Buchanan; and that they were to be formally presented to the Mexican President. At the same time, it was made clear to Mr. Forsyth that the mission was not official, but on business concerning private citizens, however important might be the ultimate results. He was also instructed to assist these gentlemen in every way in his power, and to endeavor to secure from the Mexican government proper safeguards not only for this particular work but for the interests of the United States in any transit across Tehuantepec.

This was the substance of a special note to Forsyth, signed and sent out by Cass as Secretary of State, but, if gossip is to be relied on, really written by Buchanan himself. Nay, gossip goes farther, and reports that the President said he would not entrust the writing of so important a dispatch to "a superannuated old fogy" like his Secretary of State. Gossip likewise reports unpleasant things from the City of Mexico. The two commissioners were cordially received and handsomely

entertained by President Comonfort and other Mexican
dignitaries. And after weeks of wining and dining,
they returned in October to New Orleans, triumphant,
the Tehuantepec grant confirmed by an imposing
array of those extraordinary "decrees," "pronuncia-
mentoes," or what-nots, produced in such bewildering
profusion on Spanish-American soil. So far all was
well. But news soon reached New Orleans that Soulé
and Forsyth, while not able to defeat Benjamin, had
yet ;made his task much more difficult ; and that, in
consequence, Benjamin had requested Slidell to lodge
a complaint against Forsyth at the Department of
State. At the same time Mexican newspapers began
to arrive. They said nothing of actual differences between the Minister and Mr. Benjamin, but hinted that
the latter had sedulously labored to produce the impression in Mexico that he, and not Mr. Forsyth, was
really the important personage, the confidential representative of the President, in regard to the Tehuantepec
question. And one journal, the *Trait d' Union* (September 14th), in summing up the heavy load of debts
with which the new company would have to start, concluded : "It will, moreover, have to provide for the
expenses (*frais et pots de vin*) incurred here to obtain
its privilege, which expenses amount to at least half a
million of dollars."

In regard to this uncomfortable insinuation about the
frais et pots de vin, the same newspaper published, a
few days later, a formal and indignant denial from
the commissioners of the Tehuantepec Company. In
regard to the charge that Mr. Benjamin had sought to
supplant Minister Forsyth when he found him not altogether in sympathy, we have no such satisfactory

evidence in rebuttal.   The complaints against Forsyth were not urged by Mr. Benjamin when he returned to Washington.   But it is not at all improbable that, with his whole heart set on this Tehuantepec plan, he allowed himself to speak indiscreetly of one who seemed to him to be opposing where he was in honor bound to aid.   In his zeal for the Tehuantepec Company he might well have forgotten, too, that Mr. Forsyth's first duty was to look after government interests ; that the new grant from Mexico was not so favorable to the United States as one which had been covered by the eighth article of the Gadsden Treaty, and that the Minister's opposition had been highly commendable.   It was an unfortunate little episode, closing with spiteful comments on Benjamin.   Gadsden himself wrote a letter to the papers ; its style is so bad as to be almost unintelligible (possibly the printer is partly to blame); but as it contains one of the earliest slurs upon Benjamin for his religious faith, I set down one sentence as it stands : " The mesmeric influences of Tehuantepec, and under the tribe of Benjamin, seeking its inheritance in the land of Mexican promise, seems to have been again reanimated."

A brief season of apparent prosperity came to the Tehuantepec Company.   Mr. Benjamin raised funds and actually got built a practicable road for vehicles across the Isthmus.   He coaxed a reluctant Postmaster-General into granting a contract to carry the California mails via Tehuantepec, for one year, commencing November 1, 1858.   The company provided the steamship *Quaker City*, and she started on her maiden trip from New Orleans to Minatitlan, October 27, 1858.   There was great jollification and congratulation. And there were more trips of the *Quaker City*, and the mail came through from California in twelve days less than by any other route. Then suddenly followed the evil days—Hargous Brothers floundering in financial bogs; the company well-nigh ruined; Mr. Benjamin, armed with personal letters to the Barings and others from Slidell and from the Chief Executive himself, wasting his summer vacation (1859) in the effort to get financial aid in Europe. The last hope, a hope that lingered on till the Civil War, lay in negotiations between the two governments concerned. Minister McClane, Forsyth's successor, was instructed to open the question. He did so, and had an assuring interview with Juarez; but the end of that adventurer could not then be definitely forecast, and the United States could not recognize him as *de facto* ruler while he was a mere fugitive. And so large bundles of beautifully engraved stock certificates of the Tehuantepec Company, bearing a heavy interest of dust, are probably still preserved in out of the way places, and the fruitless Company concerns Mr. Benjamin's biographer no longer.[1]

[1] *Picayune*, Apr. 21, June 16, Aug. 25, Sept. 5 and 18, Oct. 27, Nov. 11, 19, 20, 23, Dec. 8; *Delta*, June 16, Oct. 29, 1857: *True Delta*, Oct. 28, 1857, May 27, July 24, 29, Aug. 3, 1859; March 10, 1860.

CHAPTER VIII

WHATEVER kindly apologists may say in defense of President Buchanan—and it would be puerile as well as cowardly to suggest so much as a doubt of his uprightness, kindliness, and good intentions—his administration had been, to say the least, inglorious. In his foreign policy neither North nor South could take pride ; the irritation of Spain and of Mexico had been rather aggravated than allayed, nor was there any positive if unrighteous gain, such as Polk could point to, to please our own people. In his domestic policy the Kansas incident is fairly typical : the maximum of irritation to both North and South, and then no result to please either. It was manifest that some new leader must head the Democratic party, even if the "old public functionary" should wish to continue his service. Earlier than usual, therefore, the politicians seriously began the search for another Presidential candidate.

No one could doubt that the strongest man in the party was Stephen A. Douglas. But, like Clay, Webster, Seward, and Blaine, he was to lose the coveted prize just as it seemed within his grasp. Even before the enunciation of his "Freeport Doctrine," the Southern leaders had begun to doubt him ; in those debates with Lincoln, and in his action on the Kansas question, they found that which made them, almost to a man, his irreconcilable enemies. Accordingly they prepared to defeat him in the Charleston convention, or to bind him by such a platform as would secure the aims of their section. If he would have consented to such a platform, they would have trusted him. But, eager politician though he was, Douglas was too honest and sincere to palter with his principles. The result is known : the split in the Democratic party, the secession of the Southern delegates, foreshadowing secession of a more formidable sort, and the nomination of Breckinridge and Douglas by the rival factions. It was Lincoln's "house divided against itself" in fateful fashion.

Though Benjamin had not yet begun open attacks upon Douglas, he was entirely in accord with the other Southern leaders in the policy pursued at Charleston, and approved of the withdrawal of the Louisiana delegation from the convention. In a speech in the Senate, May 8, 1860,[1] he attempts to justify this action, in words whose sincerity we see no reason to question, and which recall former utterances : "Distinctly opposite interpretations, or distinctly opposite principles, if you choose, in relation to Southern rights under the Constitution, were avowed at Charleston, by men professing all to be Democrats. . . . It is unworthy of them, and unworthy of us all, that we should go before the people of this country and ask their votes in favor of one party or another, with the avowed purpose of presenting opposite sets of principles in the two sections of the Confederacy, as being the principles of a common party, and forming a common party creed. I say that I will never be a party to any such contest as that. If I go into an electoral

[1] *Globe*, 1859–1860, Part III, p. 1967.

contest, I want to know the principles of the party
with which I act, and I want, before the people of my
state, before the people of the country, to declare
those principles, to stand by them, to find them written
in letters of light, so that no man can dare misconstrue
them, and by them to stand, and with them, if need
be, fall." In the same strain he continues, that he
will support any available man who can honestly
stand on a platform satisfactory to his people : "That
far, sir, I am willing to go ; but I have no stomach for
a fight in which I am to have the choice between the
man who denies me all my rights, openly and fairly,
and a man who admits my rights but intends to filch
them." He saw little hope of finding such a platform
and such a man as the united Democracy could
support.

Nevertheless, Benjamin was one of the nineteen
Southern representatives who signed (May 17th) that
hopeless "Address to the National Democracy," [1]
urging the seceding delegates to go to Baltimore with
the Douglas faction, to await and work for some concession that will lead to reunion, and only after that
fails to join the rest of the Southern delegates at
Richmond. The signers of this document, including
Jefferson Davis, Reagan, Lamar, the senators from
Virginia, Arkansas, Georgia, and Louisiana, and
others, were unquestionably sincere in regretting the
division of the party, and in wishing to end it ; but the
Southerners, in this hour of fate, seemed to forget the
true nature of compromise, expecting all of the concessions to come from the other side. And the tone they
adopted toward the Northern wing of the Democracy,

[1] *Delta*, May 22.

and toward Douglas in particular, was not such as to calm angry passions.

The allusion to Douglas as the "man who admits my rights but intends to filch them" is patent enough; it is personally applied in a fierce and unjust arraignment of his policy on May 22d.[1] We can speak of this attack as unjust only because its bitterness is greater than the occasion called for, and because after events have reëstablished Douglas's good name in the world; for the charges made are essentially true, and the interpretation then put upon them was not unreasonable in the light of things as they seemed. The logic of events had impelled Douglas to retreat from extreme pro-Southern views whose full significance to the section he had perhaps never realized before; only when he was shown whither his own policies led did he halt, hesitate, seek a safe detour, and finally make an honest confession that he had chosen a new route that did not lead whither the South had insisted it must lead. There is, then, no reading, without a pained sense of their mingled justice and injustice, Benjamin's accusations of bad faith, of endless intrigue, of paltering with the people of both sections in words that are interpreted in one way at the North and quite another at the South.

Benjamin had this to say of Douglas's antagonist in those debates of 1858 : " In that contest the two candidates for the Senate of the United States, in the state of Illinois, went before their people. They agreed to discuss the issues; they put questions to each other for answer; and I must say here, for I must be just to all, that I have been surprised in the examination that I

[1] *Globe*, 1859–1860, Part III, p. 2233, *et seq.*

made again within the last few days of this discussion between Mr. Lincoln and Mr. Douglas, to find that Mr. Lincoln is a far more conservative man, unless he has since changed his opinions, than I had supposed him to be. There was no dodging on his part. Mr. Douglas started with his questions. Here they are, with Mr. Lincoln's answers." He then quotes the familiar answers to Douglas's seven questions, such as, that Lincoln is not in favor of the unconditional repeal of the Fugitive Slave Law; that he is not pledged against the admission of more slave states, or of any state with such constitution as the people of the state may prefer; that he is committed to a belief in the right and duty of Congress to prohibit slavery in the territories, etc.[1] "It is impossible . . . not to admire the perfect candor and frankness with which these answers were given : no equivocation—no evasion." And it is easy to present in ugly contrast the disingenuous and evasive answers of Douglas to Lincoln's questions, especially to the famous one : "Can the people of a territory, in any lawful way, against the wishes of any citizen of the United States, exclude slavery from their limits prior to the formation of a state constitution ?" Douglas certainly made a poor figure in this contrast, and in condemning the "Little Giant," the Southerner expressed the resentful feelings of his section.

In spite of his partisan bias, however, Benjamin did not forget justice and kindness. A little episode in the Senate in 1860 may serve to show something of his regard for principle as well as for the dictates of humanity. As chairman of the Judiciary Com-

[1] *Globe*, 1859–1860, Part III, p. 2237.

mittee, Benjamin reported[1] to the Senate a bill author-
izing the President to make contracts, for terms not
exceeding five years, with such organizations as the
African Colonization Society, to return to Africa
negroes taken from captured slavers. These forlorn
wretches were to be fed, clothed, and provided for till
they could look out for themselves, for a period of six
months, at a cost of not more than $100 each. An
amendment was made, extending the period of care
over the captives to one year, at the same cost; and
the bill proposed an appropriation of $200,000. There
were at the time about twelve hundred such negroes,
detained in camp, no doubt under bad conditions, at
Key West.

Mr. Davis opposed the bill, as a waste of public
money, and maintained that we should be carrying
out our treaty obligations if we merely took the
negroes back to the point whence they were shipped
and turned them loose. Brown, of Mississippi, declared he was unwilling to support them "out of the
national treasury one hour after" they got to the coast
of Africa. Mallory, of Florida, championed a scheme
that was attracting some attention in the press; *viz.*,
to "apprentice" the captives to planters for five
years. Mason, of Virginia, opposed the bill on the
ground that he thought the power of stopping the
slave-trade should belong to the states, as did Toombs,
of Georgia, on similar grounds.

Benjamin, against all of these prominent men of his
own party, took a broader and more humane view of
our obligations under the treaty with Great Britain:
"The government of the United States is bound by

[1] *Globe*, Part III, pp. 2304, 2306, *et seq.*

treaty stipulations to aid in the suppression of the slave-trade. If that treaty binds us, it is our duty to carry it out in good faith. If it does not, then we ought to refuse the performance of that duty openly and fairly, by declaring that we are not bound by the treaty, and do not mean to execute it. No one has yet taken the latter position. The treaty binds us in good faith to aid in the suppression of the slave-trade. That being the obligation of the government, the practical question alone was presented to the committee. . . . The captive Africans are on our shore; what shall be done with them? That was the simple practical question to which we looked. I desired, if possible, to avoid the constant recurrence of agitating discussions in the Senate. Finding the negroes there, I could conceive of no mode of disposing of them more expedient, viewing all the circumstances of the case, than that suggested by the President of the United States, which had been adopted by President Monroe, and afterward by himself. Until the proposition that has just been read for information, just presented by the senator from Florida,—which I shall not discuss, which I do not approve—nobody had hitherto suggested that anything else could be done with these slaves than to take them back to Africa. . . . We are not bound to go in search of the domicile of each one of the liberated captives, and take him just back to where he was originally taken from; but we take him back and put him as far on his way home as we can, and at the same time pay just regard to the dictates of humanity. . . . I do not myself construe the obligations of our government as the senator from Mississippi does. I think it was understood between

Great Britain and this country, when that treaty was made, that we would endeavor to stop the slave-trade on the coast of Africa by rendering it impossible to prosecute it; and we expected to do that by capturing vessels engaged in it.   I do not think myself—other gentlemen may take a different view of the obligation —that it would be consistent with fair dealing between this government and Great Britain to take these slaves off the ships and take them back to the barracoons to be resold.   That is my view of our national obligation.   If I am right in that view of it—and I am firmly convinced I am right, I do not say I may not be mistaken—that it is our duty under that treaty to arrest, as far as we can, the prosecution of the slave-trade, then something else must be done with these slaves besides putting them back in the hands of the slave-traders and slave-dealers on the coast."

On the final vote there were but fourteen nays, including the senators before named and some others, such as Slidell, Wigfall, and Yulee; while among the forty-one yeas were some notable Southerners, such as Chesnut, Clingman, Crittenden, Hunter, and Pearce. It would be as idle to commend their vote—praise is uncalled for in a case where duty and humanity both pointed the path—as to fancy that the vote of the opposition was due to lack of plain perceptions of duty and humanity; those on the negative side were the nucleus of the determined obstructionists of any measure likely to be pleasing to the North.

Nothing else of much note came up in the Senate in the few remaining weeks of the session.   In fact, even practiced observers at the time failed to see any momentous stir or active interest in politics during the

summer of this year. Knowing how portentous were
the results, that the black cloud upon the Southern
horizon was indeed charged with lightning, we perhaps exaggerate the enthusiasm and excitement of
the campaign of 1860. The correspondent of the London *Times* was obviously disgusted at the lack of
interest, for he wrote in August,[1] in the tone of one ag-
grieved because the play is not so thrilling as the
posters : "The most striking feature of the present
presidential contest is the comparative apathy of the
American public. They cannot be raised to the requisite degree of enthusiasm either for Breckenridge and
Lane, or Bell and Everett, or Lincoln and Douglas, or
any other man or pair of men. The old secession cry
of South Carolina, raised by Mr. Keitt, a legislator of
the Brooks school, falls as dead as the 'screamers' of
the New York *Herald*." Yet the country was gathering
heat as the time of election drew on, and sundry rum-
blings and mutterings, more among the camp-followers
than from the leaders, gave warning that the South
was preparing herself for separate existence in case
the vote favored Lincoln. Persons of apparent ra-
tionality on other topics were writing to the papers
with various hopeful plans to foil the Black Republicans. Most of them in Mr. Benjamin's own state
seem to oppose absolute secession, but not a few counsel rigid non-intercourse between North and South,—
social, political, industrial, intellectual. What was
to become of the Union under these circumstances is,
unfortunately, not stated. And commercial gentlemen
of all sorts conjure Southerners to be patriotic in their
purchases ; as, "in view of the impending crisis that

[1] Quoted in *True Delta*, Aug. 28.

Abe Lincoln may be elected," let all Louisianians buy Southern sewing machines instead of the inferior Black Republican article.[1] Occasionally some extreme fire-eater breathes destruction in a fashion that must have taxed the patience of the most submissive typesetter. Thus some injudicious parties having expressed a wish to know "his views," a well-known planter of Terrebonne Parish aimed a three-column letter at them, whose style may be imagined from the following verbatim extract:[2] "We must not, cannot, and will not submit to wrong and oppression, so we must war against and fight our enemies, and be forced against our will to fight our friends and relations. In New York at the last election, it shows the Southern states had 350,000 votes, which are our friends. . . . From these calculations and knowledge,—on very favorable terms we commence the war and battle, and, with a small band of our patriotic and brave fighting men, we can very easily whip, scare and put to flight the negro stealers and murderers with our patriotic and fighting army assisted by 350,000 in their own state, New York."

With such ebullitions, of course, Benjamin would have been as much irritated as we are; but there was little opportunity during this campaign for discovering his opinions, further than what was amply expressed in the Senate speeches of the spring; for he was absent from the state on his last great legal case in this country. Before he started for California to continue this suit, the firm of Benjamin, Bradford and Finney had been succeeded by that of Benjamin,

[1] *True Delta*, Oct. 12 ; cf. Nov. 28.
[2] *True Delta*, Dec. 16.

Bonford and Finney.[1] Mr. Bradford, in poor health,
retired from the partnership temporarily (so it was
then intended), to travel in Europe. The new firm
went on as if there had been no break, for Mr. P. E.
Bonford was no novice at the New Orleans bar. But
not a full year elapsed before it was dissolved and
the three partners were enlisted in the service of the
Confederacy.

The case of the United States *vs.* Castillero involved
the title to the famous quicksilver mine, New Almaden, discovered in 1845 by Andres Castillero, to whom
the Mexican governor, Pio Pico, had given possession,
together with three thousand *varas* of land in every
direction from its mouth. Not long after this, California was ceded to the United States (February 2,
1848). In the present suit Calhoun Benham and Ed-
mund Randolph, for the government, denied the genu-
ineness of Castillero's title papers, and the right of the
Mexican governor to make him a grant of land in
California. The counsel for the claimants were A. C.
Peachy, Reverdy Johnson, and J. P. Benjamin; the
last named, owing to his special familiarity with
such land claims and with the Spanish laws, prepared
the brief and made the leading argument. The trial
began on October 8, 1860, before the Circuit Court for
California, and Benjamin's argument ran through four
days, October 24th, 25th, 26th, and November 5th.
The legal points of the case, however, being of interest
to few, we shall omit; for though the sums involved
were so great that Benjamin received a fee of twenty-
five thousand dollars for his services, it was after all
but a private claim. The decision of the Circuit

[1] *Picayune,* July 11.

Court, January 18, 1861, was adverse to the claimants, who appealed to the Supreme Court, before which the brilliant Louisiana advocate could no longer personally appear. But the "counsel on appeal for the claimants, including Reverdy Johnson, Charles O'Conor, and J. J. Crittenden, did him the signal honor of filing a copy of his brief with the Supreme Court, when the case reached that tribunal in January, 1863, at a time when Benjamin himself was premier of the Confederate cabinet." [1] This was an honest confession that they could not hope to improve upon the cogency of the plea of the "rebel."

From far California the lawyer hastened back to find war in the political atmosphere in Louisiana and at Washington. He had not returned when the session opened, but arrived shortly afterward. During all the summer and autumn, he had been absent from his state and silent on the political issues. Now that the expected had really happened, and the "Black Republican" was actually elected President, men were forced to show whether they meant to make good the threats uttered during the campaign; and not a few had wavered, hesitated, weakened in the face of the crisis in a way that left constituencies most uncertain as to what their representatives would really do. Though known as a secession man, Benjamin had not stumped the state, making threats of disunion in case of Lincoln's election; one had to be vociferous for Southern rights to be heard above the din then making, and Benjamin was not half prompt enough in announcing his separatist views to suit the excited people.

[1] See Kohler, p. 71, and for further details of the case, 2 Black's U. S. Reports 1, vol. 67.

At one time the New Orleans papers [1] report that he is to make a strong Union speech in the Senate, and a fortnight later, more correctly, that he is counted on for a strong speech in favor of secession; certainly, however, the correspondent of the *Picayune* was right when he stated that "Mr. Benjamin opposes secession, except in the last resort."

That last resort, however, in his judgment, had been already reached. The *Delta* of December 23d, published a letter from Benjamin himself, dated at Washington, December 8th, in which he briefly and unequivocally outlines his opinions. He believed:

"1.   That the feeling of a large number, if not a majority, of the people of the North is hostile to our interests; that this feeling has been instilled into the present generation from its infancy; that it is founded upon the mistaken belief that the people of the North are responsible for the existence of slavery in the South; that this conviction of a personal responsibility for what they erroneously believe to be a sin, springs chiefly from the consideration that they are, with us, members of a common government, and that the Union itself is thus made the principal cause of hostile interference by them with our institutions.

"2.   That no just reason exists for hoping for any change in Northern feeling, and no prospect remains of our being permitted to live in peace and security within the Union.

"3.   That, therefore, the interest of the South, the very instinct of self-preservation, demands a prompt severance of all connection with a government which has itself become an obstacle to what it was designed

[1] *Picayune* and others, Dec. 11; cf. Dec. 16 and 23.

to effect, *viz.*, 'Insuring *domestic* tranquillity, and promoting general welfare.'

"4. That to effect this purpose separate state action is vitally necessary. . . .

"The opinions thus hurriedly expressed have been deliberately formed. They have been gradually forced upon me by intercourse with the accredited representatives of Northern sentiment, and each day adds to my conviction of their truth."

At this turning point in Benjamin's life the biographer may be pardoned for citing at such length a manifesto that sets forth so little of which we need have been in doubt. With the deliberate statement of his convictions in the first three articles of this creed we cannot be startled; for all of this Benjamin had said before, and was to say again, more eloquently. It does surprise us, as showing an advance to the extreme radical position of the secessionists, to find him urging separate state action, *i. e.*, secession first, and attempts to coöperate with other seceding states afterward. This, nevertheless, was no bait hastily thrown out to the extremists in Louisiana, but a deliberate opinion. He reaffirmed it in signing the address of Southern congressmen to their constituents,[1] stating their belief that "the honor, safety, and independence of the Southern people require the organization of a Southern confederacy—a result to be obtained only by separate state action; that the primary object of each slave-holding state ought to be its speedy and absolute separation from a union with hostile states." But, once admitting the right of secession, and convinced that the time had come to exercise that right, it would

[1] Dec. 14; see *Delta*, Dec. 22.

be difficult to deny that this separate action by the states was expedient, nay, that it was the only practicable way of meeting the situation. The argument to this effect is presented, though not with much cogency, in an address to the Louisiana Convention,[1] signed by Benjamin and Slidell. The strongest plea would have been the simplest: in beginning a revolution promptness not only gives vigor to the revolutionary cause but demoralizes the established forces. This, however, would have involved the confession that secession was nothing short of revolution, a confession that few of the Southern politicians cared to make, though we shall see Benjamin very distinctly resting the Southern case on the inherent right of revolution, in the last great speeches he made in the Senate.

In reviewing what we have had to say of his oratory in the Senate, there may seem to be too great copiousness of superlatives in its praise, and much iteration, nearly all of the longer orations being on the same theme—the exposition of Southern rights. By no means shall we regret the first charge as a fault; the last is self-evident. Let any one who can, regardless of political opinions, be roused to a genuine feeling for the mere grace of expression, dazzling brilliance of reasoning and withering force of sarcasm; let any one, in short, who has a love for style and an interest in forensics read this splendid series of orations, and then formulate a judicious estimate of Benjamin as an orator and expounder of the political principles in which the South believed. Such a one, I am assured, would find it difficult to express himself in strictly measured terms. And so it is that we must preface a thrilling

[1] Jan. 14, 1861; *Delta*, Jan. 26.

oration, delivered in the Senate on the last day of the
year 1860.

The first aim of this address [1] is to make clear the actual, practical situation in South Carolina now that she
has seceded ; to establish the right of secession ; and to
show the wrong and the folly of the course proposed by
the administration. At the beginning, however, before
the statement of the principal part of his aim, he refers
to his speech of May 2, 1856, and in a few simple phrases
recites the most potent of the causes for the unexampled
bitterness and violence of Southern feeling toward the
North : " Mr. President, it has been justly said that
this is no time for crimination ; and, sir, it is in no
such spirit, but with the simple desire to free myself
personally, as a public servant, from all responsibility
for the present condition of affairs, that I desire to
recall to the Senate some remarks made by me in debate more than four years ago, in which I predicted
the precise state of public feeling now, and pointed
out the two principal causes that were certain to produce that state. The first was the incessant attack of
the Republicans, not simply on the interests, but on
the feelings and sensibilities of a high-spirited people
by the most insulting language and the most offensive
epithets ; the other was their fatal success in persuading their followers that these constant aggressions
could be continued and kept up with no danger ; that
the South was too weak, and too conscious of weak-
ness, to dare resistance." Hereupon follows the quotation reiterating his disbelief in the possibility of a
peaceable dissolution of the Union. As Benjamin
intimates, and as some Northern writers are now be-

[1] *Globe*, 1860–61, Part I, p. 212, *et. seq.*

ginning to comprehend, it was not so much what the Republicans or even the Abolitionists—and the people of the South were convinced that the two were Siamese twins—had done or might do that wrought them to the pitch of frenzy and vicious, uncontrollable rage against the North; it was the things they said, and very horrid things they were, that galled. Nay, even if the North did not speak, she thought these things; and, half-conscious of being on the defensive, with the opinion of the civilized world against her, the South could not bear to be so regarded. Unless one has personally experienced that sort of utterly childish and yet wholly human temper, one can hardly account for Southern feeling.

In the subsequent portion of the speech Benjamin proceeds to a consideration of the existing situation in South Carolina, and the impending secession of seven other states. Then he squarely presents the question : Shall we recognize the fact that South Carolina has become an independent state, or shall we wage war upon her ? As to her right to become an independent state, to secede, that he plants firmly on the inherent right of revolution. "From the time that this people declared its independence of Great Britain, the right of the people to self-government in its fullest and broadest extent has been a cardinal principle of American liberty. None deny it. And in that right, to use the language of the Declaration itself, is included the right, whenever a form of government becomes destructive of their interests or their safety, 'to alter or to abolish it, and to institute a new government, laying its foundation on such principles and organizing its powers in such form as to them shall seem most likely to effect their safety and happiness.'"

But quite aside from the right of revolution, there is, he maintains, a right of secession. Once more he marshals, with force and lucidity, the historical and constitutional arguments in support of this idea. But even granting that South Carolina has no right to secede, that she is utterly mistaken, it is a patent fact that she has seceded: "You still have the same issue to meet, face to face. You must permit her to withdraw in peace, or you must declare war. That is, you must coerce the state itself, or you must permit her to depart in peace. There is nothing whatever that can render for an instant tenable the attempted distinction between coercing a state itself, and coercing all the individuals in the manner now proposed." He disposes of this idea by a *reductio ad absurdum* similar to the familiar one in Webster's reply to Hayne. For, he says, if there be anything in this notion, it should stand the test of practical application. Now suppose a violation of United States laws in South Carolina, who is to arrest the violator? There is no United States marshal there now. Suppose him arrested, who is to try him? Is there a Federal judge there? And granted the judge, where will you get a jury that will recognize your jurisdiction, much less one that will convict, in a community that has almost unanimously repudiated all connection with you?

He accuses the Republican party of putting a false and treacherous construction on the Constitution, to the prejudice of the South, as Rhadamistus swore to Mithridates that he would use neither steel nor poison against him, and kept this promise by smothering his captive. "You do not propose to enter into our states, you say, and what do we complain of? You do not pretend to enter into our states to kill or destroy our institutions by force. Oh, no! You imitate the faith of Rhadamistus: you propose simply to close us in an embrace that will suffocate us. You do not propose to fell the tree; you promised not. You merely propose to girdle it, that it die. And then, when we tell you that we did not understand this bargain this way, and that your acting upon it in this spirit releases us from the obligations that accompany it; that under no circumstances can we consent to live together under that interpretation, and say: 'We will go from you; let us go in peace;' we are answered by your leading spokesman: 'Oh, no, you cannot do that; we have no objection to it personally, but we are bound by our oaths: if you attempt it, your people will be hanged for treason. We have examined this Constitution thoroughly; we have searched it out with a fair spirit, and we can find warrant in it for releasing ourselves from the obligation of giving you any of its benefits, but our oaths force us to tax you; we can dispense with everything else; but our consciences, we protest upon our souls, will be sorely worried if we do not take your money.' That is the proposition of the honorable senator from Ohio, in plain language. He can avoid everything else under the Constitution in the way of secession; but how he is to get rid of the duty of taking our money he cannot see."

After this touch of ridicule, drawing laughter from his auditors, a short transition brings on the eloquent peroration, delivered with such dramatic effect that those who heard—and some live still—never forgot it:

"And now, senators, within a few weeks we part to meet as senators in one common council chamber of the nation no more forever. We desire, we beseech you, let this parting be in peace. I conjure you to indulge in no vain delusion that duty or conscience, interest or honor, imposes upon you the necessity of invading our states or shedding the blood of our people. You have no possible justification for it. I trust it is in no craven spirit, and with no sacrifice of the honor or dignity of my own state, that I make this last appeal, but from far higher and holier motives. If, however, it shall prove vain; if you are resolved to pervert the government framed by the fathers for the protection of our rights into an instrument for subjugating and enslaving us, then, appealing to the Supreme Judge of the universe for the rectitude of our intentions, we must meet the issue that you force upon us as best becomes freemen defending all that is dear to man. What may be the fate of this horrible contest, no man can tell, none pretend to foresee; but this much I will say : the fortunes of war may be adverse to our arms ; you may carry desolation into our peaceful land, and with torch and fire you may set our cities in flames; you may even emulate the atrocities of those who, in the war of the Revolution, hounded on the bloodthirsty savage to attack upon the defenseless frontier; you may, under the protection of your advancing armies, give shelter to the furious fanatics who desire, and profess to desire, nothing more than to add all the horrors of a servile insurrection to the calamities of civil war; you may do all this,—and more, too, if more there be—but you never can subjugate us ; you never can convert the free sons of the soil into vassals, paying tribute to your power; and you never, never can degrade them to the level of an inferior and servile race.   Never ! Never !"

Then followed, says the *Globe*, such a burst of applause in the galleries that the chair ordered the gentlemen's gallery to be closed; and immediately thereafter the Senate adjourned. At the season of Christmas holidays, and when the young were watching every move with frantic enthusiasm, the old with feelings wherein doubt, regret, fear mingled with unquenchable sympathies for the cause of their own state, many visitors had come to Washington.   Upon them, eager listeners to the speeches made by prominent leaders, no longer to persuade House or Senate, but as vindications of their course before the nation, as trumpet calls to their friends and defiance to their foes, this address of Benjamin's had telling effect. One, who came as a schoolboy on his holidays to see the sights of the capital in this time of storm and stress, told the writer of this scene at its close, and of the wild cheers of himself and his companions.   He could recite a few of the concluding phrases, though he had not read the speech since, so lasting was the impression on his memory.   Tradition has associated with the Louisianian's real farewell to the Senate, to be mentioned presently, a much quoted remark by Sir George Cornewall Lewis, but one is not so sure that it might not more fitly apply here.   "Have you read Benjamin's speech?" he is reported to have asked Lord Sherbrooke, adding, "It is better than our Benjamin [Disraeli] could have done."

The press of the day recognized this as the senator's supreme effort, and it compelled the admiration even of hostile papers. One of the Northern journals gives so interesting a pen-picture of the orator as he spoke that we must not pass it by:[1] "He made a capital speech; quiet, and if not exactly dignified, his manner was self-possessed and resolute. He went over the whole ground of Southern causes of complaint against the North as coolly and dispassionately as if arguing a case before the Supreme Court. There was no fine speaking; no appeal to the feelings; and yet the attention of the galleries was unbroken. The ladies, too, listened as closely as the reporters. He summed up his argument very calmly, read from a written paper, in a measured legal tone, the causes of difference, and then concluded. This conclusion was a telling shot. He spoke coolly of the approaching dissolution of the Union, and the contest that might ensue. He enumerated the horrors of civil war— alluded to the probability of the South's not being able to defend herself. It was all repeated over as calmly as had been his authorities. He stood in a simple position, between two desks, one foot crossed over the other, no attitude, no gesture. As he reached the close, he had one hand in his pocket, the other negligently toying with a vest chain. He balanced his head a little to and fro, in a truly professional manner. Only his black eyes showed the emotion he must have felt. They were elongated, as Rachel's sometimes became, when at her stillest, most concentrated points of acting—the quiet curse in *Camille*, for example—scintillating with light; a faint smile, just a little scornful, as he said, 'You may set our cities in flames . . . you will never subjugate us.' He let

[1] Philadelphia *Bulletin*, quoted in *Delta*, Jan. 16.

go of his vest chain, and put his other hand coolly into his pocket, and, as he half-turned to take his seat, he added: 'An enslaved and servile race you can never make of us—never! never!' This reiteration of the word 'never' was as free from emotion as if he had been insisting on some simple point of law, which could not be decided in any different way. But, free from emotion as it was, it produced the greatest effect. The whole gallery, on all sides, burst out as in one voice, in uncontrollable applause."

But once more was the silvery voice of the gifted leader from Louisiana to charm the Senate in a set address. The interval before his withdrawal from that body was filled with schemes of compromise that might, so their advocates hoped, extinguish the conflagration already begun. Among the people and the representatives of the South, there was diligent, even feverish preparation for separation from the Union; since it must come, they seemed to think delay a dishonor. They would show the insulting Yankees, who had believed this but one more Southern "bluff," that the other states were ready to stand by South Carolina, to the uttermost. Among the Republicans of set purpose, it appears, there was dogged or sullen silence, resolute and exasperating inaction. In Congress they ceased from troubling with those too righteous and too irritating disquisitions on the iniquity of slavery and of the slave-holder. They said nothing; nor would they do anything, either aggressive or of conciliatory tendency. They seemed content to block all efforts at compromise and let Southern rashness lead the South whither it would. Among the moderate men of all parties, forlorn old Whigs and

Americans, and Northern Democrats, cowed by the impending ruin of their long triumphant party, there was much despairing negotiation. The most notable attempt was the compromise proposed by Senator Crittenden, of Kentucky, who nobly, though fruit-lessly, strove to emulate the great statesman from Kentucky who had twice saved the Union when its stability seemed endangered.

The Crittenden Compromise was a sort of wet blanket or patent fire extinguisher with which certain opti-mists hoped to put out this national Vesuvian eruption. Yet, among the might-have-beens, one must not omit to consider what were the chances of success of this measure, and why it failed. If you read the story of the closing scenes in Congress, during the last months of 1860 and the beginning of 1861, in the books of the historians of the North, you will find it said that Mr. Benjamin and five other Southern senators voted against the Crittenden Compromise. An examination of the *Congressional Globe* will show that this is, in the mere letter, true; Mr. Benjamin and five other Southern senators simply refused to vote at a time when they could have defeated an amendment hostile to the very spirit of the compromise offered by Crittenden. The amendment was carried, and these senators, so it is said, left the house immediately and telegraphed to their respective states that there was no hope of set-tlement; therefore, say those who accept the state-ment unquestioned, upon these men rests the awful responsibility of making the war inevitable, of reject-ing the compromise offered them. To all of which any candid student must answer, "Positively not proven."

In the first place, it was no gracious offering from the party victorious in the late election, and wickedly rejected by truculent and selfish Southern politicians bent on embroiling the country in a civil war. On the contrary, proposed by a Southerner, it had the support of all the Southern members, exclusive of one or two extremists; and it met with the all but unanimous opposition of the Republican members of the House and of the Senate. In the Senate, particularly, they fought it by every means in their power, and sought to delay its consideration, perhaps in the hope that the exasperated South might in the meantime prejudice her cause by some violent outbreak. At last, when the question could not longer be kept from coming to a vote, and after days of debate wherein they had all too plainly exposed the unrelenting spirit in which they proposed to meet those over whom they had won a doubtful victory in electing the President, a Republican senator, Mr. Clark, of New Hampshire, moved an amendment to the Crittenden Compromise that he knew could not be acceptable to the South; and every Republican senator voted for it. And then—do you blame them?—Mr. Benjamin and those five others refused to help achieve a barren victory in the defeat of this amendment, seeing in what spirit the opposition was acting. They allowed the compromise to go a little earlier to the death that it could not long have escaped.

It is a cheerful symptom of restored health in the Union when we find one of the ablest of Northern historians, Mr. Rhodes, admitting the facts to be as we have stated them:[1] "The truth is that it was the

[1] Vol. III, p. 267.

Republicans who for a second time defeated, for weal
or woe, the Crittenden Compromise." There is another erroneous impression concerning Benjamin and
the other Southern leaders that Mr. Rhodes may help
us to correct, especially since contemporary opinions
on the same side may be cited.

What of Benjamin's brilliant talents, it may be
asked, if they were deliberately and wickedly used to
encourage the people in the fatal policy of secession ; to
fan the flame of sectional hate ; to make inevitable the
bloody and desolating war from which the South has
not yet fully recovered? That is what Mr. Blaine,
in his book called *Twenty Years of Congress* says of
Judah P. Benjamin, "the Mephistopheles of the
Southern Confederacy." That is what many on the
other side and some even on his own said, as if
the great conflict whose premonitory thunders had
been heard for a generation were the work of a little
junto of selfish politicians, such as Jeff Davis, Toombs,
and Benjamin on the one side, and Seward, Chase, and
Sumner on the other. In answer to this, Mr. Rhodes
is of opinion that the popular enthusiasm for secession
in the South quite outran the politicians : [1]   " Davis
and Toombs are always classed among the conspirators,
yet Davis was in favor of delay ; and Toombs, in spite
of his vehement talk at Washington, could not keep
pace with the secession movement in his state. The
South Carolina radicals murmured that the people
were hampered by the politicians."

In commenting on Benjamin's speech of December
31st, the Cincinnati *Commercial* said : [2]   " No one who

[1] Vol. III, p. 276.
[2] Quoted in *Delta*, January 16th.

understands the brilliant powers of Benjamin can fail to feel the deepest sorrow that a man of such splendid gifts should have abused them so miserably in a cause so hopeless. He might have saved Louisiana from the desperate experiment of secession, and rolled back the flood of Southern fanaticism from the banks of the Mississippi, thus entitling himself to the gratitude of the country, and adding to the lustre of his reputation as an orator the brighter and better fame of enlarged and elevated patriotism." To this the *Delta* replied: "Before Mr. Benjamin had returned from California, the secession movement had attained an irresistible power in this state. It was not even known what his views were, and, indeed, it was not until the state convention had been ordered by the legislature, in view of secession, that a report that he was about to make a Union speech was contradicted. The idea that Mr. Benjamin, or any other statesman, politician, or orator could have arrested or even checked this impulse grows out of that prevailing delusion at the North . . . that the secession movement originated with politicians. This is the greatest error ever committed by a sagacious people. There has been no excitement or movement in our political history with which the politicians have had so little and the people so much to do. Men in high places and honors are not eager or prompt to engage in revolutions. It happens that all the prominent politicians engaged in the secession movement occupied the highest places in the government of a great republic of thirty-three states. In connecting themselves with the secession of the South, they yield up honor and places which would satisfy the highest civil ambition.

They do so to embark on the uncertain and tempestuous sea of revolution.''

Thus calmly, in the middle of January, before the state had formally seceded, the press talked of "revolution"! The history of the world has no similar page to show, nothing that compares with this in cool audacity. As Americans, and used to free speech and a free press, we scarcely appreciate this, or realize that in any other country the leaders who thus boldly announced their determination to form a new government would have been laid by the heels long before matters reached such a crisis. But the preparations for secession were allowed to proceed without interruption, though sometimes a trifle hastened by an intimation of possible interference; and all the while the United States mail went to states that had proclaimed or were proclaiming themselves not united. At length Louisiana joined her fortunes to those of secession (January 26), but seventeen out of one hundred and twenty members in the convention remaining steadfast against immediate withdrawal from the Union. Her senators and representatives (all save one of the latter) had but awaited the command of their state to bid farewell to Washington. Accordingly, on February 4th Mr. Slidell sent up to be read by the Secretary of the Senate the ordinance to dissolve "the union between the state of Louisiana and the other states united with her under the compact entitled the Constitution of the United States of America," and delivered a speech, in explanation of his course and of the course of his state, which Mr. Blaine describes as "insolent."

Benjamin, too, made a speech, his real farewell to the Senate, and the same partisan writer speaks of its "tone of moderation as contrasted with the offensive dictation of Mr. Slidell."[1]   We could scarcely find a better chance to point out the effect of Benjamin's manner and delivery in softening what he had to say. For his colleague's address, without any but the most commonplace devices of oratory, is in its matter, one would think, far less radical, severe, and offensive than Benjamin's.   Another contemporary who heard this speech bears testimony of similar purport in a passage which will serve our purpose well to quote at some length.

General E. D. Keyes,[2] of the United States Army, was at the time a young officer in Washington, and used to visit Congress and report to General Scott the doings and sayings of the politicians, having a soldier's innate distrust of all such, whether Northern or Southern.   He writes:

"When I heard Mr. Sumner and others proclaim the superiority of the North in jurists, men of science, historians, orators, merchants, mechanics, schools and general intelligence, I felt disposed to stone them. Every speech of the Northern senators had something deprecatory in it, and that at a time when all the powers of the government were in the hands of Southern men.   Notwithstanding my hostility of sentiment, I admitted the graceful dignity and splendid elocution of the Southern senators, as well as the candid selfishness with which they told how long and grievously they had groaned over the exactions of the North.   I heard the farewell speeches of Senators Jefferson Davis of Mississippi and Benjamin of Louisiana. . . .

[1] *Twenty Years of Congress*, Vol. I, p. 249.
[2] *Fifty Years' Observation*, p. 49.

Mr. Benjamin appeared to me essentially different from Mr. Davis. Notwithstanding his incomparable abilities and the fact that he became a secessionist with great reluctance, he never excited animosity in me or in any other Northern man so far as I am aware. When I listened to his last speech in the Senate, I was transported out of myself. Such verbal harmony I had never heard before! There was neither violence in his action nor anger in his tone, but a pathos that lulled my senses like an opiate that fills the mind with delightful illusions. I was conscious that it was Senator Benjamin who spoke, and that his themes were mighty wrongs and desperate remedies; but his words I could not recite, nor can I yet recall them. Memory, however, restores the illusive pleasure they left, which is like the impression I retain of my youthful days."

And so Mr. Slidell, saying merely matter-of-fact things that the situation rendered obvious, and saying them without art, gave offense; while Benjamin, saying things that were a fierce attack upon the honesty, fairness, honor of his opponents, and saying them in that piercingly melodious voice, without apparent passion and with all the arts that rhetoric could teach to make them effective as well as beautiful, gave no offense,—rather stirred his hostile listeners to mingled admiration and regret.

This speech of February 4th[1] is one that Louisianians should read with especial pride, as a most able defense of the state against the charges that had been brought against her. So very effective is the argument that Mr. Blaine, describing the tone as "moderate," yet covers four pages in the attempt to answer it, while

[1] *Globe*, 1860–61, Part I, p. 727, *et seq.*

contenting himself with a paragraph on Slidell's offensive utterance. The theme of the greater part of the speech may be best stated by Benjamin himself:

"Sir, it has been urged on more than one occasion, in the discussions here and elsewhere, that Louisiana stands on an exceptional footing. It has been said that whatever may be the rights of the states that were original parties to the Constitution—even granting *their* right to resume, for sufficient cause, those restricted powers which they delegated to the general government in trust for their own use and benefit— still Louisiana can have no such right, because *she* was acquired by purchase. Gentlemen have not hesitated to speak of the sovereign states formed out of the territory ceded by France as property bought with the money of the United States, belonging to them as purchasers; and although they have not carried their doctrine to its legitimate results, I must conclude that they also mean to assert, on the same principle, *the right of selling for a price that which for a price was bought.*

"I shall not pause to comment on this repulsive dogma of a party which asserts the right of property in free-born white men, in order to reach its cherished object of destroying the right of property in slave-born black men; still less shall I detain the Senate in pointing out how shadowy the distinction between the condition of the servile African and that to which the white freemen of my state would be reduced, if it indeed be true that they are bound to this government by ties that cannot be legitimately dissevered, without the consent of that very majority which wields its powers for their oppression. I simply deny the fact on which the argument is founded. I deny that the province of Louisiana, or the people of Louisiana, were ever conveyed to the United States for a price as property that could be bought or sold at will. Without entering into the details of the negotiation, the archives of our State Department show the fact to be, that although the domain, the public lands, and other property of France in the ceded province, were conveyed by absolute title to the United States, *the sovereignty was not conveyed otherwise than in trust.* . . . What is the express language of the treaty ? 'The inhabitants of the ceded territory *shall be incorporated in the Union* of the United States and admitted *as soon as possible*, according to the principles of the Federal Constitution, to the enjoyment of *all* the rights, advantages, and immunities of citizens of the United States; and in the meantime they shall be maintained and *protected* in the enjoyment of their liberty, *property*, and the religion which they profess.'"

The basis of his argument is thus strong historically as against those who held that the states of the Louisiana Purchase had less right than any of the original thirteen to "resume the powers delegated to the general government." We cannot follow him as he develops his defense; but one fine outburst near the end must be cited.

"We are told that . . . the South is in rebellion without cause, and that her citizens are traitors. Rebellion ! The very word is a confession; an avowal of tyranny, outrage, and oppression. It is taken from the despot's code, and has no terror for other than slavish souls. When, sir, did millions of people, as a single man, rise in organized, deliberate, unimpas-

sioned rebellion against justice, truth, and honor?
Well did a great Englishman exclaim on a similar
occasion: 'You might as well tell me that they re-
belled against the light of heaven; that they rejected
the fruits of the earth. Men do not war against their
benefactors; they are not mad enough to repel the
instincts of self-preservation. I pronounce fearlessly
that no intelligent people ever rose, or ever will rise,
against a sincere, rational, and benevolent authority.
No people were ever born blind. Infatuation is not a
law of human nature. When there is a revolt by a
free people, with the common consent of all classes of
society, there must be a *criminal* against whom that
revolt is aimed.'

"Traitors! Treason! Ay, sir, the people of the
South imitate and glory in just such treason as glowed
in the soul of Hampden; just such treason as leaped in
living flame from the impassioned lips of Henry; just
such treason as encircles with a sacred halo the undy-
ing name of Washington!"

With this last vigorous appeal of the eloquent champion of the South, we close his career in the Senate of
the United States, a career that rendered his name
illustrious, that reflected honor on his state, and that
was long remembered as phenomenal. Senator Vest[1]
relates that, years afterward, he asked an old reporter
of the Senate who was the best equipped member of
that body he had ever known. "By all odds," he
said, "Mr. Benjamin, of Louisiana."

But before we undertake to follow him in the
stormy course of the next few years, let us for the sake
of simple justice to the honorable men who took part in

[1] Philadelphia *Saturday Evening Post.*

the Southern cause, and who conscientiously believed they were right, try to get rid of the notion that there was something monstrously wrong, some great crime in the mere fact that the South simply did not want to be any longer part and parcel of a government whose policies and whose acts she did not relish.   An unsuccessful revolution always needs all the apologies it can procure at the hands of the historian; therefore I do not fear misconception of my motives when I venture to state that there was no "crime of '61"; that there was no conspiracy of Southern politicians to wreck the Union, but a popular movement for separation too powerful to be resisted; and that it is the duty of the New South, while recognizing fully and cheerfully that the outcome was for the ultimate good of us all, to protest against the habit of holding up Southern leaders as horrible examples.   The war settled vexed questions, and in the best way, forever; the Union was not made to be broken, for

"Our Union is river, lake, ocean, and sky,
    Man breaks not the medal, when God cuts the die!"

But let us not be unjust to the civil leaders of the South any more than to those who led her marvelous armies.

CHAPTER IX

FROM Washington, Benjamin, a little apprehensive that he might be arrested if he lingered at the capital, hastened back to his home. Without his own consent, he had already been mentioned as a delegate to the Montgomery Convention of the seceded states, but received only a scattering vote, not being seriously considered as a candidate.[1] He had not long been at home before a country newspaper,[2] perhaps unaware of the fact that Benjamin was constitutionally ineligible as being of foreign birth, had hoisted on its front page a banner proclaiming its choice for executive officers of the yet unborn Confederacy: For President, Robert Toombs, of Georgia; for Vice-President, J. P. Benjamin, of Louisiana. Can one fancy a man of Benjamin's energy content to subside into a position of such hopeless inaction as that of the Vice-President? But he would not have been eligible, even if he had been willing to accept such an office. At first, on his return, he devoted himself to private affairs; to setting in order the business from which he knew he would soon be called. His reputation for fluency of speech brought him once more before the citizens of New Orleans, when, on the 22d of February, 1861, he made his last public address there; and in it, we are glad to say,

[1] *True Delta*, Jan. 30, 31.
[2] Bastrop *Weekly Dispatch*, quoted in *Delta*, Feb. 21.

there is no cheap flattery of the people's vanity, such as too many orators were then indulging in, but the truth as he saw it. A memorable occasion it was to all who know the story of Louisiana's sons in the great battles that were soon to follow. For on this anniversary of Washington's birth, the Washington Artillery, its laurels yet unwon, was to receive a flag on behalf of the ladies of New Orleans, who had made it. As Mr. Benjamin, now no longer a senator of the United States, delivered his address to the proud young soldiers, and conjured them to defend this flag with the courage befitting gallant men, he did not forget in this hour of easy gratulation to emphasize the fact that they would have need of all their courage in the coming war. "I speak, gentlemen," he said, "in the belief that our independence is not to be maintained without the shedding of our blood. I know that the conviction is not shared by others. Heaven grant that I may prove mistaken. Yet fearful as is the ordeal, and much as war is to be deplored, it is not the unmixed evil which many consider it to be."[1]

It seems a work of supererogation, and fatuously wearisome withal, to continue to pile up evidence that Benjamin knew there was going to be war. But we must remember, in the first place, how difficult it is for us to divest ourselves of the knowledge of the event. We know there was a war; but in February, 1861, nay, even in March and April, there were many in each section who thought there would be none. There were many braggarts, on each side, who with brazen vociferousness assured their people that the other side would not dare fight. It is just another exhibition of Southern

[1] *Delta*, Feb. 24 ; cf. March 26.

bluster, intended to scare us into more abject submission, said some at the North. The cowardly Yankees won't fight, and if they dare do so, one gallant gentleman is a match for five or six of the low-born counterjumpers, said many at the South. And the North, in the flush of victory, has forgotten these false prophets in her own household. The South, however, in the bitterness of defeat, has not forgotten that siren voices sang so false and flattering a song to her. And the result has been rather indiscriminate condemnation of all the politicians alike. Among them all, I fancy, Alexander Stephens is alone unharmed by this hasty judgment. Therefore it seems somewhat needful, even at the risk of appearing tedious, to show that Benjamin, at least, neither deceived his people nor was deceived himself.

In the midst of all this political excitement the course of life went on much as usual for Benjamin's sisters in the home in Nashville Avenue. Mrs. Levy could perceive that "J. P." was deeply interested in and excited by the situation. She must have felt sure that some part, and that no inconspicuous one, in the new government would fall to him; but he kept his own counsel for the present,—came and went as of old, though less frequently at this busy time, and was as cheerful and unconcerned as if there were ample assurance of peace and prosperity. At length, just after the address to the Washington Artillery, his sisters noticed him packing his belongings as if for a prolonged journey. When all was ready, he told them that he had been called to Montgomery to consult with Mr. Davis, and that he anticipated some service under the new government that would probably so occupy his time as to make it impossible for him to see much of them. It was known that Montgomery would hardly continue to be the capital of the Confederacy after the expected secession of Virginia; and so he did not wish them to move there. He explained that, in any event, his means were certain to be curtailed for a time, but provided amply for their present needs. They might, if they wished, leave New Orleans; but he advised against it, considering the city absolutely secure against attack, and adding that it would be easier for him to care for them and to communicate with them there than in some place where they had no friends. And so, bidding all an affectionate farewell, with hope of returning, if but for a brief visit now and then, he left them. It was the last time they ever saw him. For he was too busy to return in the first days of the Confederacy; and then it so turned out within little more than a year that New Orleans would not have given cordial greeting to her great lawyer, while afterward came the years of desperation when it was impossible for him to leave Richmond but as a fugitive from the land.

Mrs. Levy, however, was a capable woman, and not afraid of being left to hold her own in New Orleans. Her brother had given her sufficient money for comfort, if not for luxury, and would supply more as necessity arose from time to time. She could manage and practice economy if need be. No doubt she found the truth of what Mrs. Benjamin wrote when her husband preached more thrift: : "Oh, talk not to me of economy! it is so fatiguing." But she did not say so; and she and her daughter and sister weathered the storm in New Orleans as long as they were allowed to keep the roof over their heads. We shall catch another glimpse of the household when that city is lost to the Confederacy.

The *Delta* of February 26th announced Benjamin's nomination as Attorney-General of the Confederacy. We can agree with the editor that it was, seemingly, a most excellent choice on the part of Mr. Davis; as a matter of fact, however, it was a waste of good material. The President, long used to the customs of political patronage at Washington, and now doubly anxious to attach to his government as many of the states as possible, while pacifying as many of his political opponents as possible, selected his first cabinet rather with a view to political effect than to executive efficiency. The men chosen were not incapable; but it may be doubted if any one of them really fitted the executive department over which he was called to preside at a time when only peculiar fitness and talent could achieve success; and it is absolutely certain that several of them could not work in harmony with the President or with one another as an advisory council. Looking at this body of advisers, manifestly ill at ease in one another's society and representing widely different political views on all but the cardinal point of secession, one is reminded of the good Washington's unhappy experiment, the cabinet in which political differences, wicked and dangerous to the peace of America, were completely ignored. Mr. Davis, in his *Rise and Fall*, gives a brief statement of his reasons for the selections he made. Not one of those chosen could have been called a close friend, or even a conspicuous political ally of the President. It is apparent that he was solicitous to secure men of respectable ability, but above all to distribute the cabinet positions as equitably as might be among the states and the political factions. In this he was but following the precedent often set in the United States—Lincoln's first cabinet was so composed—and followed with safety; but such a composite group, perhaps only useless and powerless to harm when there was no occasion for more than ordinary efficiency, could work great injury at a time like the present. Though all of its members were men of some ability, though most of them had had considerable experience in legislation, not one had had any experience of executive affairs; they were all more used to arguing a case or debating a bill than to carrying out executive plans with promptness and decision.

The composition of the cabinet, then, was not fortunate. It was a pity to see a man of such capacity as Benjamin wasting his time in the child's play of Attorney-General to a government that scarcely had any courts. Beyond giving an occasional opinion to some executive officer, a matter of minutes to so ready a man, he was idle, so far as the duties of his own almost superfluous department are concerned: *Inter arma silent leges.* We shall therefore have no official action of moment to record.

Mr. Benjamin was thus frequently called upon by the President to undertake services sometimes apparently trifling, but requiring tact and delicacy. It fell to his lot to receive and entertain visitors with whom there was nothing else to do, inquisitive foreigners, or importunate office-seekers. There were plenty of the latter at Montgomery as well as at Washington; one recalls Lincoln's whimsical remark, that he felt like a man letting lodgings at one end of his house while the other was on fire. And so Mr. Davis was dogged by relentless would-be generals who had innumerable hosts of gallant and totally unequipped and undisciplined soldiers to offer; or inventors who had new weapons of destruction. Benjamin, being always affable and a good conversationalist, probably succeeded better in disposing of these people without offense than his more peremptory chief; besides he was generally accessible, and could spare more time than other prominent members of the government.

It is interesting to compare the impression he made upon two of the rather notable visitors to Montgomery, both of whom came with intent to take notes and print. Mr. W. H. Russell, the correspondent of the London *Times*, saw various members of the Confederate government on May 9th,[1] and was seemingly more favorably impressed by Benjamin than by any one else; he had more of the manner and bearing of a man of the world. And yet Russell obviously has some distrust of the "short, stout man, with a full face, olive-colored, and most decidedly Jewish features, with the brightest black eyes, one of which is somewhat diverse from the other, and a brisk, lively, agreeable manner, combined with much vivacity of speech, and quickness of utterance." He finds "Mr. Benjamin . . . the most open, frank, and cordial of the Confederates." But he rather hints that frankness and cordiality too closely border on indiscretion in speech, since, "in a few seconds he was telling me all about the course of government with respect to privateers

[1] *Diary*, Vol. II, pp. 252–256.

and letters of marque and reprisal, in order probably
to ascertain what were our views in England on the
subject"—which, in fact, he did, without telling Mr.
Russell any more than he could have got out of any
newspaper.

The other observer of the time, though not so finished
a writer as the English correspondent, is really one of
the most entertaining and useful of those who have left a
record of the impression made by current events in the
Confederacy. Mr. J. B. Jones, author of *A Rebel War
Clerk's Diary*, is very honest, devotedly loyal to the
South, and full of shrewdness; but he is likewise
narrow-minded, and intensely conceited in that seemingly modest way which affects extreme humility. It
is easy to allow the proper discount in his criticism of
the leaders, and so discounted his comments are very
valuable. He came to Montgomery, as he frankly
tells us, with the deliberate purpose of getting some
subordinate position in an important department,
where his facilities for observation might be good, and
of publishing the results of this microscopic study of
the Confederacy in book form when the war was over.
If the good man did not take himself quite so seriously,
there would be something almost uncanny about this
plan and the deliberateness with which it was carried
out.

At first Jones's comments are very favorable to
Mr. Benjamin; but something seems to have turned
him against the Jewish lawyer, whose religion, or race,
rankles in the writer's breast. The tendency to flattery on Mr. Benjamin's part, and the ease with which
his subject succumbed, is amusingly manifested in this
passage, under date of May 21, 1861, at Montgomery :

"I am necessarily making many new acquaintances, and quite a number recognize me by my books which they have read. Among this class is Mr. Benjamin, the minister of justice, who, to-day, informed me that he and Senator Bayard had been interested, at Washington, in my 'Story of Disunion.'"

Events were hastening on, during this time of comparative inactivity for Mr. Benjamin, with a speed that no Congressional action could longer hope to arrest. Three weeks before Lincoln, the untried Westerner at whose presumptive ignorance or radicalism the cultured East trembled, could be installed in office, the Confederates had inaugurated their President and Vice-President, both men of national prominence. At once, too, the Provisional Congress of the Confederacy, which Stephens[1] pronounced as able and conservative a body as he was ever associated with, had proceeded to pass the necessary measures not only for civil organization but also for military preparation in the face of the great war that their President anticipated. There has long been much dispute—what have they not disputed about?—among Confederate writers as to whether the Executive was energetic enough in pushing these preparations. One fairly moderate example may be referred to among the published articles—Mr. Rhett, in *Battles and Leaders of the Civil War*.[2] Another, not in print, has come to my notice recently, and may be cited as a typical illustration of the freakish injustice of memory and gossip.

Judge D. M. Shelby, of the United States Circuit

[1] See *War Between the States*, Vol. II, p. 325; Johnston and Browne, pp. 392, 414.
[2] Vol. I, p. 108.

Court, and formerly a partner of Leroy P. Walker, first Secretary of War under the Confederacy, relates[1] an interesting story in regard to the views of the cabinet and of Mr. Davis before the outbreak of hostilities. Mr. Walker was in the old Exchange Hotel, at Montgomery, one day, and pointed out to Judge Shelby the room near the parlor in which the first Confederate council was held, indicating even the relative positions of the ministers and the President. "At that time," said Mr. Walker, "I, like everybody else, believed there would be no war. In fact, I had gone about the state advising people to secede, and promising to wipe up with my pocket-handkerchief all the blood that would be shed. When this cabinet meeting was held, there was only one man there who had any sense, and that man was Benjamin. Mr. Benjamin proposed that the government purchase as much cotton as it could hold, at least 100,000 bales, and ship it at once to England. With the proceeds of a part of it he advised the immediate purchase of at least 150,000 stand of small arms, and guns and munitions in corresponding amounts—I forget the exact figures. The residue of the cotton was to be held as a basis for credit. For, said Benjamin, we are entering on a contest that must be long and costly. All the rest of us fairly ridiculed the idea of a serious war. Well, you know what happened."

Now there is no reason to question that Mr. Walker was honestly relating things as he remembered them; but this conversation took place many years after the events to which it referred. As a consequence, some of

---

[1] Conversation with the writer.

the statements are undoubtedly correct, others may be correct, and some are almost as certainly incorrect. There is no question about the "pocket-handkerchief" speeches, for example, of which Mr. Walker has the courage to feel a little ashamed. There is every probability that Benjamin, whose opinion we know from other sources, and who was perhaps more familiar than the rest with the great cotton trade, did present some such scheme as that suggested. The plan, too, if so presented, was likely elaborated with all of that skill at discounting the future that had enabled Benjamin to build enchanting air castles out of Tehuantepec. It is improbable that a course of action so highly desirable and prudent was rejected by all of the men present at that meeting for the reason suggested by Mr. Walker. They rejected it, no doubt, but for other and sufficient reasons, as I think, and probably not without regret. Mr. Davis, like Benjamin, felt certain that there would be war; and though he, as well as everybody else on both sides, failed to conceive of the magnitude and desperation of the contest, he had the professional soldier's instinct to lead him to desire as much as he could get in the way of military equipment. He would not have rejected Benjamin's suggestion if it had been practicable. We can only guess, of course, at the reason for the failure to act out some such policy on the part of the Confederate government; but it seems to me decidedly unfair to make a guess that exalts Benjamin at the expense of others, his associates, in a way that he would never have approved. The reasonable and sufficient ground for the rejection of this plan, if such a plan was proposed by Benjamin, is given by Captain

Bulloch.[1] The South had no shipping of her own; as soon as hostilities became imminent, neutral traders and those from Northern ports made haste to load and get away from Southern ports, lest they be seized. For two months prior to the firing on Sumter, according to Captain Bulloch's narrative, it would have been barely possible to get together enough vessels to carry out any considerable quantity of cotton on government account; and after that fatal shot, the vessels in Confederate harbors falling into the hands of the authorities were but a handful.

In an agricultural nation undertaking a great war under modern conditions, innumerable things, and immense quantities of them, had to be provided. Considering the energy and the pertinacity with which they carried on the government and the war afterward, it would require overwhelming proofs to convince us that the Confederate authorities did not make every effort they knew how to have the South in readiness in the interval before Fort Sumter fell. When that event came, perhaps by a hasty action for which the cabinet was not to blame,[2] they were not fully prepared; yet the wonder is not that they had accomplished so little, but so very much, in the way of preparation. And they acted with promptness so soon as the first blow was struck. For reasons stated by Mr. Davis in his book, and which seem valid enough, the Confederate government hastened to move to Richmond as soon as Virginia seceded. On the way there the President, Mr. Benjamin, and other members of the government addressed the people in

[1] *Secret Service of the Confederacy*, Vol. I, p. 20, *et seq.*
[2] See Rhodes, Vol. III, p. 351.

speeches of optimistic tone, according to the meagre press dispatches of the day, promising vigorous action "to expel the invader from our soil."

During the weeks of feverish mustering of troops that followed, Benjamin had little to do; his legal opinion was sometimes called for on the constitutionality of acts of the executive departments. But in the stress of war it soon became manifest that niceties of legal discrimination must be swept aside. Whether the proposed act were quite regular or not, it must be performed ; there must be no delay. In this interval when the lawyer found little need for his services, the other qualities of the man were revealed to Mr. Davis. The ever-watchful Jones noticed very soon that Benjamin was particularly in the President's good graces. Thus when the anxious group of high officials waited about the War Department telegraph office on the night of July 21st, he reports[1] that it is Mr. Benjamin who goes to Mrs. Davis at the Spottswood Hotel and returns with a soul-gladdening message from her husband on the battle-field of the first Manassas. It is Benjamin, too, who repeats the inspiring news to the reporters from memory, while his "face glowed something like Daniel Webster's after taking a pint of brandy." It is he, too, who brings a special verbal message from the President to the Secretary of War about two Northern gentlemen who had come within the Confederate lines at Manassas to look for the body of Colonel Cameron, and not under a flag of truce lest this should be construed into a recognition of the "rebels." And then (August 10), "Mr. Benjamin is a frequent visitor at the depart-

[1] Vol. I, pp. 64, 68, 71.

ment, and is very sociable; some intimations have been thrown out that he aspires to become, some day, Secretary of War. Mr. Benjamin, unquestionably, will have great influence with the President, for he has studied his character most carefully. He will be familiar not only with his likes, but especially with his 'dislikes.'"

With due allowance for this observer's anti-Semitic squint, and consequent suspicion of Benjamin, I should fancy there was truth in his suggestion that the latter had made a study of the President's character, and exerted himself to win favor. Whatever may be said of Jefferson Davis's abilities, statesmanship, devotion to public duty, and wealth of private virtues, he possessed some traits which were the very manifestation of the sincerity and honesty of the man, but which brought upon him much superficial and undeserved censure. Take him all in all, it is extremely doubtful if the Confederacy could have found a leader more suitably endowed for the military dictatorship to which its government must tend. The necessities of the situation constrained Davis to be autocratic,[1] just as similar conditions constrained Lincoln to be similarly autocratic. It was essential that colleagues in the government and officers in the army, should be absolutely subordinate and obedient to the Executive.

Again a little reflection will plainly show that of both sides this is equally true; and it is not difficult to parallel Joseph E. Johnston with McClellan, or Lee with Grant, to show that, with the first pair, the prime cause of trouble was disagreement with the Executive, while with the second the secret of success was being

---

[1] But see below, Chapter XIII.

in harmony. Of course, such a parallel is misleading if blindly followed; we do not mean to compare the men named in any way but with regard to their relations with the Presidents. Not only did Mr. Davis find it necessary, therefore, to rule with vigor or not rule at all, but his military education and predilections made the habit of command second nature. He was really of most kind disposition, but extremely reserved and severe of manner. I think the unprejudiced historian must pronounce Mr. Davis superior to any member of his cabinet in the essential qualities needed for his difficult position; but some of them did not think thus, and resented firm control, which was indispensable, as capricious and even haughty dictation.

But a few weeks of the intimate and difficult relations of the cabinet officers to the President were needed to develop this opinion in recalcitrant or insubordinate members of the new government. It was natural, therefore, that Benjamin's urbanity, and his thorough realization of the proper relations of a cabinet officer to his chief, should have won Mr. Davis's gratitude and favor, while his unusual abilities soon likewise gained the confidence of the President. Bound up, heart and soul, in what people reverently called "the cause," Mr. Benjamin was quite willing to serve loyally in any sort of capacity; willing to defer to the opinion of his leader for the good of that cause. He did not always agree with Mr. Davis; but when his opinion was overruled, he neither lost his temper and resigned his post, nor nursed injured pride in sulky and reluctant obedience. His advice was shrewd and prudent, urged with cogency of reasoning and tact. He was always cheerful, generally sanguine,

capable of an amazing amount of hard work, method-
ical and prompt. It is not to be wondered at, therefore, that Mr. Davis found him a most useful member
of the official family, and thought him fitted for almost
any post in it.

The battle of Bull Run by itself was sufficient to
demonstrate that there would be more blood shed than
many handkerchiefs could wipe up. Secretary Walker
found himself unequal to the strain imposed by his
duties,—overwhelmed by the mass of unfamiliar detail, and restive under the inevitable complaints and
the bickering of officers. Early in the fall there
began to be rumors that he would retire, and that
Benjamin would succeed him. And on September
17th, Walker having resigned, Benjamin was officially
appointed Secretary of War, *ad interim*, acting also as
Attorney-General until November 15th.[1]

Jones, now to have close relations with the new
secretary, remarks on September 16th :[2] "Mr. Benjamin's hitherto perennial smile faded almost away as
he realized the fact that he was now the most important member of the cabinet. He well knew how ardu-
ous the duties were; but then he was in robust health,
and capable of any amount of labor." And he adds :
"It seems, after all, that Mr. Benjamin is only acting
Secretary of War, until the President can fix upon another. Can that be the reason his smile has faded
almost away? But the President will appoint him.
Mr. Benjamin will please him; he knows how to do
it." And the New Orleans *Delta*,[3] though also rather

[1] *Official Records*, Series IV, Vol. I, pp. 614, 957.
[2] Vol I, p. 79.
[3] Sept. 28.

prejudiced against Mr. Benjamin, had a letter from
its correspondent at Richmond a week later, saying :
"The good effects of his presence in the War Department are already exhibited in his administration as
compared with that of his predecessor. The duties of
the War Department are, of course, excessively ardu-
ous and unremittant ; but Mr. Benjamin manages to
fulfil them all without exciting complaints of delay.
. . . He determines every question submitted to him
with the promptness and the accuracy characteristic
of his mind, while at the same time he exhibits administrative capacity of a high order and great organizing talents."

There can be no question of Benjamin's tireless industry, or of the good results to be anticipated from
habits of precision and systematic care in the war
office. Probably at no time during his life, with the
possible exception of the first years of trial in New
Orleans, had he worked so hard. Various accounts
are given of the hours he kept at his desk ; one would
fancy that he toiled from early morn till midnight, day
in and day out, with not even time for meals ; but the
fact is that Benjamin was far too sensible to waste his
energies, and the amount of work he managed to perform is far more to the point than the time he took to
do it. Under his supervision the department was
thoroughly organized for efficient service at headquarters. The immense masses of correspondence, which
had formerly been allowed to accumulate till confusion
and despair reigned, were disposed of on the day of
their receipt, if that were humanly possible. Long letters, that consumed the time of the secretary in the
writing and of his clerks in the copying, were eschewed ;

if such replies could not be avoided, and the matters were important, telegraphic answers at least were sent at once. Now every one was assigned his duty, and the secretary expected him to perform that duty. By these simple means he managed to save himself fruitless drudgery, while leaving more time for the multifarious larger problems that might and must quite properly engage the attention of a minister. But he saw to it that every letter or communication, no matter how silly, received some sort of answer. Thus, to a foolish attorney for certain "bold and daring spirits on our western border," who inquired concerning the legal possibilities of getting letters of marque to prey upon the enemy's commerce on the Ohio River, the secretary replied :[1] "In regard to the project of Mr. Crawford and other 'bold and daring spirits,' I can only say that privateering is of necessity, by the laws of Congress as well as of nations, confined to the high seas, and this service is, moreover, not under the charge of this department."

The routine work of the War Department, however, is not of sufficient interest or importance to tempt us into extended notice of it. Moreover, the President devoted much of his time and attention to the larger problems of strategy, so that these, which might repay study, concern the biographer of Mr. Benjamin very little. Neither will it suit us to chronicle the still unsettled disputes that arose between the government and its generals in the field ; or rather, we must chronicle,

[1] *Official Records*, Series IV, Vol. I, p. 669. Cf. p. 1008, for refusal to organize guerrilla companies, which " are not recognized as part of the military organization of the Confederate States, and cannot be authorized by this department."

but not discuss them. With Beauregard, and especially
with Joseph E. Johnston, Mr. Davis had quarrels, in
which there was some right on each side, and which
each side has fought out in print in a fashion that
quite relieves us of that unpleasant task. Suffice it to
say that Benjamin supported Mr. Davis. But one of
these disputes with officers of the army, since it concerns a general of such insignificance that we may fearlessly suppress his name, will serve to illustrate both
the difficulty of dealing with these absurdly sensitive
gentlemen, and one of Benjamin's faults as Secretary
of War.

This incident brings out the insolent wrath of a jealous brigadier-general, who had expected to be made
a major-general, and who resigned in a huff when
he failed of this. He wrote[1] at some length to the
Secretary of War, paying a glowing tribute to himself,
and stating that although he had been for months at
the front, almost every mail brought news of his being
overslaughed by some officer whom he "ranked in the
old service" of the United States ; that the last straw
had come in the appointment as major-general of "a
New York office-holder," and that he would "not con-
descend to submit any longer to the insults and indignities of the Executive." To this Benjamin replied
with justice, but without tact : "It is due to self-
respect that I should remark on the impropriety of
your using this department as a channel for conveying
disrespectful and insulting comments on the commander-in-chief of the army and the chief magistrate
of the Confederacy. His sole offense, according to
the statements of your letter, consists in not *selecting*

[1] Correspondence in the papers, as *True Delta*, Nov. 1 and 6.

you to be a major-general, for there is no question
of promotion involved in the appointment of major-
generals. The law expressly vests in him the power
to *choose* officers to command brigades and divisions,
and it is no disparagement to any officer, whatever
may have been his services, that the President prefers
another as a division commander. Your statement,
therefore, that you have been overslaughed, and that
you have been subjected 'to the insults and indignities' of the Executive, is based on a total misappre-
hension of his duties and your rights, according to the
laws which govern the army. Your communication
has been submitted to the President, and, by his direction, your resignation has been accepted."

Of this officer's merit and capacities we know, and
care very little; the one preferred to him did not,
indeed, prove himself very deserving. But Benjamin's
reply was ill-advised. Its tone is very severe, however justly so. And it gave the indignant officer a
chance to write another letter, which he did. One is
reminded of Mrs. Davis's comment on the secretary : [1]
"Each time that he had an angry contest with any of
his colleagues, some one was sure to say : 'How can
any one get provoked with Mr. Benjamin? he is so
gentle and courteous.' In fact the truth was that
Mr. Benjamin's courtesy in argument was like the
salute of the duelist to his antagonist whom he intends to kill if possible. He was master of the art of
inductive reasoning, and when he had smilingly established his point he dealt the *coup de grace* with a fierce
joy which his antagonist fully appreciated and resented. I never knew him in those days to be very

---

[1] Letter in *Lawley MS.*, June 8, 1898.

much in earnest without infuriating his antagonist beyond measure. Mr. Slidell, who loved him like a brother, once said to Mr. Davis, 'When I do not agree with Benjamin, I will not let him talk to me; he irritates me so by his debonair ways.'" He did not forget or lay aside the training and habits of the bar and the Senate when acting as Secretary of War, and could not forego the delightful chance to make remarks that, however just and convincing, were sarcastic and often exasperating. Much of this comment has not been preserved save in the gossip of the time, and therefore we may not record it as of reliable authority; but it seems to me that there is a touch of contemptuous sarcasm even in a reply which he submitted to a resolution of Congress asking what means were needed for the prosecution of the war. We need, he says,[1] 350,000 additional men, 500,000 rifles, over 1,000 pieces of field artillery, 2,000 tons of powder, and $200,-000,000; and since all these things are beyond our reach, he presumes Congress wants to know what is practicable: "If I am right in this conclusion, then I respectfully answer that the great deficiency under which we suffer is the want of small arms and powder. . . . In a word, what we need is the 'material' of war."

Always indifferent to the clamors of the press, and now feeling perfectly secure in the support of the President, Benjamin doubtless made himself even more unpopular than his necessarily unpopular duties required. Jones, scenting disaster to the Confederate arms, declares in January, 1862,[2] "There is no *entente cordiale*

[1] *Official Records*, Series IV, Vol. I, p. 970.
[2] Vol. I, p. 103.

between Mr. Benjamin and any of our best generals."
With such a feeling abroad against him, whether justified or not, his usefulness in his present position would
be at an end unless some signal victory in the field
should restore public confidence. But the reports of
the Secretary of War showed conditions to be anything but reassuring. With scarcely enough inferior
and antiquated muskets on hand to fit out an additional
regiment, he is badgered by state governors and officers
of the army to supply arms. What a sigh of relief when
the precious cargo of the *Gladiator*,[1] containing a few
thousand stand of arms, is safely brought through the
blockade, having been reshipped at Nassau on several
smaller and swifter vessels that might outrun the
active Yankee gunboats. For nearly three months,
Benjamin says, we have been waiting for these Enfield
rifles, have promised them to eager soldiers, and could
make use of several hundred thousand more. We
vigorously set about manufacturing muskets, guns,
powder, and with some success, considering the dearth
of mechanics and of necessary materials. We appoint,
on the secretary's recommendation, special officers to
investigate the supplies of nitre and saltpetre in the
Confederacy; to suggest means of supplementing and
improving them. But we must already, before the
first half-year of the blockade is over, offer blockade-
runners a profit of fifty per centum over the cost of
the articles specially named, with reimbursement of
all charges for "freight, drayage, package, and cost
of loading at the port of departure. . . . For
freight you will be allowed twice the current rates of
freight from the port of loading to the port of Havana.

[1] *Official Records*, Series IV, Vol. I, pp. 800, 985, etc.

. . . Payment to be made to you on arrival and delivery of cargo in a Confederate port in good order, . . . in cotton at current market prices." And in the list of articles for which these extraordinary sums will be paid, one finds not only arms and munitions of various kinds but such things as bar steel, nitric acid, sulphuric acid, and even "leather suitable for harness and bridles." One heartily sympathizes with the difficulties and the perplexities of the Secretary of War:

"When it is considered that the government of the United States—with all its accumulation of arms for half a century, and all its workshops and arsenals, public and private, and its untrammeled intercourse with foreign nations—has recently been compelled to disband a number of cavalry regiments on account of the difficulty of arming them, and has been driven to the necessity of making purchases of arms in Europe in very large quantities, and of saltpetre by thousands of tons, some faint idea may be formed of the difficulties against which this department has been and is now struggling in the effort to furnish arms and munitions for our troops. The difficulty is not in the want of legislation. Laws cannot suddenly convert farmers into gunsmiths. Our people are not artisans, except to a very limited degree. In the very armory here at Richmond the production could be greatly increased if skilled labor could be procured. In the absence of home manufactures no recourse remains but importation, and with our commerce substantially at an end with foreign nations the means of importation are limited." [1]

Meanwhile the winter was passing away with noth-

---

[1] *Official Records*, Series IV, Vol. 1, pp. 760, 768, 790–797, 820, 955–962, 970, 988, *et seq.*

ing but the most blessed inactivity, for the most part, on the Federal side. Joseph E. Johnston, with inferior forces and "Quaker" guns, made of logs, managed to keep a menacing front at Manassas. McClellan accumulated and drilled the largest fighting machine the world had seen since the Crusades, but it was so huge that he feared to use it. Meanwhile, too, the Secretary of War for the Confederacy, straining every nerve to protect the long frontier and the three thousand miles of coast with half a hundred points subject to attack, was pestered with trifling things. Thus there was endless trouble about granting passports to those desiring to go within the Federal lines. At first Benjamin, following his inclination, was liberal in showing this courtesy to "alien enemies." But there were grave political as well as military dangers in such a policy. A considerable section of the more rabid, of whom Jones[1] will serve as an example, cried out against the criminal folly of allowing these men to carry over to the foe their wealth, "the sinews of war." And it was asserted that many spies were allowed passports, only to give information to the enemy. The North had proclaimed that only two parties were there as long as war continued, "patriots and traitors." Many in the South felt the same way. But while opinion sustained the Federal Congress in expelling the demagogue Vallandigham, who furnished a text for patriotic preachment even in fiction, there was less unanimity in the South when the demagogue Brownlow was expelled from Tennessee, to become a martyr in the North.

His case may be summarized as a fair instance of the

[1] See *e. g.*, Vol. I, pp. 80, 89, 93, 97, 102, 105, etc.

leniency with which Benjamin was disposed to act. Being a preacher, Brownlow was debarred the mode of expression that would have best suited his taste; in lieu of profanity, he was driven to such circumlocutions as "that heaven-offending, hell-deserving secessionist, W. L. Yancey," his usual manner of referring to the Alabamian. In language similarly choice, he had expressed his opinions of the Confederacy and its leaders in his paper, the *Knoxville Whig*, until the Confederate forces entering Tennessee drove him to flight and concealment in the mountains. From his place of hiding he sent word to General Crittenden that he would surrender and return to Knoxville to stand trial before the civil authorities for treasonable utterances, if assured of protection against arrest by the military and court martial. General Crittenden accepted this proposition, and, under instructions from Richmond, further assured Brownlow that he would not be prosecuted, but would be simply expelled from the state. Benjamin was at the time acting both as minister of justice and as minister of war, and had been assured by the local prosecuting officers that they would be content to expel Brownlow.

But when he ventured to return, in the bitterness of factional feeling in east Tennessee there was immediate demand for his prosecution, the pledge of General Crittenden was violated, and the vituperative editor was at once cast into prison. The time for his trial coming on, the district attorney produced a letter from Benjamin, as Secretary of War (December 22, 1861), explaining the circumstances, and adding that he regretted the preacher's arrest, since "color is given to the suspicion that Brownlow has been entrapped.

. . . General Crittenden feels sensitive on this point, and I share his feeling. Better that any, the most dangerous enemy, however criminal, should escape, than that the honor and good faith of the government should be impugned or even suspected. General Crittenden gave his word only that Brownlow should not be tried by the court martial, and I gave authority to promise him protection, if he would surrender, to be conveyed across the border. We have both kept our words as far as was in our power, but every one must see that Brownlow would now be safe, and at large, if he had not supposed that his reliance on the promises made him would insure his safe departure from east Tennessee. Under all the circumstances, therefore, if Brownlow is exposed to harm from his arrest, I shall deem the honor of the government so far compromitted as to consider it my duty to urge on the President a pardon for any offense of which he may be found guilty; and I repeat the expression of my regret that he was prosecuted, however evident his guilt.''

Brownlow's very inflammatory editorials, urging the destruction of railway bridges and the burning of the houses of Southern sympathizers, had made the Confederates of the region very bitter against him; but in view of this letter the prosecution was dropped, and he went on his way, still vindictive and defiant. In a public address some months later he gave a graphic account of his experiences, and we must add another sample of his writing. He had been visited in jail by some Confederate officers who suggested that he take the oath to their government. ''Before I would take the oath to support such a hell-forsaken institution, I would suffer myself to rot or die in jail of old age. . . . A short time since I was called upon by a little Jew, who, I believe, is the Secretary of War of the bogus Confederacy. He threatened to hang me, and I expected no more mercy from him than was shown by his illustrious predecessors toward Jesus Christ. I entered into a long correspondence with this specimen of expiring humanity, but from mercy or forgetfulness on their part, I was permitted to depart with all my documents in my little valise, which I hope to publish at no distant day."[1]

The winter, as we have said, had almost worn itself away without any effort to use the immense armies of the North. But though McClellan would lie dormant on the Virginia frontier, there were other danger points for the Confederacy, and from two of these bad news came in February and March. Forts Henry and Donelson, guarding the centre of the long Confederate line, and situated respectively on the Tennessee and Cumberland Rivers where those streams were but eleven miles apart, were of vital importance to the successful operation of General Albert Sidney Johnston's plans in Kentucky and Tennessee. Early in February Grant swooped down upon Fort Henry, which had but a small garrison, and on the 6th telegraphed to Halleck: " Fort Henry is ours. . . . I shall take and destroy Fort Donelson on the 8th." The boast, unlike the self-contained Grant, was made good, but not quite in

[1] Correspondence in *Delta*, Jan. 3, 1862 ; Brownlow's speech, *True Delta*, April 6 ; cf. Nicolay & Hay's *Lincoln*, Vol. V, p. 80. For Benjamin's severe retaliatory order against the Tennessee bridge burners, sharply but I think unjustly criticised in view of similar policies of the Union commanders, see Coffin, *Marching to Victory*, p. 377, and *Official Records*, Series I, Vol. VII, p. 701.

the time he had allowed himself. Though every effort was put forth by General Johnston to strengthen the place, and though he received all the assistance the administration could give him, Fort Donelson surrendered unconditionally on February 16th, with about 12,000 men, forty pieces of artillery, and a large amount of stores. It was the severest blow yet dealt the Confederates, fatal to General Johnston's campaign, and felt as a deep disgrace on account of the conduct of the two senior officers of the garrison, who, after bungling a perfectly feasible and proper plan of retreat, had slipped away and cast upon General Buckner the responsibility of surrender.

The wave of bad news from the West was met by a similar wave from the East, and the two, meeting at Richmond, quite submerged the Secretary of War. The Confederates, having failed in the effort to keep the Federal forces outside of Hatteras, had hastily fortified Roanoke Island, commanding the passage from Pamlico to Albemarle Sound, and thus protecting not only a number of small yet useful ports, but also the approach to Norfolk from the rear. General Benjamin Huger, with about fifteen thousand men and, it was believed, ample supplies, was in command of the department at Norfolk. To General Henry A. Wise was entrusted the task of completing the poor fortifications on the island and defending it. In spite of urgent appeals for help, however, General Wise got but little from the war office or from General Huger. On February 8th the small force on the island was overwhelmed, and most of it captured. The loss in killed and wounded was slight; but a touch of tragedy that was not forgotten was the death of the gallant young

Captain O. Jennings Wise, whose life, so his father and many others thought, had been a mere sacrifice to the incapacity of those who would not supply means adequate to make the defense of the island anything but a farce. The loss of this strategic point, too, was more severe than would appear from the number of troops killed. In its consequences it was, perhaps, more irreparable than the surrender of Donelson and Henry; for the gradual loss of seaports was already making it difficult for the Confederacy to breathe, and would in time shut off the breath of life altogether.

For the loss of the Western forts the government could not receive all of the blame; this was shared by General A. S. Johnston, against whom the fickle and ungrateful press and the demagogues railed atrociously, saddening the short life of one of the most able and chivalrous officers the South produced. But the President and the Secretary of War came in for their part of this undesirable popular attention when they resolutely sustained General Johnston. In the case of Roanoke Island it was clear that General Wise was not at fault. Some other victim must be found, and his rather intemperate talk, coupled with his official report of the loss, pointed to General Huger and Mr. Benjamin. General Wise was something of a popular idol; it was he of whom the current doggerel ran:

> "Old John Brown, down in Harper's Ferry section,
> Went about his ways to raise an insurrection,
> And thought that the niggers would sustain 'im:
> But Old Governor Wise, put his specs upon his eyes,
> And sent him to the happy land o' Canaan."

When he charged, therefore, that neither General

Huger nor the Secretary of War had paid any attention to his requisitions for men and materials and ammunition ; that they had rejected with contempt his recommendations, and with insolence his assurances that Roanoke Island and no other point was the destination of the Federal expedition known to have sailed ; and that the brave men who had fallen—and people remembered that one of them was his own son—had been shamefully sacrificed to incompetence or indifference in high places, all the suppressed fury of press and politicians was turned loose upon Mr. Benjamin and General Huger. Against the former, especially, was their wrath directed, as they diligently searched through every page of his record to discover grounds for the present indictment. A fair sample of the editorial assaults upon Benjamin may be given from one of the milder papers, to show the trend of popular opinion. The Richmond *Examiner*[1] declared that the War Department had been completely taken by surprise in the case of all recent disasters :

"So curious [is] the ignorance and complacency of our government in this matter, that we are advised that, though the defense of Roanoke Island was urged upon the Secretary of War for weeks before the demonstration of the enemy was made, Mr. Benjamin insisted strenuously and to the last moment that Roanoke Island was positively not an object of the enemy's attack, but that a great battle was to come off at Pensacola, for which he was busy in preparation, sending to the gulf coast all the shot, shell, and ammunition that could be gathered. . . . With equal disregard and the same stupid complacency was treated the

[1] Quoted in *True Delta*, March 7.

protest of General Wise, made directly to the government at the time of his taking command of Roanoke Island. These are strange facts; but they are true. It is possible that the persistent delusion of Mr. Benjamin as to the designs of the enemy on the coast may be accounted for on the supposition that his mind was abused by the duplicity of the spies he employs. It is notorious that the easy credulity of the secretary has more than once been imposed upon by double-dealing spies and covert agents of the Lincoln government. . . . We are surprised by each movement of the enemy; the War Department seems to know no more of his plans and intentions than the children in the streets of Richmond; the credulity of its secretary is absolutely astonishing."

In the face of popular distrust so wide-spread, Mr. Benjamin's usefulness as Secretary of War was obviously ended. The voice of the people, besides, found a willing echo in Congress, where a special committee was called to investigate the recent misfortunes and to place the blame. The reports of the officers involved were submitted to this committee, and the secretary himself was summoned to testify. There was little hope in the reports of the officers, in the testimony of the secretary, or in the composition of the committee, that he would be exonerated. Mr. Davis, always doggedly loyal to his subordinates, even at the dear cost of his own popularity, would have ignored even Congressional censure and sustained Benjamin, but finally resolved to outwit rather than directly withstand the assailants. "It is said Mr. Benjamin has been dismissed, or resigned," writes Jones, in glee, on March 27, 1862. But next day he adds, "Mr.

Benjamin has been promoted. He is now Secretary of State." [1] Before the Congressional committee could render its fatal report against Benjamin, he had been wisely transferred to the one department for which, if for any, he was preëminently fit.

As has been anticipated, the finding of the committee was detailed and uncompromising. After a résumé of all the evidence submitted, the report concluded: "General Huger and the Secretary of War paid no practical attention to those urgent appeals of General Wise; sent forward none of his important requisitions; and permitted General Wise and his inconsiderable force to remain to meet at least 15,000 men, well armed and equipped. If the Secretary of War and the commanding general at Norfolk had not the means to reënforce General Wise, why was he not ordered to abandon his position and save his command? But, upon the contrary, he was required to remain and sacrifice his command, with no means in his insulated position to make his escape in case of defeat. The committee, from the testimony, are therefore constrained to report, that whatever of blame and responsibility is justly attributable to any one for the defeat of our troops at Roanoke Island on February 8, 1862, should attach to Major-General Benjamin Huger and the late Secretary of War, J. P. Benjamin." [2]

We must agree, at least in part, with the verdict here rendered, though our reasons for concurrence might be different from those that convinced Congress. Mr. Benjamin, in spite of his undoubted skill and

[1] Vol. I, p. 116.
[2] *Official Records*, Series I, Vol. IX, pp. 183–190; cf. pp. 122, *et seq.*, 132, 141, 164.

services in organizing and directing the routine work of the War Department, certainly had displayed no talent for the larger and more difficult work of planning or assisting in the execution of actual campaigns. He had no victory of importance to grace his administration; and here were two great disasters, to one of which, at least, the secretary had contributed by a serious error of judgment. After the war Mr. Benjamin, in a private letter to Colonel Charles Marshall,[1] furnished an entirely satisfactory and creditable explanation of his failure to respond to General Wise's appeals for ammunition: he had none to send. He had hinted strongly at that fact in one of his first replies to the general, and it is wofully manifest in the reports of the Secretary of War just before and just after the defeat. Mr. Benjamin furthermore states that he and Mr. Davis dared not present to the committee the whole of the facts about the dearth of powder, lest news of the critical condition should leak out and get to the Yankees; that by the President's consent and advice he therefore suppressed the information that would have cleared him. It would be idle to doubt the sincerity of these statements, or the good intentions of Mr. Benjamin; the readiness to shoulder popular odium for the sake of the cause is characteristic and, of course, highly commendable in one whose absolute devotion to that cause none but the unreflecting could question; but the explanation in this letter, which may be found treated in some detail in the *Life of General Wise*, cannot be accepted by us as it apparently is there. In faith, it is no excuse at all for what we consider the most important of Mr.

[1] Quoted in *Life of Wise*, by B. H. Wise, pp. 304–315.

Benjamin's faults as Secretary of War—an error of judgment. Powder or no powder in the supposedly full magazines of General Huger, it was still within the secretary's power, as the report of the committee indicated, to warn General Wise and let him save his command.

CHAPTER X

THE CONFEDERATE COMMISSIONERS

In writing of the period of Mr. Benjamin's life occupied by his incumbency of the office of Secretary of State, I shall endeavor to avoid, as far as possible, being diverted into writing a history of Confederate diplomacy or foreign relations. I shall devote myself, as largely as may be, to Mr. Benjamin's own share in these affairs. But for the coherence and clearness of the narrative, it will be necessary to outline the general course of events, both foreign and domestic, whether or not we momentarily lose sight of him personally.

As regards the general condition of foreign affairs, it becomes at once apparent that only a maritime and trading nation, with considerable commerce and a respectable navy to protect it, could be of service to the blockaded Confederacy with cotton to sell. Such nations were not numerous. In fact, since we are not attempting more than a sketch, we need mention only three from which there might be possibility of succor —Spain, France, and England. The first named, although still a slave power and therefore at first thought less likely to be hostile, could hardly be expected to be friendly to the new nation whose citizens, in the past, had been persistent filibusters. Therefore the ablest representations of a change of sentiment, now that the South was independent of the North, had no weight with Spain. Since her distrust could not be overcome, France and England alone remained, and with them the Confederacy sought to establish relations. It has been suggested that, with a Benjamin Franklin to help, it might have been possible for the Confederacy to succeed in its revolution, through foreign aid, just as the Colonies succeeded in their revolution. But a glance at history should suffice to establish the fact that this is a misleading parallel to draw between the relations of Europe and the English Colonies in 1778, and Europe and the Confederacy in 1860. Without going into details, we should note that in 1778 the traditional enemies, England and France, were still enemies; France, moreover, smarting under her loss of colonial power to England, especially in Canada, hailed with eagerness the proffered chance to deal a telling stroke that might cut off the American Colonies from perfidious Albion. France, too, was then still the leading power of the continent, with Spain, as it were, in tow, and lesser nations hardly to be considered. Leaving out of consideration all other differences, it is sufficient for our purpose to note that in 1860, France and England were on the friendliest terms; that there was no hope of fomenting the jealousy or the cupidity or the love of revenge of one against the other; and that France, no longer assured of her preëminence in Europe, could not have interposed with the same effectiveness, even had she cared to act independently of England.

What had been done by the Confederate government to make friends for itself, if none such kindly volunteered to speak first? Our answer involves the restatement of many facts that are very familiar, but not to be overlooked. It must be confessed that the Confederates had so far proceeded in a fashion likely to repel rather than to encourage alliance with foreign powers. There was among many of the leaders of the new nation an arrogant assumption that the old world must come and make suit to the Confederacy for its friendship. The more rational among them understood enough of the relations between peoples to know that such a feeling followed common interest and reciprocal advantage; that pure sentiment had never, perhaps, hurried even the most emotional and romantic of peoples into alliances that must involve costly war; in short, that there must be a *quid pro quo* to secure any alliance. They had something to give, namely, cotton; and they estimated too highly its value to the world. Cotton was indispensable to England, they said, and perhaps also to France; cotton was king. Being an agricultural people, and meaning, as soon as the war should be ended, to establish practical free trade, they thought that the precious privileges of buying their cotton and selling them in return the manufactured articles they would need, should be sufficient inducement to secure the friendship of England and of France. They forgot, apparently, that, granted the establishment of their Confederacy, a very large part of their needs could and would be more cheaply supplied by the neighboring manufacturing states of the North[1] than by any foreign competitor,—a consideration that probably did not escape France and England. They were therefore offering but a doubtful advantage in trade, and no other could be thought of. This was understood to be the true state of affairs by some, at least, of the public men at the South.[2]

[1] Cf. Benjamin to Mason, Dec. 11, 1862; see Mason, p. 360 *et seq.*
[2] Cf. *Battles and Leaders*, Vol. I, p. 108.

But the government with which Mr. Benjamin was associated proceeded for some time upon the assumption that cotton was not merely king but czar. Whether Mr. Benjamin really believed in the false doctrine of king cotton, or how far he believed in it, it is not possible to determine absolutely. We would fain have him among the sane men, like Mr. Rhett; and certainly his experience and knowledge of the old world, greater than that of most of his associates, would predispose us to the opinion that he must have known better than to imagine that the South had both the fulcrum and the lever that would move the universe at will. There is no positive proof that he actively propagated the heresy in his speeches; yet Mr. Russell, in the interview referred to in a previous chapter, reports that, "Mr. Benjamin did not appear afraid of anything; but his confidence respecting Great Britain was based a good deal, no doubt, on his firm faith in cotton, and in England's utter subjection to her cotton interests and manufactures." The same Mr. Russell, now become Sir William, adds elsewhere:[1] "Many long years afterward I walked with Mr. Benjamin from a pleasant dinner party in Mayfair, and reminded him of our conversation in Montgomery. 'Ah, yes,' he said, 'I admit I was mistaken! I did not believe that your government would allow such misery to your operatives, such loss to your manufacturers, or that the people themselves would have borne it.'" Furthermore, whether so misguided himself or not, Benjamin coöperated with a government that was. Perhaps he really believed otherwise; perhaps he pressed, in the secret meetings of the cabinet, for some such instruc-

[1] *North American Review*, 1898, p. 373.

tions to the Confederate commissioners as Mr. Rhett had outlined, and merely surrendered his own views in order that there might be harmony in the government. If this be so, it is more creditable to his loyalty than to his intelligence.

When Mr. Benjamin became Secretary of State, nearly all of the important diplomatic or quasi-diplomatic agents of the Confederacy had been appointed, and the policy of the government, following the lines indicated, had been defined, although "the policy of the State Department," writes [1] the courteous and discreet Mr. L. Q. Washington, assistant secretary and chief clerk, "can hardly be said to have taken shape and development during Mr. Toombs's incumbency." Mr. Toombs, in fact, is said to have declared that he carried the archives of the State Department under his hat—one recalls Lincoln's post-office, said to have been similarly kept. Matters had rather bettered under Secretary Hunter, who had sent out, in the autumn of 1861, the most notable emissaries of all, Messrs. Mason and Slidell, with instructions [2] to pursue a policy as rational, perhaps, as was possible without treason to King Cotton.

When these two gentlemen were inadvisedly seized on board the British ship *Trent*, Mr. Benjamin, with the rest of the Confederacy, had hoped that the incident would involve the Yankees in a war with England, and had smiled at Jones's rhetorical bombast about its bringing "the Eagle cowering to the feet of the Lion." But this hope had faded and been succeeded by others on the kaleidoscope with which the

[1] *Lawley MS.*
[2] Callahan, *Diplomatic History*, p. 133.

South was amusing itself, before Mr. Benjamin was called upon to preside at that machine. After all, even if England had shown signs of fighting in defense of her flag, it could not have pleased the new Secretary of State to read in the London *Times*,[1] that "Messrs. Mason and Slidell are about the most worthless booty it would be possible to extract from the jaws of the American lion. They have long been known as the blind and habitual haters and revilers of this country. . . . It is through their lifelong hatred and abuse of England that they come here in their present conspicuous capacity. . . . So we do sincerely hope that our countrymen will not give these fellows anything in the shape of an ovation. . . . They must not suppose, because we have gone to the very verge of a great war to rescue them, that therefore they are precious in our eyes. We should have done just as much to rescue two of their own negroes, and, had that been the object of the rescue, the swarthy Pompey and Cæsar would have had just the same right to triumphal arches and municipal addresses as Messrs. Mason and Slidell." Clearly, Mr. Mason would find the need of much suavity and cleverness if he hoped to win the confidence of the "Thunderer" and its readers.

It may be proper here to consider the personal qualifications of the two Confederate commissioners for the delicate missions to which they had been assigned. Both had the full confidence of the Richmond government. Though more intimate with Slidell, Benjamin knew Mr. Mason thoroughly; hence the most complete accord might be looked for between the gov-

[1] Jan 11, cited by Rhodes, Vol. III, p. 540, note.

ernment and both of its envoys. Of Mr. Mason first, it can hardly be far wrong to say that his political record was not such as to make him altogether *persona grata* in England. An extremist in his state rights and pro-slavery opinions, generally known as the author of the drastic Fugitive Slave Law of 1850,[1] and forcing himself to the front in speech and action whenever these questions came up,—such a record, blazoned in the press, could not be forgotten. Nor was the uncompromising Virginian solicitous to conceal his opinions in deference to the contrary view of the government to which he was sent to plead the cause of the Confederacy. It is scarcely necessary to point out that pro-slavery sentiments could not meet with the open approval of Earl Russell, unless that individual were mightily changed from the Lord John of earlier days. The political antecedents of the commissioner, therefore, were unfortunate, and not modified by present demeanor. Mr. Mason was a man of good abilities, and sterling uprightness of character, honest and reliable, lacking neither in mental capacity nor in energy. But he was unbending in temper, rather cold in manner, and sensitive about his dignity. On a mission from a government of no certain standing among the nations, and which had proffered nothing but a dangerous friendship in return for the reception it sought in England, it behooved him to approach the British authorities with extreme deference; to submit without manifesting resentment to such treatment as might very properly have been resented by an established government; to be patient and long-suffering while he sought to make good

[1] See Mason, p. 81.

the claims of his people. Such considerations could
not escape a man so intelligent as Mr. Mason, and
with good intent he endeavored to act accordingly;
but personality is often stronger than intelligence, and
in spite of himself his attitude toward the British
government was rather that of one demanding a patent
right than of one asking action that would be immensely helpful to his people and probably very costly
to England. This much, I think, may be justly said
without undue disparagement of one who loyally did
his best. His position was extremely difficult and
trying; but he should have realized that it could not
be otherwise. On the whole, therefore, the conclusion
seems justifiable that a man of greater urbanity, of
more flexible temperament and pleasing address might
have had better success.

Such a man, if he could possibly have been spared
at home, was the Secretary of State himself. Such a
man, too, in certain respects, was Mr. Slidell, who in
his dealings with the polite but rather unreliable
French authorities displayed even greater patience
and self-control than Benjamin. While his political
history would, doubtless, have been no more satisfactory in England than Mason's, he had some of the
very personal qualifications which the latter lacked.
He would have been more patient as well as more
insinuating. Although perhaps of no greater intellectual ability, and of less forceful character, than Mason,
he was a more adroit politician, and proved a better
diplomat. Yet the connections of his family and his
personality best fitted him for the post he was sent to
occupy, as he was in general of a type extremely different from the English and not likely to win their

confidence. Slidell proved a good choice for France; it is doubtful if he would have suited so well in England.

When Benjamin assumed charge of his office, official news of the reception accorded the Confederate commissioners was still lacking, for even now dispatches came through but slowly and at great hazard. Accordingly he wrote to Mr. Mason: "In the absence of reliable information as to the present condition of public affairs in England and the tone and temper of its government and people, the President does not deem it advisable to make any change in the instructions communicated to you by my predecessor."[1] The earlier dispatches, therefore, confine themselves largely to a summary of military and naval operations, lest Mason be misled by the Federal accounts. It must have been far from pleasant to tell of the loss of Forts Donelson and Henry and of Roanoke Island, which disasters, the secretary says,[2] have had the good effect of rousing the people to a proper sense of the magnitude of the struggle in which they are engaged and of the necessity for strenuous exertion. The effort to prove the blockade ineffective is still most conspicuous, as for example, in the dispatch of April 8th above referred to: "You will find annexed a list showing the number and character of the vessels which have traded between our ports and foreign countries, during the months of November, December, and January. They exceed one hundred in number, and establish in the most conclusive manner the inefficiency of the blockade which it has pleased neutral nations heretofore to respect as binding on their commerce." In his third dispatch to

[1] Dispatch to Mason, April 8; see Mason, p. 291.
[2] Dispatch to Mason, April 5; see Mason, p. 288.

Mason,[1] dated April 12th, he discusses at some length the difficulty of communicating with the envoys, and broaches the question, whether dispatches to a neutral power may properly be considered contraband of war, and if not, what is the distinction between these and dispatches to an envoy to a neutral power. That Benjamin should have wasted his time in formulating so futile a proposition, is indication of the annoyance he felt at the delays in hearing from the men whose policy he was supposed to direct. In this same dispatch we find a passage that may be quoted to show the line of argument upon which he urged Mason to proceed: "So long as England as well as the other neutral powers shall continue practically to assert, as they now do, their disbelief of our ability to maintain our government, what probability is there that our enemy will fail to rely on that very fact as the best ground for hope in continued hostilities? Without intending that their policy should be thus disastrous in its results, it cannot be doubted on reflection, that the delay of the neutral powers in recognizing the nationality of the South is exerting a very powerful influence in preventing the restoration of peace on this continent; and in thus injuriously affecting vast interests of their own which depend for prosperity and even for existence on free intercourse with the South. There is every reason to believe that our recognition would be the signal for the immediate organization of a large and influential party in the Northern states favorable to putting an end to the war. It would be considered the verdict of an impartial jury adverse to their pretensions."

This is cogent reasoning in expression of the opinion

[1] Mason, p. 293.

on which the envoys were consistently urged to insist, that recognition alone, without intervention, would end the war. If recognition had come early, indeed, it seems entirely probable that this opinion would have been justified by the event.

Presently, however, news began to arrive from the envoys. Mr. Slidell, whom we shall mention briefly first, reported an encouraging reception from the officials in Paris, and in his initial dispatch[1] had given his government a summary of political conditions that strikes the keynote for the relations between the Confederacy and France. He told the Secretary of State that there was much favor expressed on all sides for the South, and that he believed the Emperor and the higher officials to be really friendly. He perceived at once that the question of slavery was to have a powerful influence upon the foreign relations of the Confederacy, and stated that, although the public sentiment was opposed to slavery, opposition was not so earnest as in England, rather the academic opinion of a people not directly concerned. All things considered, therefore, the French government would be inclined to favor the Confederacy, and the French people would not resist the Emperor in such a policy. But, owing to political complications, particularly in the affairs of Italy and Mexico, and to financial embarrassments, France did not wish to take the initiative in any decisive action, feeling, moreover, that England, having more at stake than she, should have the lead. Such had been the fruit of reflection upon what he heard in private conversation, or read in the press; and this had been confirmed by his interviews with

[1] *Pickett Papers*, Feb. 11, 1862.

M. Thouvenel, the Minister for Foreign Affairs, and Count de Persigny, Minister of the Interior, both very non-committal but of courteous and even friendly bearing.

Meanwhile Mr. Mason had been received in something of the triumphal arch style deprecated by the *Times*, and had been a good deal misled by this enthusiastic welcome. It cannot be determined with absolute certainty, of course, what were the sympathies of the voting majority in England. The fact seems to be that, in spite of what we consider her vital interest in the speedy settlement of the war, these were not vital enough to permit of the American question's becoming a party issue. The government of the day, while not deserving great praise for its American policy, understood enough of its true duties to await manifestations of the popular will; and as yet there had been no manifestation of real popular concern in the affairs of the "kin across the sea." Mr. Mason, however, did not see this, and was disposed to attach undue political weight to the merely social courtesies that were extended to him so generously and pleasantly. The membership of the House of Lords, I suppose, was beyond question overwhelmingly in favor of the Confederacy at this time; but Mr. Mason should have remembered that, in politics at least, it was not a mere jest that had identified the House of Lords with the excellent Mrs. Partington. Contrasting the cordiality of the upper classes in England, apparently the predominating sentiment, with the cautious and cold refusals of Russell to have any official relations with him, Mr. Mason resented this attitude, and finally came to conceive the false notion that the minister alone stood in the way of foreign recognition for the Confederate States; that, somehow, he did not in this faithfully represent the will of the English people, and that he was unduly influenced by the bald misrepresentations of Secretary Seward. In his dispatch of June 23, 1862,[1] he even intimated that it might become incompatible with his official dignity to remain in London, for he had concluded that when recognition was next proposed—he did not mean to act at the present time—it should be "presented as a demand of *right*; and if refused—as I have little doubt it would be—to follow the refusal by a note, that I did not consider it compatible with the dignity of my government, and perhaps with my own self-respect, to remain longer in England."

Immediately upon the receipt of this rather alarming news, Benjamin sat down to implore Mason not to act rashly and to impress upon him the value of his mere presence in London to await eventualities; for the withdrawal was a step that should not be taken "without very grave and weighty reasons."[2] Fortunately, Mr. Mason had not acted on this impulse, and relieved the anxiety at Richmond by announcing in subsequent dispatches that he had decided not to withdraw without authorization, except in some extreme case. But the impression being made by his advices may be seen from the references in Benjamin's dispatch[3] of October 28th to the "scant courtesy" with which Mr. Mason had been treated by Earl Russell, and to the "marked contrast between the conduct of the

[1] Mason, p. 279.
[2] Dispatch September 26; see Mason, pp. 303-306.
[3] Mason, p. 339.

English and French statesmen now in office, in their intercourse with foreign agents, eminently discreditable to the former." In the next dispatch [1] he writes more fully that the offensive conduct of Lord Russell, in several particulars which he recites, would be " conclusive in determining [the President] to direct your withdrawal from your mission, but for other considerations which have brought him to a different conclusion. The chief of these is the conviction entertained that on this subject the British cabinet is not a fair exponent of the sentiments and opinions of the British nation. Not only from your own dispatches, but from the British press and from numerous other sources of information, all tending to the same result, we cannot resist the conclusion that the public opinion of England, in accordance with that of almost all Europe, approaches unanimity in according our right to recognition as an independent nation. It is true that in official intercourse we cannot look to any other than the British cabinet as the organ of the British nation ; but it is equally true that in a government so dependent for continued existence on its conformity with public opinion, no ministry whose course of policy is in conflict with that opinion can long continue in office. It is certain, therefore, that there must very soon occur such a change of policy in the cabinet of St. James as will relieve all embarrassments in your position arising from the unfriendly feelings toward us, and the dread of displeasing the United States, which have hitherto been exhibited by Earl Russell." Accordingly, the body of the dispatch contains further arguments, based on the blockade and the application

[1] October 31 ; Mason, p. 330, *et seq.*

of the Treaty of Paris chiefly, to be used by Mr. Mason when a fit opportunity should occur. The misjudgment of British public opinion is evident; how much excuse there was for such error, to which Mr. Mason's reports had contributed no little, may be seen presently.

But when this dispatch was penned, the golden opportunity in England had slipped away unnoticed, and though others were to come in the course of the strife, there were none quite so full of promise. In order to appreciate this, we must consider the fortunes of the war, and the news of American events as it came to England; for never was the diplomatic fate of a nation more absolutely subject to the chances of war than that of the Confederacy. There was no cable then; and though mail service was not much slower than now, there could not be continuous communication. Moreover the news brought by one ship might be contradicted by the next, so full of falsehoods were many of the reports printed in the Northern papers—and the Southern journals were as bad; it was only that their opportunities of misleading the outside world were much curtailed by the blockade. Let us glance at the events of the spring and summer of 1862, that we may better understand diplomatic affairs.

Upon the retreat of General Albert Sidney Johnston from Kentucky, the people of the Southwest, and of New Orleans in particular, answering his and Beauregard's very urgent appeal, put forth their utmost endeavors to rebuild another army about the nucleus of twelve or fifteen thousand left after Donelson and resultant disasters. Of men there came a plenty, of arms and material, pitifully little, and that distressingly bad; but the host gathered full of high hopes and of courage, and never did raw soldiers fight better than those under Johnston and Beauregard in the bloody fields about Shiloh Church. Though both sides claimed a victory, and with some right, the death of General Johnston and the loss of his daring spirit, were more costly to the Confederates than were their ten thousand dead, wounded, and missing to the Union army. It was then, while Benjamin was composing his first dispatches, that details of the great battle were coming into Richmond, and Jones was writing :[1]

"The President is thin and haggard ; and it has been whispered on the street that he will immediately be baptized and confirmed. I hope so, because it may place a great gulf between him and the descendant of those who crucified the Saviour. Nevertheless, some of his enemies allege that professions of Christianity have sometimes been the premeditated accompaniments of usurpation. It was so with Cromwell and with Richard III."

The anxiety of the President at this time was not without reason; for soon New Orleans fell, a loss most severe in a military way, leading to the opening of the Mississippi and the dividing of the Confederacy ; and yet more unfortunate still in its effect on foreign opinion. It was then, too, that McClellan, at last goaded into action and following a route to which the Northern armies ultimately had to return, gathered his vast army in the Peninsula while the thin Confederate line, at first under Joseph E. Johnston, and when he fell wounded at Fair Oaks, under the yet

[1] April 18, Vol. I, p. 120.

untried Robert E. Lee, faced him and baffled him throughout the month of June. But it was a perilous season for Richmond, when Lee could write to Jackson that, unless they could drive McClellan out of his entrenchments he would push up those entrenchments till his guns commanded the capital. Jackson and Lee, taking great risks which were no risks only because these men carried things through, first assailed the helpless incompetents playing at soldier in the Shenandoah Valley, and demoralized the politicians in Washington; then struck swiftly at a segregated wing of McClellan's army down on the Chickahominy, at Gaines's Mill, demoralized that general, and followed him, with many a desperate fight, through the Seven Days' Battles. McClellan "changed his base" to the James River. Doubtless it was a wise move, and effected with great military skill; but to the world it was an acknowledgment that the campaign had been a failure. Europe wondered, and, in spite of sympathies, praised Jackson's brilliant exploits; and though Malvern Hill was bloody, though it may have been tactically a mistake on the part of Lee, she saw that, after all the immense and costly preparations of the North, their plans had been utterly frustrated.

There was now a distinct lull in active operations, giving time for foreign opinion to become instructed on these events, while McClellan sat down to nurse his wounds and his wrath, and the Washington politicians sought a less timorous Napoleon. He is found, and the cry is, Make way for General Pope, he who is used to behold the backs of his enemies, and who dictates orders from "headquarters in the saddle." And again the wit of Lee and Jackson is matched, if one may so use the word, against that of Pope with some assistance from Washington, till there come in order Gainesville, Groveton,—and a second Bull Run, with the capital, on September 2d, again in panic and scrambling for its swords and guns to repulse the "rebels" believed to be following on Pope's heels. Neither Union nor Confederate armies ever after had much acquaintance with his back or front. The politicians were, for a season, brought low before McClellan, to whom they appealed for counsel and defense in this hour of peril. Not very reassuring news this, to go over to Europe, that the man who had but two months before been outwitted by Lee and Jackson, was the only officer to whom the Union could venture to entrust the army that must now be hastily gathered to protect Washington and Baltimore from the victorious Confederates, led by generals who were fast proving themselves strategists of the first rank, and who now had crossed the Potomac into Maryland.

Here was the critical moment for the Confederacy, both in its military affairs and in its hopes of Great Britain's recognition. General Lee, acting with his usual promptitude and decision, seized the moment of panic and demoralization consequent upon the second Bull Run to risk an incursion across the border. With forces far more slender than ascribed to him by panic-stricken foes, with a commissariat the very thought of which would have made the pampered Federal troops feel the pangs of starvation, and dependent for his ammunition on a long and precarious line, it was yet with a most splendid army of victorious veterans that Lee marched into Maryland. Good news was hoped for from Kirby Smith and from Bragg in Kentucky, who threatened Cincinnati and Louisville; and could his soldiers but once more do what seemed impossible,—win a victory where all the odds of numbers and equipment were against them,—General Lee meant, on the morrow of this fresh success, to offer peace to the North on the condition of the recognition of Southern independence; and by this appeal from the Washington government to the people in their hour of discouragement he and Davis quite reasonably hoped to shake, if not utterly to break, the resolution to reconquer the seceded states. Often had he, with the aid of Jackson and Longstreet, taken desperate chances, relying on the chapter of accidents, and on the probable mistakes of the less able generals opposed to them; and success had often justified him.

The authorities in Richmond were heartily in accord with Lee, and inspired by his confidence. Davis prepared to go to the field, but was asked not to expose himself. Benjamin, now learning of Mason's ill success, hoped to have news to send him on which he might base a yet stronger argument for "the acknowledgment of a fact patent to mankind"—the recognition of Confederate independence. Greater still would have been his anxiety if he could have known what was passing in England. She had watched with growing interest the campaigns of this active spring and summer; and as she watched, greater had grown her sympathy with the generals of the Confederacy and her confidence in the ultimate success of its cause. Mason took heart of grace, after the news of McClellan's retreat from Richmond, and asked for a personal interview with Russell, that he might the more forcibly present the arguments with which he was armed by his State Department; but the interview was declined: "Her Majesty's government are still determined to wait." Then, while Mason consoled himself with the thought that the *Alabama* had been allowed to sail, and that public sympathy was manifestly tending his way, came the news of Pope's defeat, and of Lee's advance into Maryland, in the early days of September. The British press considered the Federal cause hopeless, and Lord Palmerston was writing to Lord Russell that the Yankees had "got a very complete smashing," and that, in the probable event of the capture of Baltimore or Washington, the time seemed to have come when his government and France should "address the contending parties and recommend an arrangement upon the basis of separation." "I agree with you," replied Russell, "that the time has come for offering mediation to the United States government with a view to the recognition of the independence of the Confederates. I agree, further, that, in case of failure, we ought ourselves to recognize the Southern States as an independent state." But Palmerston, again cautious, as the risk of Lee's campaign became clearer, counseled delay: in case the Federal army again met defeat, then would be the time to offer intervention; but if not, "we may wait awhile and see what may follow." [1]

What followed was the news of the great battle of Sharpsburg, or Antietam, and the checking of General Lee. Though it was not a very costly defeat, the prime object of his campaign had been lost, and he

[1] Walpole's *Life of Russell*, Vol. II, pp. 349, 350, cited by Rhodes, Vol. IV, p. 338.

must seek safety on his own side of the Potomac. Then came the news that he had been permitted to withdraw his army in fairly good order, and that McClellan had been dilatory in pursuit of the Southern troops. No wonder that Benjamin, writing to calm Mason at this time, should have been urgent with him not to leave the ungracious Russell; for even the results of the campaign as they then showed would add force to the Confederate demand if it had been pressed. He could not know, of course, that Adams was thinking that his mission would end before the winter was over, and that as the October days came on, and England still heard that Lee's army was intact and McClellan still afraid of it, the tide of Southern sympathies would sweep higher and even engulf a prominent member of the British government. Gladstone, the Chancellor of the Exchequer, declared at Newcastle, October 7th, "There is no doubt that Jefferson Davis and other leaders of the South have made an army; they are making, it appears, a navy; and they have made, what is more than either—they have made a nation. . . . We may anticipate with certainty the success of the Southern states so far as their separation from the North is concerned." [1] Meanwhile Lincoln, taking advantage of Antietam in the same way that the Confederates had hoped to do, had issued his Proclamation of Emancipation, but even that was as yet coldly received in England. And while the cabinet were meditating a meeting to discuss their policy in American affairs, with every likelihood that they would decide on a course helpful to the South,

[1] Rhodes, Vol. IV, p. 339.

the clever Adams managed to convey indirectly to their ears the instructions he had received from Washington : "If the British government, either alone or in combination with any other government, should acknowledge the insurgents, . . . you will immediately suspend the exercise of your functions, and give notice of that suspension to Earl Russell and to this department." The possibilities of war with Great Britain and other powers, wrote Seward, under Lincoln's instructions, had been weighed, and did not appall the United States. The cabinet meeting was postponed, and with it the question of Southern independence ; though the British ministers might again approach the danger line marked out by Lincoln, they would not cross it.

Benjamin had no such trump card to play, nor could he know that henceforth it was beyond all human probability that any representations he might make through Mason would have any other than superficial effect. In his dispatches during the autumn of 1862 he sends constant reënforcements to the arguments already familiar to us, taking advantage of every favorable chance of battle to present in new forms (1) the inefficiency of the blockade, maintained but fitfully at many ports, and many times simply by watching and chasing vessels on the high seas bound from Nassau or Cuba, or by sinking in the mouths of harbors, contrary to the laws of nations, obstructions that might permanently injure them ; (2) the great advantages to each nation of mutual trade ; and (3) the certainty that the South could never be subdued and forced into the Union,—a fact that should be sufficiently evident from the continued reverses suffered by Federal armies in their unhallowed career of conquest. Occasionally, as in a dispatch[1] of December 11th, some variation is ventured upon this basic argument; but there is never the suggestion of any larger reward than virtue's for British recognition. Thus, in the dispatch referred to, after an able discussion of the possible trade relations in view of peace, of which he is sanguine in anticipation of the great victory for which Lee was then preparing at Fredericksburg, Benjamin instructs Mason to see what might be done even to secure action that could be construed into recognition or that might lead to intervention.

Many applications were at this time being made, so Mason had written, for permission to buy and export cotton from the Confederacy, and as he was not thoroughly informed of existing conditions and possible change of policy, he desired instructions. Benjamin advised him that the policy of the government would be, of course, to favor cotton exportation where there was some security that it would go to a neutral and not to a Yankee port. Moreover, as regards the fear entertained by foreign merchants that the Confederate authorities would themselves destroy cotton which was the property of neutrals, when in danger of falling into Federal hands, as had been done at New Orleans and at scores of other places, the Southern leaders could offer but this: if neutral governments will protect cotton belonging to their subjects and held in the Confederacy awaiting export, preventing its confiscation or destruction by the forces of the United States, the Confederate government will likewise agree to respect such property of

[1] *Pickett Papers;* see Mason, pp. 359–367.

neutrals, and to protect it; if, however, no such assurance be given, the Confederate government must continue its policy of destruction in order to prevent cotton from falling into the hands of the enemy. Of course, the assumption of any such position by England or France would have been a long step toward intervention; and the dissemination of the proposal among the English spinners would bring a fresh crop of pro-Southern sentiment, and increase the popular pressure on the ministry. As a matter of fact, Benjamin's suggestion did have its effect, for Lyons, the British Minister at Washington, and Mercier, the French Minister, made some tentative approaches to the subject of protection for neutral cotton and tobacco; but Lincoln and Seward perceived too readily whither this tended.

Here we may halt in the pursuit of the policy adopted toward England, which as yet had been chiefly fruitful of vexation and hopes deferred, to consider what had been done with the other great European nation to which the Confederacy turned with some hope of a hearing for its cause.

CHAPTER XI

DIPLOMATIC RELATIONS WITH FRANCE AND ENGLAND

WE have seen that Slidell estimated and reported with accuracy the sentiment of the French Emperor and his people. Benjamin was, through his frequent visits to France, familiar with the nature of its government, and had made a shrewd guess at the true character of its ruler. When, therefore, his impressions were confirmed by Slidell's report, he did not hesitate to adopt a policy that promised the best results. His first dispatches to the envoy may be passed over as of no particular importance, or at least not different in essentials from those to Mason already mentioned. The second, for example, April 8th,[1] reviews the blockade question, and comments on the inconsistency of France and England in recognizing the paper blockade of the Federals after insisting that the Confederacy agree to the principle of the law of nations that "blockades in order to be binding must be effective; that is to say, maintained by a force sufficient really to prevent access to the coast of the enemy." But the third dispatch, April 12th, is in principle, it seems to me, a complete abjuration of the Southern cotton heresy, which speaks no little for the influence of Benjamin over Davis and for his clever estimate of Louis Napoleon.

Omitting the earlier and more formal parts of the

---

[1] *Pickett Papers.*

document—it is one of the few that have been often printed[1]—we find Benjamin saying: "It is well understood that there exists at present a temporary embarrassment in the finances of France, which might have the effect of deterring that government from initiating a policy likely to superinduce the necessity for naval expeditions. If under these circumstances you should after cautious inquiry be able to satisfy yourself that the grant of a subsidy for defraying the expenses of such expeditions would suffice for removing any obstacle to an arrangement or understanding with the Emperor, you are at liberty to enter into engagements to that effect. In such event the agreement would take the form most advantageous to this country by a stipulation to deliver on this side a certain number of bales of cotton to be received by the merchant vessels of France at certain designated ports. In this manner one hundred thousand bales of cotton of 500 pounds each, costing this government but $4,500,000 would represent a grant to France of not less than $12,500,000, or 63,000,000 francs, if cotton be worth, as we suppose, not less than twenty-five cents per pound in Europe. . . . I do not state this sum as the limit to which you would be authorized to go in making a negotiation on the subject, but to place clearly before you the advantage which would result in stipulating for payment in cotton." The subsidy, therefore, might be even larger than that suggested; and the stipulation for payment in cotton was not a *sine qua non*. The offer was to be made, primarily, to induce France to raise the blockade, by armed inter-

[1] See Bigelow, p. 176; cf. Rhodes, Vol. IV, p. 346; my citation is from the original, *Pickett Papers;* cf. Richardson, Vol. II, p. 229.

vention if necessary ; but Slidell was given still further discretion : " If you find, then, that it would be more feasible to use the discretion vested in you to procure a recognition, than to raise the blockade, you are to consider yourself authorized to *use the same means*[1] as are placed at your disposal for raising the blockade."

This dispatch was an important triumph for the Secretary of State, and a radical departure from the policy to which the administration, so far, had seemed to commit itself. By what arguments Mr. Davis was brought to assent to this offer we can only surmise ; but we may feel assured that a step so important was not taken without his knowledge and consent. By what reasoning Benjamin brought himself to see the possible advantage of such terms to France while he was offering England only the ordinary privileges of trade, we can also guess. From the reports of wide sympathy with the Confederate cause in England he was led to believe, or confirmed in the belief, that the British government, which he knew to be dependent on popular support, would sooner or later yield to the pressure of public opinion ; and from the sketch we have given of what was taking place in England it may be seen that his confidence was not without justification. But he knew that the interest of the French people in cotton was not so vital, and besides, that their government was not a democracy, and hence not so immediately responsive to popular opinion, while the ambitious Emperor for the time controlled everything. To him, engaged in costly schemes that might eventuate in war, and anxiously seeking money to prosecute them, such a temptation might come as

[1] Italics in the original.

decisive.   All now hinged on the continued success of
the Confederate armies, and on the skill with which
Slidell might use the large powers entrusted to him.

Events in the Confederacy at this period have
already been outlined ; the one of most significance
for the negotiations with France, and at the same time
most nearly touching Benjamin himself, was the capture of New Orleans, the danger of which began to be
apparent to the Richmond authorities soon after this
dispatch was written.   But while disquieting news was
coming from that quarter, Benjamin was cheered by
a visit from Mercier ; for though he declared his visit
strictly informal and was himself very guarded, it was
made with the consent of Seward, and showed that for
some reason France was interested to learn something
of the status of affairs at Richmond.   Mercier reported
to his government that, having sailed to Norfolk on a
French vessel of war, and having received permission
to go to Richmond in a private capacity, he went at
once.[1]   " My first visit was to Mr. Benjamin, Secretary
of State, whom I had known when he represented
Louisiana in the United States Senate.   I said to him
that the purpose of my journey was merely to assure
myself, for myself, of the true condition of things ; and
that I called to beg him to aid me in attaining it.   He
answered that he would do so with the greatest pleasure,
and that he would be delighted that I should be able
to penetrate to the truth, which, judging from all that
came back to him from the North, appeared to be little
known there.   I condense, M. le Ministre, what I heard
from the mouth of Mr. Benjamin, and in conversation

[1] Report published in the papers; see N. Y. *Tribune*, Feb. 9,
1863.

with others. 'We have,' they said to me, 'relied too much on Europe and the power of commercial interests, but are determined to conquer our independence at all hazards. On this point the sentiments of our people are unanimous. They have already suffered much, but they will endure far more, if necessary, to accomplish their object. We do not disguise from ourselves that the Federals possess infinitely superior resources, and the command of the ocean; that they may in the long run make themselves masters of our ports. But in capturing our cities they will find only women, old men, and children. The whole population capable of bearing arms will withdraw into the interior, beyond the reach of gunboats, and in presence of such a resistance, the North will be obliged to yield. . . . We can, if absolutely necessary, defend ourselves, but the North cannot attack us without money. On the other hand, we will not hesitate an instant to burn our cotton and our tobacco, rather than permit them to fall into the hands of the enemy.' I have seen here all the most important personages. All have held the same language and have expressed the same sentiments. Nevertheless, among those persons several are known for the moderation of their character and for the resistance that they opposed at the outset to the movement of secession. . . . I see many reasons for not calling in question their profound sincerity at this moment."

One proof of their sincerity, most annoying to Mercier, he found in the willingness of the Confederates to burn their cotton rather than have it fall into the hands of the Federals. And, indeed, the whole tone of the dispatch, as well as others that he was writing at this time, was favorable to the South; he might almost as well have said, in plain speech, that the spirit of resistance there was indomitable, and capable of inspiring to years of patriotic sacrifice and suffering; that, therefore, the revolution would succeed, and the Emperor might merely use his own discretion as to when he would stay the arm of the North in its useless shedding of blood and destruction of property.

The substance of Mercier's interview with Benjamin was immediately published, though the formal dispatch from which we have quoted was not, of course, yet made public when Benjamin wrote to Slidell[1] that "the result of this conversation has been very fairly stated by him." If he could have read the text of the Frenchman's dispatch, his expressions of approval would have been stronger. Surely, the thing could hardly have been better for the South if Benjamin himself had written it, instead of merely injecting it into Mercier. Parts of what the French minister wrote sound almost like quotations from Benjamin, and we have no hesitation in declaring that in the long and intimate conversation between the two, the latter successfully exerted his powers of influencing the mind of his hearer with such a calm and well-reasoned statement of the Southern cause as carried conviction and left an impression not to be effaced or replaced by anything he might afterward see or hear. Though Benjamin, in reporting the interview to Slidell, does not express any elation whatever, he was doubtless aware of the favorable effect he had created upon Mercier, and of the good influence this might have on

---

[1] *Pickett Papers;* see also Mason, p. 297.

the negotiations with France. He told Slidell: "In the course of conversation he [Mercier] remarked that it would be a matter of infinite gratification to himself personally as well as to his government if his good offices could be interposed in any way to restore peace, and said that the only possible solution he saw, was *political* independence combined with *commercial* union. But, he continued, 'how can anybody talk to either side? I dare not utter to you a single sentence that does not begin with the word *independence*, nor can I say a syllable to the other side on any other basis than *union*.'" This dispatch concludes in very sanguine temper, and was designed to strengthen, as it should, Slidell's hand in the use of his offer of a subsidy: "You will spare no effort to avail yourself of the favorable opportunity presented by our recent successes in urging our right to recognition. We ask for no mediation, no intervention, no aid. We simply insist on the acknowledgment of a fact patent to mankind."

Having thus ordered his forces for a vigorous assault upon the already wavering Louis Napoleon, the Secretary of State was compelled to wait through the anxious months till he could learn what fortune had befallen Slidell; and meanwhile untoward events would come to disturb his plans. We have referred before to the delays and hazards of communication between the Confederate government and its foreign emissaries, and perhaps it would be well to consider, without needless detail, these and other difficulties that embarrassed the Secretary of State in particular. In spite of the fact that the blockade, at ports like Wilmington, was run with such frequency and safety as to establish almost regular intercourse with Nassau, Bermuda, or Havana, the vessels were not government vessels, and could hardly be considered trustworthy bearers of dispatches, unless some special passenger could be charged with the duty of transmission. The dispatches, then, were often entrusted to private persons[1] for conveyance either within the Federal lines, or to some foreign port, whence they might be forwarded, under various disguises if necessary, to their proper destinations. Until definite arrangements were completed for the sending of the dispatches from Mason and Slidell to Helm at Havana, Walker at Bermuda, or Heyliger at Nassau, and thence through the blockade at some convenient point, those coming from the commissioners, and from Slidell in particular, were frequently long delayed. Of Benjamin's dispatches to them, not a few, entrusted to persons who were either not zealous or not cautious, fell into the hands of the enemy, the bearers having neglected to destroy them when they themselves were captured. This might prove not only seriously embarrassing, but even disastrous, should secrets of real importance be contained in them. And the excited editors, always filled with vehement suspicion of the government in general and of Benjamin in particular, often, as we may have occasion to notice, held him as culpable as the careless messengers. Fair samples of the most exasperating delays at important crises, when it was vitally necessary that the secretary who was directing foreign policy should have authentic offi-

---

[1] Mrs. Davis writes me (Oct. 12, 1904) : "For purposes of defying the interception of dispatches from abroad, the French diplomatic letters were dictated to Rosine Slidell by her father, and they were addressed to me under a feigned and prearranged name."

cial reports from his ministers, are not far to
seek. Benjamin's dispatch No. 6, to Slidell,[1] dated
September 26, 1862, was one of those captured. It
opens: "Sir: Since my No. 5, of the 19th of July,
I am without any communication from you, with the
exception of your No. 2, of the 26th of February last,
which was brought to the department on the 26th of
this month by Mr. Chamberlyn, to whom you had
entrusted it. This gentleman has thus consumed seven
months in discharging the trust confided to him. Your
numbers 3, 4, 5 and 6 are still missing." The dispatch
chiefly confines itself to a relation of Lee's campaign
against Pope and against McClellan in Maryland from
the Confederate point of view, and so through its publication no important secrets were revealed; but what
a painful revelation it is that Benjamin has had to
direct, or attempt to direct, Slidell's dealings with the
French Emperor, while himself absolutely in the dark,
as far as reliable information is concerned, regarding
what has happened to that minister, what has been
his reception, what he has done toward securing
recognition, during all these eventful and most anxious months of the spring and summer of 1862. Things
were never again quite so bad as this; still, in a dispatch of October 30th, we find Benjamin regretting
"that none of the letters of Mrs. Slidell for Mrs. Davis,
announced in your private letter to the President, have
ever been received. I may add that the date of the
last letter received by me from my own family [*i. e.*, his
wife, in France] is the tenth of May." At Slidell's
end, too, there were sometimes delays, vexatious, dan-

[1] *Pickett Papers;* cf. in general Callahan, pp. 51, 97; dispatch
published in N. Y. *Times*, Jan. 18, 1863.

gerous, or costly, as the case might be; thus the first sentence of his dispatch written on December 27, 1862, and received by Benjamin on February 27, 1863, informed the Secretary of State that he was "without any dispatch from you later than 15th April." More than eight months without instructions! It is fortunate that the most important advices had been sent before April 15th; fortunate, too, that Slidell was discreet and able enough to act judiciously even without further instructions. This case, however, is, I believe, the worst; as a rule, communication within three months could be relied on—incredibly good, and much to be thankful for, in view of the conditions we have noted, yet truly disheartening when we remember that these things took place not a century ago, in the days of clumsy sailing ships, but in the full tide of the age of steam.

Associated with this difficulty of communication with the outside world, and not a little conditioned by it, were other petty hindrances and embarrassments that hedged about Mr. Benjamin. For knowledge of current events in the great world, absolutely indispensable to one who would give intelligent direction to affairs of state, he was largely dependent on Northern or on foreign newspapers, since the press of the South was suffering from the same stoppage of communication as he; and these outside sources of information might well be regarded with suspicion, sometimes of ignorance, sometimes of partisan bias and deliberate intent to deceive. Those who imagine "yellow journalism" a disease of these latter days are much in error; the thing, if not the name, was certainly distressingly prevalent during the Civil War, as a glance at contemporary newspapers would suffice to show. A mild case indeed, and that in a journal which one would have thought proof against it, is familiar : Horace Greeley's New York *Tribune*, with its flaring headlines proclaiming the "Prayer of Twenty Millions" for an immediate emancipation, [1] which was certainly far from being the prayer of any such number of the Northern people at the time, and which was designed to hurry the President into action that would then almost certainly have been rash and impolitic. This, purposely selected as a mild instance, is the type of newspaper exaggerations and misrepresentations against which Benjamin had to be on his guard in making deductions from the Northern press. The more important and representative newspapers were kept on file.

"The State Department," says Assistant Secretary Washington, [2] "had frequent copies of the New York papers ; but the secretary did not depend on them for foreign intelligence. The London *Times*, *Daily Telegraph*, and other London journals, besides the magazines, were regularly received at the department and most carefully scanned, especially the debates in Parliament." "I have long been in receipt at the department of the *Times*, the *Saturday Review*, *Economist*, and *Examiner*, as well as of the principal quarterly reviews, and *Blackwood's Magazine*," writes Benjamin to Mason ; and continues : "The most striking articles from the *Herald*, *Post*, and other London dailies are cut out and forwarded by Mr. Hotze." [3] The libraries

---

[1] Aug. 20, 1862.   [2] *Lawley MS.*
[3] Mason, p. 472, dated April 18, 1864; cf. pp. 418, 445, 463, 468, etc.

at Richmond being utterly inadequate, Mr. Mason was commissioned to purchase and send forward books that would prove helpful, especially works on international law and Hansard's *Debates*, which were at last and after great difficulties safely received. "Mr. Benjamin's studies and training," continues Mr. Washington, "especially fitted him for [his] position. He had a thorough acquaintance with history, with both the common and the civil law, with international law and modern precedents, with the classics, ancient and modern ; the French language and general literature ; and with the commerce, institutions, and political conditions of foreign states. He was, indeed, a citizen of Louisiana, but yet far more a cosmopolitan. . . . He was always a student and he kept up his habit of reading. One work that he read with much care and pleasure at this time was Sir Robert Phillimore's then recent work on international law." There was need of a man of wide reading and shrewd judgment to keep up an intelligent acquaintance with the affairs of the world under conditions such as those we have given.

Before Benjamin could hear what effect had been produced upon Louis Napoleon by his offer of a subsidy, there occurred some little things within his ken that, not unnaturally, filled him with suspicion. With these affairs we shall deal briefly before attempting to picture more carefully the course of policy pursued by Slidell. The essential facts in the case are presented in a dispatch from Benjamin to Slidell, dated October 17, 1862 ; this was one of those captured by the Federals, and extensively circulated in Northern newspapers—for example, in the New York *Times* of January 18, 1863.

M. B. Théron, the consular agent of France and Spain at Galveston, had written to the governor of Texas, on August 18th: "Will you be kind enough to inform me *confidentially* of your personal opinion on the following questions:

"1. The annexation of the Republic of Texas to the United States, was or was not a good political measure?

"2. The act of disunion and of the junction of the state of Texas to the Southern States, was or was not another good or bad politic taken by the state?

"3. The reëstablishment of the old Republic of Texas will or will not be beneficial to our beloved adopted country?

"Your answer to these questions, sir, will serve me as a guide in my political correspondence with the governments which I have the honor to represent."

To this astonishing document Governor Lubbock answered with decision: "Permit me to say that the annexation of Texas to the United States was a good political measure. As to your second question, I answer most emphatically that 'the act of disunion and of the junction of the state of Texas to the Southern States' was a good and proper political step. In reply to your third inquiry, I have to say that the reëstablishment of the old Republic of Texas will not be beneficial to our beloved adopted country."

Questions and answers, moreover, were forthwith sent to President Davis by the governor, creating no little perturbation in the mind of the Secretary of State. The mere questions from such a source, to acquire information that might be "a guide in political correspondence with" France and Spain, were of themselves enough to arouse suspicion. Besides there were special facts known to Benjamin that further alarmed him; and while he and Davis were discussing this thing, a bit of apparently circumstantial evidence came to confirm their fears of a French intrigue. Senator Oldham, of Texas, wrote a rather long letter to Mr. Davis, the substance of which was that M. Tabouelle, vice-consul of France at Richmond, had, in a conversation with him, made careful inquiries as to the resources of Texas, and suggested the possibility of her "supporting a powerful and independent people, and asked [him] whether [he] thought it would not be to the interest of the state to assume an independent nationality." Considering that there had yet been little news from Slidell, and none but of old date; that Napoleon "the Little" was known to be emulous of the great uncle, and would probably enjoy a chance to recover part of what had once been considered Louisiana; that he was, moreover, just at this moment known to be bent on some scheme that would establish French influence over Mexico; and considering that Benjamin knew how traditional French policy had favored the independence of Texas in 1846, it is hardly to be wondered at that he penned a dispatch to the commissioners filled with grave suspicions. Benjamin wrote to Slidell:

"In plain language, we feel authorized to infer that the French government has, for some interest of its own, instructed some of its consular agents here to feel the way, and if possible to provoke some movement on the part of the state of Texas which shall result in its withdrawal from the Confederacy. It is difficult, if not impossible, on any other hypothesis, to account for the conduct of these agents. . . .

"In endeavoring to account for such a course of action on the part of the French government, I can only attribute it to one or both of the following causes: 1. The Emperor of the French has determined to conquer and hold Mexico as a colony, and is desirous of interposing a weak power between his new colony and the Confederate States, in order that he may feel secure against any interference with his designs in Mexico. 2. The French government is desirous of securing for itself an independent source of cotton supply, to offset that possessed by Great Britain in India, and designs to effect this purpose by taking under its protection the state of Texas, which, after being acknowledged as an independent republic, would, in its opinion, be in effect as dependent on France, and as subservient to French interests as if a French colony. . . .

"One other suggestion occurs to me, which you may receive as purely conjectural on my part. It is known to me personally that at the date of the annexation of Texas to the United States, Mr. Dubois de Saligny, the present French minister in Mexico, and who was at that time French chargé d'affaires to the republic of Texas, was vehemently opposed to the annexation, and was active in endeavoring to obstruct and prevent it. Even at that date the dispatches of Mr. Guizot, which I have had an opportunity of reading, were filled with arguments to show that the interests of Texas were identical with those of France, and that both would be promoted by the maintenance of a separate nationality in Texas. The intrigue now on foot, therefore, accords completely with a policy in regard to Texas that may be almost said to be traditional with France; and it is not impossible that the movement of the consular agents here has received its first impulse from the French legation in Mexico, instead of the cabinet of the Tuileries. . . .

"An enlarged and generous statesmanship would seem to indicate so clearly that the establishment of Southern independence on a secure basis (and with a strength sufficient to counterbalance the power of the United States, as well as to prevent extensive French colonization on our Southern border) would promote the true interests of Great Britain, that we find it difficult to account for her persistent refusal to recognize our independence. The knowledge of a secret attempt on the part of France to obtain separate advantages of such vast magnitude may perhaps induce a change in the views of the British cabinet. . . . If you come to the conclusion that these conjectures are well founded, you are at liberty to make known to Her Majesty's government the facts herein communicated, either through the British minister at Paris, or by concert with Mr. Mason."

In a postscript, written three days later, Benjamin informs Slidell that he has become convinced that M. Tabouelle was not acting in concert with M. Théron, nor was in any way a party to the suspected intrigue; hence the order for his expulsion from the Confederacy, which had accompanied a similar order for the expulsion of M. Théron, had been revoked. "It is barely possible," he continues, "though I think not probable, that Théron may have acted on his own ideas of what he supposed would be agreeable to his superiors, and not in consequence of instructions. The whole matter is one of great delicacy, and I must leave it to your own discretion how best to treat it, after endeavoring to satisfy yourself whether Théron's movements were dictated by the French cabinet."

The revelation of Benjamin's mistrust by the capture of this dispatch would, of course, quite spoil the French designs, if any, and necessitate a denial of their bare existence. So things turned out; and then, the possible danger being gone by, Benjamin's suspicions could be made to appear unjust, his fears exaggerated and ridiculous, his excitement that of one who has found a mare's nest. Nevertheless, this has always seemed to me a well-written dispatch, and one justified by the facts as they appeared to him. Indeed, it has not yet been shown that there were no grounds for his doubts of Louis Napoleon, and that he did not make a very shrewd guess at the true state of affairs.[1] Certainly, the dealings of the Emperor with Slidell, which we must now take up, were such as to show him "for crooked counsels fit."

On April 14th, Slidell had written the Secretary of State a detailed account of the interview between the Emperor and Mr. Lindsay, a member of the British Parliament, in regard to Southern affairs. Lindsay and Roebuck were among the most persistent champions of the South in Parliament, and the former now presented the cause to the Emperor most urgently, hoping to elicit from him at least an expression of opinion, perhaps also something more definite. In the first interview, April 11th, Napoleon had expressed his earnest desire to see the war ended, and stated that his government had twice made representations to that effect to the British government, but had received no definite response; such being the case, "he could not again address the English ministry through the official channels without some reason to believe that his representations would receive a favorable response; . . . that he was prepared to act promptly and decidedly; that he would at once dispatch a formidable fleet to the mouth of the Mississippi, if England would

[1] See Rhodes, Vol. IV, p. 346, for similar suspicions on the part of Adams.

send an equal force; that they would demand free egress and ingress for their merchantmen."

In his conviction that the Union could never be restored, he authorized Lindsay to report the substance of this conversation to Lord Cowley, British ambassador at Paris. Lindsay having seen Lord Cowley, and having ascertained that he was of the opinion that the proper time for intervention had passed, had another interview with Napoleon, and was urged to see Lords Russell and Palmerston on his return to England, and communicate to them what had been discussed; nay, it was even suggested that he see Lord Derby and Disraeli, leaders of the opposition. It would not be proper, of course, for the Emperor to hold communication with them, but Lindsay might let them know what the former's views were. Mr. Lindsay, become a confidential diplomat, was rather offended when Lord Russell, in reply to a note stating that the writer was charged with an important message from Napoleon, declined to receive any communication from a foreign power except through the regular channels. He saw Disraeli, however, who "fully concurred in the views of the Emperor," and added that, "if France would take the initiative, any course she might adopt to put an end to the present state of American affairs, would be undoubtedly supported by a large majority in Parliament, and knowing this, Lord Russell would give a reluctant assent, to avoid what would otherwise certainly follow: a change of ministry." These things Mr. Lindsay discussed with the Emperor in another interview, on April 18th, of which Slidell wrote again, on the same date. Napoleon seemed even more favorably disposed than before, said Lindsay, and thoroughly displeased by the inaction of the English authorities, his own impulse being to make a friendly appeal to the Federal government, and to accompany the appeal, if necessary, with a demonstration of force, to open the ports. "The taking of New Orleans, which he did not anticipate, might render it inexpedient to act," said the Emperor; "he would not decide at once, but would wait for some days for further intelligence."

Before Slidell had anything more of importance to say in his dispatches to Benjamin, there came the news of the fall of that city. The large French element in the population, more considerable in its proportions then than now, the extensive and almost intimate relations in trade and even in social intercourse still kept up between the Creoles and the old country, as well as the sentiment that could so easily be roused in behalf of this lost child of France,—all these things had been of weight in influencing Napoleon, if he should make any attempt to raise the blockade, to do so for the benefit of New Orleans. Now there was neither need nor excuse for that demonstration in force at the mouth of the Mississippi; for Seward was assuring Mercier that the blockade there was over, and that the port would be opened with only such delay as formality might necessitate. Nevertheless, the good intentions of the French Emperor seemed still assured, and still persisted in, though a new excuse for action must now be found, if he ventured to move independently of England.

Slidell wrote another encouraging dispatch on July 25th, giving an account of his own long interview with Napoleon, on the 16th of that month, and with

Thouvenel on the 23d.[1] It was at this time that, as
soon as the turn of the conversation presented a
favorable opportunity, Slidell first spoke of the cotton
subsidy: "I then stated to the Emperor what I had
been instructed to propose. It did not seem disagree-
able. He said, how am I to get the cotton? I replied,
of course that depends on Your Majesty; he will soon
have a fleet in the neighborhood of our coast strong
enough to keep it clear of every Federal cruiser"—
this latter being in reference to the Mexican expedition. "When speaking of the cotton subsidy," continues Slidell, "I told the Emperor that the proposition
was made exclusively to France, my colleague at
London not being aware of my authority to make it."

The exact terms of the offer are not given, since the
whole affair was rather of the nature of friendly conversation at a private audience than a deliberate application for the aid of France; but the suggestion was
presented to the Emperor, in the hope that he would
think it over and discuss it with his ministers, to
whom a more formal approach would then be made.
Accordingly, one week later, when Slidell conceived
that sufficient time had elapsed for this to percolate
through official channels from the Emperor, he sought
an interview with Thouvenel, Minister for Foreign Affairs, and made a definite proposition, which seemed
to interest the latter very much. After discussing
the proffered advantages to France, "as I was taking
leave, M. Thouvenel asked me to give him a brief

---

[1] References, unless when otherwise stated, are to my own notes
from the *Pickett Papers;* but on Slidell's interview, cf. Callahan,
p. 151, *et seq.;* Bigelow, p. 116, *et seq.;* and Richardson, Vol. II, pp.
270–272, 288, etc.

written memorandum of the propositions, in confidence, for his own use and that of the Emperor. I sent him one unsigned, copy of which you will find herewith. . . . He asked me if any similar propositions had been or would be made to England. I replied, 'Certainly not'; that our commissioner there was ignorant of them, although I intended to give him the information as soon as I found a safe opportunity."

The memorandum submitted to the French minister, which, like other vital parts of this dispatch, Slidell was careful to put in cypher, reads: "Cotton to the value of one hundred million francs, estimated on the basis of the prices current at Havre on 23d July, deducting freight and all other ordinary charges. Free importation during the war of all merchandise under French flag, without payment of duties or imposts of any kind, and for a limited term after the war of every sort of merchandise of French origin. As the Confederate States are now without almost every article of merchandise of foreign fabric or origin, importations must necessarily yield enormous profits, and their proceeds at a moderate calculation represent at least five hundred thousand bales of cotton to be shipped to France. Havre will then be the great *entrepôt* of cotton. Alliances defensive and offensive for Mexican affairs. For this last commissioner has no express instructions, but he has large discretion."

Whether or not Slidell had exceeded the warrant of his instructions in this last matter, which he had also broached in the same manner to the Emperor, is, perhaps, open to question. Certainly, the tone of Benjamin's dispatch of October 17th, quoted from above, was not in accord with a proposal of alliance, offensive and defensive, for the conquest of Mexico. But Slidell's offer was not disavowed, nor was disapproval of it expressed. When Benjamin wrote on October 17th he did not know what use the envoy had made of the authorization to buy French recognition; moreover, his suspicions of France then concerned Texas; there is no positive disapproval of the French design to conquer Mexico. Therefore, I should say that Benjamin would have sustained the commissioner in this offer if the object aimed at had been attained through it.[1]

During the summer, however, Napoleon kept away from Paris, politics, and Slidell, as far as possible; and when cornered, said the time was not propitious for action. At length Thouvenel was replaced by Drouyn de l'Huys, and Slidell must seek favor with the new minister, whom he found (October 26th) "ignorant of [the] purport" of the propositions made to his predecessor and to the Emperor, "but they seemed to impress him strongly." Having thus paved the way for further negotiations with the new servant, Slidell again got a chance at the master, and found him quite as full of fair promise as ever. "The Emperor asked why we had not created a navy; he said that we ought to have one; that a few ships would have inflicted fatal injury on the Federal commerce, and that with three or four powerful steamers we could have opened some of our ports. I replied . . . that the great difficulty was not to build but to man and arm them, under the existing regulations for the preservation of neutrality; that if the Emperor would

---

[1] Mason distinctly approved of, and in fact, suggested a similar alliance, September 4, 1863; see Mason, p. 447.

only give some kind of verbal assurance that his police would not observe too closely when we wished to put on board guns and men, we would gladly avail ourselves of it. He said, 'Why could you not have them built as for the Italian government? I do not think it would be difficult, but I will consult the Minister of Marine about it.'"

With what comprehension and delight this hint was received at Richmond we can readily imagine. Then, too, Slidell's dispatch of November 11th, must have echoed, a *sursum corda*, in the hearts in that city; for it reported that the Emperor had written to Mercier on October 30th, directing him to intimate to Seward in no uncertain terms the opinion of Napoleon that the independence of the Confederate States was "*un fait accompli*"; and also that a circular had been sent to the European powers (England and Russia) inviting their coöperation in an appeal to Washington and to Richmond for a suspension of hostilities and raising of the blockade.

And now, while cheering news came from Slidell, the fortunes of war again opportunely befriended the Confederacy. Another well-meaning but incompetent Federal officer, reluctantly forced into a command to which he felt himself unequal, confronted Lee at Fredericksburg. With a gallant and hopeless assault upon the fortified heights held by the Confederates, Burnside had wasted the blood and shattered the confidence of his splendid army. It is another crushing blow for the Federals in their insane endeavor to conquer the South, said the press of Europe; while the victor, grieved at the slaughter, wrote to his wife on Christmas Day: "But what a cruel thing is war;

to separate and destroy families and friends, and mar
the purest joys and happiness God has given us in this
world ; to fill our hearts with hatred instead of love for
our neighbors, and to devastate the fair face of this
beautiful world ! I pray that, on this day when only
peace and good-will are preached to mankind, better
thoughts may fill the hearts of our enemies and turn
them to peace." [1]   His army, he continues, was never
in better condition, and he only regrets that the withdrawal of Burnside beyond the Rappahannock without
another fight baffled hopes of such a victory as might
have proved decisive.

Throughout the winter and early spring of 1863,
despite the increasing privations of the people and the
sufferings of the soldiers, the tone of sentiment in the
South was optimistic.   Why does the Emperor lose his
precious opportunity in vacillation ? writes Benjamin
to Slidell, on March 24th : "This war may not last
beyond the present year, perhaps not beyond the
sickly season of a Southern summer, and yet he suffers
himself to be restrained from decisive action by
alternate menaces and assurances uttered with notorious mendacity by the leaders of the frantic mob
which now controls the government of the United
States."

In an earlier dispatch he had informed Slidell of
the visit of Erlanger to Richmond to negotiate for the
Confederate loan.   Instead of $25,000,000, the govern-
ment took only $15,000,000, at 77, interest seven per
cent. ; and would perhaps have declined that, but for
the belief that the placing of the loan in France at this
time might have some good political effect. [2]

---

[1] R. E. Lee, *Letters of General Lee*, p. 89.   [2] See Mason, p. 351.

Napoleon, however, was no longer really vacillating; he had gone as far as he dared to go without England's company, though he continued to dally with the Confederates for some time. On January 8th, taking advantage of the still fresh tidings of the Federal disaster at Fredericksburg, and of the undoubted distress among French operatives consequent upon the cutting off of the cotton supply, Slidell sent to the Emperor, through his private secretary, Mocquard, a renewed demand for the separate recognition of the Confederacy by France. Napoleon dictated a courteous note, to be delivered through Mercier at Washington, offering friendly mediation between the belligerents, and suggesting an armistice. It was duly presented to Seward, and by him to Lincoln, early in February, receiving a calm and polite refusal, accompanied by reasons, quite in contrast to the menacing words with which the mere suggestion of such interference on the part of the British government had been met.[1]

In England itself at this same time the effect of the victory of Lee over Burnside was not a little offset by the constantly increasing influence of Lincoln's Emancipation Proclamation, which had now received the final touch, on January 1, 1863, that was to start it on its way, no longer a mere piece of "campaign thunder," but an active force working for the disintegration of slavery at home and for its discrediting abroad. True, the opinion of the upper classes and of many influential journals was that the President's Proclamation was a hypocritical and iniquitous attempt to curry favor and to stir up a slave rebellion. Thus the *Times* declared that Lincoln was calling "to his aid the

[1] Rhodes, Vol. IV, p. 348.

execrable expedient of a servile insurrection. Egypt is destroyed, but his heart is hardened, and he will not let the people go"; then the *Saturday Review* fulminated against "the American lawgiver [who] not only confiscates his neighbor's slaves, but orders the slaves to cut their masters' throats"; and Mason was writing to Benjamin,[1] "This, I think, will be the judgment passed upon it [*i. e.*, the Proclamation] by all except the most ignorant classes in England."

Mason was partly right, for even Lord Russell was commenting on the Proclamation to Lord Lyons as a very questionable war measure, and one that seemed to embody no principle really hostile to slavery, but merely "vengeance on the slave owner." However, in spite of aristocratic criticism of Lincoln's act, it met with increasingly hearty approval from the mass of the people; and in this same dispatch Mason gives a more judicious opinion: "Though I doubt not a word from the minister, suggesting that the time has arrived for recognition, would meet with unanimous response in the affirmative, both from ministerial and opposition benches in the House of Commons, I do not think Lord Palmerston is disposed to speak that word. Nor will the Tories make an issue with him on American affairs. The fact is that parties are so nearly balanced in the House, and, as it would seem, in the country, that they are very wary in measuring strength with their opponents." In other words, neither party was willing to risk favor with the people by any such espousal of the Confederate cause as would provoke resentment.

In the meanwhile public mass meetings expressed

[1] Dispatch of January 15; see Mason, p. 371.

sympathy with the North, and the period of acute distress among the cotton operatives was painfully passing. To them the war could no longer be made to appear a war for Southern independence and against Northern conquest; neither they nor their betters in England understood much about the constitution of the Union, but they instinctively disliked slavery: the war was now a war for the abolition of slavery.

Benjamin fully understood the advantage that his adversary would derive from the dissemination of the idea that the war was really a war of emancipation; but that idea had been disseminated. The slavery question cropped up, about this time, in a new form. Intimations having been received in Richmond from Mason [1] that the opinion was freely expressed in England and elsewhere that the successful establishment of the Confederacy would be followed by the repeal of the clause of the Confederate Constitution prohibiting the African slave trade, Benjamin wrote an elaborate circular (dated January 15th), which he sent to Mason as well as the other representatives abroad. Instructions had recently (November 19th) been furnished to Mr. L. Q. C. Lamar, as commissioner to Russia, from whom the Confederacy might get an introduction into the society of nations; but Mr. Lamar found no welcome awaiting him. He sent word to the Russian officials that he had come, and, like Bob Acres, was told, in substance, "Well, you can go away again." This had not yet happened, however, when Benjamin forwarded him a copy of the circular, and this copy fell into the hands of the enemy, and was pub-

[1] Mason, p. 373.

lished.[1] There was no secret in the paper, nor can it in justice be regarded as anything but an entirely proper and judicious statement of the position assumed by the Confederate government; yet it was susceptible of misrepresentation, and was misrepresented.

In substance, Benjamin's circular stated that the Confederate government had no control whatever over the slave-trade, which was undoubtedly true:

"The states, by the Constitution, . . . unanimously stipulated ' that the importation of negroes of the African race from any foreign country other than the slave-holding states or territories of the United States of America is hereby forbidden; and Congress is required to pass such laws as shall effectually prevent the same' (Article I, section 9). It will thus be seen that no power is delegated to the Confederate government over this subject, but that it is included in the . . . class . . . of powers exercised directly by the states. . . . Any attempt on the part of the treaty-making power of this government to prohibit the African slave-trade, in addition to the insuperable objections above suggested, would leave open the implication that the same power has authority to permit such introduction. No such implication can be sanctioned by us. The government unequivocally and absolutely denies its possession of any power whatever over the subject, and cannot entertain any propositions in relation to it. While it is totally beneath the dignity of this government to give assurances for the purpose of vindicating itself from any unworthy suspicions of its good faith on this subject that may be disseminated by the agents of the United States, it may not

[1] Cf. Callahan, p. 95; N. Y. *Times*, April 1, 1863.

be improper that you should point out the superior efficacy of our constitutional provision to any treaty stipulations we could make. . . . A treaty might be abrogated by a party temporarily in power in our country, at the sole risk of disturbing amicable relations with a foreign power. The Constitution, unless by an approach to unanimity, could not be changed without the destruction of this government itself. . . .

"The policy of the Confederacy is as fixed and immutable on this subject as the imperfection of human nature permits human resolve to be. No additional agreements, treaties, or stipulations can commit these states to the prohibition of the African slave-trade with more binding efficacy than those they have themselves devised. . . . We trust, therefore, that no unnecessary discussions on this matter will be introduced into your negotiations. If, unfortunately, this reliance should prove ill-founded, you will decline continuing negotiations on your side, and transfer them to us at home, where, in such event, they could be conducted with greater facility and advantage, under the direct supervision of the President."

The Confederacy was not to have the opportunity of making a treaty with any power; but, in contemplation of successful negotiations, it was proper that the Secretary of State should instruct his subordinates that the Confederate President and Senate were incompetent to consider at all a treaty involving the slave-trade. If taken in good part, his words bear no sinister interpretations; but just as ill-informed or malevolent critics had carped at Lincoln's Proclamation of Emancipation because it decreed abolition only where his authority was not recognized, *viz.*, within the Confederacy, while it maintained slavery in those places under his control, even so the evil-disposed saw in this paper the hint that the South would, if it could, reopen the slave-trade. Its capture and publication, therefore, were unfortunate.

Meanwhile, Benjamin had received Slidell's dispatch containing the hint that the Confederates might build vessels of war in France. Instructions were sent him to make sure of the Emperor's good faith in the matter, which then passed for a time under the control of the Secretary of the Navy and of his most important representative in Europe, Captain Bulloch.[1] But to Benjamin Slidell still reported the steps in the negotiations. After an interview with a shipbuilder, who sought him out, and who was known to be in the confidence of the Emperor; after an interview with Drouyn de l'Huys, who intimated that he would shut his eyes and not see what was not called to his attention; and after further reassuring promises from the Minister of Marine and from Louis Napoleon himself, through the shipbuilder, "that there would be no difficulty on the subject," Slidell felt confident that all would be well. Captain Bulloch, kept informed by him, then made provisional contracts for the building and equipping of four corvettes of the *Alabama* type, and later for two ironclad men-of-war. It was no wonder that Benjamin was "entirely convinced of the hearty sympathy of the Emperor," or that he wrote to Slidell (June 22d) contrasting the bullying of England by Seward and Adams with their self-restraint toward France, and praising "the acumen of Mr. Seward in discovering

[1] For fuller accounts, see Bulloch, Vol. II, Chap. I; Bigelow, *passim;* and Slidell's dispatches, *Pickett Papers.*

where it was safe to threaten, and where it was prudent to refrain.''

While his efforts thus seemed to be rewarded with some success in France, and while there was still prospect of more *Alabamas* slipping away from England, the trend of public opinion and the attitude of the British government were not so favorable. Considerable effort had already been made to influence popular feeling in Europe through the newspapers. Mr. Benjamin sent out Edwin De Leon, "for the special purpose of enlightening public opinion in Europe through the press," and with him the Secretary of State kept up a correspondence. A considerable fund of secret-service money was put at his disposal, and he was instructed to use it in subsidies where it might prove effective. De Leon was a journalist of some experience, and was expected to accomplish a great deal with the papers, especially in France and England, where he went first. Having done there all that he conceived necessary for the time, he wrote, suggesting that with more funds he might be more useful. Benjamin replied on December 13, 1862: "I will take measures to forward you additional means to enable you to extend the field of your operations, and to embrace, if possible, the press of Central Europe in your campaign. Austria, and Prussia, as well as the smaller Germanic powers, seem to require intelligence of the true condition of our affairs, and of the nature of our struggle, and it is to be hoped you may find means to act with efficiency in molding public opinion in those countries."

It was at this time, we recall, that Benjamin was sending out Lamar in the vain hope of finding Russia willing to receive a Confederate envoy. He and De Leon discovered that Central Europe was hopelessly against them where it took any interest whatever in the matter. The most promising fields were France and England, and there De Leon carried out Benjamin's wishes as best he might by publishing scraps of Southern news and pro-Southern articles in papers and reviews. His usefulness in France, however, was somewhat curtailed by his having incurred the not unreasonable resentment of Mr. Slidell, who complained to Benjamin [1] of the agent's preposterous assumption of diplomatic airs, and consequent interference with him, and seriously questioned the extent of his knowledge of and influence over Parisian journals. With this, however, we have nothing to do further than to mention it. In England several agents were relied upon quite as much as De Leon to mold public opinion. Mr. Mason himself understood this to be part of his duty, and called attention to another [2] who helped, though not, of course, a Confederate emissary; this was Mr. James Spence, who figured prominently in the negotiation of the cotton bonds of the Confederacy, and whose speech for the South was always at command. But, feeling that back-stairs dealings with the press did not accord with the diplomatic status he wished Mr. Mason to assume, Benjamin confided the press matters and other non-diplomatic business to Henry Hotze, who, like De Leon, had been a journalist, and who now, as commercial agent of the Confederacy in London, was to occupy a very difficult and necessary post. With his activities in other direc-

---

[1] Cf. Callahan, p. 97.   [2] Mason, pp. 271, 295.

tions, in connection with other departments of the Confederate government, we need not deal; what was expected of him by the State Department may be best learned through a few extracts from one of Benjamin's dispatches:[1] "You are aware that your position of commercial agent was conferred principally with the view of rendering effective your services in using the press of Great Britain in aid of our cause; and until our recognition all other objects must be made subordinate to that end. . . . Your plan of engaging the services of writers employed in the leading daily papers, and thereby securing not only their coöperation, but educating them into such a knowledge of our affairs as will enable them to counteract effectually the misrepresentations of the Northern agents, appears to be judicious and effective; and after consultation with the President he is satisfied that an assignment to the support of your efforts of two thousand pounds per annum out of the appropriation confided to him for secret service will be well spent."

But the Confederacy could not thus purchase golden opinions; despite the earnest efforts of the London *Index*,[2] a weekly paper chiefly sustained by the various press agents, its best advocates there were the honest British love of fair play and the inspiring victories of the Confederate generals. When the latter continued, so did the admiration of the English; but as the slaughter of one Northern army was relentlessly followed by the bringing forward of another to the slaughter, as the deadly and heroic blows of the armies of the South seemed to leave no more wound than

[1] January 16, 1863; see Rhodes, Vol. IV, p. 356, note.
[2] Callahan, p. 92.

upon water, the confidence of her foreign friends was shaken.

In military affairs, during the spring and summer of 1863 as one year before, the Confederacy seemed ever on the eve of attaining such success as would end the contest victoriously for her, and yet never quite succeeded. At Chancellorsville, on May 3d, Lee shattered another Federal army and discredited another Federal general; but though "Fighting Joe" Hooker's reputation was gone, Lee had lost the worth of many a brigade in "Stonewall" Jackson, who there fell mortally wounded after one more triumphant demonstration of his genius. While in the Southwest the Federals had yet made poor use of their possession of New Orleans, and had been driven back from Vicksburg, their armies now gathered in fatal folds about that last great stronghold on the Mississippi, and Lee in Virginia once more staked all upon a daring campaign of invasion. But Vicksburg surrendered on the fourth of July, while each side was resting from the shock of Gettysburg. Again, as at Antietam, Lee had failed in a task that was too great; and this time, though his splendid army held its fragments together and safely crossed the Potomac, it had suffered a defeat from whose consequences nothing but his skill could have saved it.

Just before the news of these disasters reached England the Southern sympathizers there had made another demonstration. Mr. Roebuck introduced into Parliament a resolution that the government should enter into negotiations with the other great powers looking to intervention in American affairs, and supported it by a speech strongly in favor of the Confedcracy, in which he detailed an interview with Napoleon to show that that monarch "was stronger than ever in favor of recognizing the South." But the motion was debated in no friendly spirit by members of the dominant party; the reference to Napoleon was ill-judged, and led to denial, charge, and countercharge between him and Roebuck; and it was subsequently withdrawn by its author on July 13th. Hotze wrote Benjamin ten days later that the defeat at Gettysburg, coupled with the fall of Vicksburg, had spread very general dismay. And Confederate securities, buoyant in early spring, were now unsteady, and soon on the downward grade. [1]

Before this time, however, the secretary was being wrought up to the conviction that there was little present hope of recognition from England, and the strained relations with the British consuls in the Confederacy were rapidly approaching a crisis. In a dispatch to Mason, [2] June 6th, Benjamin gives very dispassionately his side of the case, which we shall quote, with the prefatory statement that this particular quarrel was with Mr. Moore, British consul at Richmond, who had exerted himself in behalf of two men seeking to evade military service under the false pretense—there seems no doubt of this—that they were British subjects, and who had expressed himself very indiscreetly in connection with the matter:

"The President," says Mr. Benjamin, "has not deemed it necessary to interpose any obstacle to the

---

[1] *Pickett Papers;* Mason, pp. 419–427, 431, *et seq.*; Rhodes, Vol. IV, pp. 374–376.
[2] Mason, pp. 432, *et seq.*

continued residence of British consuls within the Confederacy by virtue of exequaturs granted by the former government. His course has been consistently guided by the principles which underlie the whole structure of our government. The state of Virginia having delegated to the government of the United States by the Constitution of 1787, the power of controlling its foreign relations, became bound by the action of that government in its grant of an exequatur to Consul Moore. When Virginia seceded, withdrew the powers delegated to the government of the United States, and conferred them on this government, the exequatur granted to Consul Moore was not thereby invalidated. . . . On these grounds the President has hitherto steadily resisted all influences which have been exerted to induce him to exact of foreign consuls that they should ask for an exequatur from the government as a condition of the continued exercise of their functions. It was not deemed compatible with the dignity of the government to extort, by enforcing the withdrawal of national protection from neutral residents, such inferential recognition of its independence as might be supposed to be implied in the request for an exequatur. The consuls of foreign nations, therefore, established within the Confederacy, who were in the possession of an exequatur issued by the government of the United States prior to the formation of the Confederacy, have been maintained and respected in the exercise of their respective functions, and the same respect and protection will be accorded to them in the future so long as they confine themselves to the sphere of their duties and seek neither to evade nor defy the legitimate authority of this government within its own jurisdiction.

"There has grown up an abuse, however, the result of this tolerance on the part of the President, which is too serious to be longer allowed. Great Britain has deemed it for her interest to refuse acknowledging the patent fact of the existence of this Confederacy as an independent nation. It is scarcely to be expected that we should, by our own conduct, imply assent to the justice or propriety of that refusal.

" Now, the British minister accredited to the government of our enemies assumes the power to issue instructions to, and exercise authority over the consuls of Great Britain residing within this country : nay, even to appoint agents to supervise British interests in the Confederate States.   This course of conduct plainly ignores the existence of this government, and implies the continuance of the relations between that minister and the consuls of Her Majesty resident within the Confederacy which existed prior to withdrawal of these states from the Union.

" It is further the assertion of a right on the part of Lord Lyons, by virtue of his credentials as Her Majesty's minister at Washington, to exercise the power and authority of a minister accredited to Richmond, and officially received as such by the President.   Under these circumstances, and because of similar action by other ministers, the President has felt it his duty to order that no direct communication be permitted between the consuls of neutral nations in the Confederacy and the functionaries of those nations residing within the enemy's country."

Benjamin exposes in diplomatic phraseology what must have been in plain speech an intolerable situation ; with the British consuls under the authority of and receiving their instructions through the British minister in Washington, friction could hardly have been avoided.   The fact that Moore's exequatur was now revoked is but a symptom of the growing irritation against England, which was to be further increased by a similar incident.   In the autumn of 1862 Mr. Magee, British consul at Mobile, had assisted the state of Alabama to send through the blockade, on a British man-of-war, a large sum in specie to pay interest on the state bonds to foreign creditors. Immediately upon learning of this flagrant breach of the Queen's proclamation of neutrality, Lord Lyons dismissed Mr. Magee, in spite of the earnest protest of Mr. Benjamin against a policy which could not but react injuriously upon the credit of the state of Alabama. In reporting the affair to Lord Russell, the British minister at Washington conceded the reasonableness of Mr. Benjamin's objection to "the connection between this legation and the consulates in the South, [as] embarrassing and inconvenient, with regard both to the government of the United States and to the *de facto* government of the Confederate States."

"Mr. Benjamin's complaint concerning the dismissal of Mr. Magee by Her Majesty's government," he continued, "is less reasonable. . . . To export specie from Mobile was a manifest breach of the blockade of that port. . . . But it is not surprising that this affair should have increased the susceptibility of the Confederates with regard to the connection between this legation and the Southern consulates."[1]   Just after the culmination of the quarrel with Moore, this Mobile affair developed a sequel. Benjamin informed Mason[2] in a dispatch of June 11th, that he had just learned that a Mr. Cridland, who had sometimes acted as consul at Richmond during Moore's absence, had gone to Mobile and there exhibited credentials and served the part of consul to succeed Magee, under instructions from Washington. This was immediately resented, while Mason was directed

---

[1] Callahan, p. 177, *et seq.*; Montague Bernard, *Neutrality of Great Britain*, p. 472.
[2] Mason, p. 436.

to lay before the British government the views of the Confederate authorities, expressed temperately but without hesitation. Mr. Cridland was informed that he could not be permitted to "exercise consular functions at Mobile, and it [was] intimated to him that his choice of some other state than Alabama for his residence would be agreeable to this government."

As the summer wore on and Mr. Mason continued to report an unfriendly attitude on the part of Great Britain, and especially as it became manifest that the two Confederate rams building at Birkenhead would hardly be allowed to repeat the *Alabama's* bold trick and escape, it became equally manifest that even the attempt at diplomatic relations with England would soon have to cease. The powerful rams at Birkenhead would have been of incalculable service to the Confederacy; for with such vessels, as the famous *Virginia* (or *Merrimac*) had demonstrated, the fleet of wooden blockading boats before Charleston, Wilmington, and Mobile might have been brushed away, or blown "as high as the sky, to let King Cotton and his army pass by." When the first fears of interference with the construction of these vessels arose, Benjamin had instructed Mason to arrange for their transfer to French or other neutral flags, and Captain Bulloch had, with great address, succeeded in selling them to French owners, with whom he had a secret understanding that the men-of-war, once safely out of British waters, should be resold to the Confederacy.[1] But though the blind was well constructed, Benjamin apparently perceived that it would never successfully undergo the scrutiny of

[1] Bulloch, Vol. I, pp. 376–460; Rhodes, Vol. IV p. 377, *et seq.*

Adams. At all events, without waiting for further
news of the efforts to get the vessels out of Birkenhead,
he wrote to Mason : [1]

" The perusal of the recent debates in the British
Parliament satisfies the President that the government
of Her Majesty has determined to decline the overtures made through you for establishing, by treaty,
friendly relations between the two governments, and
entertains no intentions of receiving you as the accredited minister of this government near the British
court.

" Under these circumstances, your continued residence in London is neither conducive to the interests
nor consistent with the dignity of this government, and
the President therefore requests that you consider your
mission at an end, and that you withdraw, with your
secretary, from London.

" In arriving at this conclusion, it gives me pleasure
to say that the President is entirely satisfied with your
own conduct of the delicate mission confided to you,
and that it is in no want of proper effort on your part
that the necessity for your recall has originated.

" If you find that it is in accordance with usage, to
give notice of your intended withdrawal to Earl Russell,
you will, of course, conform to precedent in that respect."

Reluctant to risk the loss of any advantage that
might accrue through a possible, if improbable, change
of attitude on the part of the British government,
Benjamin accompanied this formal dispatch with a
private note for the eyes of the envoy alone, leaving it
to his discretion as to whether the order to withdraw

[1] Mason, p. 449.

from London should be obeyed immediately or disregarded, "in the event of any marked or decisive change in the policy of the British cabinet before your receipt of the dispatch. Although no such change is anticipated, it is not deemed prudent to ignore altogether its possibility, and it is in this view of the case that discretion is left you as to your action. In the absence of some important and marked change of conduct on the part of Great Britain, however, the President desires that your action on the instructions in [the dispatch] be as prompt as convenient."

The authorization to withdraw, hardly unwelcome, was received by Mr. Mason on September 14th. Nothing had softened the heart of Russell—which, indeed, had been but further hardened against the South after the reading of Adams's famous note of September 5th, in regard to the imminent escape of the two rams at Birkenhead : "It would be superfluous in me to point out to your lordship that this is war." The vessels, so desperately needed in the Confederacy, were detained. But the prudent envoy waited to consult with Slidell about the propriety of obeying the instructions to withdraw, of which he himself had no sort of doubt. There was, indeed, nothing else to do, and so, on the 21st, Mr. Mason addressed a note to Lord Russell communicating the instructions received from the State Department and taking formal leave. According as one views it,—believing, on the one hand, that England's course saved the world from another such calamity as war between her and the United States ; or holding, on the other, that Seward and Adams were merely uttering empty threats and that the proverbially haughty Briton humiliated his nation by tameness under such threats—there is a note of the pathetic or of the sarcastic in Lord Russell's reply (September 25th), that the reasons which had induced him to decline Mason's overtures were "still in force," and that he regretted that "circumstances have prevented my cultivating your personal acquaintance, which, in a different state of affairs, I should have done with much pleasure and satisfaction." Five days later the Confederate commissioner shook the dust of London—if there be any—from his feet.[1]

So terminated, in utter barrenness, the attempt at diplomatic intercourse with England on the part of what Lord Russell used to style, offensively, "the so-called Confederate States." Shortly after Mason's withdrawal, and, indeed, before news of it had been received in Richmond, the difficulty about the British consuls reached its culmination. Again it was through an interference with the military service of the Confederacy that another British consul, Mr. Fullarton, at Savannah, offended. There was much correspondence between him and Governor Brown, of Georgia, and with the Confederate government; we may most readily dispose of it by turning to a dispatch of Benjamin to Slidell, dated October 8th, reviewing the history of the relations with British consuls, and enclosing a copy of the final letter to Mr. Fullarton from the Secretary of State.[2] In this Mr. Benjamin writes to the consul: "Your letters of the 1st and 3d instant have been received. You inform this government that, 'under your instructions you have felt it

---

[1] Mason, pp. 451–456.
[2] This dispatch was captured and published; see N. Y. *Times*, Oct. 20, 1863.

to be your duty to advise British subjects, that while they ought to acquiesce in the service required so long as it is restricted to the maintenance of internal peace and order, whenever they shall be brought into actual conflict with the forces of the United States, whether under the state or Confederate government, the service so required is such as they cannot be expected to perform.' . . .

"In a communication from the acting British consul in Charleston, to the military authorities, he also has informed them that" [his instructions are similar to Fullarton's]. . . .

"It thus appears that the consular agents of the British government have been instructed not to confine themselves to an appeal for redress, either to courts of justice or to this government, whenever they may conceive that grounds exist for complaint against the Confederate authorities in their treatment of British subjects (an appeal which has in no case been made without receiving just consideration), but that they assume the power of determining for themselves whether enlisted soldiers of the Confederacy are properly bound to its service; that they even arrogate the right to interfere directly with the execution of the Confederate laws, and to advise soldiers of the Confederate armies to throw down their arms in the face of the enemy.

"This assumption of jurisdiction by foreign officials within the territory of the Confederacy, and this encroachment on its sovereignty cannot be tolerated for a moment; and the President has had no hesitation in directing that all consuls and consular agents of the British government be notified that they can no longer be permitted to exercise their functions or even reside within the limits of the Confederacy.

"I am directed, therefore, by the President to communicate to you this order, that you promptly depart from the Confederacy, and that in the meantime you cease to exercise any consular functions within its limits."

Coming so closely after the breaking off of such relations as could, in diplomatic fiction, be presumed to subsist through Mason's official presence in London, this expulsion of the British consuls might very easily be made to appear an act of petulant retaliation. Undoubtedly the feelings of the Confederate Secretary of State were considerably exacerbated against England; but we have seen that the existing relations with the British consuls had long constituted a serious embarrassment. This awkward situation had now terminated as it could hardly have failed to terminate. Its coincidence with Mason's recall, however, was unfortunate. Among some of the people there seems to have been not a little exultation at what they erroneously considered a slap in the face for England after all her insolence to Mr. Mason; they rejoiced that the government, as they thought, at last showed real spirit in its resentment of such insufferable bad manners. And a few, like the Richmond *Enquirer* (October 15th), opined that "we may now expect, ere long, to see a British minister at Richmond, and British consuls asking exequaturs from Mr. Benjamin; for England never neglects her subjects, nor leaves them without the shadow of her wing and the guardianship of her flag. The sooner the better; we do not want to hurt either her or her subjects."

CHAPTER XII

DARK DAYS IN RICHMOND

IN treating of the larger questions of Confederate diplomacy, it has been difficult to make clear what duties there could have been sufficient to occupy during long hours, as tradition says, so ready a worker as the Secretary of State; for the writing of a dispatch or two in the course of a month to Mason and Slidell was surely no great tax upon his time. Even if we stretch the thing as much as possible, and include the names of all the diplomatic and consular agents the Confederacy employed, the purely ministerial duties of Mr. Benjamin, in the way of writing and answering dispatches,—remember that he had no ambassadors to receive nor diplomatic tea-parties to attend in Richmond—might seem at first glance but slight.

Quite true, these various agents muster a larger roll than perhaps one would fancy; besides, the bulky volumes and packages, catalogued to the number of eighty-four, now preserved in the United States Treasury building at Washington, and containing letters, dispatches, instructions to and from Mason, Slidell, Rost, Mann, Lamar, Preston, Lynch, Heyliger, Helm, Hotze, and the rest, make the impression that it would be somewhat of a task to read them, and perhaps also, therefore, to have to write or digest them. Our respect for the labor involved in Mr. Benjamin's position, if won through such considerations, is further added to when we discover that many matters not in any way akin to diplomacy help to swell these volumes, and that, much of the mere transcribing and copying of dispatches, as well as the translating of cypher and the general routine work, had to be done by the secretary himself and his assistant, Mr. Washington; for clerks were few, and not always to be entrusted with secrets.

Making all allowances, however, the affairs of state alone would not have occupied Mr. Benjamin's time. Tradition has long had it that Davis, finding his co-adjutor always willing and able, got in the habit of referring to the State Department everything that did not beyond any hope belong to some other; and that he consulted more freely with the Secretary of State than with any other member of the cabinet. Of the latter supposition we have, of course, no possible direct proof, though there is, as I have stated in a previous chapter, every reason to believe it correct. To the considerations there offered, it should, I think, be sufficient to add here that both Mrs. Davis and Mr. Washington, in their reminiscences, speak of the prolonged conferences between Benjamin and Davis. As concerning the tradition that many duties not necessarily appertaining to his office were assigned to Mr. Benjamin, confirmation sufficient is found in the miscellaneous nature of the contents of the archives of the department, as well as in current journalistic gossip and in those same reminiscences of contemporaries. And in estimating the necessary work of the Secretary of State, one should not forget to include the selection and polemic defense of a policy in the larger domestic affairs of the Confederacy. The Secretary of State was the proper intermediary in communications between the general government and its members, the state governments. Of this sort of intercourse there was, too, an appalling abundance, as one may see even in what has been published in the invaluable *Official Records of the War of the Rebellion*. Contrary to the impression that long prevailed, Mr. Davis was most scrupulous and sincere in his efforts to keep well within the limits assigned to the Executive in the Confederate Constitution, and to avoid needless encroachments on the sphere of local authority; to those who doubt this statement, not having here space for more elaborate discussion, I would merely suggest reflection on a few facts.

In the North, the writ of *habeas corpus* was suspended, during the first year and more of the war, by mere executive decree; arbitrary arrests were made hundreds of miles from the scene of hostilities by the simple command of Seward and Stanton; and later Congress authorized the suspension of the writ during the war. In the South, Mr. Davis neither claimed nor exercised this unusual power which, in the four years of strife and in the country that was invaded, was employed for periods aggregating less than eighteen months, and then by authority of the Confederate Congress.[1] Maintaining a regard so genuine for constitutional limitations, and at the same time carrying on the government and getting things done, often necessitated the writing of lengthy and skilful arguments to convince reluctant governors and other officials whom one could not ride over roughshod. Though Mr. Davis could hold his own,—none

[1] For fuller treatment of this and similar topics, see Rhodes, Vol. V, pp. 453–458, 470–475.

better, in this sort of pen-fight,—it was not infrequently a physical impossibility for him to devote his energies to this instead of to the real battles. Accordingly, it was commonly believed, and no doubt correctly, that Mr. Benjamin wrote many of the very able letters defending the policy of the government, and that he it was who formulated these policies and drafted them into laws.[1]

We could wish it more detailed and specific, but it is a pleasant picture of the Secretary of State that is given by Mr. Washington,[2] confirming some of the conclusions I have drawn :   "I was brought into close relation with Mr. Benjamin, occupied the adjoining room [at the department] to his, and shared his confidence and friendship to an unusual extent.   This enables me not only to estimate him as a public official, but to weigh and appreciate his many personal gifts and admirable qualities. . . .   A man of society, his tact in personal intercourse was unfailing, his politeness invariable.   In all the trials and anxieties of the great struggle, I never saw his temper ruffled or embittered.   His opinions were generally decided but courteously expressed, even when he differed most widely from others.   In his most unguarded moments I cannot recall that he ever uttered an oath or a violent expression.   He was ever calm, self-poised, and master of all his resources.   His grasp of a subject seemed instantaneous.   His mind appeared to move without friction.   His thought was clear.   His style, whether in composition or conversation, was natural, orderly,

---

[1] For his authorship of the Presidential Messages, see the letter to Mason, in Chapter XIV.
[2] *Lawley MS.*

and perspicuous. I do not affirm that his composi-
tions were wholly unstudied, but, whatever art there
was, he had the art to hide. I have known him often
to compose a long dispatch or state paper with great
rapidity with hardly a word changed or interlined in
the whole manuscript. Sometimes, but very rarely,
he was unwell, and then he would not work or write
at all. Ordinarily, he loved work and absorbed it not
only in his own department, but from other branches
of the service.

"Mr. Benjamin's habit was to arrive at the department about 9 A. M. and to stay until 3 P. M., unless
he had some special work to complete, when he
remained longer. But usually he left at three. He
dispatched business rapidly and permitted no work to
lie over or accumulate. As the President's offices
were near by, he was much with Mr. Davis. I spent
about an hour with him nearly every day at
the department, but rarely saw him at any other
time. . . .

"Mr. Benjamin identified himself wholly with the
struggle and with the administration. He was personally devoted to Mr. Davis, and probably had more
influence with him than any other man. . . . I
am sure that Mr. Benjamin kept Mr. Davis advised of
all the important operations of the State Department;
but its management, its instructions, correspondence,
and policies were those of its accomplished head. In
selections for positions abroad, the President, of course,
had the final decision."

Though obviously more concerned with the non-
official Mr. Benjamin than this quotation from Mr.
Washington, there is something to my purpose in Mrs.

Davis's letter,[1] from which I shall now quote, endeavoring to keep away from the alluring passages that tell merely of the man : " Mr. Benjamin and Mr. Davis . . . had had, up to the year of secession, little social intercourse ; an occasional invitation to dinner was accepted and exchanged, and nothing more. . . . It was to me a curious spectacle ; the steady approximation to a thorough friendliness of the President and his war minister. It was a very gradual *rapprochement*, but all the more solid for that reason ; and when finally many of their constituents objected to Mr. Benjamin's retaining the portfolio of war, because of some reverses which no one could have averted, the President promoted him to the State Department with a personal and sore sense of the injustice done to the man who had now become his friend and right hand during the severe labors which devolved upon the government officials in that desperate and hapless conflict of numbers against right.

"Mr. Benjamin was always ready for work ; sometimes, with half an hour's recess, he remained with the Executive from ten in the morning until nine at night, and together they traversed all the difficulties which encompassed our beleaguered land. . . . Both the President and the Secretary of State worked like galley-slaves, early and late. Mr. Davis came home fasting, a mere mass of throbbing nerves, and perfectly exhausted ; but Mr. Benjamin was always fresh and buoyant. . . . There was one striking peculiarity about his temperament. No matter what disaster

[1] This and other references, are to private letters to me, and to *Lawley MS.*

befell our arms, after he had done all in his power to prevent or rectify it, he was never depressed."

On all observers whose reminiscences are available, the most vivid and lasting impressions made by what they saw of Mr. Benjamin in Richmond are, that he was always cheerful, and that he worked very hard. Dr. Hoge, for example, writes: [1] "He entered very little into the social life of the city. Even had he been disposed to do so he could not have had time for it. He was one of the hardest workers in the cabinet, going to his office early in the morning and often remaining there until after midnight. No matter what his toils or how late his vigils, every morning as he came by my house at nine o'clock (having breakfasted before leaving his) he was dressed faultlessly, and always with a bright, cheerful aspect. Mrs. Hoge often said as she saw him pass, 'There goes Mr. Benjamin, smiling as usual.'"

Though we are credibly informed that life is not all "beer and skittles" anywhere, and though that statement would seem painfully true as applied to the war-shaken capital of the Confederacy, nevertheless the beer and the skittles were not utterly wanting there. Among a certain set, indeed, composed chiefly of reckless blockade runners and others who took desperate chances in the gamble for fortune, there was, on occasion, such riotous living as contrasted painfully with the undoubted privations of the many, at some seasons, in a city that knew what a bread riot was (April 2d, 1863), and excited the righteous wrath of the more scrupulous and patriotic citizens. Of this set, however, not even scandal could accuse Benjamin

[1] *Lawley MS.*

of being one. Though Dr. Hoge fancied he had too little opportunity for amusements, Mrs. Davis and others mention his taking part in the social life of the more dignified and proper set. This participation in the gaieties by which Richmond, from time to time, sought to relieve the strain of war, was, however, but occasional. As a rule, the routine of Mr. Benjamin's life was very simple, his manner of living unostentatious, though as comfortable as his means and the exigencies of the situation permitted.

"There were no formal receptions or dinners by the President or any of the cabinet," writes Mr. Washington. "They lived very plainly. Mr. Benjamin lived in a very modest way at the west end of Richmond, with a 'mess,' as it was called, of Louisiana congressmen—Honorable Duncan F. Kenner, Charles M. Conrad, and others; but while he liked social intercourse with a few friends, he did not care for crowds or general society." Of his associates at this time we learn further from Mrs. Davis: "He had living with him a very well-educated and elegant young brother-in-law, Jules St. Martin, whom he loved dearly." This is the same interesting man of whose desperate difficulties with the English tongue Mr. Russell makes mention, in his account of the visit to Mr. Benjamin at Montgomery. Mrs. Davis continues: "When Mr. Benjamin came to Richmond, Mr. St. Martin came also, and the two set up a comfortable house, where they entertained their friends in as elegant a manner as blockaded *bon vivants* could do." Here were received some of the few notables who managed to find their way through the blockade; and Mr. Benjamin's friends were always welcome to share what he had.

As times grew harder, however, the feasts at the secretary's table were somewhat suggestive of that famous lemonade brewed for Mr. Swiveller and herself by "The Marchioness." His family, with a comparative plenty of those broiled chickens in which they knew he delighted, heard with much comic distress, through a gentleman who dined with the Secretary of State, that the board on that occasion was graced with plenty of corn bread and a doubtful sufficiency of bacon. Of course the rather fastidious Mr. Benjamin was pleased to be included among those intimate friends who, toward the end of the war, used to receive from Mrs. Davis "verbal invitations somewhat in this fashion, 'Do come to dinner or tea; we succeeded in running the blockade this week' which meant 'real coffee' after dinner, preserved fruits, loaf sugar, good tea, and sometimes some anchovy toast, which was always acceptable to Mr. Benjamin's palate. He used to say that with bread made of Crenshaw's flour [a noted miller of Virginia], spread with paste made of English walnuts from an immense tree in our grounds, and a glass of McHenry sherry, of which we had a scanty store, 'a man's patriotism became rampant.'"

Of Mr. Benjamin's family we have not heard since the outbreak of the war, when some of its members were in New Orleans, and his wife and daughter in France. There the latter remained, and were supported by frequent remittances from him, which, though not so lavish as they had formerly been, were adequate. Mrs. Levy and her daughter, Mrs. Popham, and Miss Harriet Benjamin, in New Orleans, could not but view with alarm the approach of the Federal fleet. Mrs. Kruttschnitt, another sister, was more fortunate in being secure against molestation, her husband being of foreign nationality, and, indeed, German consul. After the fall of the city, Mrs. Levy and her household, who had been given no warning to move from New Orleans by Mr. Benjamin, found themselves in a condition rather precarious; though not molested for some time, they were, at best, cut off from their base of supplies, and from direct communication with the one who had so zealously looked after their comfort and their safety. But immunity on the part of women known to be related to the hated Confederate Secretary of State could not long be expected under the rule of such heroes as the North bestowed upon New Orleans. The stern necessities of war, even to the limit of Sherman's emphatic epithet, the South will concede ; but with what honest pride shall she not boast that her soldiers' record is free from stains of purely wanton and cowardly persecution of defenseless women and children. What now followed for Mrs. Levy and her household, which I shall relate as nearly as possible as it was told me by her daughter, is not tragic, merely petty and spiteful, of just the measure of the men responsible for it.

"One night in the summer of 1862," said she, "about nine o'clock, there came a knock on the door that startled the family. Riley, the colored diningroom man, went to answer it, and returned with fear in face and accent, to announce that 'there's a Yankee right at the door.' Mrs. Levy and Miss Harriet fled, leaving me to face the young Federal lieutenant whom I found there, and who told me that he had merely been sent to warn us that the house was needed by the military authorities, and would be taken possession of in the morning and used as a hospital for General Weitzel's men. 'This will do,' he said, after inspecting the rooms with a candle while I followed, protesting vainly. 'If you wish to leave at once, you may take away such things as you absolutely need; a squad of men will be sent to protect you to-night.' We began packing up at once, and fortunately, when the dreaded soldiers came, the men proved to be Germans who had known Mr. Popham. By humoring them and plying them with what was left of some rare old Bourbon and Cognac, once highly prized by Mr. Benjamin and his guests, we prevailed on them to move nearly all of the furniture to the house of a neighbor, kindly put at our service, which was practically empty. Owing a small amount to the German groceryman whose yard adjoined ours, I pulled some palings off the fence and drove the cow into his yard. By this payment in kind, our only debt was cleared.

"All through the night we worked, packing and moving. In the morning, as Mrs. Levy was sitting on a bundle of our belongings, almost the last, on the front porch, another squad of soldiers, with an insolent young fellow in command, came to relieve the complaisant guard of the past night. 'Madam,' said the officer, 'are you the sister of the arch rebel, Benjamin?' Mrs. Levy timidly admitted that she was. 'Then you are not to remove anything from this house. It is a military necessity.' Fortunately this individual was relieved later in the day by a more reasonable officer, who permitted us to remove the few remaining things that we needed. After a few days of discomfort and uncertainty, we rented two rooms in the French quarter of the city, where we lived for some weeks, till a letter, delivered we knew not how, came from Mr. Benjamin, advising us to make our way out into the Confederacy, where we could be in communication with him. An honest debtor, scorning to take advantage of the chance to slip out of his obligation, paid to me a note for $900; this was all we had, and all we could hope to have till we could again get in communication with Mr. Benjamin."

After adventures that would be full of interest if we had time to recount them, and which many poor refugees could duplicate if their tales were told, Mrs. Levy and her little family made their way to La Grange, in Georgia. Here they settled, and lived in comfort, considering the privations that all were subjected to. Mr. Benjamin sent them money, "as much as he could spare, and provisions, denying himself, we feared, to promote our comfort."

All of this vicarious punishment of the "arch rebel," be it remembered, was of "military necessity," by military authority; the confiscation of his property, even to the books in his deserted law office, under act of Congress, came later. With indignities and insults and even serious privation menacing not only his own womenkind but the many friends of a lifetime in New Orleans, it would be little wonder if Mr. Benjamin's personal feelings were thoroughly roused as he wrote to Mr. Mason[1] describing the "nature of the tyranny exercised over that unfortunate city by the brutal commander who temporarily rules over it."

From righteous denunciation of General Butler, and proclamation of his outlawry (December 23, 1862)—

---

[1] July 19, 1862; Mason. p. 296. For confiscation of the library, see *Picayune*, June 7, 1865.

which it must have been a pleasure to proclaim, even if barren of results—we must return to the now brief story of Confederate foreign relations.

As soon as the Secretary of State was officially informed that Mr. Mason had found it expedient to withdraw from London, he notified the envoy[1] that the President desired him and his secretary to remain on the Continent, preferably at Paris, in readiness to be dispatched wherever their services might be presumed to be useful. On this wandering commission Mr. Mason continued during the remainder of the war; there was never again any really hopeful opportunity to employ him in diplomacy, though he was freely consulted by Mr. Slidell, and, in a private capacity made several trips across the channel, attending to such small matters as Mr. Benjamin might direct or his own zeal might suggest.

Of Mr. Slidell's mission, too, the hope is soon to be lost. The historian gives a fuller account,[2] but we may condense it: Louis Napoleon played a dishonest game with both parties, and when caught at it by the United States, promptly sacrificed the Confederates. Under his assurances, as I have noted, the Confederate agents had contracted for the building in France, at Nantes and Bordeaux, of four cruisers and two ironclads. Work was progressing satisfactorily, when a clerk abstracted papers showing the design and the ownership of two of these vessels and sold them, with what other information he possessed, to Mr. Dayton,

[1] Mason, p. 457.
[2] See Bigelow, *France and the Confederate Navy*; Bulloch, *Secret Service of the Confederacy*; and Callahan, *Diplomatic History of the Confederacy*.

United States minister at Paris.   Armed with positive
proofs of the hostile destination of the vessels, Mr.
Dayton confronted the French authorities, and forced
tne government to take steps that would effectually
prevent these ships from getting out of French ports
to cruise under the Confederate flag.   The first disquieting rumors about the cruisers were sent by Slidell
in dispatches of November 15 and 19, 1863, telling of
his note of remonstrance to Napoleon; of his personal
interview with Drouyn de l'Huys, upon whom his
representations seemed to have some effect; and of the
channels through which the fatal secret had reached
Dayton.

Mr. Benjamin, more perturbed by troublous times
in domestic politics than by unforeseen disaster from a
quarter deemed so safe, and having exhausted himself
in re-fashioning the well-tried arguments that had so
far proved of no force to move European powers to
intervention, had been permitting himself to indulge
in a little digression[1] upon the admirable courage and
patience of Mr. Davis under severe criticism from his
own people: "In all cases without exception, however, our chief magistrate is compelled to bear in
silence any amount of clamor and obloquy, for in nine
cases out of ten a disclosure of facts would injure the
public interest.   At moments like the present, when
the calamities and distresses of a long war have created
in weak and despondent souls the usual result on such
natures, by making them querulous, unjust, and clam-
orous, when men even with good intentions, but ignorant of the facts on which alone judgment can be based,
join in denunciation of those in authority, it is a

---

[1] *Pickett Papers;* dispatch to Slidell, December 9, 1863.

spectacle really sublime to observe the utter abnega-
tion of self, the exclusive reliance on the *mens conscia
recti*, the entire willingness to leave his vindication to
posterity which are displayed by the President."

Within little more than a week (December 18th)
after this, Mr. Benjamin had received Mr. Slidell's
warning. Waiting a fortnight for further developments, he was, for once, despondent from the very
first when he wrote to Slidell on January 8, 1864:
"Painful solicitude is . . . felt, lest in this instance also, we may meet with the double-dealing from
which we have suffered severely since the beginning
of our struggle. Hopeful as I am in temper, there
was something in what passed in the interview to
which you refer [*i. e.*, with Drouyn de l'Huys] that
indicated a desire to escape from plighted faith, and a
scarcely disguised impatience of the burden and
responsibility imposed by previous engagements, which
fills me with distrust. The same effect has been produced on the President."

The actual determination to detain the vessels was
not reached till months later; but Benjamin never
doubted that he had been tricked and would be for-
saken by Louis Napoleon, though at first he prudently
refrained from severity of censure. When the end
came, however, he wrote:[1] "We cannot resist the
conclusion that there has been bad faith and deception
in the course pursued by the Emperor, who has not
hesitated to break his promises to us in order to escape
the consequences resulting from his unpopular Mexican
policy. . . . We feel, therefore, the necessity of
receiving with extreme distrust any assurances what-

[1] June 23, 1864.

ever that may emanate from a party capable of the
double-dealing displayed toward us by the Imperial
Government." From this time, though dispatches
continued to be written to Slidell as commissioner to
France, for all practical purposes the attempt to enlist her aid may be said to have ceased.

To all men not wilfully blind, so we think now, it
must have appeared clear, in the summer of 1864, that
the South could not win her independence, and that it
were best to make whatever terms possible to avert
further useless shedding of blood. But, with resolution which some will call stubborn and some heroic,
the Southerners still fought on, and their leaders still
spoke confidently of the impossibility of conquest by
the North. Mr. Benjamin held to this idea, and gave
it expression on all occasions, public and private. He
writes to Slidell (April 18th) of his "thorough conviction" that independence is near, through the utter
"inability of the United States to continue a contest
in which its resources, both of men and money will
have been exhausted in vain." He speaks in equally as
confident a strain to the Reverend Colonel Jacques and
Mr. Gilmore, unofficial peace envoys from the United
States, who, through passport from Lincoln to Grant
and Grant to Lee, visit Richmond on July 16th ;[1] and
he writes to his sister, Mrs. Kruttschnitt, who was
within the Federal lines at New Orleans : "31 October,
1864.—As for myself, my health is good, my spirits
unimpaired, and I look with undiminished confidence
to our future happy reunion around a common fire-
side."

Other portions of this letter, thoroughly character-

[1] Mason, p. 517; Callahan, pp. 227, 228.

istic of the man in his domestic relations, are so interesting that I shall quote them here, with no further apologies for the digression. There is news of all members of the family, and loving solicitude for their welfare, but with the exception of the brief passage just cited, there is scarce an allusion to himself, and none to political questions :

"An opportunity presents itself, my darling Penny, for writing to you more fully than in the various scraps that I have been able to send you from time to time, and I do hope that you will receive this safely.

"First, let me relieve your affectionate heart, by saying that we are *all* well and in good spirits. I had letters quite recently from Sis, Hatty, and Leah [Mrs. Levy, Miss Harriett Benjamin, and Mrs. Popham]. Sis and Leah are no longer with the family in which they were living, but have obtained board at a very moderate rate in the home of a farmer in the neighborhood of La Grange, where they pass their time somewhat dully, perhaps, but where the table is abundant with all the products of a prosperous farm, and where the people are very kind and good, and consider themselves in great part repaid by the tuition of their little children, in which Sis and Leah amuse themselves. Prior to this last change of residence Sis was not pleasantly situated, and I am very glad that she was able to find another refuge for herself and L. I am able, fortunately, to supply them with funds from a source which I do not choose to risk writing about further than to say that it is outside of the Confederacy.

"Hatty is still with her old friends, who seem much attached to her and will not hear of her leaving them. She is close enough to Sis to make frequent visits practicable, and I furnish her with a moderate contribution toward the household expenditure of the family where she lives.

"Our dear Joe [his brother, in the Confederate army] is still in the trans-Mississippi, and was unluckily unable to accompany Dick Taylor when he crossed to this side, in consequence of his ill health. At my last accounts he was much better. . . .

"Lionel [Mrs. Levy's son] is well and in good spirits. He is judge-advocate of the military court, with the rank of captain of cavalry, and his correspondence with his mother, sister, and myself is pretty regular.

"I have very encouraging letters from wife and daughter, and my wife writes me that our daughter's health is greatly improved and that she is now at last sanguine of a radical cure.

"I heard of you lately through Mrs. Brand, who has gone to Europe, and to whom I was able to be serviceable in return for her great kindness to Sis and Hatty in their trouble. I have never heard whether you received the photograms of my wife and daughter that I sent you by a lady who promised to deliver them in person, but Mrs. Brand informed me that she thought she remembered your mentioning the receipt of them. . . .

"And now, my darling, I must talk of you and your own precious treasures. I suppose that Ernest and Julius, and my saucy little coquette, Becky, have long since lost all memory of me. Your other little one I have never seen, but it seems to me you might manage to send me some *cartes-de-visite* with the portraits of all of you, including my dear Kitt. How does he come on? What does he spend his time about? There must be very little business possible for him. And how gets on the garden? and the ponies? and who are your neighbors? By the way, I live only two doors from Mrs. G——, your old neighbor, who is well and very frequently talks of you. . . .

"We get letters from you so very seldom that I am sure you do not avail yourself of all the opportunities, though Sis and Hatty sometimes hear from you indirectly. A very sure and good way to send me letters would be to get some person going to Havana to take a letter for me and deliver it to C. J. Helm to be forwarded. As our letters never contain a word of anything but family matters there would be no risk, even if they were captured. I think this could be easily managed. I got one letter from you about four months after its date, from one of the officers of a French vessel that left New Orleans last winter.

"Now I must bid you good-bye, my own darling, with a thousand kisses for you and the dear little ones, and a thousand affectionate remembrances to Kitt, from one who loves you dearly, and need not sign his name."

No plea for such a letter is necessary; its simplicity and sincerity of affection are eloquence enough. And yet it is of such a man that we are asked to credit imputations of diabolical cruelty, complicity in schemes nefarious in the eyes of all civilization. We are asked to believe that Mr. Davis and Mr. Benjamin sent agents to Canada with instructions to burn New York City. The facts, or the evidences of fact, are that on April 27, 1864, Mr. Davis issued the following commission:

"HONORABLE JACOB THOMPSON, SIR:—Confiding special trust in your zeal, discretion, and patriotism, I hereby direct you to proceed at once to Canada, there to carry out such instructions as you have received from me verbally, in such manner as shall seem most likely to conduce to the furtherance of the interests of the Confederate States of America which have been intrusted to you.

"Very respectfully and truly yours,
"JEFFERSON DAVIS." [1]

[1] *Official Records*, Series IV, Vol. III, p. 322.

To Clement C. Clay, a similar commission was issued at the same time; and funds to the amount of $900,000 were furnished Thompson. The instructions given being verbal, we have no record of them other than the memory of the persons concerned.

Mr. Benjamin made a fair statement of the principal object of the mission in a dispatch to Mr. Slidell, April 30th:[1] "We have sent Jacob Thompson of Mississippi, and Clement C. Clay of Alabama, to Canada on secret service, in the hope of aiding the disruption between the Eastern and Western states in the approaching election at the North. It is supposed that much good can be done by the purchase of some of the principal presses, especially in the Northwest."

If we add to the instructions for "aiding the disruption between the Eastern and Western states," the duty of aiding in plans for the rescue of Confederate prisoners confined on Johnson's Island and at other points near the Canadian border, we shall probably hit the truth as regards the objects of this mission. We hear nothing further of importance about it—the sweeping devastations of Sheridan in the Shenandoah Valley and the victories at Mobile and Atlanta discountenanced the peace party at the North—until November 27th, when fires undoubtedly of incendiary origin broke out simultaneously, or nearly so, in several New York hotels and theatres. They did little damage, but caused great excitement. In the official *Records of the Rebellion*, published by the United States government,[2] we find what purports to be a letter from Jacob Thompson, found in the Con-

---

[1] *Pickett Papers*, pkg. 80, p. 193; see Callahan, p. 225, note.
[2] Series I, Vol. XLIII, Part II, p. 930.

federate archives, dated Toronto, December 3, 1864, and indorsed, "Received Feb. 13, 1865. J. P. B." Here Mr. Thompson describes the plans to burn New York, as of his authority, and regrets their miscarriage. The inference is that they were approved by Mr. Benjamin, and were, indeed, the attempt to carry out instructions received from the Confederate authorities. [1]

The general denial of the imputation of designs so revolting by Benjamin and Davis has had, and will have, little power to convince so long as the embers of the great war still glow. As food for reflection, however, were it not well to consider what one of the South's most bitter enemies said when high Confederate officials were accused of complicity in the assassination of Lincoln? Thaddeus Stevens remarked: "Those men are no friends of mine. They are public enemies and I would treat the South as a conquered country and settle it politically upon the policy best suited for ourselves. *But I know these men, sir. They are gentlemen, and incapable of being assassins.*" [2]

As far as Mr. Benjamin is concerned, we need no better defense, as has been stated, than his past honorable record to repel a calumny as baseless as that other clumsy one that he had proposed to the British consul in New York that the Confederacy might return to the shelter of the mother country. [3] But for information I append Mr. Washington's statement, made in 1897 :

[1] Cf. Rhodes, Vol. V, pp. 320, 330–341 ; Schouler, Vol. VI, p. 521. Headley, *Confederate Operations in Canada*, pp., 264–283, glories in the attempt and describes his participation in it.

[2] Southern Hist. Soc. Papers, Vol. I, p. 325; quoted by Rhodes, Vol. V, p. 158, note; italics mine.

[3] N. Y. *Times*, Jan. 29, and Feb. 5, 1884; cited by Kohler, p. 78.

"I was present at the time when Mr. Thompson received his instructions from Mr. Benjamin. They were oral and largely suggestive and informal. Much was left to his discretion, and wisely; for he was an experienced and conservative man. But there was not a word or a thought that looked to any violation of the rules of war as they exist among civilized nations. As a matter of fact, Mr. Davis, Mr. Benjamin, General Lee, and the other leaders of the Confederacy, believed to the last that it was not merely right, but the wisest and best policy to maintain and respect every one of the humane restrictions in the conduct of the war which are upheld by the publicists. They did not believe with the United States War Department that any and all destruction of an enemy's property was justifiable.[1] So holding, the lives of Dahlgren's captured officers and men, despite public clamor, were spared, though they came with a known and proven program of sacking Richmond and murdering Mr. Davis and his cabinet.[2] It was not strange, however, that those who burned Atlanta, Jackson, Columbia, and a score of Southern towns, besides a belt of country in South Carolina over forty miles wide, should assume that the Confederate government would retaliate in kind."

As the year 1864 drew to its close, with Grant stubbornly holding to his campaign of hard blows and not to be diverted, with Sherman piercing the heart of Georgia, and, above all, with the ranks of Lee's army rapidly thinning and not to be easily refilled, Mr. Benjamin realized that the affairs of the Confederacy

[1] See ante, Chap. IX.
[2] Cf. Rhodes, Vol. V, p. 514.

were in desperate plight, and that only desperate measures might save the day. He set himself to the task, not an easy one, according to rumor, of convincing Mr. Davis that they must now play their trump cards. First, the ranks of the army must be filled up, and to do this the South must follow Lincoln's example and enlist the negroes. Secondly, European intervention, involving the raising of the blockade, must be had; since other means had failed, the Confederacy must try to move England and France by promising emancipation of the slaves.

Some had favored enlisting negroes long before this; thus in August, 1863, Mr. Micon, of Florida, had proposed the drafting of slaves. But Mr. Benjamin deemed the proposal premature, and inadvisable, since, as he pointed out, they would have to be paid for; and would cost at least $2,000 each, or, if hired, $30 per month, whereas white soldiers received but $11. The organization of negro men in this way might be highly dangerous; and the labor of the slaves was needed in the mines and in the fields.[1] Now, however, the complexion of affairs had changed, and General Lee himself spoke favorably of employing negroes as troops. Reluctantly won over by the representations of the Secretary of State and others, Mr. Davis recommended the prompt passage of such legislation as would empower him to enlist the able-bodied men. There followed, naturally, a long wrangle in Congress and in the press; and though Lee made it known that he favored such a measure, and though his influence doubtless had more to do with its ultimate adoption

[1] See *Pickett Papers, Domestic Letters*, August 18, 1863; summary in Callahan, p. 245.

than that of any other man, all the odium of it attached to Mr. Benjamin. It was only another foolish device, of his, men said, for foreign effect. At this time the attacks upon the score of his religion were redoubled. From their bitterness it was hard to discriminate between the Southern editors and *Harper's Weekly*, describing him as "a lifelong oppressor of [the negro] race, avenging upon them the mediæval torture of [his] own kind." When the President issued a proclamation appointing March 10th as a day of fasting and prayer, the fanatical objected because the Jewish Secretary of State signed and sealed it in his official capacity.

In spite of his unpopularity, however, his oratory had not lost its power. On February 3d, Stephens, Campbell and Hunter met Lincoln and Seward in what is known as the Hampton Roads Conference. It was, said Lincoln, to secure "peace to the people of our one common country"; it was, said Davis, to secure "peace to the two countries"; hence it secured peace to no one then, and has brought forth a pen and ink controversy since.[1] When the Confederate commissioners returned from this fruitless conference, with the answer, in substance, "no terms but absolute submission to the will of the conqueror," Mr. Davis delivered what Stephens considered probably the master oration of his life in an enthusiastic mass meeting at Richmond, to support the administration in continuing the desperate conflict. Three days later (February 9th), at another meeting, Mr. Benjamin made his last political

[1] For fair statement, see Rhodes, Vol. V, pp. 67–73; for Benjamin's contribution to the controversy after the war, see So. Hist. Soc. Papers, Vol. IV, p. 212.

address. Its substance only is known, since there is no
sort of adequate report in any of the papers; it was a
well-timed and skilfully urged plea in behalf of the
policy of emancipating and arming the negroes. Even
when championing a measure so unpopular, the unfor-
gotten art of the orator told upon his audience, made
up largely, says Mrs. Davis, of "officers and men who
had ridden in from the front to hear what had happened. He sent those who had come discouraged and
desperate, knowing as they did the overwhelming forces
which confronted them, back to camp full of hope and
ardor, and I think made the most successful effort of
his life." [1]

But the noisy furore of mass meetings, as some
of the papers remarked, did not furnish any recruits
for Lee's army; and as the enthusiasm ebbed, critics
and "croakers," always plentiful when the tide turns,
seemed to single out Mr. Benjamin as the chief cause
of the woes from which the country suffered. Long
since recovered from the soreness of defeat, and justly
proud, after serious retrospect, of the marvelous endurance of the South in an unequal contest, intelligent
Southerners have done justice to the ability and sincerity of Mr. Davis and of his chief adviser. But the
watchful Jones, who had intimated that both Seward
and Benjamin were "alike destitute of principle and
of moral or physical courage," was now doubtless
correct in his opinion that the country, demanding "a
change of men in the cabinet, [found Mr. Benjamin] the

[1] Letter in *Lawley MS.*; Mrs. Davis writes me (Oct. 12, 1904),
that she was an auditor, in an adjoining room, when the cabinet
met to hear the report of the Commissioners, and that it was Benjamin who suggested and insisted upon a public meeting, "to feel
the pulse of the people."

most obnoxious of all."[1]   Still, in this hour of stress as
always, Mr. Davis stood by him.   Congress fumed and
fretted, and passed no act that could save the Confederacy; but it did not oust the Secretary of State.
Jones, who had fancied that smile fled from his lip,
saw it return again.

Meanwhile that other desperate expedient to which
Mr. Benjamin had persuaded the President was being
tried in Europe: the offer to emancipate the slaves in
exchange for recognition.   Mr. Davis felt, and very
properly, that he had no authority under the Constitution to promise them freedom, nor, indeed, to interfere
in any way with slavery; a point which Benjamin readily conceded, for was it not so argued by himself in the
circular sent out to the Confederate commissioners on
January 15, 1863?   He justified the usurpation of an
unconstitutional authority by reasons exactly similar
to those adduced by Lincoln, and sanctioned by history, to justify a like usurpation on his part.   Indeed, such measures need no excuse other than their
necessity.   Mr. Davis was convinced, and began to
concert with Benjamin the means of carrying out the
idea.   The South, generally, of course, was not ready
for such desperate remedies; but some leaders had
already advocated emancipation, and General Lee was
believed to favor it.   So bitter was the feeling among
the majority of the people against a government that
seemed to sanction such acts as were committed by
Hunter, Sheridan, and Sherman, that there would have
been less difficulty than is thought in reconciling them
to the movement, if once they could be convinced that
this would save them from subjection to the North.

[1] *Diary*, September 27, 1863, and March 9, 1865.

Still, until the popular mind could be prepared for their reception, it was of the highest importance that the new designs of the Secretary of State should be kept secret.

A gentleman known personally to Mr. Benjamin, Duncan F. Kenner, of Louisiana, one of the wealthiest slave-owners of his state, and avowedly not at all averse to emancipation, was decided upon as the special envoy who should undertake the negotiations in Europe. Mr. Mason and Mr. Slidell might not be thoroughly in accord with the new ideas, or might not be in a position to reach the English and French authorities with whom they had had such unpleasant experiences. But some intimations were given them of a change of policy in a dispatch, the "supreme effort of Confederate diplomacy," from whose carefully measured and sonorous periods there will yet ring many a proud echo in the hearts of those who still cherish a pathetic pride in the lost cause, and who, accepting the issue as it was decided, still believe with General Lee, "we had . . . sacred principles to maintain and rights to defend, for which we were in duty bound to do our best, even if we perished in the endeavor." " The Confederate States," wrote Benjamin,[1] "have now for nearly four years resisted the utmost power of the United States with a courage and fortitude to which the world has accorded its respect and admiration. No people have poured out their blood more freely in defense of their liberties and independence, nor have endured sacrifices with greater cheerfulness than have the men and women of these Confederate States.

[1] Dispatch to Slidell, December 29; to Mason, December 30, 1865; see Mason, pp. 541–545; Callahan, pp. 247–267; Lee's *Letters*, p. 151.

"They accepted the issue which was forced on them by an arrogant and domineering race, vengeful, grasping, and ambitious. They have asked nothing, fought for nothing, but for the right of self-government, for independence."

He continues, that in this war the Confederacy has fought for Europe as well as for herself, and yet is left unaided. With skill he points out the peculiar interest of France in checking the arrogance at Washington: "It needs no sagacity to predict that in the event of success in their designs against us, the United States would afford but a short respite to France from inevitable war; a war in which France would be involved not simply in defense of the French policy in Mexico, but for the protection of the French soldiers still retained by the Emperor Maximilian under the treaty with him, for the maintenance of his position on the Mexican throne."

And finally, in a sort of peroration that Mason used in a closing effort to move Palmerston, and wherein one cannot fail to feel, rather than actually read, despair: "While unshaken in the determination never again to unite ourselves under a common government with a people by whom we have been so deeply wronged, the inquiry daily becomes more pressing, What is the policy and what are the purposes of the Western powers of Europe in relation to this contest? Are they determined never to recognize the Southern Confederacy until the United States assent to such action on their part? Do they propose, under any circumstances, to give other and more direct aid to the Northern people in attempting to enforce our submission to a hateful union? If so, it is but just that we should be apprised of their purpose, to the end that we may then deliberately consider the terms, if any, upon which we can secure peace from the foes to whom the question is thus surrendered, and who have the countenance and encouragement of all mankind in the invasion of our country, the destruction of our homes, the extermination of our people. If, on the other hand, there be objections not made known to us, which have for four years prevented the recognition of our independence, notwithstanding the demonstration of our right to assert, and our ability to maintain it, justice equally demands that an opportunity be afforded us for meeting and overcoming those objections, if in our power to do so.

"We have given ample evidence that we are not a people to be appalled by danger, or to shrink from sacrifice in the attainment of our object. That object —the sole object for which we would ever have consented to commit our all to the hazards of this war—is the vindication of our right to self-government and independence.

"For that end no sacrifice is too great save that of honor. If, then, the purpose of France and Great Britain have been, or be now, to exact terms or conditions before conceding the rights we claim, a frank exposition of that purpose is due to humanity. It is due now, for it may enable us to save many lives most precious to our country by consenting to such terms in advance of another year's campaign.

"This dispatch will be handed to you by the Hon. Duncan F. Kenner. . . . It is proper . . . that I should authorize you, officially, to consider any communication he may make verbally on the subject embraced in this dispatch as emanating from this department under the instructions of the President."

Mr. Kenner, given full and confidential instructions, and entrusted with most ample powers—to negotiate treaties, to sell cotton, to purchase ships, to supersede or to act with Mason and Slidell—made his way in disguise through New York to Europe, where he arrived in the latter part of February. Though a man of much native ability and shrewdness, and thoroughly educated, he had no diplomatic experience, and preferred, perhaps for other reasons of policy, to make international moves through Mason and Slidell. Through the latter he had an interview with the French Minister for Foreign Affairs, who, as usual, would give an answer "in two weeks," while the Emperor still proposed to act only in concert with England. Returning to London with Mason on March 3d, Mr. Kenner entered into negotiations with bankers for the sale of cotton, conditional on recognition, while Mason sought and obtained an interview with Lord Palmerston in order to sound him. In accordance with the plan of action agreed upon with Mr. Kenner and Mr. Slidell, Mr. Mason did not make a direct proposition to Lord Palmerston, but with considerable adroitness so directed the conversation that there could be no mistaking his meaning, as he read the significant conclusion of Mr. Benjamin's dispatch,—that the Confederacy would abolish slavery if that were the obstacle to recognition. "Lord Palmerston listened," says Mr. Mason in a dispatch of March 31st, "with interest and attention while I unfolded fully the purpose of the dispatch and of my interview. In reply he, at once, assured me that the objections entertained

by his government were those which had been avowed;
and that there was nothing (I use his own word)
' underlying' them." [1]

The great sacrifice, therefore, had been offered in
vain. Whether it would have availed anything if proposed earlier in the struggle is an open question; now,
certainly, it was too late, for, three days after the time
when Mason was recording Palmerston's reply, General
Lee fell back from the lines before Richmond, and the
Confederate government, fugitive and desperately
maintaining for a few weeks the show of organization,
may be said to have come to an end with the fall of
that city.

[1] Mason, pp. 552-560.

CHAPTER XIII

STARTING LIFE ANEW

"NOTHING will end the war," Mr. Benjamin had written to Mr. Mann, February 1, 1864, "but the utter exhaustion of the belligerents, unless by the action of some of the leading powers of Europe." Reluctant were he and Mr. Davis alike to believe that the Confederacy was exhausted, and till the news came from General Lee, on April 2d, that Richmond could no longer be held, both refused to despond. For some weeks, however, the packing of government archives had been going on quietly, and Mr. Benjamin had been preparing to destroy the secret service papers whose capture would compromise persons within the power of the enemy; so that when the inevitable moment came, and General Lee's message was delivered to Mr. Davis in St. Paul's Church, all was ready for immediate removal to some spot that might, for the time, be safer.

So many have pictured for us the last scenes of Confederate Richmond that we need not linger over them here. Mr. Benjamin and other officers of the government went to Danville, where a halt was made and temporary headquarters were opened. The devoted Dr. Hoge, wishing to continue his duties as a chaplain "so long as the Confederate flag flew," had come out from Richmond on the night of April 2d. "The next forenoon," he says,[1] "while walking on the streets in

[1] *Lawley MS.*

Danville I met Mr. Benjamin. . . . After greeting him I asked him where he was staying. He told me he had not secured accommodations anywhere. It was a new thing, I doubt not, in his experience to be uncertain about his immediate movements ; it had always been his good fortune to lay his plans skilfully and execute them as well. I told him I was the guest of a most estimable and hospitable gentleman, J. M. Johnston, an officer in one of the Danville banks, with whom I was on such terms that I could invite any friend of mine to his house with the assurance of receiving a cordial welcome. Mr. Benjamin thanked me warmly, but said that even if my host would welcome him he could not think of intruding on me by occupying a part of my room. . . . Finally, on my assurance that, so far from incommoding me, it would be a great pleasure to have such a roommate, he consented, and accompanied me to Mr. Johnston's house. Just as I anticipated, the whole family gave Mr. Benjamin a cordial welcome, and he was quickly made to feel at home."

Here an anxious week was spent, during which the secretary managed to make himself a thoroughly agreeable guest, and to win Dr. Hoge's heart by the many "little things" in which he showed his native regard for the feelings of others, his thorough gentleness and courtesy. When he found it to be the custom of the family to have prayers read, he attended punctually, seeking neither to evade nor to obtrude, but accepting it all naturally. There was little to do but talk, and in this he consistently suggested cheerful themes, and "never made a remark . . . that jarred upon a principle or sentiment, even," of his reverend

friend. They discussed topics literary and artistic:
" We had some friendly arguments about the place
Tennyson would occupy in history. He was a passionate admirer of Tennyson, and, I think, ranked him
above all the English poets, Shakespeare excepted.
When I would suggest that Tennyson had never written anything equal to *Comus*, or *Il Penseroso*, or
L'Allegro, or to Dryden in his vigorous and masterly
use of the English language, or to some of the stanzas
of *Childe Harold*, he would always be ready with a
reference to some passage of his favorite author to con-
fute my statement. He seemed to be as familiar with
literature as with law, and among our public men I
cannot recall one who was a more accomplished belles
lettres scholar."

But the sublime serenity and courage of those who
could thus resolutely keep up their hearts by brilliant
talk in the midst of shipwreck is only a gleam of sun-
shine to darken the clouds of disaster. It is not well,
indeed, to fiddle while Rome burns. But if there be
one thing above another with which the South may
honestly comfort herself it is that her people of unbroken spirit did *not* sit down and weep.

> "Sires have lost their children, wives
>   Their lords, and valiant men their lives;
>   One what best his love might claim
>   Hath lost; another, wealth or fame.
>   Woe is me, Alhama!"

It was by a people who would not allow themselves
to brood over what they must now live without, that
the damage and the loss must be repaired and made
good.

On Monday, April 9th, Mr. Benjamin beckoned Dr. Hoge quietly aside, after a general conversation with the ladies in which he had joined with customary cheerfulness. When they were out of hearing, he said: "I did not have the heart to tell those good ladies what I have just learned. General Lee has surrendered and I fear the Confederate cause is lost." He added, that he would accompany the President to Greensboro, whither they must retreat at once; but he evidently considered the cause hopelessly ruined, for he told Dr. Hoge that he would, if the worst came, use every means to escape capture, having resolved never to be taken alive. Since various stories of theatrical effect, hinting at suicide by pistol or (this more in keeping with the Mephistophelian or Borgian character ascribed to him at the North) the concealed poison of a ring, have been circulated, it may be as well to add that Dr. Hoge distinctly states there was no such puerility in his calm statement of his determination.

Burton Harrison, private secretary to President Davis, has told entertainingly of the subsequent adventures of the fugitive government,[1] with which we shall soon have done. At Greensboro they halted but a few days, and from there on, the railroad, poor as it was, must be abandoned. The little procession was made up of army wagons, ambulances, carriages, and mounted men, among whom were the President and most of his cabinet. Mr. Benjamin, however, being short and stout, and unused to horseback riding, joined General Cooper, another very stout individual, Jules St. Martin, and Attorney-General Davis, in an ambulance drawn by a pair of broken-down old grays. Mr.

[1] *Century Magazine*, November, 1883.

Harrison records that, one night, he rode up to this forlorn vehicle and found it stuck fast in a mud-hole. He went off to get help to haul it out, and "returning to them again, I could see from afar the occasional bright glow of Benjamin's cheerful cigar. While the others of the party were perfectly silent, Benjamin's silvery voice was presently heard as he rhythmically intoned, for their comfort, verse after verse of Tennyson's ode on the death of the Duke of Wellington!" He was the life of the party, said one of these fugitives afterward, and his good humor helped them all to bear the trials of the road. From Greensboro to Charlotte, and thence to Abbeville they went. Mr. Benjamin, when the need came, "dexterously got himself into the saddle upon a tall horse, and, with short legs hanging but an inconsiderable distance toward the ground, rode gayly off with the others of the President's following." But when the news of General Johnston's surrender arrived, and Mr. Davis had announced his determination to try to make his way to Texas and join Kirby Smith, Mr. Benjamin, writes Mrs. Davis,[1] "came to him and said: 'I could not bear the fatigue of riding as you do, and as I can serve our people no more just now, will you consent to my making an effort to escape through Florida? If you should be in a condition to require me again, I will answer your call at once.' This was his considerate manner of saying all was lost in his opinion." Having left in charge of some friends near Abbeville a trunk containing the whole of his personal belongings except what he wore, he parted from the President at the

[1] Letter in *Lawley MS.*; similar accounts in Davis's *Rise and Fall*, Vol. II, p. 694.

house where they stopped for breakfast ("Vienna," says Dr. Hoge), near Washington, Ga., and from this point we can trust him to tell, in a series of letters to Mrs. Kruttschnitt, his own story of the perils of the next three months:

"*Nassau, 22d July, 1865.*

"My darling Sister :—I arrived here last evening all safe and sound, and will depart in two hours on board the schooner *Britannia* for Havana, whence I shall take the first steamer for Europe. I cannot, therefore, write you a quarter of what I should like to tell you, but must do the best I can and hope that this letter will be allowed to reach you.

"I separated from President Davis near Washington, Georgia, early in May, last, having been requested by him to make my way through Florida to this place or Havana, and after attending to some public business, to rejoin him in the Trans-Mississippi District, by the way of Matamoras and Texas.

"I started on my journey on horseback, and knowing it to be a hazardous one, I determined to disguise myself and assume a false name. I cannot begin to give you the details of my adventures. I found my most successful disguise to be that of a farmer. I professed to be traveling in Florida in search of land on which to settle, with some friends who desired to move from South Carolina. I got a kind farmer's wife to make me some homespun clothes just like her husband's. I got for my horse the commonest and roughest equipment that I could find, and I journeyed as far as possible on by-roads, always passing around towns and keeping in the least inhabited districts. My progress was necessarily slow, about thirty miles a day, till I reached central Florida. I had intended going to East Florida and trying to cross the Gulf from Indian River, but I learned that there was not a vessel to be found there, and that the risk of detection would be great. I heard also of the proclamation in which a large reward was offered for the capture of the President, who was most outrageously accused of having connived at the assassination of President Lincoln. Everything satisfied me of the savage cruelty with which the hostile government would treat any Confederate leader who might happen to fall into their hands, and I preferred death in attempting to escape, to such captivity as awaited me, if I became their prisoner.

"I made my way, therefore, to the western coast of Florida, and was nearly a month in procuring a small boat and securing the services of two trusty persons to accompany me in the perilous effort to cross the Gulf of Mexico in a little open boat. I finally departed on the 23d June, and after a voyage of about six hundred miles in a yawl-boat open to the weather, with no place to sleep, and exposed to frequent squalls, some very severe, I happily arrived at the Bemini Isles on the Bahama reef, on Monday the 10th instant. Here my risk of capture was at an end, and I deemed it safe to take passage in a small sloop, loaded with sponge, for Nassau. We left Bemini on Thursday afternoon, the 13th, and on Friday morning about half-past seven o'clock, the sloop foundered at sea, thirty miles from the nearest land, sinking with such rapidity that we had barely time to jump into a small skiff that the sloop had in tow before she went to the bottom.

"In the skiff, leaky, with but a single oar, with no provisions save a pot of rice that had just been cooked for breakfast, and a small keg of water, I found myself at eight o'clock in the morning, with three negroes for my companions in disaster, only five inches of the boat out of water, on the broad ocean, with the certainty that we could not survive five minutes if the sea became the least rough. We started, however, quite courageously for the land, and without any signs of trepidation from any one on board, and the weather continuing very calm we proceeded landward till about eleven o'clock, when a vessel was discerned in the distance, which was supposed to be a small schooner and which we felt sure of reaching if the weather continued calm. We made for the vessel, the three negroes using the single oar by turns in sculling our little boat, and by five o'clock in the afternoon were safely on board H. B. M. Light House Yacht *Georgina,* a fine large brig, on board of which we were warmly received, and treated very kindly by Captain Stuart. The vessel was on a tour of inspection of the Bahama lighthouses, but Captain Stuart turned out of his way to put me back at Bemini, where I arrived for the second time on Saturday, the 15th. I immediately chartered another sloop to bring me here, and we started the same afternoon. The voyage is only about one hundred miles, but we were so baffled by calms, squalls, and head winds, that we were six days making it, and I arrived last evening only to learn that if I do not depart this morning for Havana, I may be detained a month before I get another chance to leave this island. I am thoroughly exhausted, and need rest, though in perfect health, but I must not yield to fatigue under the circumstances, and so I am passing this morning in writing letters to go by the *Corsica* steamer for New York on Monday, as I know how intense must be the anxiety of all I love on both sides the Atlantic, until news is received of my safety.

"In passing through Georgia I left with a friend nine hundred dollars in gold, all that I could spare, to be sent to Sis and Hatty at La Grange. I trust they received the money, as they must have suffered if they had none but Confederate notes. I don't know how to write to them, and must trust to you, my darling, to send them this letter or a copy of it, that they may be relieved of all solicitude on my account.

"I can as yet give you no idea of my plans or purposes. Until I reach England I can't tell what my condition is. I may be penniless, but I have strong reason to hope that some six or seven hundred bales of cotton which I own, reached Europe in safety. If so, I shall be beyond want for some years, and can supply all the needs of my dear sisters, and await events before determining my future course. If, however, I find that I have nothing left, I shall use my pen for a support for the present, in the English press, if I can so manage, as I have every reason to believe that I would find ready employment in that way.

"I am contented and cheerful under all reverses, and only long to hear of the health and happiness of those I love. I send you a thousand kisses, my own sweet sister, which you can distribute among your little darlings for me. Write me at once all the news about the family, and address me to care of Fraser, Trenholm and Company, Liverpool.

"I will write again from Havana. My best and kindest memories for dear Kitt."

In the interest of the narrative, we shall not pause now to draw attention to such things as his unfailing care for the well-being of those dependent on him. We may supplement the story by noting, from an "interview" with H. A. McCleod,[1] that he was one of the two brave boatmen who sailed from Manatee with Mr. Benjamin, "an awful nervy man." Furthermore, from a letter to Mr. Bayard,[2] describing the incidents of the escape, we learn that the reason for the sudden foundering of the sloop was her being too tightly packed with wet sponge which, expanding as it dried, burst the seams of the vessel; and that in the strong current of the Gulf Stream, and in the main channel where they were in hourly danger of being "saved" by some Federal cruiser, they came near being swept past the Bemini Islands. There was yet more to come:

[1] Galveston *Daily News*, May 27, 1884.
[2] Oct. 20, 1865.

" Havana, 1st August, 1865.

"I wrote to you from Nassau, my darling sister, and sent you a long account of my perils and sufferings in effecting my escape from the Yankees. I left Nassau on the day after my arrival there (on the 22d July), and arrived here on the 25th, after a very favorable passage, the first lucky weather that I have had on my voyages. I have now recovered entirely from my fatigue, have had time to provide myself with comfortable clothing, and have been received here with great kindness and attention. I shall leave for England by the steamer of the 6th (my birthday), and hope to see my wife and daughter once more by the 1st of September.

"This letter will be carried to you by Alexander Benjamin, a young kinsman with whom I made acquaintance in Nassau. It seems that he is a grandson of Emanuel Benjamin, our uncle, and is therefore second cousin to us. I have been very much pleased with him, and am greatly indebted to him for the unwearied kindness and attention with which he set himself to work to supply my numberless wants when I arrived at Nassau. He was the chief clerk of Mr. Heyliger, who was the agent of the Confederate government at Nassau, and is an excellent man of business, as well as a gentleman in manners, feelings, and deportment. Every one in Nassau spoke of him in high terms, and I beg, my love, that you will give him a warm and cordial welcome for my sake. I am quite taken with him.

"Since my arrival here, General Kirby Smith has arrived from Mexico, but is unable to give me any news of my dear Joe and Lionel. I am quite anxious to hear of them, and beg that you will not fail to give me any news of them, as well as of our poor forlorn sisters, by the very first mail for Liverpool. If you give your letters to Mr. Benjamin, he will know how to forward them without fear of their being intercepted. I trust that Sis and Hatty have been able to reach New

Orleans in safety, and I take it for granted that they would return there as their best refuge. From what I have learned since my arrival here I have very strong reason for believing that I have saved about 600 bales of cotton, and in that event I will have no difficulty in providing for them so as to place them above want.

"I did not write you in my last of the narrow escape I had from water-spouts when in my little boat at sea. I had never seen a water-spout, and often expressed a desire to be witness of so striking a phenomenon. I got, however, more than I bargained for. On the night before I reached Bemini, after a day of intense heat, the entire horizon was black with squalls. We took in our sail, unstepped the mast, and as we were on soundings, we let go the anchor in order to ride out the squalls in safety. They were forming all around us, and as there was no wind, it was impossible to tell which of them would strike us. At about nine o'clock, however, a very heavy, lurid cloud in the west dipped down toward the sea, and in a single minute two large water-spouts were formed, and the wind began blowing furiously directly toward us, bringing the water-spouts in a straight line for our boat. They were at the distance of a couple of miles, and did not seem to travel very fast. The furious whirl of the water could be distinctly heard, as in a long waving column that swayed about in the breeze and extended from the ocean up into the cloud, the spouts advanced in their course. If they had struck us we would have been swamped in a second, but before they reached us the main squall was upon us with such a tremendous blast of wind and rain combined that it was impossible to face the drops of water which were driven into our eyes with such violence as to compel us instantly to turn our backs to it, while it seemed that the force of the wind was so great that it would press our little boat bodily down into the sea. The waves were not high, the strength of the blast being such as to keep the surface of the water compressed. On turning our backs

to this tremendous squall, judge of our dismay on seeing another water-spout formed in another squall in the
east, also traveling directly towards us, although the
wind was blowing with such fury from the west.   There
must have been contrary currents at different heights
in the air, and we had scarcely caught sight of this new
danger, when the two spouts first seen passed our boat
at a distance of about one hundred yards (separated
from each other by about a quarter of a mile), tearing
up the whole surface of the sea as they passed, and
whirling it furiously into the clouds, with a roar such
as is heard at the foot of the Niagara Falls.   The western blast soon reached the spout that had been coming
toward us from the east and checked its career.   It
wavered and broke, and the two other spouts continued
their awful race across the ocean until we lost sight of
them in the blackness of the horizon.   A quarter of
an hour after, all was calm and still, and our boat was
lazily heaving and setting on the long swell of the
Bahama Sea.   It was a scene and picture that has become photographed into my brain, and that I can never
forget.

"We are all in intense anxiety on the subject of our
honored and noble chief, Jefferson Davis.   By the
last accounts there was every probability that those in
power at Washington would succeed in getting rid of
him by the tortures inflicted on him in prison, and that
the delay in trying him was intended to give time for
this moral assassination.   No nobler gentleman, no
purer man, no more exalted patriot ever drew breath ;
and eternal infamy will blacken the base and savage
wretches who are now taking advantage of their brief
grasp of power to wreak a cowardly vengeance on his
honored head.

"On looking over the New Orleans papers I see that
many of our old friends are returning, and I specially
note that Payne, Huntington & Co. have resumed
business.   Don't fail to let me know if my dear friend
Wash [Huntington] is in New Orleans, and if so, give

him a thousand memories of love and friendship for me, and say that I will write to him from Liverpool. You can read to him those parts of my letters that don't refer to family affairs.

"I long, dearest, beyond expression to see you all once more, and to have your darling chicks gathered round the knee of 'Uncle Ben.' You must write me fully about them all, as well as about your own health, and dear Kitt's health and purposes—whether he is going into business, etc., etc."

The sequel of the story is given in the next letter:

"17 Savile Row, London, 29th September, 1865.

"I have received . . . a whole volume of letters from home within the last few days. . . . I can only answer now in a general letter for you all, but a little later I will be able to regularize my correspondence. As you will all want to know what my movements are, and what I expect to do, I will begin with myself, as all egotists do, and then pass on to the family matters.

"You must have heard through the papers that my adventures and perils were not ended at Havana. On my voyage to England the small steamer which conveyed me to St. Thomas arrived two or three days before the larger vessel which was to take us to Southampton. I consequently had an opportunity of seeing the scenes of my early childhood, but of course my memory was very indistinct, as I was a mere infant when we left that island for Wilmington. We left St. Thomas at about 4 P. M., on the 13th August (I think that was the day), and at about half-past nine o'clock that night, when we were about sixty miles at sea the ship was found to be on fire in the forehold. The fire proved to be a very serious one, the boats were all prepared and provisioned for our abandoning the ship if necessary, and the vessel's head was at once turned back toward St. Thomas. By dint of great exertion and admirable conduct and discipline exhibited by all on board, the flames were kept from bursting through the deck till we got back to the harbor of St. Thomas, where we arrived at about three o'clock in the morning with seven feet of water in the hold poured in by the steam pumps, and the deck burned to within an eighth of an inch of the entire thickness. By the aid of other vessels in the harbor the fire was extinguished : the burned cargo removed : the forehold cleared of ashes and cinders, and in two more days we started afresh and reached England without further accident. If the fire had been discovered only one hour later, it would have been impossible to extinguish it, and I would have been cast adrift on the ocean for the third time in a little open boat.

"I was compelled to remain a week in London on public business before crossing the Channel to see my family, and on my arrival in Paris had the happiness of embracing them in perfect health, my daughter being now radically cured of her lifelong disorder, and looking as blooming as a rose. I also found letters from Jules giving an account of his visit to New Orleans, and of his seeing you all, and he even committed the gross flattery of writing to my wife that 'Ben's sister is charming.'

"I am now back in London partly on public and partly on private business. I am almost fixed in my purpose to practice my profession as barrister in London, but have not yet quite decided, because I still lack information about the rules and regulations for the admission of strangers, and the delay may perhaps be so great as to deter me. It will also be necessary for me to become naturalized.

"I have been treated with great kindness and distinction, and have been called on by Lord Campbell and Sir James Ferguson, the former a peer and the latter of the House of Commons, both accidentally in London, for the 'whole world,' as they say, is now in the country, this being the 'long vacation' in London,

Both assured me that I would meet the utmost aid and sympathy, and would be called on by a large number of the leading public men here, as soon as they returned to town.   Mr. D'Israeli also wrote to a friend of mine expressing the desire of being useful to me when he should arrive in town, and I have been promised a dinner at which I am to be introduced to Gladstone and Tennyson as soon as the season opens here.

"I have also received news that one hundred bales of my cotton are safely at sea, so that I shall have the means of living for two or three years, and am thus quite easy for the time being, and with good prospects ahead.   In Paris, I dined with Slidell and was introduced to some bankers who hinted that if I wished to live in France, it would be easy to obtain an honorable and lucrative position in the financial circles, but this is far less tempting than my old profession.   My old friend, Mme. de Pontalba,[1] also is imperious in her urgency that I should remain in France, and promises all sorts of aids and influence in my behalf, but I repeat that nothing is more independent, nor offers a more promising future, than admission as a barrister to the bar of London.

"I had the pleasure of meeting Bradford for a few hours in Liverpool a day or two ago.   He goes to New Orleans and you will have a chance of hearing that I look as well and as 'young' as ever.   So now enough of self. . . .

"I want you to send me *cartes de visites* of all the family, for those which I received in Richmond are in my trunk which is concealed on the other side, and I may perhaps never recover it.

"I am glad that Joe has gone to work again.   I do not doubt his success, for it is impossible that the negroes should not at some early day be ruled under a system which will compel them to labor for their liv.

[1] Well known in New Orleans, as are the "Pontalba Buildings" around Jackson Square.

ing, and if so planting will be very profitable for years
to come.   .   .   .

"I am quite anxious to hear from Kitt. Tell him to
write me fully and frankly.   If he sees a fair opening
for business, and if a moderate capital be required to
aid him in establishing it, I think I could readily find
him a silent partner on this side who would be willing
to advance it on favorable terms.

"I don't think that our dear Sis and Hatty should
remain in La Grange, separated from all they love. It
seems to me that they could take a house in New Orleans in connection with Lionel as formerly ; and with
their industry and economy the expenses would be
small, and I am sure I will be able to help them to
some extent, say about seventy-five dollars a month,
and in the meantime something better may turn up.
They must feel very desolate and lonesome, and it is
not necessary that they should be rendered unhappy
by such a trial."

These admirable letters give us so full a chronicle
that there is little for me to add, except by way of
comment. In addition to their service for the narrative, they yield us a glimpse into that happy private
life which was so religiously cherished, and guarded as
if it would be profaned by the public gaze. Over all
the members of the family he would extend his care ;
and while in the midst of misfortunes himself, he does
not forget to think and devise for them. To the facts
we may add that he arrived at Southampton, as he
writes to Mr. Bayard, " on the 30th August, nearly
four months after my separation from the President,
during which time I had spent twenty-three days seated
in the thwart of an open boat, exposed to a tropical sun
in June and July, utterly without shelter or change of
clothes. I never, however, had one minute's indisposi-

tion nor despondency, but was rather pleasantly exalted by the feeling of triumph in disappointing the malice of my enemies." It is an altogether remarkable feat of endurance, this escape, for a man used to a sedentary life and already in his fifty-fourth year. Nor is the buoyancy of spirit, the indomitable will to make a fresh start in the world, less remarkable.[1]

Arriving in London, one of his first cares, with Mr. Mason and others, was what one might call completing the obsequies of the Confederacy, counseling with them as to winding up the affairs of their offices, disposing of papers, etc. Deeply and sincerely grieved at the sufferings of his people, and especially at the hardships of the imprisonment to which Mr. Davis was subjected, he wrote at once to Mrs. Davis, sending the letter to the care of Mr. T. F. Bayard. Feeling, too, that Mr. Davis should be defended from the mean calumnies that were being spread, he wrote a long letter to the London *Times* (September 12th), which is an admirable defense of the Confederates against the charge of deliberate cruelty to prisoners. This very painful topic has been much discussed; no one, I suppose, now believes that Jefferson Davis starved the Federal prisoners at Andersonville and denied them salt and medicines; if so, it is peculiar that "Lee's Miserables" were subjected to similar privations, and that the eminently humane government of the United States declared contraband of war, and seized wherever possible, every drug that could relieve the sick, every anesthetic that could soothe the tortures of the

[1] The London *Times*, in its obituary, May 9, 1884, comments on this "elastic resistance to evil fortune" as perhaps a race characteristic.

wounded under the knife of the surgeon.   Mr. Benjamin's letter [1] on the subject is marked by those characteristics that almost invariably distinguish his writings
at a time when the greatest violence of language was
deemed the proper thing on both sides : perfect coolness, calm logic, dignified expression.   That his words
do not lack force we may judge from this paragraph,
concerning the responsibility for the refusal of the
Federals to exchange prisoners of war, which kept Andersonville full, and Confederate armies empty :   "It
requires no sagacity to perceive that every motive of
interest as well as of humanity operated to induce us to
facilitate the exchange of prisoners, and to submit
even to unjust and unequal terms in order to recover
soldiers whom we could replace from no other source.
On the other hand, interest and humanity were at war
in their influence on the Federal officials.   Others
must judge of the humanity and justice of the policy
which consigned hundreds of thousands of wretched
men to captivity apparently hopeless, but I can testify
unhesitatingly to its sagacity and efficacy, and to the
pitiless sternness with which it was executed.   Indeed
this refusal to exchange was one of the most fatal
blows dealt us during the war, and contributed to our
overthrow more, perhaps, than any other single measure.   I write not to make complaint of it, but simply to
protest against the attempt of the Federals so to divide
the consequences of their own conduct as to throw on
us the odium attached to a cruelty plainly injurious
to us, obviously beneficial to themselves."

On the passage across the Atlantic, it is evident, Mr.
Benjamin's political opinions had not suffered a sea

[1] Reprinted in the N. Y. *Times*, Sept. 27, 1865.

change, nor did they ever. General Taylor said that the Confederacy was dead, and he was tired of sitting by the corpse, and had come away. Mr. Benjamin, too, accepted as decisive the ruin of the cause; but not only was he ever ready to speak in its defense, and ever ready to help fellow-sufferers in the shipwreck, but he also relished conversations that would revive old memories. From his private letters—he never entered politics nor made a political address again—I shall quote, from time to time, little references to conditions existing in his old home.

For the present, however, the pressing business was to provide for the bodily needs of the day and to make some plan for the future that would repair a fortune now gone for the second time. He had staked all on the Confederacy, and nearly all was lost. Much of his money, earned at the bar in New Orleans, had been in real estate, a form of investment that could not very readily be made available, and that, moreover, could not be concealed from the enemy. As intimated in the letters to his sister, he had tried at the last to save in cotton all that he had left. But when he got to England the "six or seven hundred bales," which would have been a large fortune, had shrunk to about one hundred, and these had not yet arrived. He was practically penniless when he landed, and must provide for immediate needs by his wits, unless he would consent to borrow. The editor of the *Daily Telegraph* writes that Mr. Benjamin came to him with a letter of introduction, obtained through Bennett Burleigh, and continues :[1] "I gave him forthwith occasional work in writing leaders on subjects of international law or in-

[1] *Lawley MS.*

ternational policy." Personal support being thus provided for, he was relieved to find that his one hundred bales of cotton had really come out safely ; though a poor remnant of fortune for him, it would be sufficient to supply the needs of those dependent on him. As for himself he could submit to close living till better times should arrive. Those ever loyal friends, the Bayards, wrote to offer him pecuniary assistance, to which he replied (October 20th) : "I cannot describe to you, my dear friend, how deeply I am touched by the kind and generous offer of yourself and son, and if I needed aid, there is no one from whom I could consent to receive pecuniary assistance sooner than yourselves. Fortunately this is not the case. I was very poor when I landed here, and had barely enough to support my family for a few months. I have been lucky enough to receive, however, a hundred bales of cotton that have escaped Yankee vigilance ; and the price here is so high that it has given me nearly twenty thousand dollars, besides which I have made already almost ten thousand dollars by means of information furnished by a kind friend in relation to the affairs of a financial institution, in which I invested my little fortune, and which has already increased in market value fifty per cent.—so you see I am not quite a beggar."

But his misfortunes were not at an end. Some six months later the failure of Overend, Gurney & Co. swept away much of this little accumulated capital, and made more urgent the need for adding to his income, and meantime for strict economy on his own part. He had written home (December 20th) : "Tell Sis and Hatty, to write me and let me know how money matters are getting on, and not to hesitate to write me if they are the least in want, as I can always find a few hundred dollars without pinching myself, and I have no fears of my ability to make a handsome competence at the bar here." He felt he must, if humanly possible, live up to this obligation; to do so he had to pinch himself, though those at home did not know of it at the time. Mrs. Bradford, who was much in London during these months of struggle before he could earn a competence at the bar, reports that he lived as simply as he could in bachelor's quarters, dined furtively, sometimes on bread and cheese, at cheap restaurants where it would hardly do for him to be seen, if he hoped to maintain the dignity expected of a barrister, and cultivated the habit of walking (he did not like it), since the penny 'bus was beneath a barrister's rank, while cabs were somewhat above this one's means. He used to dine with Mrs. Bradford almost every Sunday; and after manifest enjoyment of such a good dinner, in a moment of post-prandial relaxation once confessed to her something of these little economies. But he was not of a sort to make a parade of his troubles, nor did he let them mar either his good humor or his confidence in the ultimate success of his venture at the English bar.

That a man of fifty-four, who had always used his energies to the full limit of endurance, and who must start anew the battle of life after four years of such labor as he had undertaken during the war, should reject all offers of pecuniary assistance and all easier modes of making money to begin again the practice of law in a foreign land is, I think, a truly astonishing exhibition of pluck. As soon as opportunity offered, he started to look into the requirements for admission to the bar, hoping to take up his studies at once. "But I find one cannot be allowed to commence in the middle of a term, and as the next term only begins on the 11th January, I shall spend Christmas and New Year with my wife and child, and return early next month [letter dated December 20th] to commence my new life." On January 13, 1866, he entered as a student at Lincoln's Inn, and shortly afterward was admitted to "read law" under the instruction of Charles Pollock, later Baron Pollock, who himself tells some little incidents in connection with this extraordinary pupil, to which we may turn after quoting Benjamin's own humorous description of the Inns of Court as then conducted. He writes to his old partner in New Orleans (February 21, 1866) :

"My dear Bradford : . . . . . I am now entered as a student at Lincoln's Inn and do not expect to be called to the bar till next fall. I found on inquiry that it would be more difficult than I had anticipated to get a dispensation from the rules of the different Inns of Court, all of which require the keeping of twelve terms ; *i. e.*, three years, before a call to the bar. These terms are kept, as you are aware, simply by eating a certain number of dinners in the hall of the Society or Inn, that is to say, six dinners in each term. I felt, of course, that I was not at all prepared to practice under the English law, and after consultation with friends, I concluded that the best plan was to enter Lincoln's Inn, to keep *four* terms, employing myself in close study, and at the end of that time (having in the interim made as much interest as I could manage with the Benches of the Inn), to apply for a special exception and relaxation of the rules in my favor. In the meantime I am making enough to pay for my personal expenses by an engagement to contribute one leading article a week to one of the daily papers, for which I am paid £5 per week, and am thus enabled to devote the small sum that I was able to save from the wreck to the maintenance of my family till I can obtain some practice at the bar. I think I have enough with close economy to get through three years, and by that time may be able to secure a decent practice. I could now make £600 or £800 a year by consenting to become sub-editor of the paper I refer to, but that would take up nearly all my time and prevent my preparation for the bar. I therefore restrict myself to one article a week, although they offer to pay me for as many more as I choose to write, not exceeding three a week.

"It will, I know, interest you to learn what were the forms, etc., attending my admission to the Inn. So I shall even incur an extra postage and enclose you the regulations. I had to pay, on admission, the following sums : stamps £25 2s 6d, lectures £5 5s 0d, admission fee £5 12s 6d, printed form £1 1s 0d, making a total of £37 1s 0d. I had then to deposit £100 as security that I would pay for my dinners. The next step was to enter a barrister's chambers with a view to learn the course of practice, and for this the fee was £105. I am now in the chambers of Mr. Charles Pollock, son of the Chief Baron of the Exchequer, Sir Frederick Pollock. I am very kindly treated on all sides, and was invited by the Chief Baron to spend a day with him at his country seat at Hatton. We went down on Saturday P. M. and returned on Monday morning, and I spent a most charming day, the old gentleman, although eighty-three years old, being as lively and sportive as a boy.

" You would be greatly amused to see our dinner at Lincoln's Inn. There are tables at the head of the room for the Benchers, who are the old leaders of the bar, such as Lord Brougham, Lord St. Leonards, Sir Roundell Palmer, Sir Hugh Cairnes, etc., etc. Next come tables for the barristers, of whom some forty or fifty always are found at dinner. Next the students, to the number of about one hundred and fifty, includ-

ing your humble servant, all seated at long tables, and
dressed in stuff gowns, which the waiters throw over
us in the antechamber before we enter the dining-hall.
To each four persons, who constitute a mess, the waiter
serves a dinner composed of soup, one joint and vegetables, one sweet dish, and cheese. A bottle of sherry
or port at choice is allowed to each mess (fiery stuff it
is), and bitter beer *ad libitum*. The charge for the
dinner is two shillings. No one at mess helps another,
but the etiquette is each in turn helps himself, one being first for soup, the next first for the joint, and so on.
One dines almost every day with some stranger, but
the rule is that all are presumed to be gentlemen, and
conversation is at once established with entire abandon, as if the parties were old acquaintances.

"When called to the bar, I shall take the Northern
Circuit, which includes Liverpool, where I hope to get
my first start with the aid of some of our old clients
there."

The late Baron Pollock, whose reminiscences I have
before referred to,[1] tells of the impression Benjamin
made upon one of his sisters on that visit to his father,
when Mr. Mason accompanied him. She had expected
to see a man of the conspirator type, or perhaps like
Jefferson Davis : "To my surprise, when he entered
the room, I saw a short, stout, genial man, of decidedly
Jewish descent, with bright, dark eyes, and all the politeness and *bonhomie* of a Frenchman, looking as if
he had never had a care in his life." Baron Pollock
also tells how, having at first declined Benjamin as a
pupil because he already had two in his small chambers, he was brought to reconsider this decision by his
father's remark that the American had no need to learn
law, only to see something of the practice of the Eng-

[1] *Green Bag*, Sept., 1898.

382 JUDAH P. BENJAMIN

lish courts and to meet members of the bar. And one of the first pieces of work Benjamin did in his office impressed him strongly with the learning and readiness of the student. The Metropolitan Police, to whom he was counsel, sent him a paper asking his opinion, " 'as to the searching of prisoners,' involving the right of the police to search such persons in their custody before they have been convicted of any crime, for different purposes, —as, for instance, to find dangerous weapons, stolen property, or possibly to take from a drunken man his watch or other valuables for their protection. I was leaving for court and threw it across the table to Benjamin, saying, 'Here is a case made for you, on the right of search' (alluding to the *Trent* affair) . . . Benjamin took the papers, and at once set to work to consider the authorities and deal with the questions with such purpose that when I returned from court they were all disposed of. The only fault to be found was that the learning was too great for the occasion, going back to first principles in justification of each answer. Many years after, I was told that the opinion was held in high respect, and often referred to by the police at the Home Office."

With all the proverbial English conservatism and respect for established rules, the authorities were wise and generous enough to see that it would be absurd to tax the digestion of such a man by the perfunctory eating of six dozen dinners as a fit preparation for the practice of a profession in which he was already a veteran. The only obstacle might have been his foreign nationality ; but this was readily disposed of, for he had been born of British parents and under the British flag, and once a Briton always a Briton was an axiom that swept aside, as if they had never been, the forty-odd years of citizenship, and the services in the Senate of a foreign power. "By the influence of Lords Justices Turner and Giffard, of Page Wood (Lord Hatherly), and Sir Fitzroy Kelly, Benchers of the Society, the Secretary of the Confederacy was dispensed from the regular three years of unprofitable dining, and called to the bar of Lincoln's Inn in Trinity term, (June 6) 1866." [1]

[1] London *Times*, May 9, 1884.

CHAPTER XIV

A NEW HOME AND NEW FAME

BEFORE attempting to give such a condensed sketch as our limits allow of the phenomenal success of this young barrister of fifty-five, it will be well to sum up the peculiar advantages and disadvantages of his position. First, of the disadvantages, the chief and most obvious are his being a stranger, an exile under a political ban, past the prime of life, and poor. The poverty his own skill and tireless industry could be relied upon to offset and finally to overcome; and the buoyant youthful spirit that had always been his was yet unimpaired. His past record, politically, in America, while it might earn him the sympathy of those who had favored the Confederacy, did, it is alleged, make the government slower to accord him the fitting reward of his abilities, and so may be said to have impeded his progress. His being an alien was kindly forgotten; he himself testifies to the cordiality and consideration with which a generous bar always treated him. "From the first days of his coming," said Sir Henry James, "he was one of us."

As for the advantages, the obvious are his own ability and determination to succeed. But we should not forget the long years of peculiarly varied experience in America, nor the special training in French and Spanish law. Moreover, from the difference in the practice of the English courts, with solicitors and barristers, the one preparing the facts of the case and the other concerned only with the law and the pleading, he derived another advantage; for in his old home, of course, he had been both solicitor and barrister, and so was familiar with the duties of each and habituated to more careful and thorough preparation than, perhaps, may have been customary with his British brethren. On these points Baron Pollock speaks as follows:[1] "One great and early advantage held by Benjamin was this—that he was . . . educated within the state of Louisiana, . . . and, the law taught and administered within it was that which took its origin in the code of Justinian, and was afterward adopted by the nations of Europe, and continued to be the law of France until the Code Napoleon. The principles and practice of this great system of law Benjamin knew and appreciated thoroughly, and he was at all times ready to point out its leading features, and how they differed in principle from English law. This also gave him a distinct position superior to his brother advocates when arguing, before our judicial committee of the privy council, appeals from those of the English colonies of French origin which were ceded to England before the code. . . . The profession and duties of barrister and solicitor, which in England are separate, are in America discharged by one and the same person. . . . Benjamin . . . had for years been a member of . . . a legal partnership. His clients were numerous, their business being principally of a mercantile character, and few men had a sounder or wider range of knowledge and experience of the law-merchant, including shipping, insurance, and foreign trading, than Benjamin,

[1] *Green Bag*, Sept., 1898.

long before he ever thought of leaving America and coming to England."

Here now is the late Confederate secretary entering on his new career, with such special advantages and disadvantages as I have sought to indicate. After some little delay and trouble in securing suitable chambers, he settled in those he was to occupy, 4 Lamb Buildings, for the remainder of his active life. "Unlike most newly-called men," says Baron Pollock, "he was not long allowed to be idle, although for some time he was more occupied in answering cases and advising on evidence than by holding briefs in court. One of the first—if not the very first—pieces of work which Benjamin did will illustrate his great experience and untiring energy. An old established ship insurance club was desirous of having its rules, which were very lengthy, remodeled. The annual meeting of the club was at hand, and the time remaining was so short that two experienced counsel, who had for some years past acted for it, declined the service, although some considerable fee was marked on the papers. Benjamin's name was mentioned, and the instructions were sent to him late one evening. Most men would probably have looked up the rules of other similar clubs in order to collate them and exhaust every source of improvement. Not so Benjamin. His own knowledge of the requirements told him what was wanting; and the very next morning, commencing after an early breakfast, and never pausing for a midday meal, he worked on steadily, and, shortly before eight, the hour at which he usually dined, the rules were complete, written out in his own neat hand, *currente calamo*, with scarce an alteration or correction from beginning to end, as if he

had been composing a poem.   I doubt if any draughts-
man within the walls of the two Temples could have
done this so efficiently within the same time."

To Mr. Mason, with whom he had formed a closer
friendship during the trying months immediately succeeding his arrival in England, he wrote [1] briefly of
his beginnings in the new field : "I have as you know
been called to the bar, and have chosen the Northern
Circuit, which embraces Liverpool.   I have attended
assizes once at Liverpool, and have no reason as yet to
complain, though I have done very little, as my call
was just before the long vacation.   But Michaelmas
term commences on the 29th inst., and I may have a
chance to appear in some cases.   My time is spent in
close study, and we have not had a game of whist since
your departure.   I am as much interested in my profession as when I first commenced as a boy, and am
rapidly recovering all that I had partially forgotten in
the turmoil of public affairs."

As he had hoped, he was not long without practice
in the courts, beginning in this Michaelmas term.   At
the close of his career before the bar he gratefully recalled the day when he first appeared as junior counsel to Sir W. B. Brett, "before the late Lord Justice
Lush, to whom I had not then the honor of being
known, [but] that learned judge wrote me immediately
a kind and affectionate note, congratulating me on
seeing me holding my first brief, and expressing a
hope it would be the precursor of many more.   I had
no reason to suppose that he even knew me, and yet he
was prompt to recognize that a word from him would
be of inestimable value to me at that time as an en-

[1] Oct. 25, 1866.

couragement." [1] From the first, too, he determined that his necessities should not be allowed to cheapen his services. It is related that a well-known firm of solicitors, whose favor might be most valuable to him, sent in a batch of papers with a request for his opinion, and a fee of five guineas. When their clerk called for them a few days later he remarked that there must be some mistake; the tape had not even been untied. "Not at all," said Mr. Benjamin, "the fee proffered covered taking in the papers, but not examining them." The "mistake" was remedied when the clerk returned with an additional five and twenty guineas. [1]

In no way, however, can I give the reader a clearer conception of the years of struggle for a livelihood, nor of the gallant, tender heart that made the fight, than by the letters he was writing to his family and friends at this time. Since the more important happenings of his daily life are all chronicled therein, we may once again almost dispense with other narrative; while into their very texture, so that excision would likely remove something vital, are woven the loving, playful, half-boyish allusions to little incidents and doings of the home circle in New Orleans of which he was an actual member no more. The one from which I shall now quote is to Mrs. Kruttschnitt, and dated, 4 Lamb Buildings, Temple, 11th April, 1867, after he had been almost a year at the bar. The first page or two deal with matters of family interest,—how he has "fallen desperately in love with your little blossom Alma, whom I have never seen, but I can imagine from the

---

[1] London *Times*, July 2, 1883.   [2] *Generation of Judges*, p. 196.

photograph what a darling cherub she must be"; how he must know all that each and every member of the household is doing; how she must send him Mr. Kruttschnitt's articles on microscopy, "for I like to read everything, although I know little or nothing about the microscope; . . . he would write nothing but the conscientious result of careful and accurate observation."

Then he turns to his own affairs: "I have been spending the last month on circuit at Manchester and Liverpool, and only got back this morning to chambers in the Temple. I give you at the head my address, which will be unchanged now for a long time, as I have taken a seven years' lease. . . . As I have so little to do at the bar compared with my former professional life, I am turning author and have in preparation a law work which will be ready for publication I hope in November or December next, and will bring me into more prominence with the profession and perhaps secure a more rapid advance in getting business. As poor Kitt's article gave you the face-ache, I shall not upset you entirely with my law book; but I suppose some copies of it will reach New Orleans, and you can read the title-page and look at the outside without much risk of serious injury. . . .

"I must now close, darling, and leave open for you my letter to Hatty for the rest of the news. Tell Alma to mind not to get close to me, for I'll eat her up, and then she can't squeeze my life out."

On June 5th he writes to Miss Harriet Benjamin four full pages of his fine script that tell about the famous Paris Exhibition of that year (he had but a two days' glimpse of it), which we have not space to quote. It

is only by an occasional allusion we learn from him
that he made good his promise to help, as always, in
the support of his sisters. "I got the letter of Lionel
acknowledging the remittance," he says, and he continues :

"I have been over to Paris, for two or three
days to see my family before their departure for
the south of France, where they will spend the summer, and we will rent our apartments during the
Exhibition. . . .

"We have all been in great jubilee here at the news
of our poor President's release from his shameful captivity. I have not yet had a letter from him but am
expecting one every day, as I am eager to learn how
he is, whether his health is improving, and whether
his constitution has been undermined by his sufferings.

"I am getting along tolerably well in my profession,
barely making my expenses, but I think I see that my
reputation is growing and that the future is brighten-
ing. I work hard, but it is a happy life for me to be
absorbed in my studies and business, and to have no
harassing anxieties to disturb my labors. I am getting
too old to care now for anything except ease and tranquillity, with means sufficient to live in comfort, but
without any desire for splendor, or show, or what are
called pleasures."

The pretense of complete absorption and the satisfaction of all cravings in hard work was, doubtless, for
the benefit of the home folk,—whom it did not deceive. They knew that he was capable of hard work,
indeed, but that, as he himself confessed, he "loved to
bask in the sun like a lizard," being always by nature eminently sociable and fond of worldly pleasures.
After some brief excursions into aristocratic circles,
however, during the first six or eight months of his

stay in London, when he had the felicity of dining
with his political idol, Gladstone, and of meeting a
"crowd of titled and fashionable guests," whose "tone,
manners and customs I found just what I would have
expected,—quiet, easy, courteous and agreeable"—he
resolutely declined social attentions. "I have no time
to yield to pleasures," he wrote home in the letter[1]
from which I have quoted, "till I have secured some
lucrative business." General Taylor was rather put
out with him, says Mrs. Bradford, because he declined
the honor of meeting the Prince of Wales.

But though too busy to yield to pleasure for himself,
he yet had time to spare to give others pleasure. A
typical little passage from a letter of February 22, 1868,
shows the great lawyer busily engaged in hunting up
rare stamps for his small nieces and nephews in New
Orleans : " I searched in vain for some time," he writes
with all the exuberant joy of the youngster who has
treasure trove, . . . "but by a very lucky chance
my eye fell on the little advertisement that I enclose,
and I lost no time in going to the place, which I believe is the only place in this great world of a city
where they could be found. So now they will get
Chinese, and Egyptian, and Turkish ! ! !"

It is worth noting that, once the suggestion was made
to him that stamps would please the children, he seems
never to have forgotten it ; there are stamps of all kinds
sent in numerous letters for the next dozen years,—till
the children at home, indeed, must have been far too
grown up to care about them, though they would not
hurt "Uncle Ben's" feelings by intimating as much.
In this same letter he continues : "I am looking forward

[1] Dec. 20, 1865.

to the day when restored peace to our unhappy South will enable me to devote a long vacation to a full month's visit to you all, and when I shall have nothing to do but be petted and *stuffed*, and get no scoldings unless my appetite fails."

He gives sage counsel about the boys, with quite as much interest and affection as if they were his own,— how they "must be made to take an education, not be allowed to fancy a profession or business yet, for boys are really incapable of forming judgments of such things, and only long to get into business in order to seem grown up; let it be a good education first; if you will, let them come to me; after they are fitly educated, then business or a profession, what you will." Here he adds something of more personal bearing: "My book is nearly finished, but the nearer I get to the end, the more fastidious I become about correcting, amending, and improving it. I do not think it will be out before June; but who told you that it had a jaw-breaking name? It is a simple Treatise on Sale under the English law, which is very different from the law of Louisiana, and the subject quite a difficult and troublesome branch of professional learning here."

The book over which he was toiling, and from which, not without good reason, he expected much increased reputation, was the famous "Treatise on the Law of Sale of Personal Property, with Reference to the American Decisions, to the French Code and Civil Law." It went through three editions before the author's death, and became a classic on both sides of the Atlantic as "Benjamin on Sale." The selection of the subject in itself showed acuteness of judgment; for this extremely difficult question had not been adequately discussed ; and in its treatment, involving, as the preface explained, "an attempt to develop the principles applicable to all branches of the subject," there was wide scope not only for the accumulations of varied learning and experience incident to such a life as Benjamin's had been, but for the display of that power of comprehension, of logical and perspicuous development of first principles for which he was remarkable, though the English public had yet seen but little of it in him. It was this intellectual power, the clear perception of essential rules in their practical application, that won for the book its immediate popularity with the legal profession, and, we may add, has preserved that high standing. Soon after its publication, "Baron Martin, when taking his seat one morning upon the bench, asked to have Mr. Benjamin's work handed to him. ' Never heard of it, my Lord,' was the answer of the chief clerk. ' Never heard of it !' ejaculated Sir Samuel Martin ; 'mind that I never take my seat here again without that book by my side.' " [1]

We shall see from the letters how grateful to the author was the vogue of the work, and how it brought him speedily more practice with increased reputation. But the first one from which I shall quote has again to do with family affairs : [2] " Tell darling little Alma that uncle won't have her laughed at, and that she is perfectly right in saying that the 'Syringe came down like a wolf on the fold,' and that when I come to play with her on my lap, I'll just give the 'schlague' to any one that makes her cry. I want her for my own pet. . . . I will not permit myself to doubt that I

[1] London *Daily Telegraph*, Feb. 10, 1883.
[2] June 21, 1869.

shall have the chance of embracing you all next year."
But at the beginning of the next year,[1] in a long letter
in which he sent many messages to little Alma, and
rare stamps saved by his daughter Ninette for her
cousin Julius, and some accumulated American stamps
from his own correspondence to buy Alma ice-cream;
in which he reviewed and commended the progress of
his nephews; in which he hoped Mrs. Levy would be
consoled for her rheumatism by a little grandson, he
wrote:

"I long beyond measure to see you all once more,
but I am plainly to be disappointed this year. The
simple truth is that I cannot afford the visit. I had
anticipated from the growth of my reputation at the
bar here and from the assurances of those who ought
to know, that I would already have been in the receipt
of an income sufficient for support at all events. But
the growth of business here is so very slow, and the
competition so severe, that the attorneys give their
briefs, whenever they possibly can, to barristers who
are connected or related in some way with them or
their families; and in an old country like England
these family ties are so ramified that there is hardly an
attorney who has not in some way a barrister whom it
is his interest to engage. I therefore have but little
chance for a brief whenever it *can* be given elsewhere, and this accounts for the difficulty under which
any one in the world must labor, if not connected in
some way with the attorneys and their families. I cannot get along with less than £1,400, say about $7,000
a year, including my professional expenses at the
Temple for rent, clerk hire, bar-mess, robing-room,
wigs and gowns, etc., etc., which are endless. I had
hoped strongly that by this year at furthest I should be
able to make both ends meet, but I have not yet

[1] Feb. 8, 1870.

reached that point, though I see a more decided increase in my receipts than I have hitherto perceived. If I had not written my book, I should be 'nowhere' in the race, but that has done me an immensity of good, and will give me further fruits of business and reputation, though I barely clear the costs of publication and make no money out of it. I think from the present aspect of things that I shall *nearly* succeed in not getting behindhand this year, and if so, my subsequent career will become more rapidly prosperous, if I preserve my health, which is excellent,—quite as good as ever. I am now Queen's Counsel for the County of Lancashire only, which is very important as far as Liverpool business is concerned, but I hope within twelve months to have the same promotion for all England, so that my London business will be much more profitable, and I shall then feel perfectly easy in my mind as to pecuniary matters. I write these things *for no one but the family*, but I can keep no secrets from you all, knowing how much you will be interested in all that concerns me."

The same hopeful tone distinguishes his reference to himself in a long letter to Mr. Mason,[1] from which we may quote. The greater portion of it is taken up with news of and inquiries for his old associates of the Confederacy, and with a reply to a request from Colonel Charles Marshall, of General Lee's staff, for certain data ; I omit all but the passages of special significance :

"I am doing here in London not only as well but even better than I dared to hope, and am now at last in receipt of an income sufficient for my family, with a fair prospect of again laying up a little store for them when I am no longer able to work, in the place of what

[1] Feb. 8, 1871.

our Northern friends confiscated for me. I have, however, worked very hard, and have been closely straitened for means while striving to attain my present position. Now as regards the other part of your letter. Please say to Colonel Marshall that I perfectly remember our acquaintance during the war, and that I deem him entitled in every respect and on every ground to apply to me for information, or for any other service I can render him ; and above all for any aid that I can afford in the pious labor he has undertaken. Upon some points I can give him information, but upon others my memory is a blank, *as to order of dates and such like details.*   I have hardly anything to which I can refer to refresh my memory, but I have the *original* report made by the Commissioners who went to Hampton Roads, and a bound copy of the President's Messages to Congress, which you (who were in our secrets) know to have been written by me, as the President was too pressed with other duties to command sufficient time for preparing them himself."

Returning to more personal matters, we find that in the course of the same year in which he wrote thus to Mr. Mason, he was able to give an even better report of his financial condition to his own family.[1] But coupled with this is the first mention of ill health. He had been singularly free from even trifling bodily ailments all his life, though now he says :

" After getting through my work on circuit I left for Paris on the 23d August, and have had a good long vacation of over seven weeks, and am now back to hard work. A good part of my vacation, however, was spoiled by an attack of neuralgic or rheumatic pains in the side and back which kept me in nearly constant pain for several weeks ; but, fortunately, by the aid of hot sulphurous baths, I got rid of the attack

[1] Oct. 15, 1871.

and have been free from it now for three weeks, so that I hope there will be no relapse. Singularly enough, Natalie had been suffering from a similar attack, only much more, for several months. She was in bed for two months unable to use the knee joints at all, but she also has recovered, from the same treatment, and when I left them at the beginning of the week, the whole family were in excellent health and spirits. . . .

"I am happy to tell you, my darlings, that although my success at the bar is absurdly exaggerated in some accounts that I have seen in the newspapers, I have really 'turned the corner' at last, and that my receipts for the last twelve months have exceeded ten thousand dollars, so that I have been able to lay up something after paying expenses. It is now probable that there will be a substantial increase for the future, and that if my health lasts, I shall in four or five years feel that I am 'safe,' and that in the event of my death a comfortable subsistence will be secure for my family. I think my reputation at the bar is increasing and I can see that my circle of clients is daily widening."

A little later he writes to Miss Benjamin :[1]

"I am sadly in arrears with my correspondence with you all, and I know that my dearest Penny has good reason to scold, but I have really for some time past been under *high pressure* of work, and I avoid as much as possible using my eyes by gaslight. I don't mean to say that there is anything the matter with them, but I have so much writing to do, that they get fatigued before I finish my day's work, and then it is not a pleasure to continue writing. . . .

"I have been in Paris for two or three days since I last wrote you. I ought to have had the whole of Christmas week for my holiday, but a client got hold

[1] Feb. 21, 1872.

of me and gave me one hundred guineas for three days of my time, and I could not afford the luxury of a holiday at that rate, so I was cheated out of half my week. . . .

"Pen says that she will celebrate her silver wedding and Ernest's majority next year, and if I dared look forward so far, it would rejoice me beyond measure to be of the party. But while the political excitement lasts, and while the Senate rejects amnesty bills, and the South is kept crushed under negro rule, it sickens me to think of the condition of things. After the Presidential election it may be that the general amnesty bill will pass; but it is a wonder to me that so much bitterness against the conquered can endure after the lapse of seven or eight years."

The longed-for amelioration in the pitiable condition of Louisiana did not come so soon, nor was he sufficiently secure of his position at the bar to take the vacation and go to New Orleans in the summer of 1872; but a letter of August 10th gives the most cheering news he had yet sent home:

"I have had high professional promotion lately. A number of the judges united in recommending to the Lord Chancellor that I should have a 'patent of precedence,' which gives me rank above all future Queen's Counsel and above all Sergeants at Law (except two or three who already have such patents), and Her Majesty upon the transmission of this recommendation by the Lord Chancellor, who endorsed it, was pleased to issue her warrant directing that such a patent should be granted to me.

"I received it in person from the Lord Chancellor at his own house, and he gave it to me with some very flattering expressions. I need hardly say that as the law journals and the *Times* have contained some articles on the subject it will be of immense value to me

in my profession in various ways, both in increased income and in greater facility of labor; for you must
know that a 'leader' who has a patent of precedence
has not half as hard work as a 'junior,' because it is
the business of the junior to do all the work connected
with the pleadings and preparation of a cause, and the
leader does nothing but argue and try the causes after
they have been completely prepared for him.

"As the ladies always want to know all details of
ceremonies, I will say for the gratification of the feminine mind that my patent of precedence is engrossed
on parchment, and to it is annexed the great seal,
which is an enormous lump of wax as large and thick
as a muffin, enclosed in a tin box, and the whole together contained in a red morocco box highly orna-
mented. As nothing of this kind is ever done under a
monarchy without an endless series of charges, etc., it
cost me about £80, or $400, to pay for stamps, fees,
presents to servitors, etc., etc. Now for the reverse
side of the medal.

"I have now to wear a full bottomed wig, with
wings falling down on my shoulders, and knee breeches
and black silk stockings and shoes with buckles, and
in this ridiculous array, in my silk gown, to present
myself at the next levee of Her Majesty to return
thanks for her gracious kindness. In the same dress I
am also to be present at the grand breakfast which the
Lord Chancellor gives to Her Majesty's Judges and to
the leaders of the bar every year in October (at the end
of the month), when the Michaelmas Term begins.
Fortunately, I have three months for bracing up my
nerves to the trial of making myself such an object,
and as it is usual to have photographs made of one's
self on these occasions I will send some to enable you
all to laugh at 'how like a monkey brother looks in
that hideous wig.'

"Before I forget it, I must just mention that I don't
want anything of this sort that I write for the family
to get into the papers, for if it were repeated here, it

would be known that such details must have originated with me, and I should be suspected, to my great mortification, of writing puffs of myself, than which nothing is deservedly regarded with more contempt. Of course, the *fact* of my promotion being announced could do no harm, but none of the details which can come *only* from *me* must get into the papers."

Much encouraged by this signal manifestation of the estimate placed upon him in his new home—there were, of course, congratulatory letters, and flattering articles in the press and law reviews—Mr. Benjamin went to work with renewed zest. It was said that he owed his success to the argument in the case of Potter *vs.* Rankin, in the House of Lords, when Lord Hatherly was so impressed with his ability that he at once ordered the patent made out. Certainly, it became before many more years almost a matter of course that in every important case taken to the Courts of Appeal, Privy Council or House of Lords, Mr. Benjamin, Q. C., should be retained as counsel.

Curiously enough, "the doctors disagree" in their diagnosis, if we may so call it, of his peculiar talents as a lawyer. Several, including the writer of the excellent sketch in the *Times* of May 9, 1884, concur that Mr. Benjamin was not markedly successful before a jury. Since our account of the purely legal part of his life is designedly condensed, let us here disregard chronology to give such of the facts about technical or professional matters as may be presumed to interest the lay reader. The character of Mr. Benjamin's practice in America, as has been repeatedly stated, was principally civil, not criminal, involving especially points of commercial law. In England it would be natural to expect him to follow the same bent, even if we did not recall that he expected, and did get, much of his earlier business through Liverpool merchants. The writer in the *Times* states—and I quote him as giving a fair summary from one who was a contemporary :

"When he first settled in London he practiced in all the courts, and made many masterly addresses to juries ; but in the very peculiar and difficult art of examining and cross-examining witnesses and managing a case at *Nisi Prius*, he did not shine. This requires a special experience of the peculiar class of jurymen who are to be influenced. . . . But in arguments before the court which depended on the scientific treatment of legal questions Mr. Benjamin's superiority became early established. After a few years he confined himself to these. Anson *vs.* the Northwestern Railway was his last case at *Nisi Prius*. Thenceforward he restricted himself to the Court in Banc or Courts of Appeal, but was likewise often taken into Chancery to argue before an Equity Judge. Still later, feeling the absolute necessity of restricting his exertions, Mr. Benjamin refused to go into any court other than the House of Lords and the Privy Council except for a fee of 100 guineas, and a client having demanded a consultation at his own house, the fee of 300 guineas was fixed. The Privy Council was, perhaps, his favorite tribunal ; his wide acquaintance with foreign systems of law qualified him in an eminent degree to deal with the cases from the colonies and dependencies of Great Britain which come before the Judicial Committee in Downing Street. His great faculty was that of argumentative statement. He would so put his case, without in the least departing from candor, that it seemed impossible to give judgment except in one way. It must be confessed that this was a dangerous power, and sometimes imposed on himself. His 'opinions' were, in consequence, sometimes unduly sanguine or at least seemed so in cases which he had not the opportunity of arguing himself. When he did argue he often justified by his advocacy advice which had seemed the hardiest. The *Franconia* was perhaps the best-known of his cases. It dealt, to some extent, with international law, in which, having been not only a lawyer but a statesman, he was at home; but it was a criminal case, and so of a class with which he was not usually concerned. More characteristic examples will be revealed by a glance at the columns of the *Times* between 1872 and 1883, or by dipping into the pages of the 'Appeal Cases.'   Here we find him arguing questions about bills of exchange, a husband's liability for his wife's debts (Debenham *vs.* Mellon), the duties of the charterer of a ship, the explicit rights of the Caledonian and North British Railways under their acts, the reopening of accounts closed in New Zealand nine years before, the perjury of Thomas Castro, otherwise Arthur Orton, otherwise Sir Roger Tichborne, etc."

Regarding his non-success,—comparative, of course —as a jury lawyer, other English observers concur with the *Times*. Some note that his accent was decidedly American, and his voice not pleasant,—a view we must believe mistaken considering the unanimous testimony to its beautiful timbre before he crossed the Atlantic, though it is fair to note that Mrs. Davis remarks, [1] "When I saw him in England much of the

---

[1] As elsewhere, from private letters to the author, and in *Lawley MS.*

well-remembered music of his voice had fallen silent."
Others, however, commented on his wonderful power
of exposition, of presenting facts : "He makes you see
the very bale of cotton that he is describing as it lies
upon the wharf at New Orleans." [1] And Baron Pollock gives several anecdotes, too long to quote, to illustrate his skill in handling witnesses, remarking, in
direct contradiction of the opinions offered above:
"Although not eloquent as a speaker, he always
showed a great experience in the conduct of a *Nisi
Prius* issue, and thoroughly knew the rules of the game ;
clear in the statement of facts, an effective cross-exam-
iner, and cautious in the extreme of expressing any
false or figurative surroundings, he presented his client's
case with great force to a jury." [2] On the whole, therefore, it would seem that the predilection for courts which
tried without juries, and his unquestioned mastery of
that sort of pleading, misled those who thought that he
was not, or would not have been, so successful in handling juries.

In conclusion, Lord James of Hereford comments
upon Mr. Benjamin's "mode and method of argument
[as] peculiar and strange to" the English Judges when
he first came. "His habit was to commence his arguments with an abstract lecture upon the law affecting
the case before the court. Most elementary principles
would be very minutely explained. If the court differed from or doubted any of his propositions, the
tribunal was informed that they certainly were wrong,
and that it was desirable they should have the state of
the law more fully explained to them." Sir Henry

[1] *Daily Telegraph*, February 10, 1883.
[2] *Green Bag*, Sept., 1898, p. 400.

James, as he then was, took occasion in private to call Mr. Benjamin's attention to a fault that might work him harm : "Right well he accepted all I had to say, and agreed that he had not yet fallen into our ways." [1]

His custom, noted even while he was practicing in New Orleans, of beginning his arguments by a bold statement of the propositions he intended to maintain, which sometimes needed all of his subtlety of logic in order to seem reasonable at all, was indirectly responsible for one little episode that made a deep impression in England. It was in the case of the London and County Bank *vs.* Ratcliffe, which Mr. Russell Roberts, one of the junior counsel, declares to have been exceedingly puzzling in its facts, that Mr. Benjamin had his difficulty, May 19, 1881. As senior counsel for the appellants in the House of Lords, Mr. Benjamin insisted on proceeding with his argument as he had planned it, in spite of signs of impatience on the part of the members. At length, upon his stating one of the propositions that he meant to defend, Lord Selborne, the Lord Chancellor, remarked *sotto voce*, but in a tone that reached the counselor's ear : "Nonsense!" Changing color slightly, says Mr. Roberts, from whom I take these facts,[2] Mr. Benjamin "proceeded to tie up his papers. This accomplished, he bowed gravely to the members of the House, and saying, 'That is my case, my Lords,' he turned and left the House." The junior counsel was therefore compelled to go on as best he might. "On the following day the respondent's counsel were heard, and a reply being called for, Mr. Horace Davey, Q. C., on the 23d day of May, rose to address the House, Mr. Benjamin being absent. On

[1] *Lawley MS.*   [2] *Lawley MS.*

Mr. Davey's rising, the Lord Chancellor said, 'Mr. Davey, it is unusual for the House to hear three counsel for the same party, and we have already heard Mr. Benjamin and Mr. Russell Roberts. I notice Mr. Benjamin's absence, however, and I fear that it may be attributable to his having taken umbrage at an unfortunate remark which fell from me during his argument, and in which I referred to a proposition he stated as 'nonsense.' I certainly was not justified in applying such a term to anything that fell from Mr. Benjamin, and I wish you to convey to him my regret that I should have used such an expression.' . . . Mr. Davey conveyed to Mr. Benjamin what had been said by Lord Selborne, and induced him to write a note to Lord Selborne acknowledging the apology."

This little incident has echoed in nearly every one of the English reminiscences of Mr. Benjamin. The prompt and unhesitating resentment of an affront to his dignity (all the more unwarranted in view of his own unvarying courtesy) even from the Woolsack made a strong impression, and increased respect for him. It is no doubt fortunate that the occasion for this action on his part arose late in his career, when he was firmly established in the front rank, perhaps at the head of the bar ; for if it had come earlier, he would assuredly have acted in the same way ("he was like fire and tow," says Mrs. Davis, "and sensitive about his dignity"), and then popular approval might not have been so certainly on his side.

Having thus run ahead of the man in surveying the course of the lawyer, let us hark back to some of the details of his life during these years. On August 9, 1874, he wrote to Mrs. Kruttschnitt :

"As soon as the assizes are finished, say about 26th to 28th of this month, I leave at once for Paris for the marriage of Ninette, which will take place early next month. Of course I cannot but feel anxious at thus giving up my only child, but, as far as human foresight can predict, I have assurance that the match will prove happy. Captain de Bousignac, her intended, is represented on all sides as one of the most promising officers of the French army. At the age of thirty-two he has acquired a distinguished position on the general staff from his merits both as an artillery and engineer officer ; he is of excellent family, irreproachable habits, beloved by all around him for his frank, gay and amiable character, and I know no better test of a man than his possession of the affection of those most intimate with him. . . . He is stationed at Versailles in the war department, only half an hour from Paris, and as long as he remains there, the new couple will live with us. . . . By giving up all my savings I have been able to settle on Ninette three thousand dollars a year, so that her future is now secure against want, and I must now begin to lay up a provision for the old age of my wife and self. I undertake this new task with courage, because we shall not require a great deal, and the practice of my profession is now so much more lucrative than it ever was before, that I hope in two or three years to see the end of necessary labor, and to be able to work as little or as much as I please."

In the next letter, October 24th, he gives a full account, almost feminine in its attention to detail (though he declines even the attempt at describing the toilettes), of the wedding, which took place on September 7th. The bride spent most of that winter with her mother, Captain de Bousignac coming to and from Orleans, whither he had been transferred ; in the spring they opened apartments of their own in that place.

That Benjamin set to work with a will to add to his savings, and that in doing so he did not forget to continue his generosity to all who had any claim on him, may be seen from a letter of March 17, 1875, in which he sends a present of one thousand dollars for one of his nieces about to be married, and says of himself: "I have just finished the trial of a cause which lasted eight days, and on Sunday I was at my desk from breakfast till two hours past midnight, with only an interval of half an hour for taking some light food, as one cannot *dine* when so deeply absorbed." In the same letter he records his satisfaction with his daughter's match; "her husband is all that I could desire." And it may be added that the years did not diminish his gratification. He recurs once more to the hope of coming to America: "You say, my dearest, that I never now speak of visiting you all. I never *can* consent to go to New Orleans and break my heart with witness-ing the rule of negroes and carpet-baggers. I have hoped year by year that some change would be effected which would place decent and respectable men at the head of the administration of affairs, and it seems to me that the time is now fast approaching. I long and yearn to press you all to my heart once more, and for some of us at least age is creeping on and not much time is to be lost."

"I don't know what you mean," he writes to Miss Benjamin some months later (June 6th), "by saying you suppose that I am having a little holiday. I am scarcely able to get to dinner before nine or ten o'clock at night once a week, and generally my whole Sunday is also occupied." And in the next sentence, as if apologizing for this complaint of his hard work, he

goes on : " But I am in depressed spirits on account of
the condition of poor Jules," his brother-in-law, who
was wasting away with the same disease that ultimately
caused Mr. Benjamin's death.   Her brother's distress-
ing state greatly affected Mrs. Benjamin, with whom he
lived, and who had no other companion now that her
daughter had gone.

Many a page might be filled with the little things
from these home letters, but I must give only gleanings
here and there.   He constantly refers to his professional progress with a pardonable pride in the successes
achieved, and yet modestly withal.   For example:[1]
"I have been acquiring a good deal of reputation
lately in a great cause that I had to argue before fourteen judges, presided over by the Lord Chief Justice of
England, in behalf of the captain of a German ship, the
Franconia.   As it involved a question of international
law, the papers were full of it, and I received many
compliments."   Early in 1877 (March 18th) he announces that he does not have it so hard now :
"I very seldom have to work after seven in the
evening, and from ten in the morning to seven in the
evening is no excess of labor " !   Two years later,[2] he
announces that he has cut off a large part of his practice in the lower courts, " confining myself chiefly to
the House of Lords and other Appeal Courts.   .   .   .
I am beginning again to go into society, which I had
relinquished for years, and to accept invitations to
dinner which I had habitually declined.   I am all the
better for it."   During this year he was building his
house, at No. 41 Avenue d'Jéna, Paris, and writes
amusing letters about his difficulties in getting things

[1] July 16, 1876.   [2] March 23, 1879.

done. "I was *maliciously* pleased," he writes[1] to Mrs. Kruttschnitt, "with your account of your tribulations with the workmen in your house, as I have gone through the same trouble for weeks, and left Paris with everything in dire confusion. . . . . The Paris workmen of all classes began 'strikes,' and first the joiners, next the plumbers, next the gas-fitters, next the 'fumistes,' or fireplace and stove workers, next the plasterers, etc., etc., refused to do any work, while my contractors were in utter despair, unable to advance a step." By desperate exertions, they managed to get into the bedrooms, leaving the rest to be completed, with the attendant confusion and discomfort : "We all came to the conclusion that no violence of language or feeling could do justice to the occasion, so we finished by laughing at each other's doleful faces and went on in the best way we could. . . . We shall be housed like princes, but the cost will be greater than I supposed, and including the additional furniture, etc., etc., I don't get off for less than $80,000. However, all is now paid for."

Benjamin took special pride in this comfortable mansion, the first that he could really call a home of his own, since the happy days of "Bellechasse" ; and as the years wore on he chafed more and more under the strain of his practice, began to yield to the weight of age, and longed with increasing ardor for absolute retirement from the great world. He writes, just before the Easter holidays in 1880 : "I have felt work more this winter than ever before, and in addition to advancing age, which of course must tell on me, I attribute much to the dreadful weather which we had

[1] Nov. 6, 1879.

early in the season and which carried off *very* many persons advanced in life. . . . We are in the midst of the turmoil of a general election here, and it amuses me to look on, as I do not take the slightest part in politics and shall never again be induced to emerge from the quietude of private life. Half my brethren of the bar are candidates, and great efforts have been made to induce *me* to become a candidate, but I laugh them off, and *both* sides claim me, because I belong to *neither*."

It was very shortly after this that, while on a brief visit to Paris in May, he met with an accident from which he never fully recovered. Though sometimes, in moments of depression, feeling his age, he was still far from seeming a man on the verge of seventy, and usually moved with a step as elastic as if he were yet in his prime. He tells very briefly what happened, in a letter to Mr. Bayard, written when the more serious consequences were just making themselves manifest:[1]

"I now feel able to answer your welcome and affectionate letter of 28th March. I have been *very* ill, but am now greatly improved, though I am told I must not hope for complete recovery. . . . In May, 1880, I was thrown to the ground with great violence in a foolish attempt to jump off a tram-car in rapid motion. My right arm was torn from the socket, the shoulder blade broken, and the left side of the forehead fractured ; indeed, but for my hat, which fortunately remained on my head and acted as a buffer, I must have been killed."

In fact, he had stepped off the swiftly moving tram as he had been in the habit of doing thirty years before

[1] Aug. 2, 1883.

in New Orleans; the thirty years made some difference, however, and furthermore, losing his presence of
mind when he first stumbled, he held on to the hand-
rail of the car, and was dragged a considerable distance. As he wrote to Mr. Bayard, his recovery from
the initial effects of the accident was surprisingly
rapid. He was hard at work again in London the
following winter, and his physician promised him a
cure, though not immediate. He wrote cheerfully of
the régime prescribed : "I am made to take a liqueur
glass of cognac pure three times a day, to take a preparation of iron at each meal, to drink my claret without water, and altogether to accustom myself to getting
a little 'tight' every day. I shall soon be an accomplished 'tippler,' and then my 'cure' will be complete." [1]

Indeed, for a time it seemed so ; for after a successful year, he spent a "very pleasant summer vacation,
[1881] three weeks at Bagnéres-de-Luchon, a most
charming watering place in the Pyrenees, and a month
at Biarritz, a beautiful seashore resort. I had the
pleasure of having my dear child with me the whole
time, and her husband, after a flying visit of one day
at Luchon, got leave of absence and spent a fortnight
with us at Biarritz." Moreover, on a little trip to
some friends near Toulouse, there were dinner parties
almost every day, "followed by extempore music and
dancing in the evening, and this 'old man' was made
to dance by invitations from the young ladies, who refused to dance at all if *he* would not. What do you
say to that ?" [2] Of his profession he wrote :[3] "I still

---

[1] Oct. 24, 1880.   [2] To Miss Benjamin, Nov. 4, 1881.
[3] Nov. 27, 1881.

keep up my old jog-trot, but my work is less absorbing. I have cut off a good deal of my practice preparatory to withdrawing, but my withdrawal now depends entirely on our success in getting Ninette and her husband back to live with us, as I should hardly know what to do with myself in the 'big house' all alone with my poor wife, who is constantly fretting for her daughter when the latter joins her husband." In spite of efforts, which we may well believe to have been quietly courageous, to shake off his infirmities, they increased alarmingly in the course of the next year. His heart became seriously involved, and he was in such a state that he could hardly walk. He went over to spend the Christmas vacation as usual with his family, and in his own words let us tell of the close of a career unique, so far as I know, in history :

"*41 Avenue d'Jéna, Paris, 12 February, 1883.*
"My darling Penny :
"You will see by the above heading, that I am still here and this will be my address in future, for *I have left the bar and shall practice no more.*

"For the last few months, new and strange symptoms developed themselves in my condition. I was troubled with an oppression in breathing and palpitation of the heart ; my feet became swollen and remained so : my legs were so weak that they could scarcely sustain my body, and Natalie insisted on a consultation of the most eminent physicians of Paris, which took place just a week ago. After a close and careful examination of all the vital organs, and auscultation by the most experienced, it was discovered that the diabetic affection had injured the heart, which had become enlarged, and the great valve of the aorta had ceased to act efficiently so as to expel as it should do, the blood which had passed through the heart. In this state of things they advised an energetic course of treatment which I am now undergoing, but they specially insisted on complete repose, and declared that the fatigue and excitement of arguing causes were particularly prejudicial and must be discontinued.

"I had of course no alternative, but directed my clerk to announce my retirement, to return all my briefs to my clients, and to repay all fees received in matters which I am unable to finish.

"I cannot tell you how greatly I have been surprised and how deeply I have been moved by the effect of this announcement. Every leading London newspaper,[1] with the *Times* at the head, has made my retirement a matter of national concern and regret, and my table is covered with piles of letters (some sixty or seventy at least) from my brethren of the bar, expressing the warmest sympathy and regret, and hopes of my recovery, and assurances of warm friendship, etc., etc. For the last few days I have hardly kept my eyes free from tears on reading these testimonials to the rectitude and honor of my professional conduct, *such as no member of the English bar has ever received.* . . .

"If my treatment is at all successful as the doctors anticipate, I shall go to London for a week or two in about a month to close up all my business, get rid of the lease of my lodgings and chambers in the Temple, sell my furniture and law library, etc., and return here free from all preoccupation that can cause care, or fatigue, or excitement; and having nothing to do except to assume my new character of 'an invalid old gentleman' taking care of his health."

The expression of sympathy on the part of his fellow-barristers was later to take a form yet more remarkable. In a letter to Miss Benjamin, of March 1st, he writes: "I have just received a signal honor

[1] The best is the sketch in the *Daily Telegraph*, Feb. 10, 1883.

from the English bar. A letter from the Attorney-General informs me that he has received a requisition signed by more than eighty Queen's Counsel, and by all the leading members of the bar of England, desiring him to offer me a public dinner in order to take a 'collective farewell' of me and to testify their high sense of the honor and integrity of my professional career, and of their desire that our relations of personal friendship should not be severed. The correspondence will be made public. This is the *first* time that such an honor has been extended to a barrister on leaving the profession."

As he had planned, he went back to London in the spring and closed his offices. Fees to a large amount for unsettled causes were returned to the clients, and business affairs were put in order with that perfect attention to detail which had helped so much to make his fame. But no temptation could possibly induce him to practice again, though it is said a fee of two thousand guineas was offered him. The formal announcement of his retirement, made on February 9th, was treated as final. There only remained the more personal farewell to the members of the bar at the dinner given in his honor.

The great banquet[1] took place in the hall of the Inner Temple, on Saturday evening, June 30, 1883, with Sir Henry James, the Attorney-General, in the chair ; Lord Selborne, the Lord Chancellor, on his left ; and Mr. Benjamin on his right. There were present all that England ranked highest in the legal profession, including such names as that of Lord Coleridge, the Lord Chief Justice, who had wanted Benjamin on the

[1] See London *Times*, July 2, 1883.

bench; the Master of the Rolls, Sir. W. B. Brett, who had seen him begin his career in English courts and now came to do honor to the culmination of that career.   There were the Justices of all the high courts, and a list of titles such as Englishmen are always pleased to see in social Theban phalanx, but which mean less to us than the "more than two hundred members of the bar," without distinction of party,— both the old who had perhaps been distanced in the race by this wonderful little Jew from America, and the young to whom his name was a shibboleth of brilliant success.   Many a rival must have been overcome in the course of Mr. Benjamin's rise before the English courts; yet not one manifested any ill feeling.   It is testimony eloquent on two points—the generosity of the British lawyer, and the scrupulous regard for the rights of his opponents which had always marked the man they had met to honor.

The toasts, not the viands, were of course the *pièces de résistance* of the dinner; but in this place I shall note only his own response.   It was brief, and marked by fastidious simplicity of diction, a characteristic example of his manner when deeply moved; and as his sweet voice recited the simple and sincere story of his illness, of his gratitude to the generous bar of England, and of his regret at feeling that he should meet most of them no more, the great throng of gentlemen listened with rapt attention and manifest sympathy. I shall quote but a fragment of what he had to say: "The feelings of joy and gratification [at this testimonial] are counterbalanced—more than counterbalanced—by the reflection, unutterably sad, that to the large majority of those present my farewell words to-night are a final earthly farewell—that to the large majority of you I shall never again be cheered by the smiling welcome, by the hearty hand-grasp, with which I have been greeted during many years, and which had become to me almost the very breath of my life. It was on the 16th of.December, 1832, that I was first called to the bar; and on the 7th of December last I had accomplished fifty years of professional life."

After recounting the causes of his retirement, and doing homage to those who had made possible his success he gratefully concludes: "From the bar of England I never, so far as I am aware, received anything but warm and kindly welcome. I never had occasion to feel that any one regarded me as an intruder. I never felt a touch of professional jealousy. I never received any unkindness. On the contrary, from all quarters I received a warm and cordial welcome to which, as a stranger, I had no title, except that I was a political exile, seeking by honorable labor to retrieve shattered fortunes, wrecked in the ruin of a lost cause. . . . I must conclude by thanking you all from the bottom of my heart for the kind reception you have given me ever since I first came among you down to this magnificent testimonial, the recollection of which will never fade from my memory, and on which I shall always love to dwell. I thank you all."

Little remains to be told; he was not spared to enjoy even a full year of that home-life for which he had so long yearned and in procuring which he had performed what must always seem prodigious labors. The summer he spent chiefly at Le Mans, where Captain de Bousignac was stationed; and here he appeared to improve so much that his family were hopeful of many more years for him. It is hard to say what he felt himself; for he was resolutely cheerful always, took the brightest view of things, and wrote home the most reassuring letters. Yet there is a touch of melancholy here and there that shows he could not really have cherished many false hopes. The winter was a hard one, and in addition to the depressing effect of the weather, Mrs. Benjamin was seriously ill. A painful operation became necessary, and he sat by her side and held her hand during the terrible ordeal. As the spring came on he did not rally. On April 23d he wrote to Mr. Lawley: "I have been very ill (but I believe I have turned the corner this time), otherwise I could not have left unanswered your sympathetic and affectionate letter; but I have been quite unable to write. For more than two months, I have alternated between my bed and my armchair; but if we can only get rid of this glacial temperature and dry east wind, I shall get some strength. What I require is warmth—will it never come?" He had not turned the corner: on Tuesday, May 6, 1884, the great and kindly gentleman died at his house in Paris.

CHAPTER XV

CHARACTER AND ACHIEVEMENT

As was fitting for one who, in spite of exalted station, had always been singularly unostentatious, the funeral of Mr. Benjamin was very simple. Services were held at midday on Saturday, May 10th, at the Church of St. Pierre de Chaillot, and the body was interred in the great cemetery of Père La Chaise. I shall not pause in this place to discuss the question of Mr. Benjamin's religion, to which I shall recur. For that which he had chiefly labored, the comfort of his family, it was found that there was ample provision. His will, written entirely by his own hand, and dated April 30, 1883, devised legacies, all free of state dues, amounting to a total of £18,000, apportioned in various sums to his three sisters, to his brother Joseph, and to nieces and nephews. The residue of his estate he left to "my said dear wife Natalie and to our only child Ninette, wife of Captain Henri de Bousignac, now captain in the One Hundred and Seventeenth Regiment of the line of the French army. If either my said wife or my said daughter should die before me, the survivor is to be my sole residuary devisee and legatee. I have no real estate in England, but I have in France the family mansion or hotel at No. 41 Avenue d'Jéna, Paris, in which I have resided since my withdrawal from the bar, and in which I contemplate residing the rest of my life." The will further appointed as executors, John George Witt and Lindsey Middleton Aspland, two London barristers, by whom it was proved on June 28, 1884. The personal estate, consisting of various securities, was appraised by the executors at £60,221 9s 1d. Owing to the fact that Mr. Benjamin died abroad, and had become domiciled there, at first some doubt was felt as to where the will should be proved, in France or in England. In view of the insistence in its phraseology on his residence in Paris, he evidently meant that place to be his domicile. But it was discovered that under a statute which he doubtless had in mind, "the will of a British subject domiciled abroad may be proved in England without any proceeding in the foreign country"; hence all difficulties were removed. It was a curious fact, noted by legal writers at the time, that "he was all his life a British subject, had been a senator of the United States and the Confederate Attorney-General, became domiciled in England, and died a domiciled Frenchman." [1]

The ample fortune thus left to those for whom he had made it was the third one wrought out from the brain of this man, who had begun as a penniless lawyer's clerk in New Orleans something more than fifty years before. The steps in the accumulation of this great wealth, for which, he told Mr. Lawley, he had worked harder than ever in his life before, not barring even the toilsome years in Richmond, are made plain for us through his fee-book, [2] wherein he kept a record of his earnings from 1867 to 1882. The full array of

[1] *A Generation of Judges*, p. 202; *Albany Law Journal*, Vol. 30, p. 62.
[2] *Lawley MS.*; see appendix.

figures would be but dry reading, and perhaps puzzling; I therefore give some of the items only. In the
first year, 1866–1867, his fees amounted to £495 12s 3d.
Two years later (1869), in the course of the year when
his book appeared, they had doubled: £1,074 (I omit
the shillings and pence). And in 1871, when he wrote
that he had "turned the corner," they were £2,100.
Before the end of his next year the first promotion as
Queen's Counsel had come, and bore fruits at once; for
now the figures are more than doubled in one year:
£5,623.   From that time on the increase in receipts is
very rapid, till we reach £13,812 in 1876; £15,742 in
1878; and in 1880 the maximum of £15,972. The
total for the sixteen years is £143,900, or, expressed in
round figures and in American currency, something
more than $700,000. Popular fancy, dazzled by the
rapidity of Mr. Benjamin's success, had placed his
earnings at a much higher figure; they are surely sufficiently amazing, however, without fantastic incre-
ment.   It is probable that, during his most fortunate
years, from 1877 to 1882, his profits in England exceeded those of the best years in New Orleans; for
though the American lawyer, then as now, got larger
single fees than his British brother, there was in
Benjamin's case always a division with partners in
America, while in England he had no one to divide
with, and by an automatic arrangement even the English barrister's clerk is provided for by a percentage
of the fees.   Benjamin's chief clerk, it is said, got in
one year from his percentage £1,200; and upon his
retirement was presented by him with £500.

Mere ability to make money, however, is but a poor
gage of real legal ability.   I have given in the course

of the preceding chapter sufficient comment and sufficient evidence in support, I trust, to establish the fact that English lawyers held the very highest opinion of his intellectual powers. None among his contemporaries, indeed, ranked above him; and it was generally agreed that only the peculiar circumstances of his career in England prevented his occupying the bench. There was always a little hesitancy lest the government of the United States be offended; and, as one writer remarks, when he was young enough for the bench he was too young at the bar, when old enough at the bar he was already too far advanced in years.[1]

Connected with his ability as a lawyer, at least in America, was his power as a speaker and as a writer. I have mentioned some of the English criticisms upon his delivery; certainly no fault was ever found with it in America. On the contrary, all unite in testifying to the exquisite melody of a voice that, though soft, yet penetrated; to the distinctness and faultlessness of a rapid enunciation; and to the perfection of simplicity in manner and carriage, the complete absence of oratorical tricks and histrionic gestures. And in the style of his writings, whether speeches for the general public audience, speeches in the Senate, state papers, or legal arguments, one finds the same characteristics I have rather frequently noted: lucidity, simplicity, directness of statement, with sentences usually short, and with little extrinsic ornament. As significant of this, I cannot forbear calling attention to the fact that, in all the numerous citations I have made from the many varieties of his writings there is scarce a foreign phrase; though familiar with French, he seeks the fit

[1] *Generation of Judges.*

English word; nor does he resort frequently to Latin, and to Spanish and German not at all. In this respect, as indeed in his fine feeling for style in general, he is a good model for those who find the limits of their native tongue too narrow to contain their thought. His speeches read well, and indeed, as a recent writer has remarked,[1] would entitle him to rank with Sumner, Beecher, Phillips, or Yancey, as one of those who "stirred multitudes, aroused passions and fired the public heart in terms not less eloquent than the loftiest productions of Fox or Pitt, of Patrick Henry or John Adams."

In considering Benjamin as an orator and as a statesman one cannot forget the other great member of his race who at the same time held sway as statesman, orator, and novelist in England. But the resemblances between Judah P. Benjamin and Benjamin Disraeli are largely superficial and of no significance. The fastidious dandy whose waistcoats used to startle the House, whose Oriental imagination overflows in *Lothair*, whose very name, indeed, carries something of exotic suggestion with it, has little but his race, and his success, in common with the hard-working, accurate, modestly attired American lawyer. Their geniuses were of different types; if it be an axiom and a commonplace to say that the style is the man, I risk it in this case, and need do no more than ask the reader to compare a page of *Lothair's* or *Vivian Grey's* exuberance with the cautious repression of some of the passages quoted from one whom Americans may call "our Benjamin."

In personal habits, Mr. Benjamin was in one sense,

indeed, an "exquisite," though not of the Beacons-
field school.   Always fastidiously neat, he was careful of his dress, and disliked anything in it that would
attract attention.   Simple black was therefore his preference; and the letter describing his costume as
Queen's Counsel will show that he never got over his
democratic dislike of fuss and feathers; he even had a
distaste for the formal black evening coat, since it
usually went with a "function."   A similar neatness
characterized his business habits; and of these his clear
and almost faultless handwriting, so frequently commented on, is typical.   Mr. Witt, his executor, has
this to say of traits that seem to have impressed themselves on everybody who came in contact with Mr.
Benjamin, Q. C., probably the hardest working member of the London bar: "If you called on him in his
chambers, you were perfectly sure to find him seated
at his table, writing a letter with a gold pen, in the
best of style, with nothing on the table except the
note-paper and a tidy blotting pad.   No papers lit-
tered about—no untied briefs.   He welcomed you with
the air of a man who had nothing just then to do except to enjoy a chat.   If he wanted to find a paper for
you, he unlocked the proper drawer in his table, and
at once handed you the document.   What a contrast
to the fussy, no-time-for-anything people, busybody
feeble folk, one usually comes across.   Every one
knows the sort.   They cannot spare you a minute;
they are overwhelmed with work; their papers strew
the table, the chair, and the floor.   Mr. Benjamin was
never in a hurry, never important with this big thing
and that big thing—never pretentious, always the same
calm, equable, diligent, affable man, getting through

an enormous mass of work day by day without ostentation and without friction. Another trait—he left no documents. When I first became friends with him he told me that on his starting in law business in New Orleans, his partner taught him that the secret of human happiness was the destruction of writing. 'Never,' said he, 'keep any letter or other document if you can possibly help it. You only give yourself infinite trouble, and if you die, you bequeath a legacy of mischief. Of course you may have a piece of business going on which compels you to preserve correspondence for a time, but do not keep it a moment longer than is absolutely necessary.' He did not preach without practicing. When he died, he did not leave behind him half a dozen pieces of paper. . . .

"He was absolutely free from vanity. His manner was simple to a degree. He was not in the least self-conscious. He never gave himself airs—in friendly intercourse, in society, and in court, the last thing that was in his mind was himself. The subject under discussion, the case under argument, absorbed him, and left no room for other thought." [1]

Mr. Witt and others tell us, too, of Mr. Benjamin's "amiability of disposition"; his "desire to help his brother barristers in the pursuit of fame and fortune"; his "kindness of heart," which, combined with his "high sense of honor" and that rightly beloved English "fair play," immediately disarmed hostility, and conciliated the good will of every one. Baron Pollock, to give a specific instance, tells how Benjamin unhesitatingly and with precision gave him an opinion, in friendship, on a difficult point of law; and how,

[1] *Lawley MS.*

some days later, he quite unexpectedly found himself opposed to Mr. Benjamin as counsel in arguing a case, used the arguments with which his fellow lawyer had furnished him, and won.   Mr. Benjamin was in all ways of most generous disposition, desirous to aid his friends in any perplexity, to give his time for mere courtesy's sake, or to give his brain, or to give money. He was lavish in his expenditures for private charity, always willing to help, it is said, the forlorn who appealed in the name of the dear "lost cause" or of religion.   Of course, specific instances of this sort are hard to give, especially in the case of one so reticent to outsiders; but a fair sample seems to me to be: "Tell Lionel that I have sent an order on him for one hundred dollars in favor of Mrs. L——, the widow of a former District Judge in New Orleans whom I knew in old times and who wrote me a most pitiful story of her distress. . . . He can draw on me for the amount."[1]

More than the cold giving of money—have we not high authority for thinking so?—was the gentleness of spirit, the consideration for the feelings of others. One little incident, related by Mrs. Davis,[2] will illustrate what I mean.   At a party in Richmond he happened to observe a poor girl who had retired to a corner and was having a very unhappy time over that greatest of feminine tragedies—her gown was not right: "Mr. Benjamin passed, and though he had rarely spoken to her saw her embarrassment, and sat down by her.   After a little desultory ball-room talk he said, 'How very well you are dressed' (we did not

---

[1] Letter to Mrs. Kruttschnitt, March 23, 1880.
[2] Private letter and *Lawley MS.*

say 'gowned' in that day), 'I could not suggest any
improvement in your costume.' He told me afterward
how the poor little creature brightened up, and how
he took some 'grist to her mill' in the shape of
partners. 'Thus,' said he, 'I made two green blades
to grow where only one had been before.'"

"No shade of emotion in another," continues this
lady whose warm friendship has stood the test of years
and separation, "escaped Mr. Benjamin's penetration
—he seemed to have a kind of electric sympathy with
every mind with which he came into contact, and very
often surprised his friends by alluding to something
they had not expressed nor desired him to interpret.
. . . Perhaps I attach too much importance to the
humanism of great men, but I have observed that this
quality is oftenest found wanting in men of great intellect. Looking down from their great elevation the
sorrows of the humble in the valleys beneath would
naturally escape them; but the gracious sympathy of
men mentally endowed beyond their fellows is especially beautiful when it is used to lighten the griefs of
their less gifted friends."

Another instance of his thought for others given by
Mrs. Davis is somewhat comical, and also serves to
display his own fondness for good things to eat. He
was, indeed, a gourmet, not a large eater, but most
fastidious in his taste, relishing extraordinarily dainty
and highly seasoned dishes; he "loved 'lollipops,' as
he called candy, like a child." On one occasion he
was enjoying some special luxuries at Mrs. Davis's
table, in Richmond days, when "he stopped midway
in a criticism upon *Les Miserables* of Victor Hugo
(which had just reached the Confederacy) and whis-

pered to me: 'I do not enjoy my dinner, for Jules
(his brother-in-law, who lived with him in Richmond)
would like these dishes so much, and he is young and
values such things.' I begged him to let me send
some of the dinner to his house; but he declined, saying: 'The papillottes would fall flat and the salad
would wilt; but if I might take him some cake and
lollipops, I should feel very happy.' He would not
allow a servant to carry them, but took them in a
parcel covered with a napkin, and walked home beam-
ing with the hope of conferring pleasure upon his
beloved Jules."

Loyal to friends and to family, steadfast in adherence to political principles and ideals, he was yet not
a patriot of the highest type. The citations from his
letters have shown that he kept up a lively interest in
the political conditions at the South; indeed, few
political prophets have ever estimated a situation with
greater accuracy than the writer of these words, in a
letter to Mr. T. F. Bayard, November 11, 1865: "If
the Southern states are allowed without interference
to regulate the transition of the negro from his former
state to that of a freedman, they will eventually work
out the problem successfully, though with great difficulty and trouble, and I doubt not that the recupera-
tive energy of the people will restore a large share of
their former material prosperity much sooner than is
generally believed; but if they are obstructed and
thwarted by the fanatics, and if external influences are
brought to bear on the negro and inflame his ignorant
fancy with wild dreams of social and political equality,
I shudder for the bitter future which is in store for my
unhappy country."

There can be no question that the wisdom and the political experience of Judah P. Benjamin would have counted for a host in helping the South to solve the problems with which his sagacity foresaw that she would be burdened. He had not, as I have tried to make clear, led his section into the war ; but during the fatal years of that war no one man had had a greater share in directing the destinies of the South, save the President alone. That President, saddled with the odium of drastic policies rendered necessary by the war, and held responsible for disasters which neither he nor any other man could, in all human probability, have averted, was captured by the foes of the Confederacy and imprisoned and menaced with death : he emerged the South's martyr. Because he abode with his people and had suffered in their name, his enemies were silenced, his shortcomings and offenses were forgiven and forgotten. Had Mr. Benjamin remained, too, though there was the probability of imprisonment and the menace of death, was there not also the certainty of such gratitude to him from the impulsive people whom he knew so well, had served so long ? The perfect patriot is so much of the soil that he cannot survive transplantation. Of such, to note only two examples from among the Confederates, was Alexander H. Stephens of the politicians, and General Lee of the soldiers, with a host of others who followed the example of good citizenship set by them. But of that lofty, Puritanic type of patriotism Mr. Benjamin could not boast. Thus remains a flaw in his character which I would not seek to conceal, whatever excuses I may find to urge.

Perhaps we shall not altogether do injustice to his point of view if we suggest that it was, so to speak, the outcome of professional training. He was a born lawyer, and the excursion into politics was merely an episode. Having, as it were, taken a brief for the South, he earnestly and zealously fought for his client as long as his abilities could avail. When the cause was lost, after he had done all that in him lay to win it, he accepted the decision as absolving him from further useless effort. Though he felt for the South, he thought that there rested no obligation upon him to share her adversities. Material and other interests, too, impelled him to seek a new home. His fortunes were ruined ; if imprisoned, or even if not imprisoned, he could not hope to repair them speedily in a country in the condition of the South after the war. And he had many dear ones dependent wholly or in great part upon him for support. His wife and daughter lived in France and would not live elsewhere. If he remained, there was the certainty of long continued separation from them, and of inability on his part to supply their needs.

The exercise of heroism is far easier, and far pleasanter to contemplate, from a safe distance than *in medias res*. For his own fame, doubtless, heroism would have been the best course, nor do I by any means imagine that he did not understand this. But the predominant trait in the man, as I have sought to show, was devotion to his family. "Not for himself, for he cared little for money, but for those he loved," writes one who knew him intimately in England, was he determined to make another fortune. And if we consider these things, endeavoring to give them bearing as if upon our very selves, we shall not, perhaps, judge him hastily and harshly.

The fact that Mr. Benjamin's wife and only child lived in France for years before he went to England, and that they continued to live there while he was just across the Channel, cannot fail to excite comment. The responsibility for this state of things rests not at all upon him; for no husband could have been more affectionate, more attentive to the whims and fancies of his wife, or been a more lavish provider. Those family letters from which I have quoted only the parts bearing particularly on the man, are filled with all sorts of affectionate allusions to Mrs. Benjamin: he is anxious not to disappoint Natalie and Ninette, who will be waiting for him at the station in Paris to-morrow evening, and have a party of pleasure on hand; he is sorry that he has to go off alone to a watering-place, for his health, since Natalie cannot bear the spa and is waiting for him in the Pyrenees; he is worried because Natalie must be left so much alone with poor sick Jules, it is very depressing to her spirits; it is sad that she must be so much parted from Ninette, for she frets so for her; Natalie and Ninette "are as busy as bees deciding on shades of color for the decorations, patterns of paper for every room" (in the house at 41 Avenue d'Jéna), and "I am leaving my study and library on the ground floor unfurnished this year, as it will not be ready in time to be of any service to me till next vacation"; and "the two together are as busy as bees, finishing the furnishing and ornamentation of the 'grand salon' and threatening to give several soirées during the winter on the pretext that they want to establish intimate relations with certain grand personages who can aid in the more rapid promotion of the Captain,"—and so on, and so on, the sum of it all being that there is ample and multiform evidence of his taking the most active and helpful interest in anything that might add to their comfort or contribute to their pleasure.   On the other hand, close searching, and a faith that one might call blind rather than simply charitable, is necessary to discover that Mrs. Benjamin manifested the least solicitude about his comfort.   He wrote to Mr. Bayard [1] that he hoped soon to have attained such a position that he might move his family to London.   No doubt he sincerely desired to do so ; almost every letter home has some allusion to the irksomeness of separation from his wife and daughter.   He hesitates even about permitting himself to hope for that chance to visit New Orleans, since he owes his vacations to his family ; and he spent with them every spare moment of time. But Mrs. Benjamin, self-indulgent and indulged by him, could be happy nowhere except in Paris.   By a strange perversion of truth, the English are called "insular" ; the greatest nomads, the most cosmopolitan nation, perhaps, that the world has known, mind you, are held up as horrible examples of Philistine insularity, to combine terms that may convey my meaning.   The truly insular, surrounded by a veritable Chinese wall of self-satisfaction, are the French ; the homage of the barbarians to their dazzling Grand Monarch and other like astonishing phenomena has encouraged in them what one may call the Narcissus habit.   Mrs. Benjamin was a typical Frenchwoman,

[1] Sept. 11, 1869.

in tastes, and in point of view. She did not, probably, understand at all that she was playing a selfish part; but economy was "fatiguing," and she could no more consent to live in the wilds of barbarous London (almost within hail, too, of the Champs Elyseés) than in the seclusion of "Bellechasse."

She was not without kindly feelings toward his family in New Orleans, to whom she sent messages and presents. But all of her real affection was centred in her daughter, to such a point, indeed, that she was somewhat jealous of Captain de Bousignac, and utterly miserable when he took his wife away with him. The daughter, too, was incapable of reciprocating the wealth of affection displayed by her father; she was in temperament more like her mother than like him. Both survived him a number of years, the mother dying in 1891; the daughter, without living children, in 1898. About one thing only did Mrs. Benjamin, good Catholic that she was, seem solicitous—that her husband should be deemed safe within the fold of the Church.

Was Mr. Benjamin a convert to Catholicism? On his deathbed Catholic rites were performed over him, and the services of that Church consecrated his funeral. Surely, they could do him no harm; he was probably, however, as thoroughly unconscious at the time of the first rites as at the time of the last, though he would very likely, also, have consented smilingly to anything that could give comfort to his wife and daughter. Surely, too, for one who had led an upright and kindly life, with loving sympathy and charity and gentleness to those who passed his way,—Jew and Gentile alike, in this day, will concede that there could be some hope of the mercy of God, with or with-

out forms and ceremonies. It is incumbent upon us,
however, to glance again at the question of Mr. Benjamin's religion, since it is beyond doubt that the fact
of his being a Jew by birth has quickened interest and
curiosity about him. After a careful examination of
such data as could be discovered, I see no reason to
alter the opinion expressed in a preceding chapter,[1]
nor have I much of consequence to add to what is said
there. A more detailed investigation than I can give
is that by Mr. Max J. Kohler, in his admirable monograph,[2] with whose conclusions I agree. Mr. Benjamin early ceased to conform to the observances of
the faith to which he was born; but he never entirely
lost either his belief in or his memory of the tenets of
that faith; he neither obtruded nor sought to conceal
his Jewish birth, of which, indeed, he was proud. He
rarely attended any religious services, but he would,
on occasion, hear good Presbyterian doctrine from
Dr. Hoge, or be edified on the proper relation subsist-
ing between Church and State in Westminster. I have
it on the best authority (if, indeed, any other evidence
than the fact of Benjamin's own intelligence were
needed), from one very intimate with him, that he
was always a firm believer in immortality and in a
personal God; the authority I consider good especially
since the person is a non-believer, and distinctly recalls long and always good-humored (that's a wonder, in theology) controversies with him. In concluding this subject I shall refer to an anecdote that is
related, in slightly varying forms, by several people.

[1] Chapter II, p. 46.
[2] Publications Am. Jewish Hist. Soc., No. 12; cf. *Jewish Ency-
clopedia.*

Since it is told about both Disraeli and Benjamin, I doubt its authenticity as regards either of these great Jews; but since it is a fine bit of the retort that fulminates and blasts, I give it. Being contemptuously referred to by an opponent in debate (some place the scene in the Senate, some on the hustings in Louisiana) as "that Jew from Louisiana," Benjamin retorted: "It is true that I am a Jew, and when my ancestors were receiving their Ten Commandments from the immediate hand of Deity, amidst the thunderings and lightnings of Mt. Sinai, the ancestors of the distinguished gentleman who is opposed to me were herding swine in the forests of Scandinavia." [1]

It is universally stated by those who remember Mr. Benjamin, that he was a brilliant and witty conversationalist, with a fund of rich and varied information, a marvelous facility in quotation, and withal a thorough knowledge of the poetry at his tongue's end, a stock of anecdotes, not too freely used, and a mastery of repartee. Where so many see the same thing, we must give them credence; and yet the examples of Mr. Benjamin's wit are few; perhaps this is because there was no Boswell or Lady Holland to record his witticisms. Of courteous, gallantly phrased repartee Mrs. Davis gives a good example. She had disagreed with him on some trivial point and declined to argue about it: "I playfully said, 'If I let you set one stone, you will build a cathedral.' He laughed and answered, 'If it should prove to be the shrine of truth, you will worship there with me, I am sure.'" Of quicker flash is his answer to Gambetta, whom he met at dinner in Paris, and who said, with what a theatrical toss of his mane we can well

[1] Cf. *Saturday Evening Post*, Oct. 3, 1903, and Kohler, p. 83.

figure to ourselves : "Messieurs les journalistes anglais sont les rois de la terre"—alluding especially to the power of the *Times*. Benjamin replied : "Parfaitement, et ils ne sont jamais détrônés."

But of humor there is an abundance in his letters ; humor of a tender and playful sort that reached the heart of those to whom it was addressed, and that will hardly bear transplanting from the home garden. They refer very frequently to the children of whom he was specially fond, and who returned the affection. Mrs. Bradford says that in 1872 she found him one day, when she was a little late for dinner, lolling on the lounge and reading, with as much zest as her boy, whose playfellow he was, the *Arabian Nights*.   He longed for a grandchild, but was always disappointed, for none of Mme. de Bousignac's children lived beyond a few hours after birth.   On one occasion, when his hopes were high, he wrote home :   " We have decided that it is to be a boy and that he is to become a Marshal of France, so *that* anxiety is off my mind." "Those dear little folks," he writes to Mrs. Levy when mentioning her young grandson, as at least a palliative for rheumatism, "twine themselves so 'round the heart that everything else seems trifling and unimportant in comparison."   "I have been away for so long, alas !" he writes to Mrs. Kruttschnitt, "that I can't figure to myself, as the French say, how [your children] look as grown up, and then your sweet little things that I don't know at all ! Send me a list of them ! I ain't joking, I want a list with ages. Of course I know their names ; but I want to realize if I can their ages."   "Give Johnny [his great-nephew] a

[1] Letter from Sir Campbell Clarke, *Lawley MS.*

kiss for his lock of hair for Uncle Ben, and as I can't
send him a lock of mine, having none to spare, I send
him the postage stamps to buy candy. Tell him to
give a piece to J. P." [1]

The letters are full of indignant comments on the
stubbornness of that "dear old lady," Mrs. Levy, who
will not subside into the indolence becoming to one of
her years, but insists on gardening in spite of cold and
wet, and contracts rheumatism. If she *will* raise toma-
toes, it's a pity she could not send them here : "I have
to pay eight cents apiece for them." But shortly, to-
matoes have gone down; "they only cost seven cents
now." To Leah, also, the loving playful references
are frequent: "Sis writes me . . . that dear
Leah's health is not as good as she could wish. This
will never do ! How can we get on for 'sauce' if she
fails us ? It is my opinion that she requires a vast deal
of gaiety and society to get rid of her superabundance
of that article, and that if she does not avail herself of
every occasion, it will strike inward like the measles,
and prove fatal."

When his wife and daughter send a goodly list of
presents to various members of the family, he says :
"It has been a labor of love for them, and my Lordship was not permitted to say a word on the subject,
except to select the box for Sis and the buttons for
Lionel ; and I venture to say that my superior taste
will be self-evident, when compared with that of the
'inferior sex.'" When he himself, after a very successful year, wrote to wish them all a Happy New Year (December 14, 1877), and enclosed a draft for five hundred
dollars, specifying how the sum was to be distributed
he stipulated : "I make one general condition—

Ernest is to pay for a bottle of champagne to drink the health of your loving brother on New Year's Day ; so *his* present is to pay a couple of dollars out of his own pocket. And Kitt is to give a 'grande séance scientifique et amusante' exhibiting the glories of microscopic research."

The same humorous vein crops out in several of the few letters to friends that have been preserved. "My dear Mrs. Bayard," he writes,[1] "it seems that Mrs. Benjamin took it into her head to-day to have made for you a cake of the kind she thought you liked, and I found her determined when I came home, that *I* should write you a line in *her* place, as she was unwilling to *ventilate* her English in writing. I obey like a good husband —— So much for *her*. For myself, I beg to place myself on the very top of the list of your warmest friends, and at the feet of your charming daughters. Please don't let Bayard have any of the cake." And in a pleasant, chatty letter to Mrs. Bradford,[2] with whom he had frequent arguments as to the genius of the Laureate, after quoting a verse which he expects her to scorn, he continues : "This puts me in mind of the indignation with which your soul must be inflamed by the *Times*' criticism on Tennyson's new poem which I propose to get by heart and use as a weapon of offense against you whenever I am too much provoked. I have not yet read it, however, and anticipate with delight selecting 'pretty' passages for your special delectation. Honest confession is, however, good for the soul, and I will avow at the expense of your

[1] To Mrs. T. F. Bayard, not dated, but probably during the summer of 1881.
[2] Oct. 26, 1872.

triumph that I *do* wish Tennyson would let King Arthur alone for the present and take up some other subject for his Lady Muse.

"The English people are as raw and fretful as their worst enemies could wish over the San Juan award. In private conversation I observe the very great soreness which is felt, and I begin to see that I was not wrong in the forecast, that arbitration is not like spermaceti, the sovereign ointment for an inward bruise. . . .

"I give up the English climate—wreak your vengeance on it, and enjoy your triumph. It has rained incessantly for a fortnight, yet an Englishman has had the assurance to ask me to spend the day with him in the country to-morrow (Sunday), because the 'country looks beautiful in its autumn dress, and we will have a delightful walk.' Of course I wrote him an insulting reply."

Surely, this was no dark conspirator hatching sinister plots, but a gentle, generous, and lovable man, from whose exquisite private life I have drawn the veil, I trust, with reverent hand. He had great wealth, made honestly by his own labor, and expended most freely for the pleasure of those he loved. From the bitter accusations uttered in the heat of politics I have not sought to shield his memory by concealing them; rather have I given them place in these pages, confident that the record of good deeds, of kindly thoughts, of great and honorable preferment that could be placed beside them, would be answer sufficient. And in judging the character of Judah P. Benjamin, after a career brilliantly successful in so many fields, a career that began as a penniless private tutor, rose to

a climax that would have ruined a weaker man in the
fearful ordeals of the Civil War, and culminated in

> "That which should accompany old age,
>   As honor, love, obedience, troops of friends,"

I shall let his English admirers give their judgment,
after they had met him in their courts for sixteen
years. "You know how Mr. Benjamin came among
us," said Sir Henry James at the farewell dinner, [1]
"and how we received him. *Ejectum littore egentem ac-
cepimus;* but no regret, no self-reproach has ever come
to us for having given him place within our kingdom.
He knocked at our doors and they were widely opened
to him. We found place for him in our foremost
rank ; we grudged him not the leadership he so easily
gained—we were proud of his success, for we knew
the strength of the stranger among us, and the bar is
ever generous even in its rivalry toward success that is
based on merit. And the merit must have been there,
for who is the man save this one of whom it can be
said that he held conspicuous leadership at the bar of
two countries ? To him this change of citizenship and
transition in his profession seemed easy enough. From
the first days of his coming he was one of us. We had
been taught by the same teachers, Coke and Black-
stone. . . . But he was one of us not only in this
common knowledge. The honor of the English bar
was as much cherished and represented by him as by
any man who has ever adorned it, and we all feel that
if our profession has afforded him hospitality, he has
repaid it, amply repaid it, not only by the reputation

[1] London *Times,* July 2, 1883.

which his learning has brought to us, but by that which is more important, the honor his conduct has gained for us. But he became one of us in fuller spirit yet; not only the lawyer but the man was of us. Rivalry with him seemed to create rather than to disturb friendship, and it was within the walls of our courts that Mr. Benjamin first found those friends who sit around him to-night. And how strange and quick must have been his power to make them! Mr. Benjamin sees here no small gathering of men who have come in friendship to his side. To other men it may be given also to have many friendships, but they take a lifetime to form. They commence in childhood and strengthen and increase as life goes on. The years are few since Mr. Benjamin was a stranger to us all, and in those few years he has accomplished more than most men can ever hope in a lifetime to achieve."

APPENDIX

Since professional men may take an interest in the matter, the appended extract from Mr. Benjamin's fee-book (*Lawley MS*) gives the figures for his earnings at the English bar.

	£	s	d
1867	495	12	3
1868	703	0	8
1869	1,074	7	2
1870	1,480	3	0
1871	2,100	17	0
1872	5,623	7	4
1873	8,934	3	11
1874	9,861	1	4
1875	11,316	0	0
1876	13,812	9	4
1877	14,741	3	7
1878	15,742	6	6
1879	14,632	5	2
1880	15,972	4	10
1881	14,632	3	2
1882	12,789	5	3
Total,	143,900	10	6

BIBLIOGRAPHY

In the subjoined list of books, periodicals, and other sources, no attempt has been made to include those having but slight or inconsiderable notices of Mr. Benjamin. Those found most useful to the writer, whether for direct evidence or as supplying the necessary historic background, are included. The references in the footnotes are usually to the name of the author, or to a condensed title; where authorities are frequently referred to, the bibliography shows the title used for reference in the footnotes. Entries are made in alphabetical order, and for convenience the authorities are classified under five heads, as I, Books, Pamphlets, and Cyclopædias; II, Newspapers; III, Periodicals; IV, Public Documents and Official Publications; V, Private Sources.

I. Books, Pamphlets, and Cyclopædias

A Generation of Judges. By their Reporter, 1886.

Alfriend, Frank H. Life of Jefferson Davis, 1868.

American Annual Encyclopædia (Appleton's), 1861, 1884.

Bancroft, Frederick. Life of William H. Seward, 1900.

Barnes, T. W. Memoir of Thurlow Weed, 1884.

Battles and Leaders of the Civil War, 1884–1887.

Bernard, Montague. Historical Account of the Neutrality of Great Britain during the American Civil War, 1870.

Bigelow, John. France and the Confederate Navy—1862–1868. An International Episode, 1888.

BLAINE, JAMES G. Twenty Years of Congress : From Lincoln to Garfield, 1884.

BREWER, DAVID J. The World's Best Orations, 1899.

BULLOCH, J. D. Secret Service of the Confederate States in Europe, 1884.

CALLAHAN, J. M. The Diplomatic History of the Southern Confederacy, 1901.

COFFIN, CHARLES C. Marching to Victory, 1863, 1889.

CORTHELL, E. L. The Atlantic and Pacific Ship-Railway, 1886. Pamphlet.

COX, S. S. Three Decades of Federal Legislation, 1885.

CURRY, J. L. M. Civil History of the Government of the Confederate States, 1901.

CYCLOPÆDIA OF AMERICAN BIOGRAPHY. Appleton's. Edited by James Grant Wilson and John Fiske, 1891.

DAVIS, JEFFERSON. Rise and Fall of the Confederate Government, 1881.

DAVIS, (MRS.) VARINA A. H. Jefferson Davis—Ex-President of the Confederate States of America. A memoir by his wife, 1890.

DE LEON, J. C. Four Years in Rebel Capitals, 1892.

DIRECTORIES. Directories of the cities of New Orleans and Lafayette, etc., for the years : 1835, 1838, 1841, 1842, 1844, 1846, 1850, 1851, 1853–1856, 1858–1861.

EADS, JAMES B. The Tehuantepec Ship-Railway, 1883. Pamphlet.

HAMILTON, J. A. H. Article, "Benjamin, Judah P.," Dictionary of National Biography, 1888.

HEADLEY, J. N., Confederate Operations in Canada and New York, 1806.

HOLST, HERMANN E. VON. Constitutional and Political History of the United States. Translated by John J. Lalor, 1889-1892.

HURD, JOHN C. The Law of Freedom and Bondage in the United States, 1858–1862.

JOHNSTON, ALEXANDER. American Orations : Studies in American Political History, 1897.

JOHNSTON, R. M., AND BROWNE, WILLIAM H. Life of Alexander H. Stephens, 1884.

444 BIBLIOGRAPHY

JOHNSTON, WILLIAM PRESTON. The Life of General Albert Sidney Johnston, 1880.

JONES, J. B. A Rebel War Clerk's Diary at the Confederate States Capitol, 1866.

KEYES, E. D. Fifty Years' Observation of Men and Events, Civil and Military, 1884.

KOHLER, MAX J. Judah P. Benjamin: Statesman and Jurist. Publications of the American Jewish Historical Society, No. 12. Pamphlet, 1905.

———— Article, "Benjamin, Judah P.," Jewish Encyclopædia.

LEE, GUY CARLETON. The World's Best Orators, 1900. (Vol. X, pp. 99–110.)

LEE, CAPTAIN ROBERT E. Recollections and Letters of General Robert E. Lee, 1904.

LEOVY, H. J. The Ante-Bellum Bench and Bar. Transactions of the Louisiana Bar Association, 1900. Pamphlet.

McPHERSON, EDWARD. Political History of the United States during the Great Rebellion, 1865.

MASON, VIRGINIA. The Public Life and Diplomatic Correspondence of James M. Mason, 1904.

MORSE, JOHN T., JR. Abraham Lincoln. American Statesmen Series, 1893.

NICOLAY AND HAY. Abraham Lincoln : a History, 1890.

POLLARD, E. A. The Lost Cause, 1866.

———— Life of Jefferson Davis. With a Secret History of the Southern Confederacy, 1869.

POORE, BENJAMIN PERLEY. Reminiscences of Sixty Years in the National Metropolis, 1886.

RHODES, JAMES FORD. A History of the United States from the Compromise of 1850, 1904.

RICHARDSON, JAMES D. A Compilation of the Messages and Papers of the Confederacy, including the Diplomatic Correspondence, 1861–1865. Published by permission of Congress by James D. Richardson, 1905.

RUSSELL, WILLIAM H. My Diary North and South, 1863.

SABINE, JOSEPH. A Dictionary of Books relating to America. (Vol. II, pp. 64, 65.)

SCHOULER, JAMES. A History of the United States of America under the Constitution, 1899.

SCHWAB, J. C. The Confederate States of America. Financial and Industrial History of the South during the Civil War, 1901.

SCOTT, H. W. Distinguished American Lawyers, 1897.

SEWARD, FREDERICK W. Seward at Washington, 1846–1872, 1891.

STEPHENS, A. H. The War Between the States, 1868–1870.

STEVENS, HENRY. The Tehuantepec Railway : Its Location, Features, and Advantages under the La Sére Grant of 1869, 1869. Pamphlet.

TEHUANTEPEC, ISTHMUS OF. Memorial setting forth the rights and just reasons which the government of the United States of Mexico has for not recognizing the validity of the privilege for opening communication by the Isthmus of Tehuantepec. Published by the Minister of Relations, 1852. Pamphlet.

TOMPKINS, H. C. Judah P. Benjamin. Alabama State Bar Association Reports, 1896. Pamphlet.

TRASTOUR, P. Summary Explanation respecting the Tehuantepec Canal, 1856. Pamphlet.

WHITAKER, JOHN. Sketches of Life and Character in Louisiana, the portraits selected principally from the Bench and Bar, 1847.

WILLIAMS, J. The Isthmus of Tehuantepec. Results of a Survey under the direction of Major J. G. Barnard for a railroad to connect the Atlantic and Pacific Oceans, 1852.

WISE, B. H. Life of Henry A. Wise of Virginia, 1899.

II NEWSPAPERS

The most valuable source for materials upon Mr. Benjamin's life prior to the Civil War is the collection of newspapers on file at the City Hall in New Orleans. At one period a particular journal may be of great use, and then become utterly valueless ; hence it is impossible within brief limits to indicate the periods covered by the journals named below. But the following list includes those that have been consulted for various periods; specific references are given in the footnotes in all cases of importance :

The New Orleans *Argus ;* the New Orleans *Bee ;* the New Orleans *Courier ;* the New Orleans *Crescent ;* the New Orleans *Delta ;* the New Orleans *True Delta ;* the New Orleans *Jeffersonian ;* the New Orleans *Picayune ;* the New Orleans *Times ;* the New Orleans

Tropic; the London *Daily Telegraph,* February 10, 1883; the London *Times,* July 2, 1883, and May 9, 1884.

The files of the New York *Times* and *Tribune,* 1861–1865, are of course very useful, as publishing especially intercepted Confederate correspondence ; but specific references to the particular copies of these and other newspapers are given in the footnotes.

III. PERIODICALS

Albany Law Journal. Vol. 27, p. 182 ; Vol. 28, pp. 41, 61, 82 ; Vol. 29, pp. 382, 422 ; Vol. 30, p. 62.

ALDIS, O. F. Article, "Louis Napoleon and the Southern Confederacy." *North American Review,* Vol. 129, pp. 342, 344.

The Athenæum. 1888, Vol. I, p. 599.

BIGELOW, JOHN. Article, "The Confederate Diplomatists," *Century Magazine,* Vol. 20, p. 413.

CALLAHAN, J. M. Article, "The Confederate Diplomatic Archives." The Pickett Papers. South Atlantic Quarterly, Vol. 2, No. 1, January, 1903.

DAWES, HENRY L. Article, "Has Oratory Declined?" *The Forum,* Vol. 18, p. 148. October, 1894.

DE BOW, J. B. *DeBow's Commercial Review of the Southern and Western States,* Vol. I, 164, 167, 498 ; II, 322–345, 442; V, 44–57, 357–364; X, 94–96 ; XII, 312; XIII, 45, *et seq.,* 236, *et seq. ;* XIV, 1–23 ; XXI, 209–212; XL, 1–6.

"Diary of a Public Man." *North American Review,* Vol. 129, pp. 133, 134, 139, 263, 264, 271.

Gulf States Historical Magazine. Vol. II, No. 1, July, 1903.

HARRISON, BURTON N. Article, "The Capture of Jefferson Davis," *Century Magazine,* Vol. 27, pp. 130–140, November, 1883.

Jewish Chronicle. May 9, 1884.

Jewish World. May 16, 1884.

KOHLER, MAX J. Article, "Jews and the American Anti-Slavery Movement," American Jewish Historical Society Publications, Vol. II, No. 9, p. 52.

Law Journal. March 10, February 17, and July 14, 1883 ; May 17 and July 5, 1884. (See London *Times,* among Newspapers.)

Law Times. Vol. 75, p. 188, July 7, 1883 ; Vol. 77, p. 47, May 17, 1884. (See London *Times*, among Newspapers.)

LEBOWICH, JOSEPH. Article, "Judah P. Benjamin : a Bibliography," *The Menorah Monthly*, November, 1902; pp. 305–312.

New York Public Library Bulletin. Confederate Attorney-General Records. Vols. I and II.

POLLOCK, CHARLES, BARON POLLOCK. "Reminiscences of Judah Philip Benjamin," article in" *Fortnightly Review*, Vol. 69, pp. 354–361, March, 1898 ; also in *The Green Bag*, Vol. X, pp. 396–401, and *Littell's Living Age*, Vol. 217.

Records of the American Catholic Historical Society of Philadelphia, Sept. 1903.

RUSSELL, SIR WILLIAM H. Article, "Reminiscences of the Civil War," *North American Review*, March, 1898, p. 373.

Solicitor's Journal, May 10 and July 7, 1884.

Southern Historical Society Papers. Vols. IV, VII, and XIV.

STERN, DAVID. Article, "Judah P. Benjamin," *North Carolina University Magazine*, January, 1902, pp. 56–61.

SUMNER, J. O. Article, "Materials for the History of the Government of the Confederacy," American Historical Association Papers, Vol. IV.

SWALLOW, W. H. Article, "Retreat of the Confederate Government," *Magazine of American History*, June, 1886.

VEST, G. G. Article, "A Senator of Two Republics : Judah P. Benjamin," Philadelphia *Saturday Evening Post*, October 3, 1903.

IV. PUBLIC DOCUMENTS AND OFFICIAL PUBLICATIONS

References to the law reports—Louisiana Annuals, United States Supreme Court Reports, and English Reports—are here omitted, since the mere record of cases in which Benjamin appeared would be necessarily extended, and of slight interest to any but legal students.

Acts and Resolutions of the Provisional Congress of the Confederate States of America.

The Congressional Globe, 1853–1861.

Journal of the Proceedings of the Convention of the State of Louisiana begun and held in the City of New Orleans on the 14th day of January, 1845. Published by Authority. New Orleans, 1845. (Less full than *Proceedings*, below.)

Journal. Louisiana Constitutional Convention of 1852.

Pickett Papers. Confederate Diplomatic and Consular Correspondence, now preserved in the Treasury Department, Washington, D. C. These papers, so named because obtained chiefly from Colonel John T. Pickett (see *Callahan*, Chapter I), have not yet been published in complete form; for portions of important dispatches to and from Benjamin, see references to *Official Records, Mason, Richardson, Bigelow,* and *Callahan.*

Proceedings and Debates of the Convention of Louisiana which assembled at the City of New Orleans, January 14, 1844 (should be 1845). Robert J. Ker, reporter. New Orleans, 1845.

Statutes at Large of the Confederate States of America.

United States Senate Reports. 44th Congress, 1st Session, Vol. I. (Report on Confiscated Lands of J. P. Benjamin.)

War of the Rebellion. A Compilation of the Official Records of the Union and Confederate Armies. Washington, 1880. Referred to as *Official Records.*

V. Private Sources

1. Collection of manuscript materials made by the late Mr. Francis Lawley, of London, with a view to his writing the life of Benjamin. He completed no more than the bare rough draft of opening chapters, with an outline of the proposed treatment. But the collection includes a number of letters, usually of slight intrinsic value, from Mr. Benjamin, numerous very valuable special contributions from those who knew Mr. Benjamin in England, (*e. g.* Lord James of Hereford and Mr. Witt), letters, copies of newspaper clippings, copies of his fee-book, contributions of great interest from such persons in America as Mrs. Davis, Mr. L. Q. Washington, and the Rev. Dr. Hoge, etc., and from some of the contemporaries of Benjamin at school and college. Particular articles in this collection are referred to by title, with reference to the *Lawley Manuscript* in the footnotes.

2. *Family Letters.* A collection of letters covering the years 1864–1883 from Mr. Benjamin to members of his family in New Orleans, kindly put in the hands of the writer by Mr. E. B. Kruttschnitt, of New Orleans.

3. *Bayard Letters.* A small collection of very interesting and important letters from Mr. Benjamin to Messrs. James A. and Thomas F. Bayard, with notes upon Mr. Benjamin made by the latter, all carefully copied and furnished to the writer by Mrs. W. S. Hilles (*née* Bayard), of Wilmington, Del.

3. *Miscellaneous letters and notes* made from conversations with Mrs. Jefferson Davis, Mrs. E. A. Bradford, Judge D. M. Shelby, Mrs. Leah Popham (niece of Mr. Benjamin), Mr. E. B. Kruttschnitt (his nephew); a few letters from Benjamin to James M. Mason, in possession of Miss Mason.

INDEX

Born to a long line of Natchez Butlers, PIERCE BUTLER (1873-1955) was a true son of the South. He was educated at Tulane, the Sorbonne, and Johns Hopkins University, taking his Ph.D. in English but maintaining an active interest in history as a member of the American Historical Association. Butler served as Professor of English, History, and French, finally becoming Dean of Tulane University. As a scholar and prominent figure in New Orleans, he came into close contact with Judah P. Benjamin's friends and relatives and was well equipped to write about the controversial Confederate leader.

BENNETT H. WALL is Lecturer in American History at the University of Georgia. A member of the Organization of American Historians and a past President of the Louisiana Historical Association, he has served as Secretary-Treasurer of The Southern Historical Association for the last twenty-seven years. He has contributed numerous articles to professional journals and is co-author with George S. Gibb of *Teagle of Jersey Standard.*